Author in Love...

Tempted to make a stupid joke here...

But I'm not going to do it!

Naoshi Komi

NAOSHI KOMI was born in Kochi Prefecture, Japan, on March 28, 1986. His first serialized work in *Weekly Shonen Jump* was the series *Double Arts*. His current series, *Nisekoi*, is serialized in *Weekly Shonen Jump*.

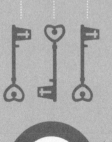

NISEKOI:
False Love
VOLUME 2
SHONEN JUMP Manga Edition

Story and Art by
NAOSHI KOMI

Translation ✒ Camellia Nieh
Touch-Up Art & Lettering ✒ Stephen Dutro
Design ✒ Fawn Lau
Shonen Jump Series Editor ✒ John Bae
Graphic Novel Editor ✒ Amy Yu

Published by VIZ Media, LLC
P.O. Box 77010
San Francisco, CA 94107

10 9 8 7 6 5 3 4 2 1
First printing, March 2014

www.shonenjump.com   www.viz.com

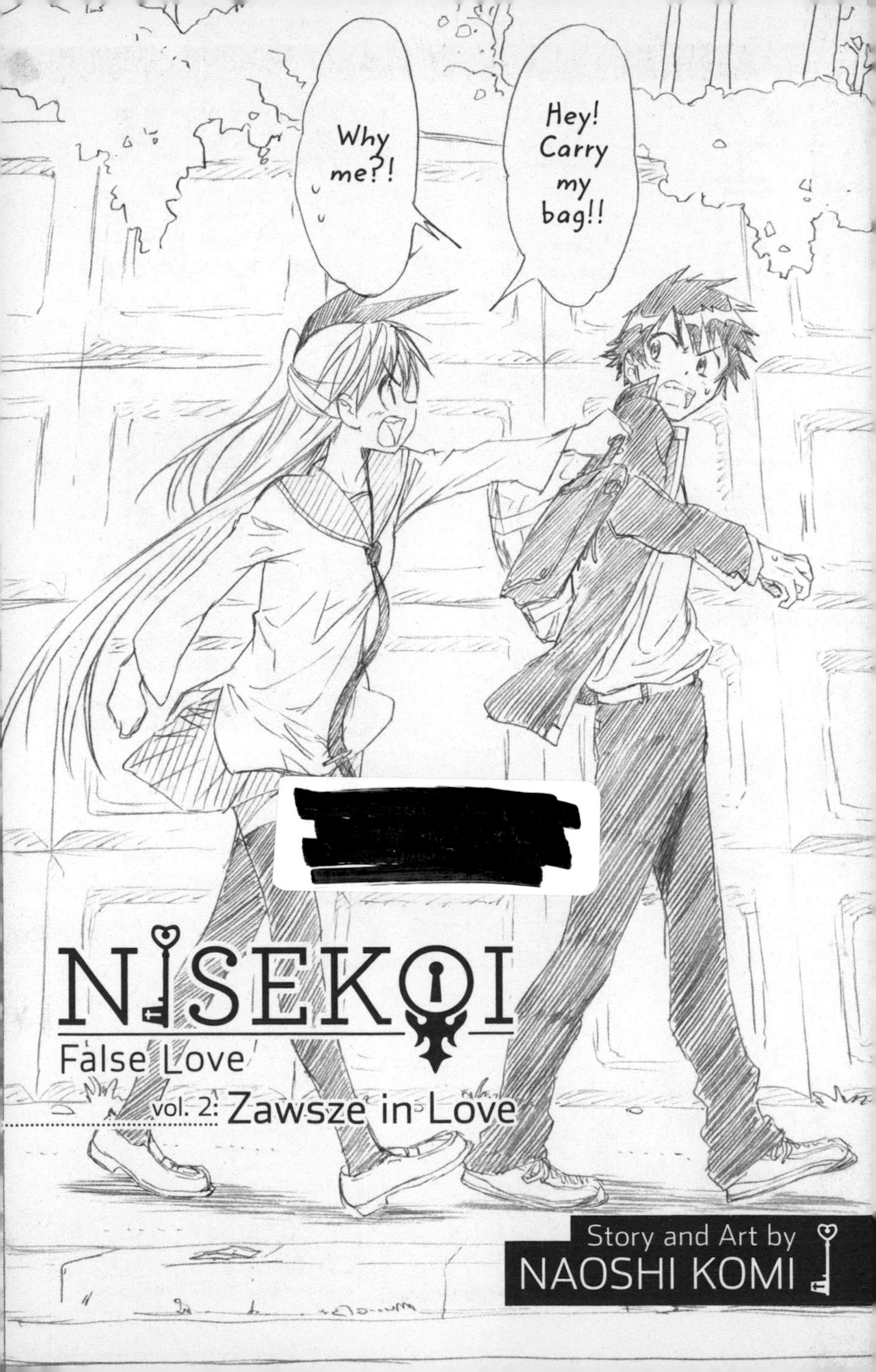
Hey! Carry my bag!!
Why me?!

[redacted]

NISEKOI

False Love

vol. 2: Zawsze in Love

Story and Art by
NAOSHI KOMI

CHITOGE KIRISAKI

A half-Japanese bombshell with stellar athletic abilities. Short-tempered and violent. Comes from a family of gangsters.

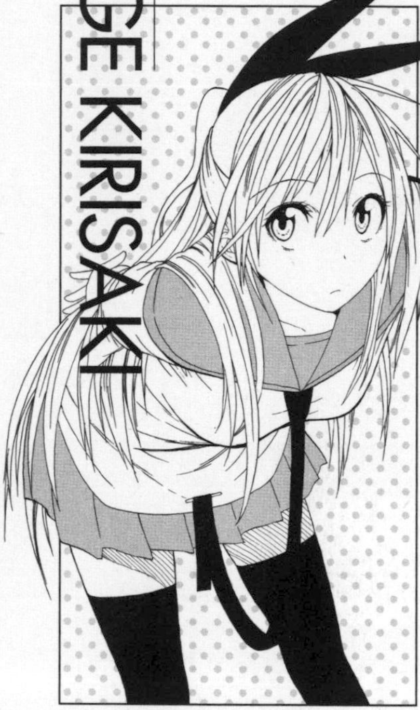

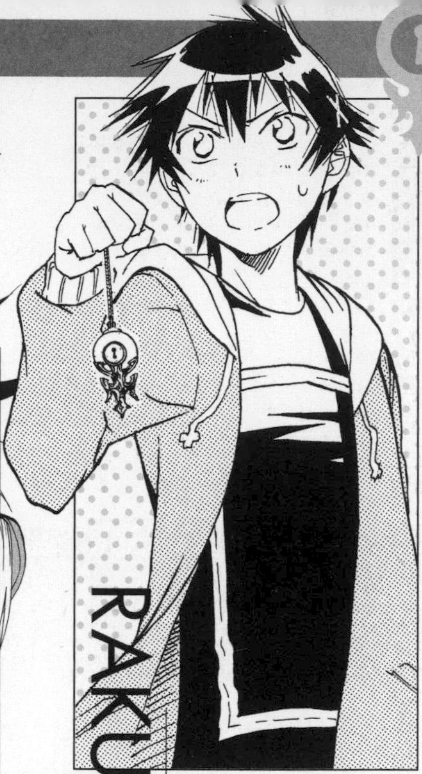

RAKU ICHIJO

A normal teen whose family happens to be yakuza. Cherishes a pendant given to him by a girl he met ten years ago. Has a crush on Kosaki.

RURI MIYAMOTO

Kosaki's best gal pal. Comes off as aloof, but is actually a devoted and highly intuitive friend.

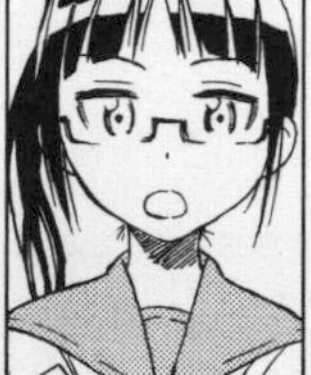

SHU MAIKO

Raku's best friend. Outgoing and girl-crazy. Always tuned in to the latest gossip at school.

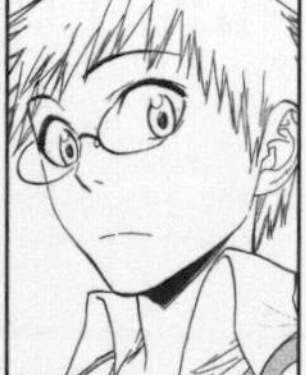

CLAUDE

Executive member of the Beehive and protector of Chitoge. Suspicious of Raku and Chitoge's relationship.

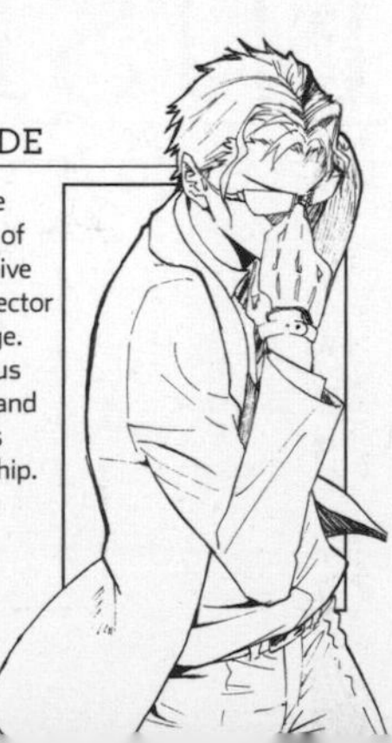

THE STORY THUS FAR

Raku Ichijo is an ordinary teen... who just happens to come from a family of yakuza! His most treasured item is a pendant he was given ten years ago by a girl whom he promised to meet again one day and marry.

When super-babe Chitoge Kirisaki transfers into Raku's class, it's clear from the get-go that they don't get along. Meanwhile, tensions are escalating between a gang called the Beehive and the Shuei-Gumi, the yakuza syndicate led by Raku's father. To prevent an all-out turf war, Raku's father coerces Raku into a false love match with the daughter of the Beehive gang's boss. To Raku's horror, she turns out to be Chitoge!

When Raku and Chitoge are forced to go on a date together, they run into Kosaki Onodera, Raku's crush. Kosaki is convinced that the two are a genuine couple, and Raku is anxious to clear up the misunderstanding. But with Chitoge's bodyguard Claude scrutinizing his every move, that's easier said than done!

KOSAKI ONODERA

A girl Raku has a crush on. Beautiful and sweet, Kosaki has no shortage of admirers. She's a terrible cook but makes food that *looks* amazing.

SHUEI-GUMI MEMBERS

Consider Raku their future leader. Their enthusiastic support of Raku and Chitoge's relationship often makes Raku's life difficult.

CHITOGE'S FATHER

Leader of the Beehive, a gang with designs on the Shuei-Gumi's turf.

RAKU'S FATHER

Leader of the Shuei-Gumi, the yakuza syndicate at war with the Beehive.

NISEKOI
False Love
vol. 2: Zawsze in Love

TABLE OF CONTENTS

chapter 8: The Visit 7

chapter 9: Up Close 27

chapter 10: Swimming 49

chapter 11: The Keyhole 69

chapter 12: Out of the Bag 89

chapter 13: Zawsze in Love 109

chapter 14: We're Even 127

chapter 15: Rival 147

chapter 16: Showdown 167

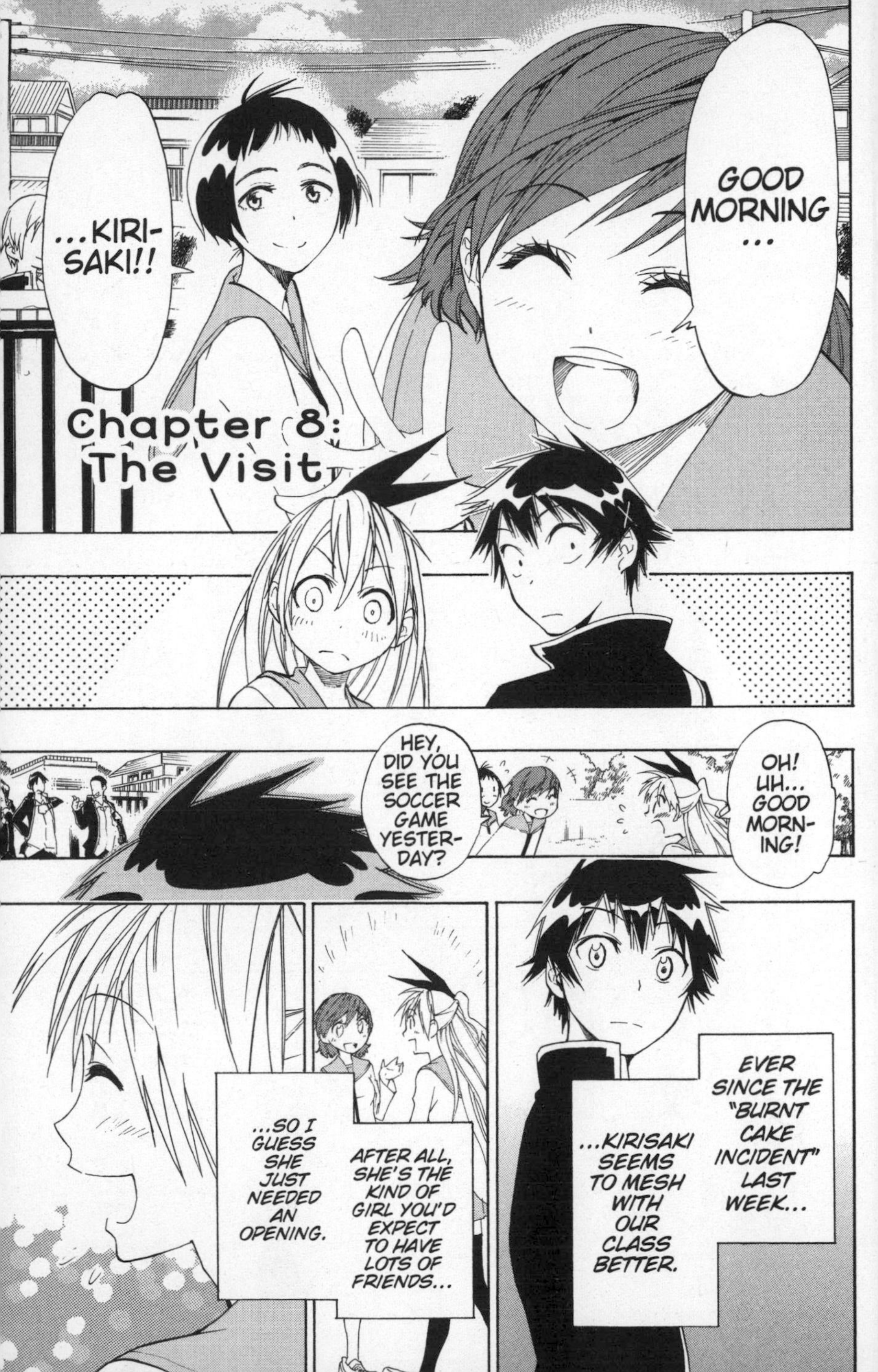
GOOD MORNING...
...KIRISAKI!!
Chapter 8: The Visit
OH! UH... GOOD MORNING!
HEY, DID YOU SEE THE SOCCER GAME YESTERDAY?
EVER SINCE THE "BURNT CAKE INCIDENT" LAST WEEK...
...KIRISAKI SEEMS TO MESH WITH OUR CLASS BETTER.
AFTER ALL, SHE'S THE KIND OF GIRL YOU'D EXPECT TO HAVE LOTS OF FRIENDS...
...SO I GUESS SHE JUST NEEDED AN OPENING.

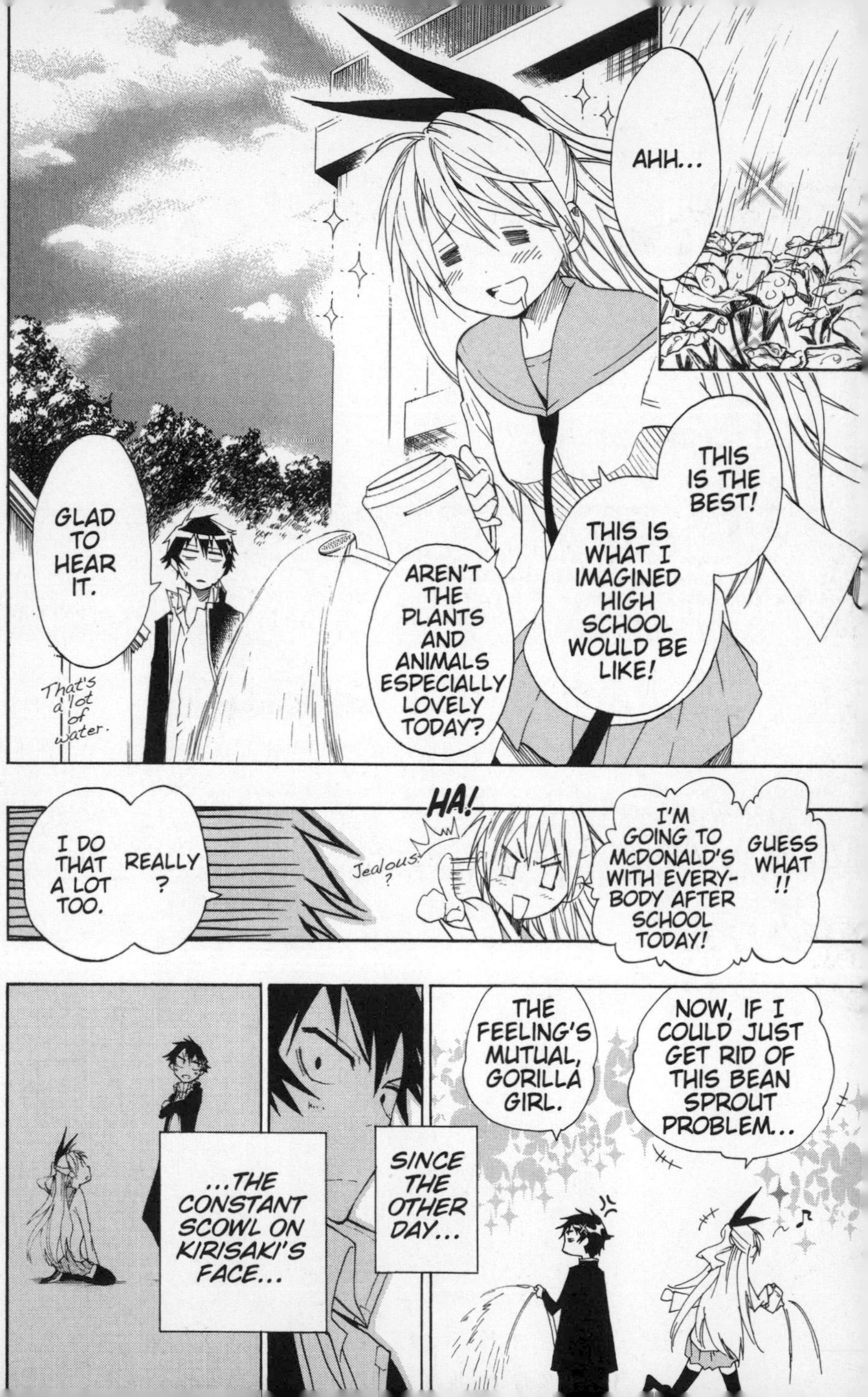
AHH...
THIS IS THE BEST!
THIS IS WHAT I IMAGINED HIGH SCHOOL WOULD BE LIKE!
AREN'T THE PLANTS AND ANIMALS ESPECIALLY LOVELY TODAY?
GLAD TO HEAR IT.
That's a lot of water.
GUESS WHAT!!
I'M GOING TO McDONALD'S WITH EVERY-BODY AFTER SCHOOL TODAY!
HA!
Jealous?
REALLY?
I DO THAT A LOT TOO.
NOW, IF I COULD JUST GET RID OF THIS BEAN SPROUT PROBLEM...
THE FEELING'S MUTUAL, GORILLA GIRL.
SINCE THE OTHER DAY...
...THE CONSTANT SCOWL ON KIRISAKI'S FACE...

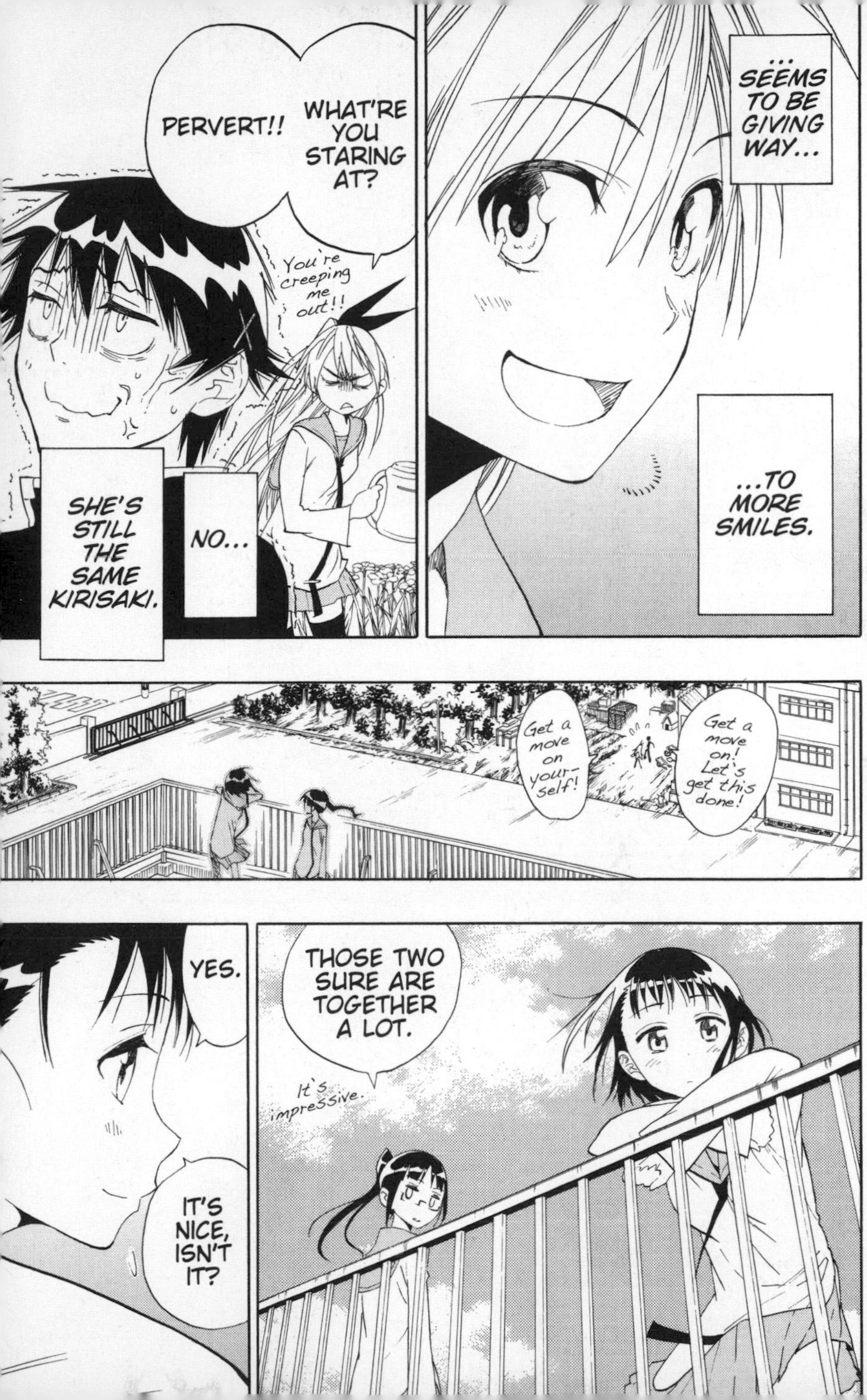
...SEEMS TO BE GIVING WAY...
...TO MORE SMILES.
WHAT'RE YOU STARING AT?
PERVERT!!
You're creeping me out!!
NO...
SHE'S STILL THE SAME KIRISAKI.
Get a move on! Let's get this done!
Get a move on your-self!
THOSE TWO SURE ARE TOGETHER A LOT.
It's impressive.
YES.
IT'S NICE, ISN'T IT?

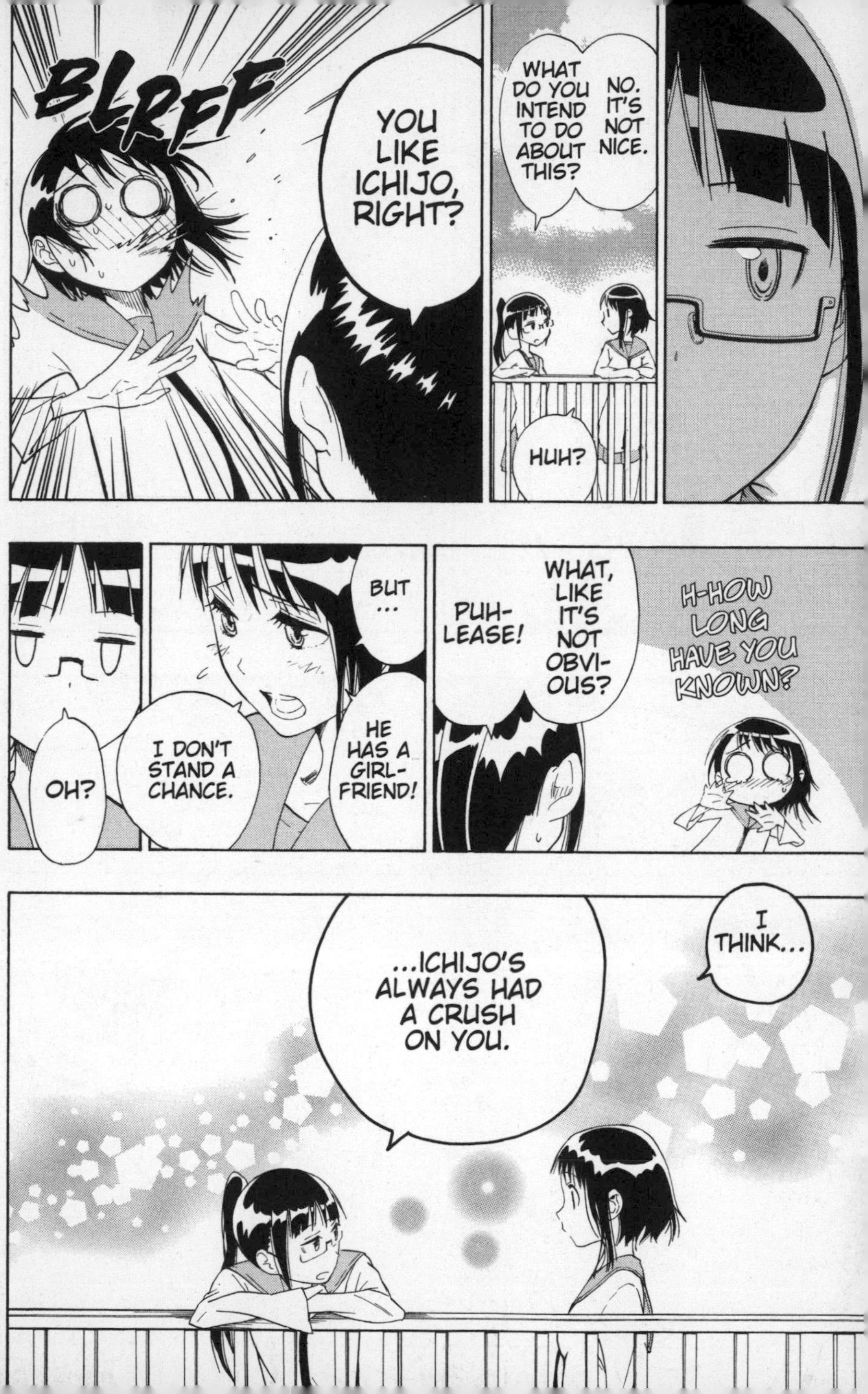
NO. IT'S NOT NICE.
WHAT DO YOU INTEND TO DO ABOUT THIS?
HUH?
YOU LIKE ICHIJO, RIGHT?
BLRFF
H-HOW LONG HAVE YOU KNOWN?
WHAT, LIKE IT'S NOT OBVIOUS?
PUH-LEASE!
BUT...
HE HAS A GIRL-FRIEND!
I DON'T STAND A CHANCE.
OH?
I THINK...
...ICHIJO'S ALWAYS HAD A CRUSH ON YOU.

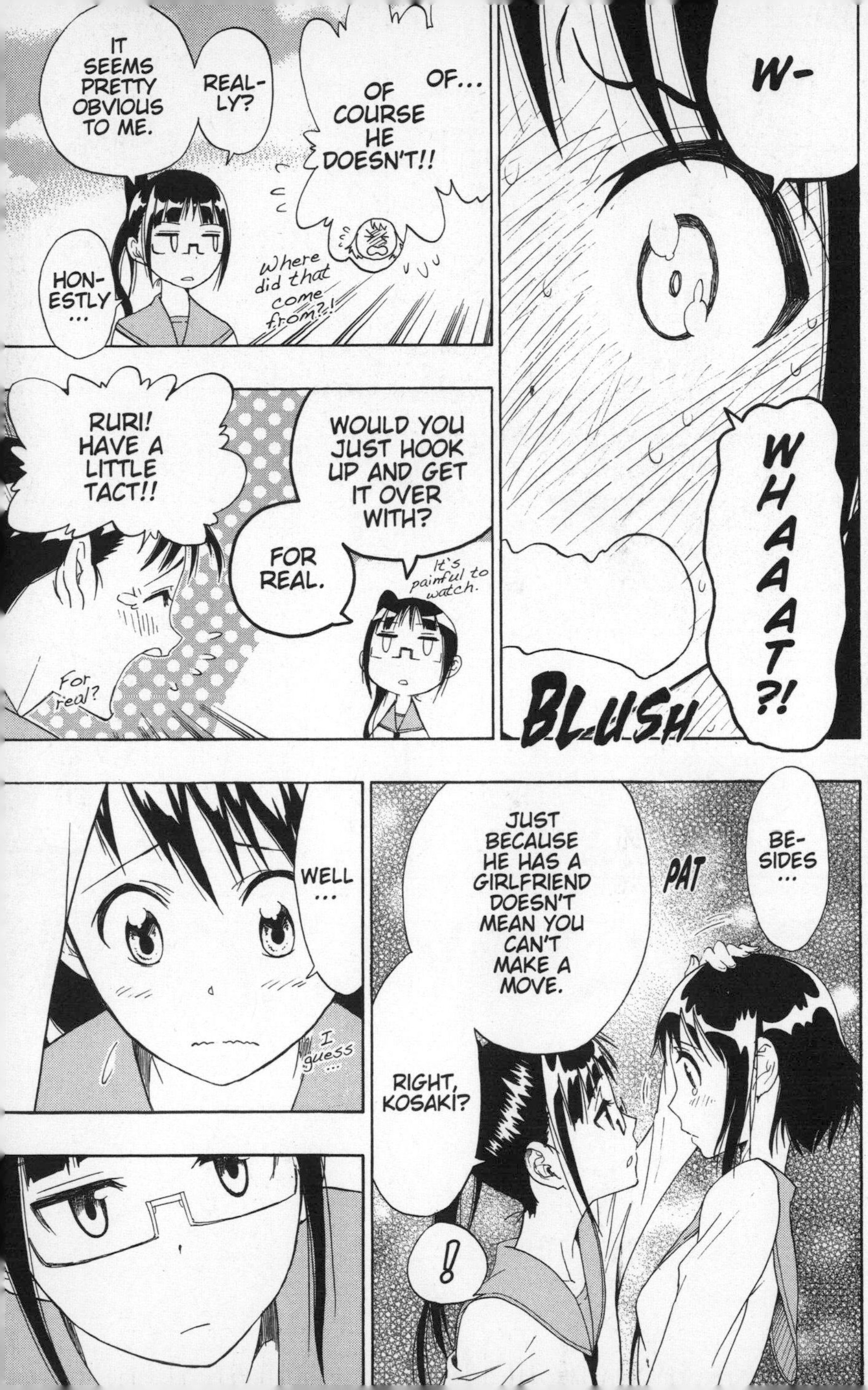
W-
WHAAAT?!
BLUSH
OF...
OF COURSE HE DOESN'T!!
REAL-LY?
IT SEEMS PRETTY OBVIOUS TO ME.
Where did that come from?!
HON-ESTLY...
WOULD YOU JUST HOOK UP AND GET IT OVER WITH?
FOR REAL.
It's painful to watch.
RURI! HAVE A LITTLE TACT!!
For real?
BE-SIDES...
PAT
JUST BECAUSE HE HAS A GIRLFRIEND DOESN'T MEAN YOU CAN'T MAKE A MOVE.
RIGHT, KOSAKI?
!
WELL...
I guess...

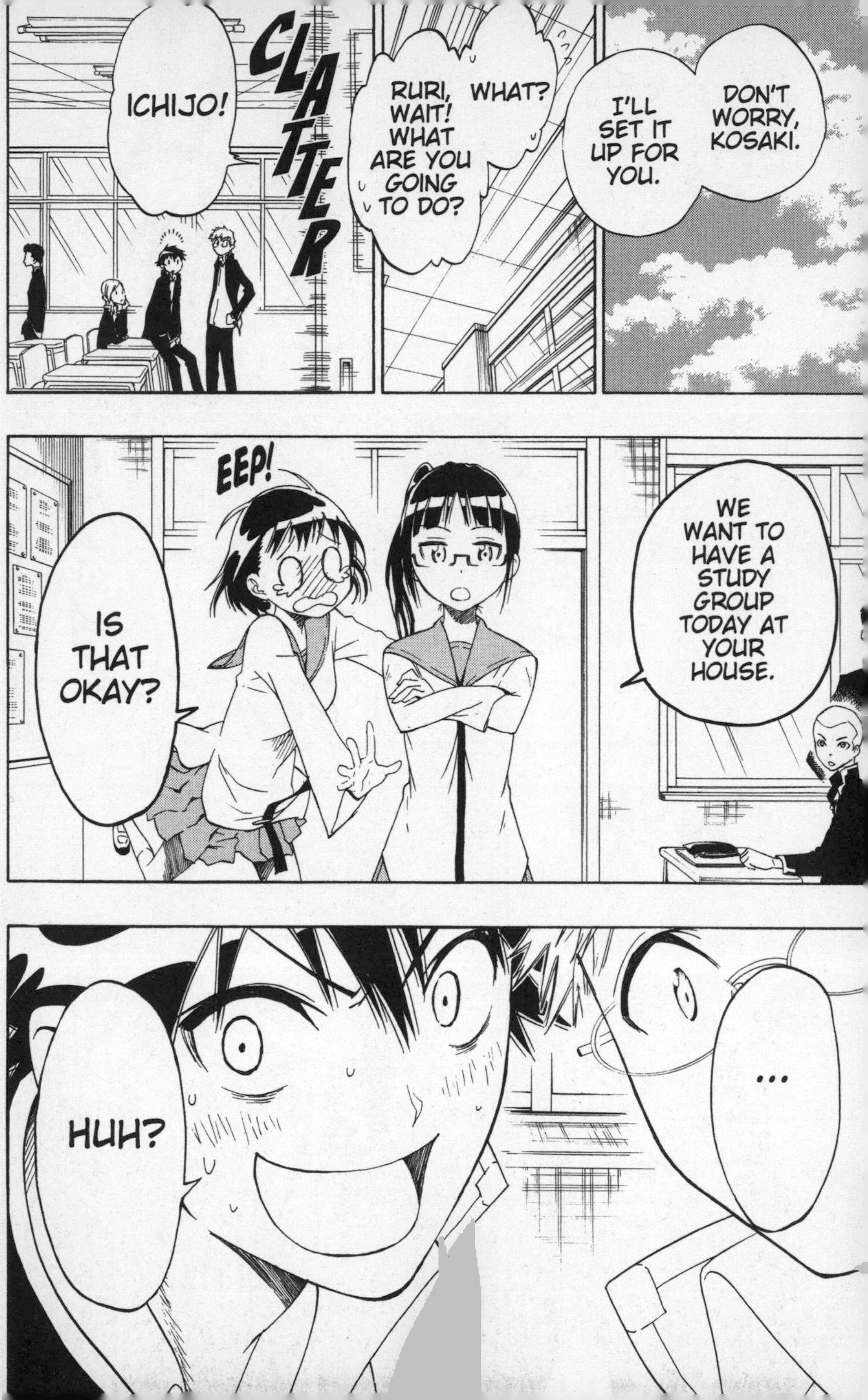
DON'T WORRY, KOSAKI.
I'LL SET IT UP FOR YOU.
WHAT?
RURI, WAIT! WHAT ARE YOU GOING TO DO?
CLATTER
ICHIJO!
WE WANT TO HAVE A STUDY GROUP TODAY AT YOUR HOUSE.
EEP!
IS THAT OKAY?
...
HUH?

Chapter 8: The Visit

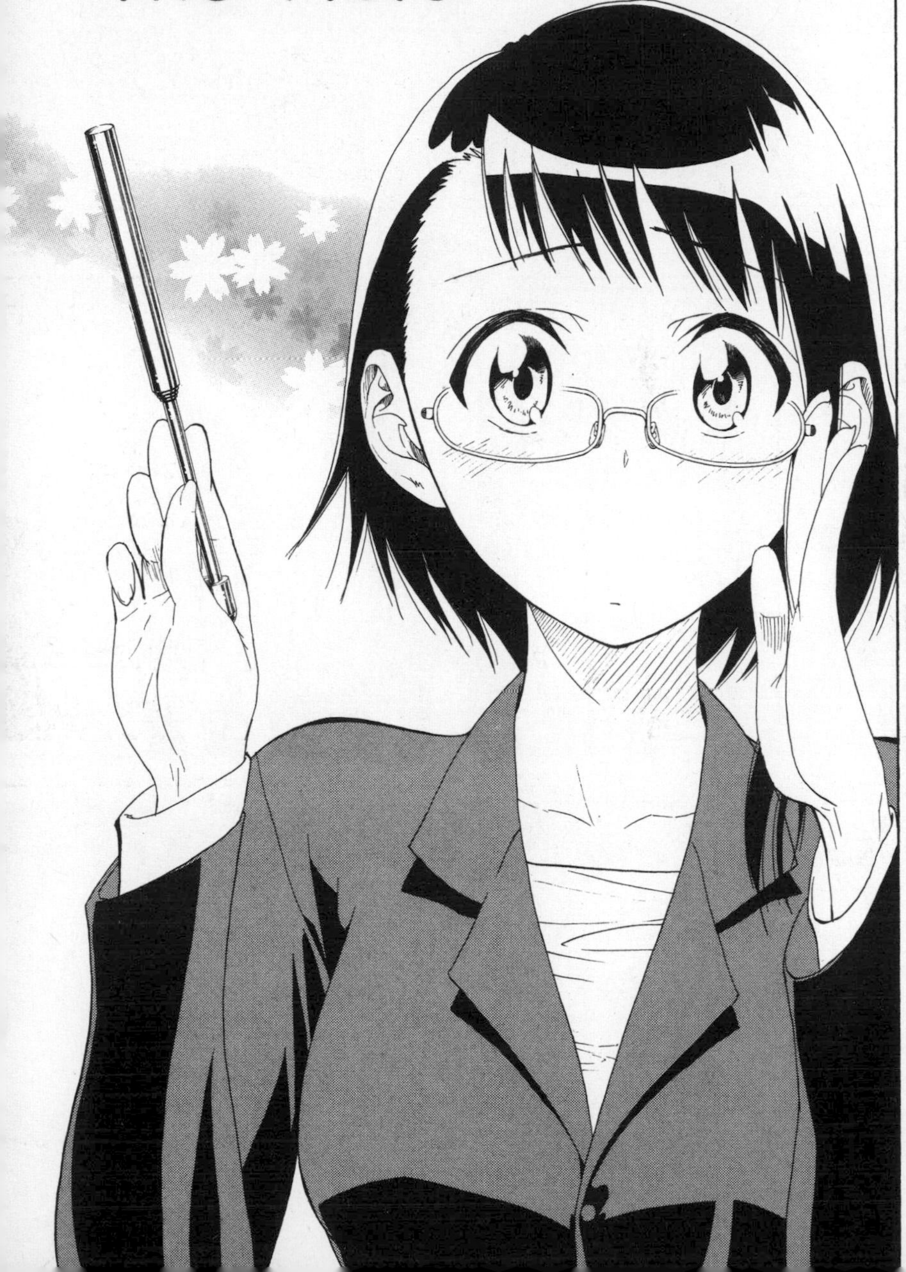

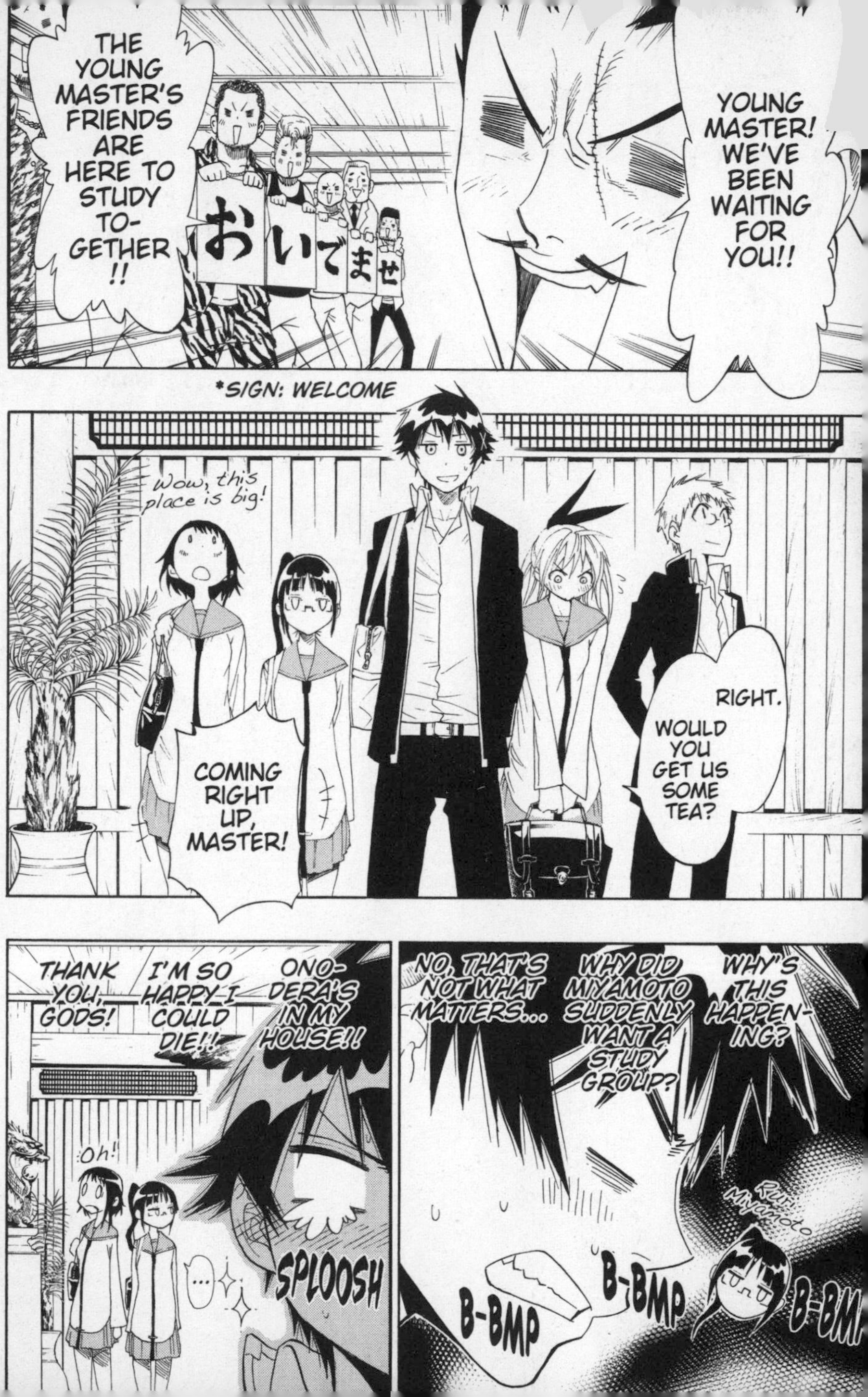
YOUNG MASTER! WE'VE BEEN WAITING FOR YOU!!
THE YOUNG MASTER'S FRIENDS ARE HERE TO STUDY TO-GETHER!!
おいでませ
*SIGN: WELCOME
RIGHT.
WOULD YOU GET US SOME TEA?
Wow, this place is big!
COMING RIGHT UP, MASTER!
WHY'S THIS HAPPEN-ING?
WHY DID MIYAMOTO SUDDENLY WANT A STUDY GROUP?
NO, THAT'S NOT WHAT MATTERS...
Ruri Miyamoto
B-BMP
B-BMP
B-BM
ONO-DERA'S IN MY HOUSE!!
I'M SO HAPPY I COULD DIE!!
THANK YOU, GODS!
Oh!
...
SPLOOSH

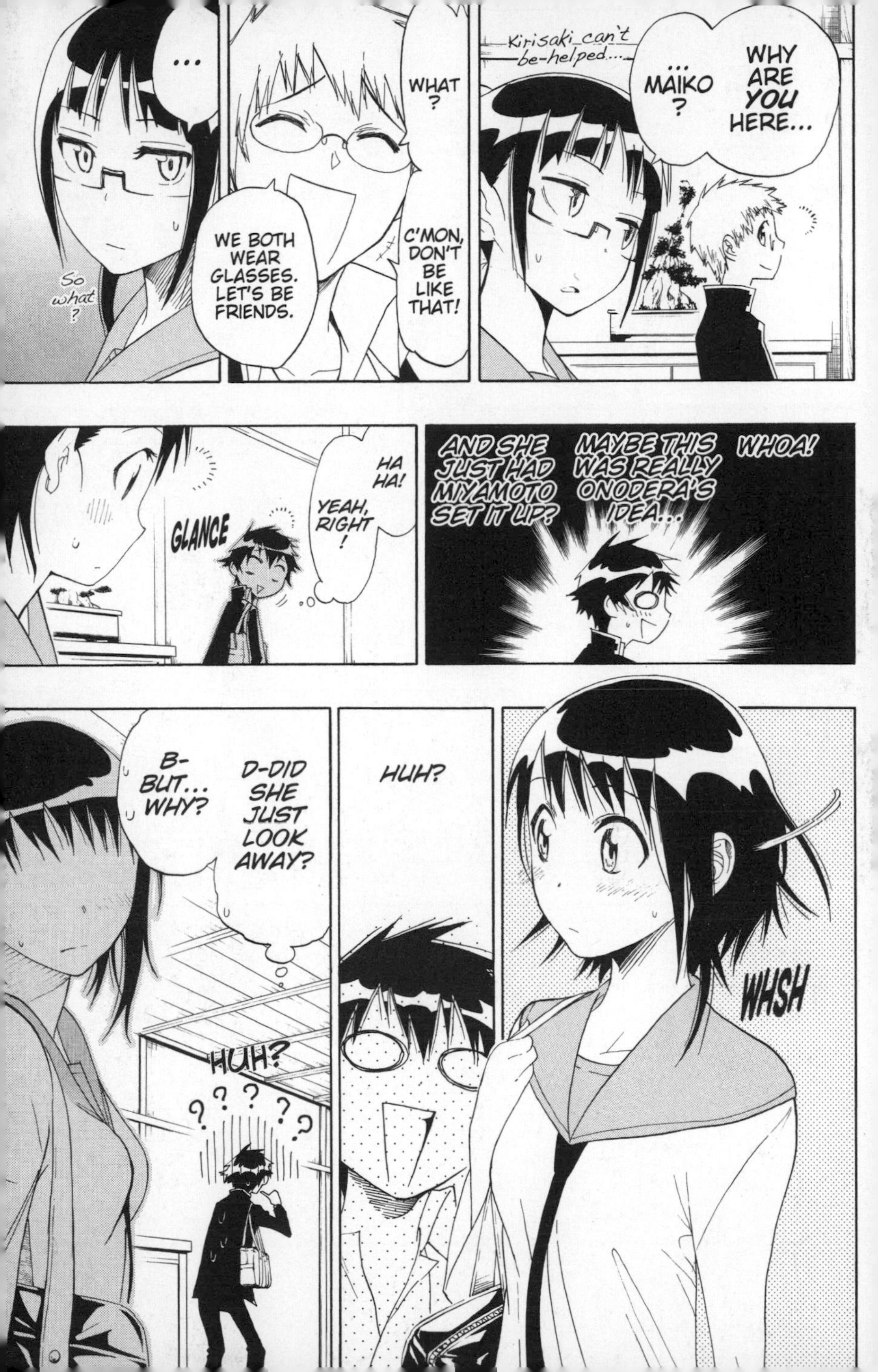
WHY ARE YOU HERE...
...MAIKO?
Kirisaki can't be-helped....
WHAT?
C'MON, DON'T BE LIKE THAT!
WE BOTH WEAR GLASSES. LET'S BE FRIENDS.
...
So what?
WHOA!
MAYBE THIS WAS REALLY ONODERA'S IDEA...
AND SHE JUST HAD MIYAMOTO SET IT UP?
HA HA!
YEAH, RIGHT!
GLANCE
WHSH
HUH?
D-DID SHE JUST LOOK AWAY?
B-BUT... WHY?
HUH?

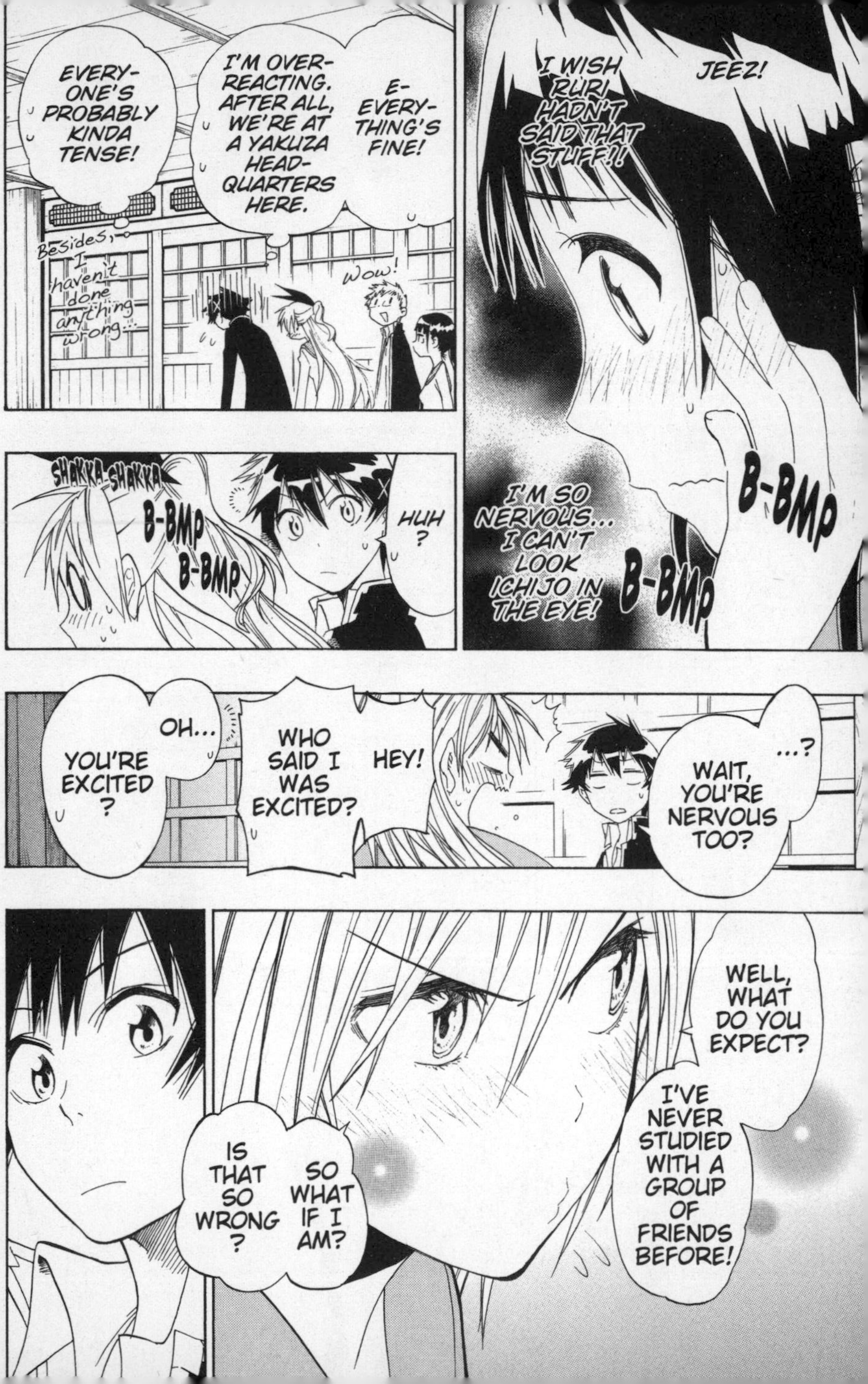
JEEZ!
I WISH RURI HADN'T SAID THAT STUFF!!
B-BMP
I'M SO NERVOUS... I CAN'T LOOK ICHIJO IN THE EYE!
B-BMP
E-EVERYTHING'S FINE!
I'M OVER-REACTING. AFTER ALL, WE'RE AT A YAKUZA HEAD-QUARTERS HERE.
EVERY-ONE'S PROBABLY KINDA TENSE!
Besides, I haven't done anything wrong...
Wow!
HUH?
B-BMP
B-BMP
SHAKKA SHAKKA
...?
WAIT, YOU'RE NERVOUS TOO?
HEY!
WHO SAID I WAS EXCITED?
OH...
YOU'RE EXCITED?
WELL, WHAT DO YOU EXPECT?
I'VE NEVER STUDIED WITH A GROUP OF FRIENDS BEFORE!
SO WHAT IF I AM?
IS THAT SO WRONG?

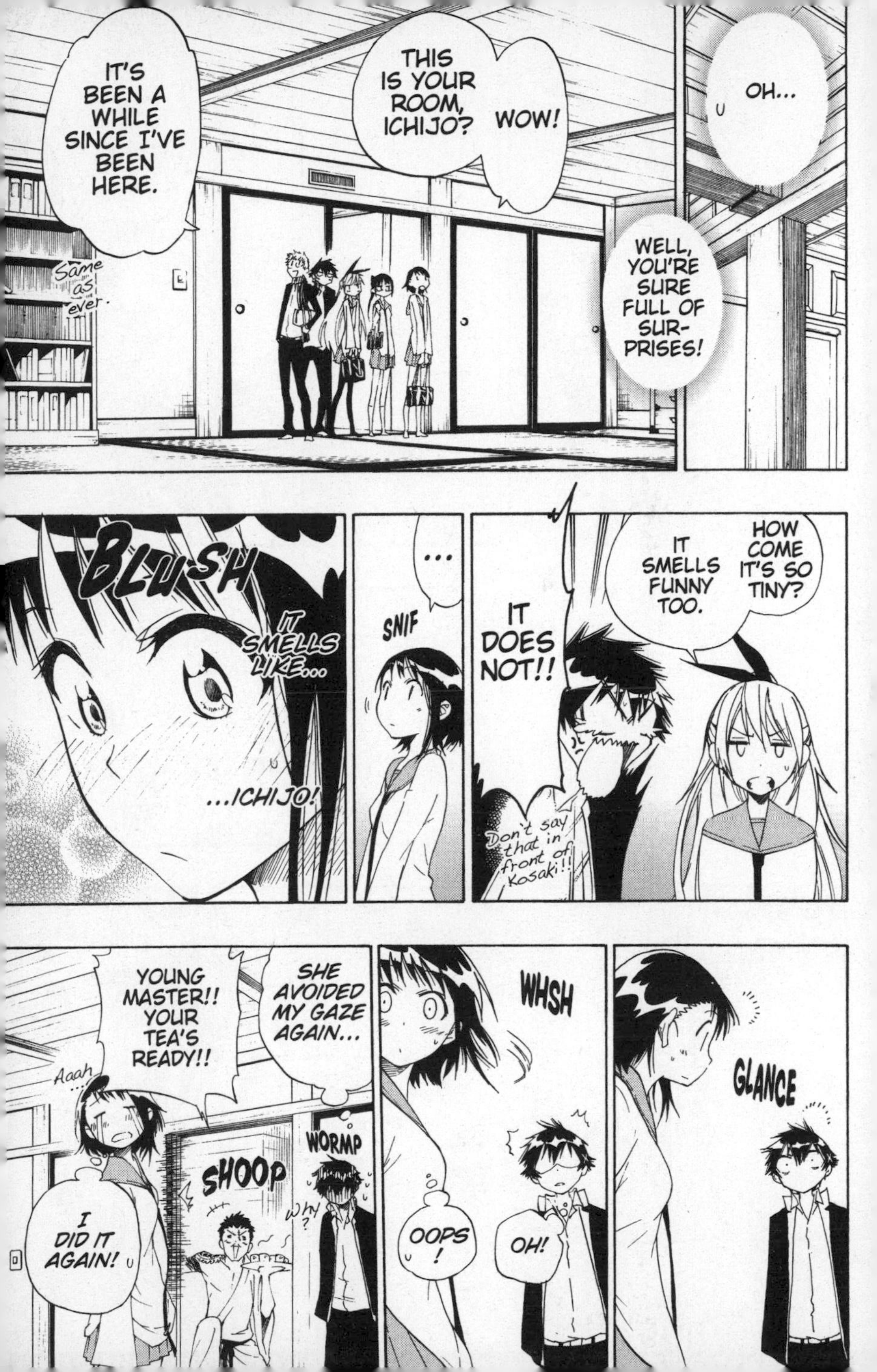
OH...
WELL, YOU'RE SURE FULL OF SURPRISES!
WOW!
THIS IS YOUR ROOM, ICHIJO?
IT'S BEEN A WHILE SINCE I'VE BEEN HERE.
Same as ever.
HOW COME IT'S SO TINY?
IT SMELLS FUNNY TOO.
IT DOES NOT!!
Don't say that in front of Kosaki!!
...
SNIF
BLUSH
IT SMELLS LIKE...
...ICHIJO!
GLANCE
WHSH
OH!
OOPS!
SHE AVOIDED MY GAZE AGAIN...
YOUNG MASTER!! YOUR TEA'S READY!!
WORMP
Aaah...
SHOOP
Why?
I DID IT AGAIN!

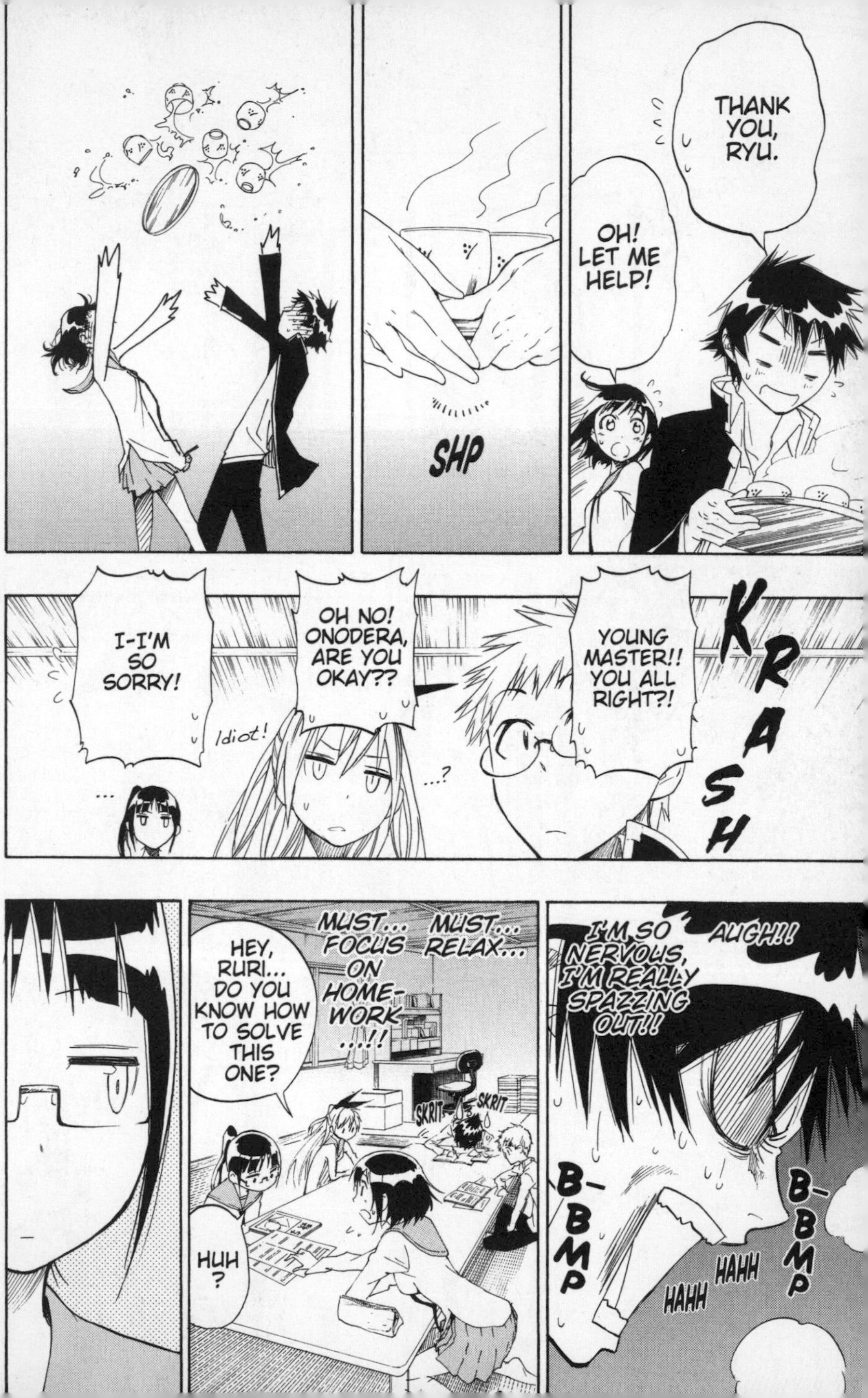
THANK YOU, RYU.
OH! LET ME HELP!
SHP
KRASH
YOUNG MASTER!! YOU ALL RIGHT?!
OH NO! ONODERA, ARE YOU OKAY??
...?
Idiot!
I-I'M SO SORRY!
...
AUGH!!
I'M SO NERVOUS, I'M REALLY SPAZZING OUT!!
B-BMP
HAHH
HAHH
B-BMP
MUST... RELAX...
MUST... FOCUS ON HOME-WORK...!!
HEY, RURI... DO YOU KNOW HOW TO SOLVE THIS ONE?
SKRIT
SKRIT
HUH?

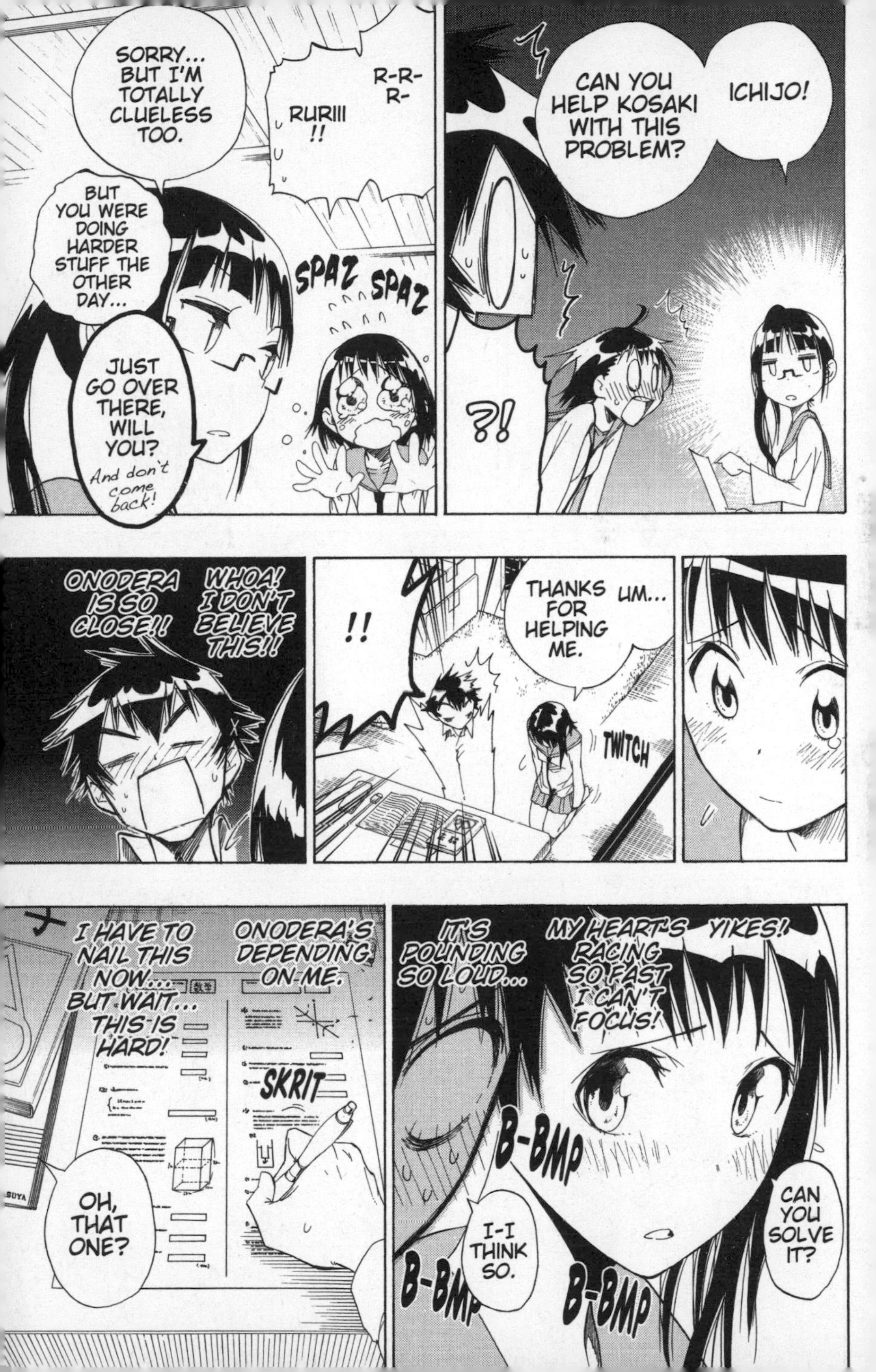
ICHIJO!
CAN YOU HELP KOSAKI WITH THIS PROBLEM?
?!
R-R-R-
RURIII !!
SORRY... BUT I'M TOTALLY CLUELESS TOO.
SPAZ SPAZ
BUT YOU WERE DOING HARDER STUFF THE OTHER DAY...
JUST GO OVER THERE, WILL YOU?
And don't come back!
UM...
THANKS FOR HELPING ME.
!!
TWITCH
WHOA! I DON'T BELIEVE THIS!!
ONODERA IS SO CLOSE!!
YIKES!
MY HEART'S RACING SO FAST I CAN'T FOCUS!
IT'S POUNDING SO LOUD...
CAN YOU SOLVE IT?
B-BMP
I-I THINK SO.
B-BMP
B-BMP
ONODERA'S DEPENDING ON ME.
I HAVE TO NAIL THIS NOW... BUT WAIT... THIS IS HARD!
SKRIT
OH, THAT ONE?

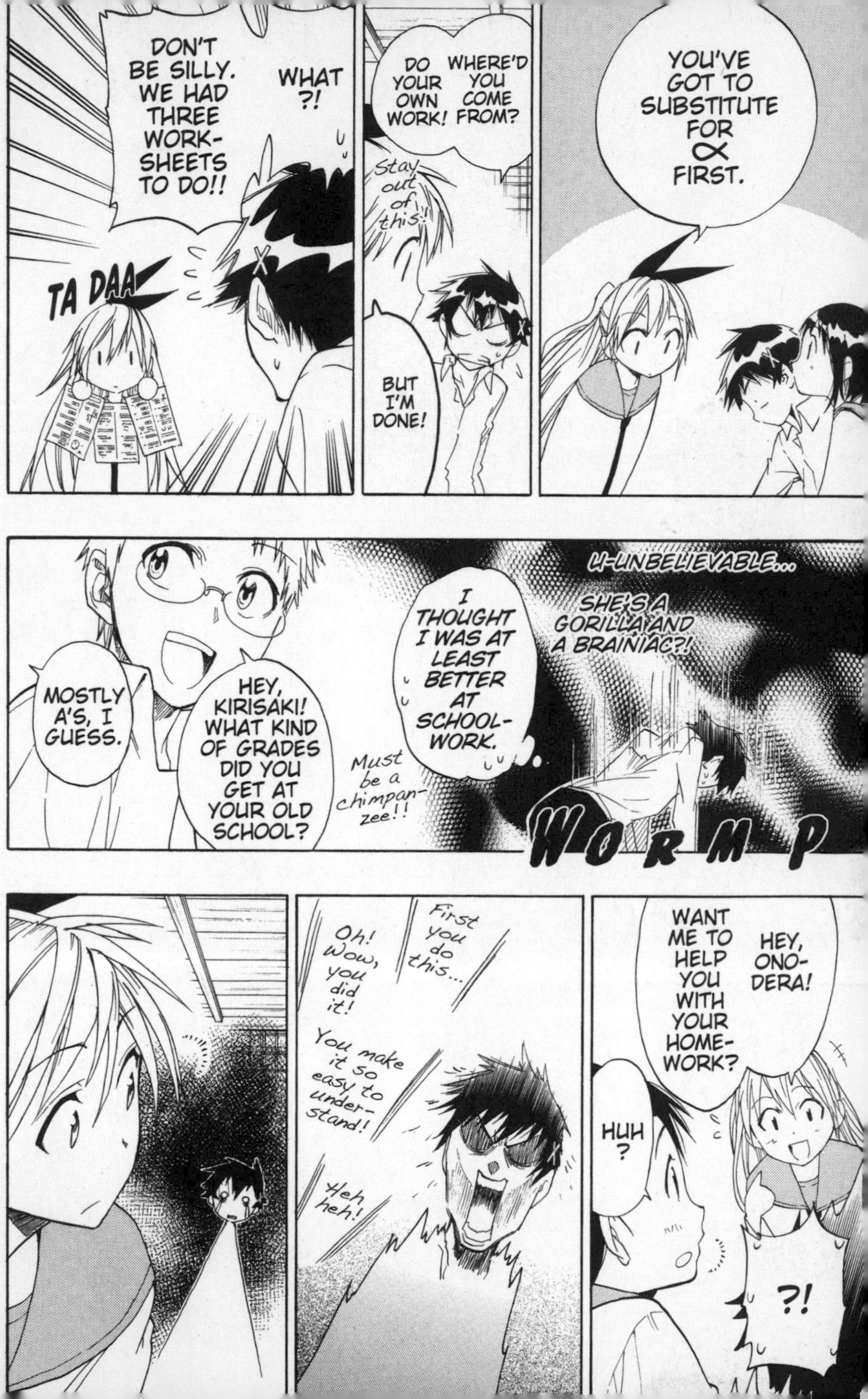
YOU'VE GOT TO SUBSTITUTE FOR α FIRST.
WHERE'D YOU COME FROM?
DO YOUR OWN WORK!
Stay out of this!
BUT I'M DONE!
WHAT ?!
DON'T BE SILLY. WE HAD THREE WORK-SHEETS TO DO!!
TA DAA
U-UNBELIEVABLE...
SHE'S A GORILLA AND A BRAINIAC?!
I THOUGHT I WAS AT LEAST BETTER AT SCHOOL-WORK.
WORMP
Must be a chimpan-zee!!
HEY, KIRISAKI! WHAT KIND OF GRADES DID YOU GET AT YOUR OLD SCHOOL?
MOSTLY A'S, I GUESS.
HEY, ONO-DERA!
WANT ME TO HELP YOU WITH YOUR HOME-WORK?
HUH ?
?!
First you do this...
Oh! Wow, you did it!
You make it so easy to under-stand!
Heh heh!

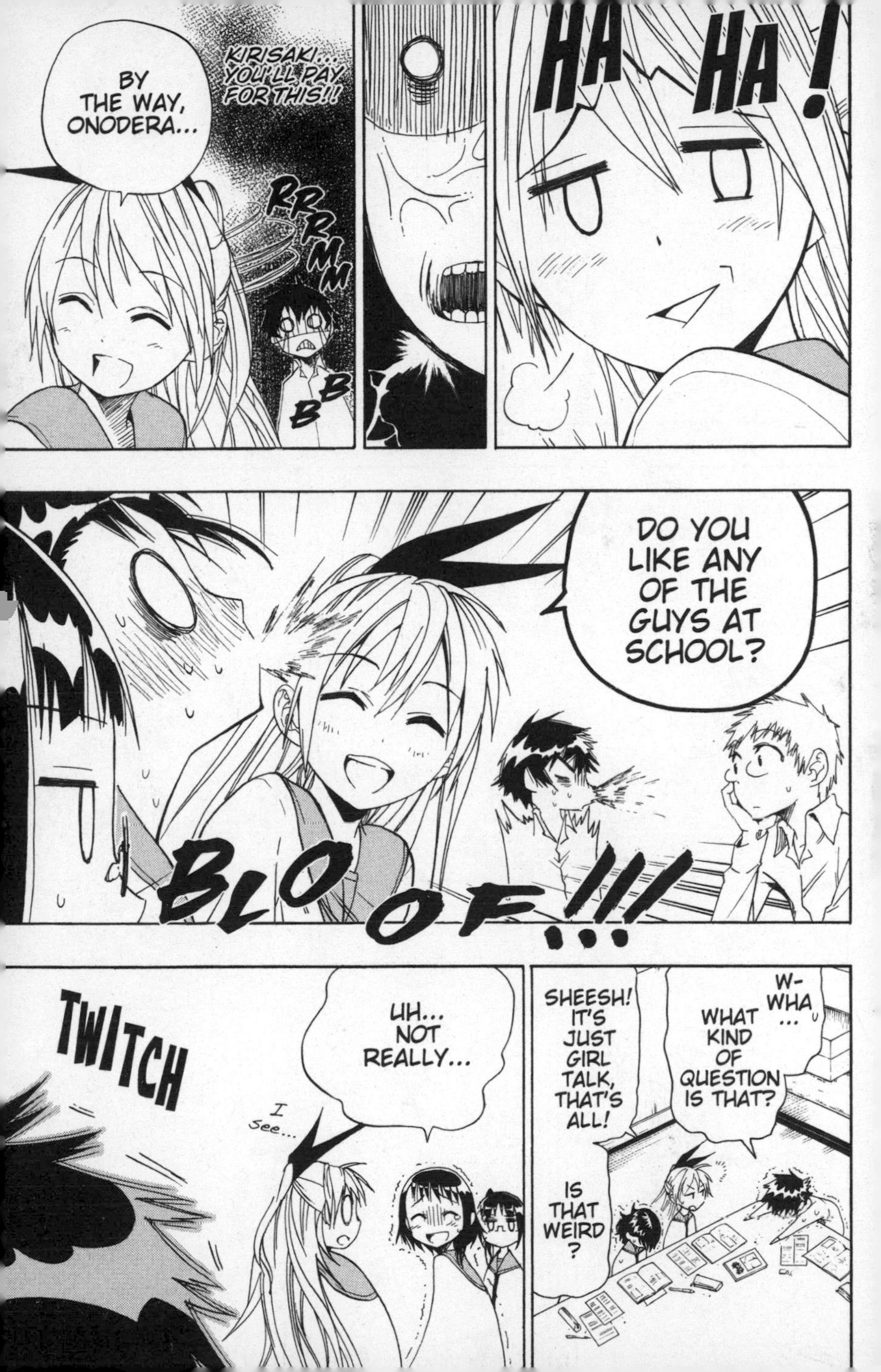
HA HA!
KIRISAKI... YOU'LL PAY FOR THIS!!
BY THE WAY, ONODERA...
RRRMMM
BB
DO YOU LIKE ANY OF THE GUYS AT SCHOOL?
BLOOF!!!
W-WHA...
WHAT KIND OF QUESTION IS THAT?
SHEESH! IT'S JUST GIRL TALK, THAT'S ALL!
IS THAT WEIRD?
UH... NOT REALLY...
I see...
TWITCH

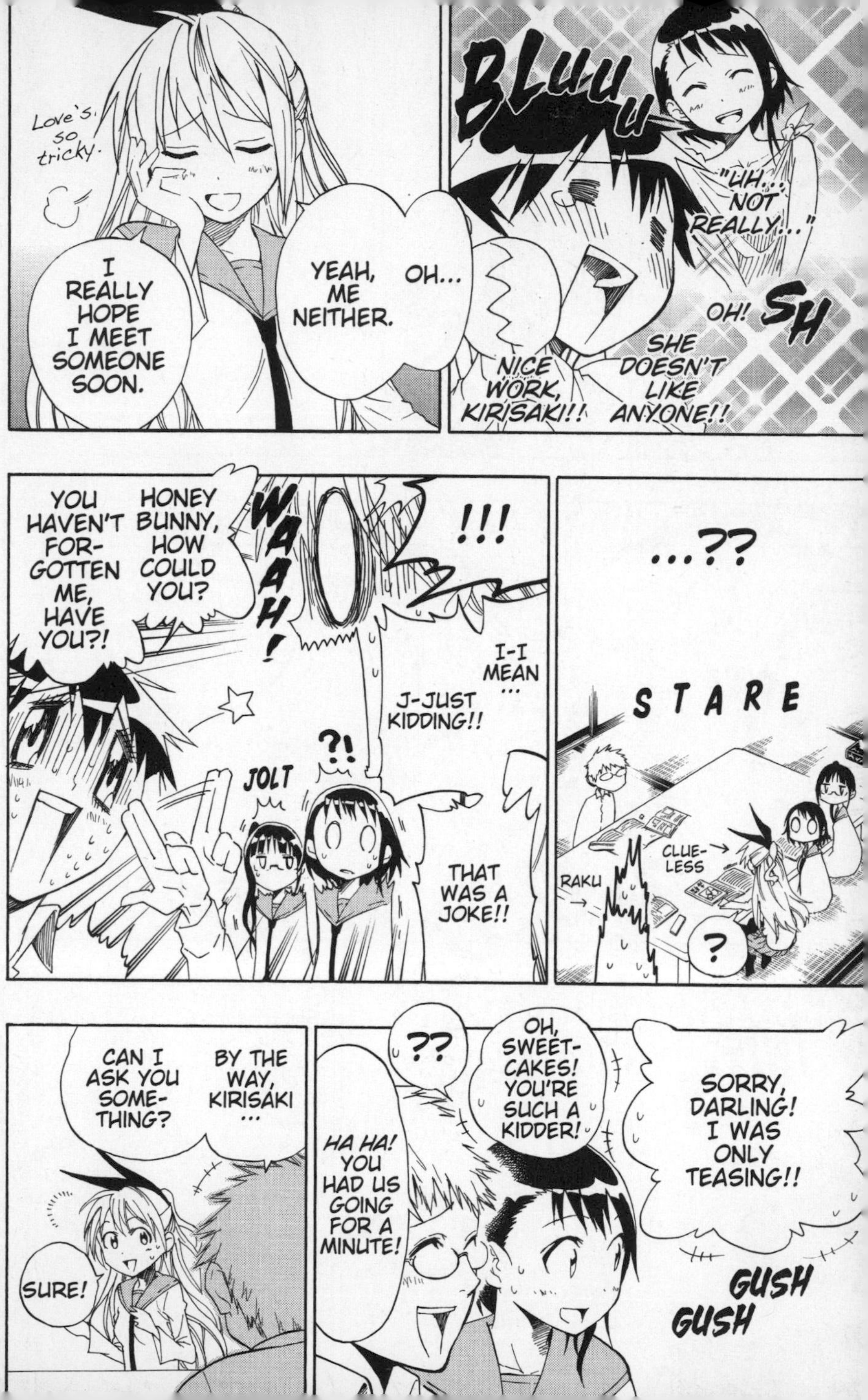
BLUUUU
"UH... NOT REALLY..."
OH!
SH
SHE DOESN'T LIKE ANYONE!!
NICE WORK, KIRISAKI!!
OH... YEAH, ME NEITHER.
Love's so tricky.
I REALLY HOPE I MEET SOMEONE SOON.
...??
STARE
CLUELESS
RAKU
?
!!!
HONEY BUNNY, HOW COULD YOU?
YOU HAVEN'T FORGOTTEN ME, HAVE YOU?!
WAAAH!
I-I MEAN...
J-JUST KIDDING!!
THAT WAS A JOKE!!
?!
JOLT
SORRY, DARLING! I WAS ONLY TEASING!!
OH, SWEET-CAKES! YOU'RE SUCH A KIDDER!
??
HA HA! YOU HAD US GOING FOR A MINUTE!
GUSH GUSH
BY THE WAY, KIRISAKI...
CAN I ASK YOU SOMETHING?
SURE!

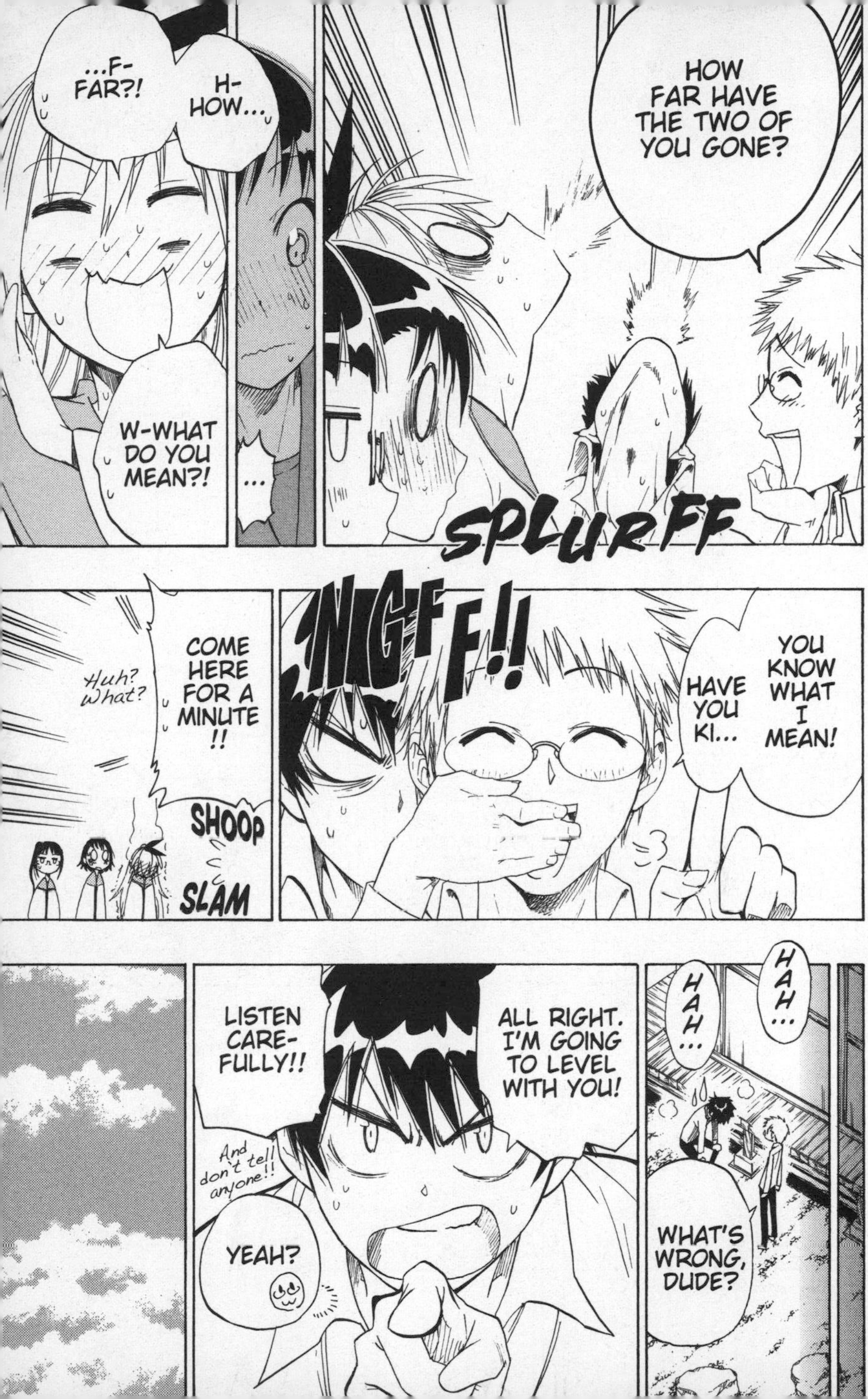
HOW FAR HAVE THE TWO OF YOU GONE?
SPLURFF
H- HOW...
...
...F- FAR?!
W-WHAT DO YOU MEAN?!
YOU KNOW WHAT I MEAN!
HAVE YOU KI...
NGFFF!!
COME HERE FOR A MINUTE!!
Huh? What?
SHOOP
SLAM
HAH...
HAH...
WHAT'S WRONG, DUDE?
ALL RIGHT. I'M GOING TO LEVEL WITH YOU!
LISTEN CARE-FULLY!!
And don't tell anyone!!
YEAH?

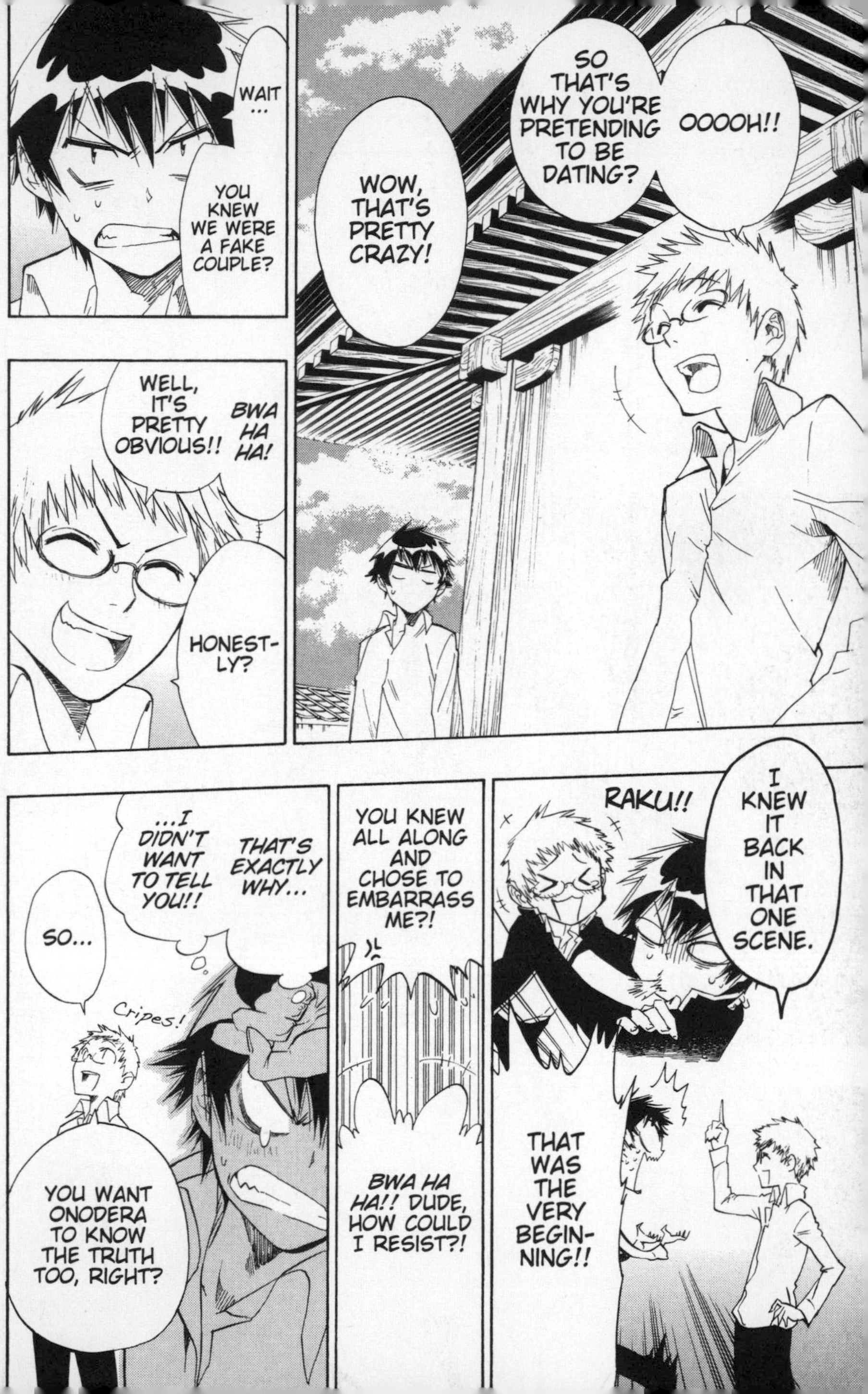
OOOOH!!
SO THAT'S WHY YOU'RE PRETENDING TO BE DATING?
WOW, THAT'S PRETTY CRAZY!
WAIT...
YOU KNEW WE WERE A FAKE COUPLE?
BWA HA HA!
WELL, IT'S PRETTY OBVIOUS!!
HONEST-LY?
I KNEW IT BACK IN THAT ONE SCENE.
RAKU!!
THAT WAS THE VERY BEGIN-NING!!
YOU KNEW ALL ALONG AND CHOSE TO EMBARRASS ME?!
BWA HA HA!! DUDE, HOW COULD I RESIST?!
THAT'S EXACTLY WHY...
...I DIDN'T WANT TO TELL YOU!!
SO...
Cripes!
YOU WANT ONODERA TO KNOW THE TRUTH TOO, RIGHT?

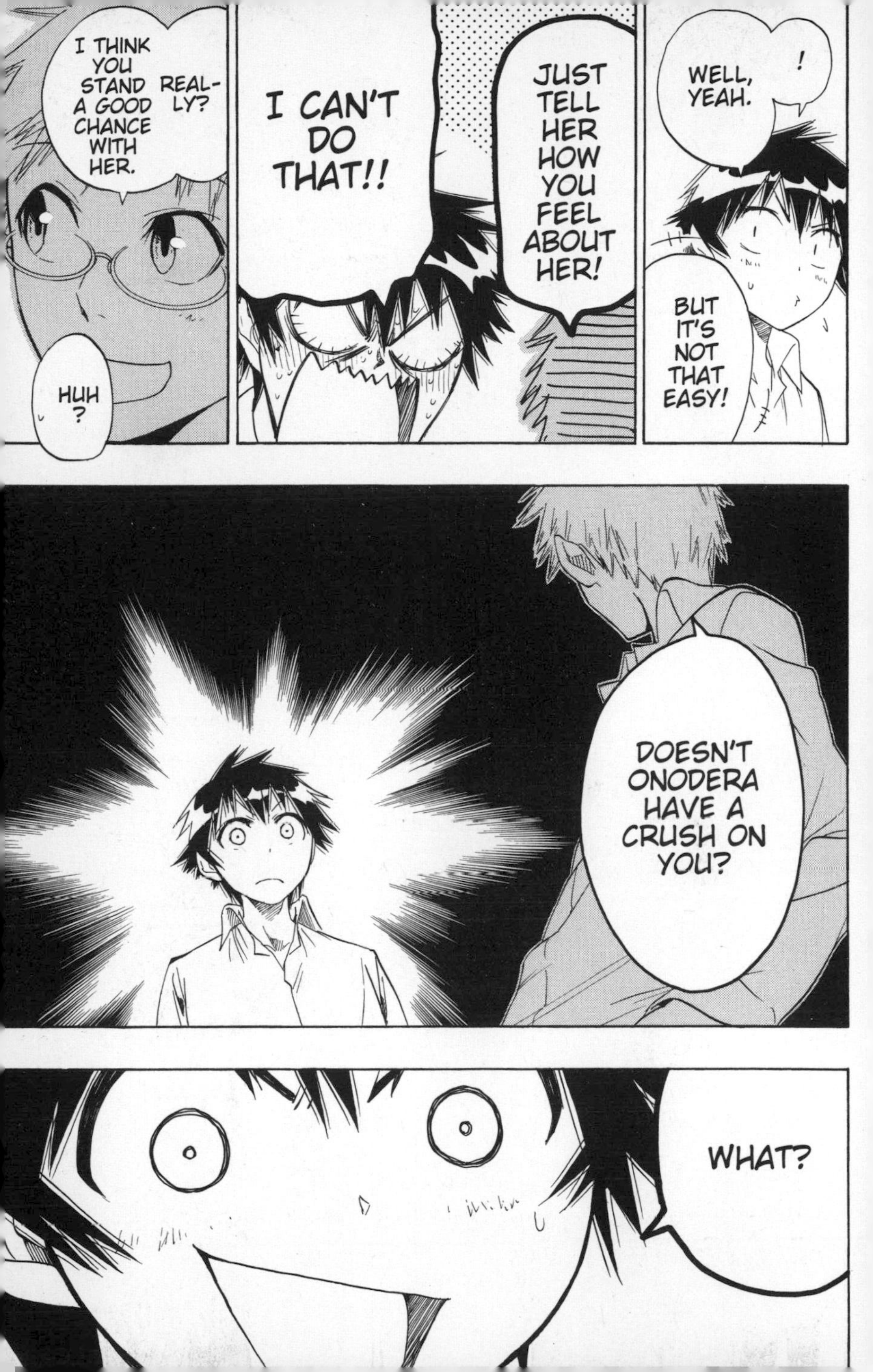
!
WELL, YEAH.
BUT IT'S NOT THAT EASY!
JUST TELL HER HOW YOU FEEL ABOUT HER!
I CAN'T DO THAT!!
HUH?
I THINK YOU STAND A GOOD CHANCE WITH HER.
REAL-LY?
DOESN'T ONODERA HAVE A CRUSH ON YOU?
WHAT?

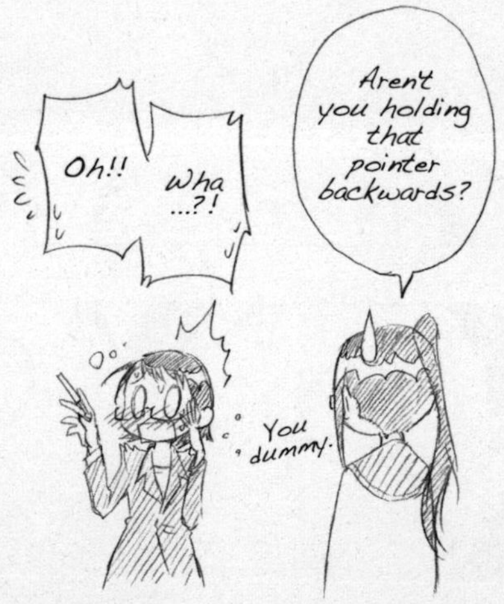
Aren't you holding that pointer backwards?
Wha ...?!
Oh!!
You dummy.

Chapter 9: Up Close

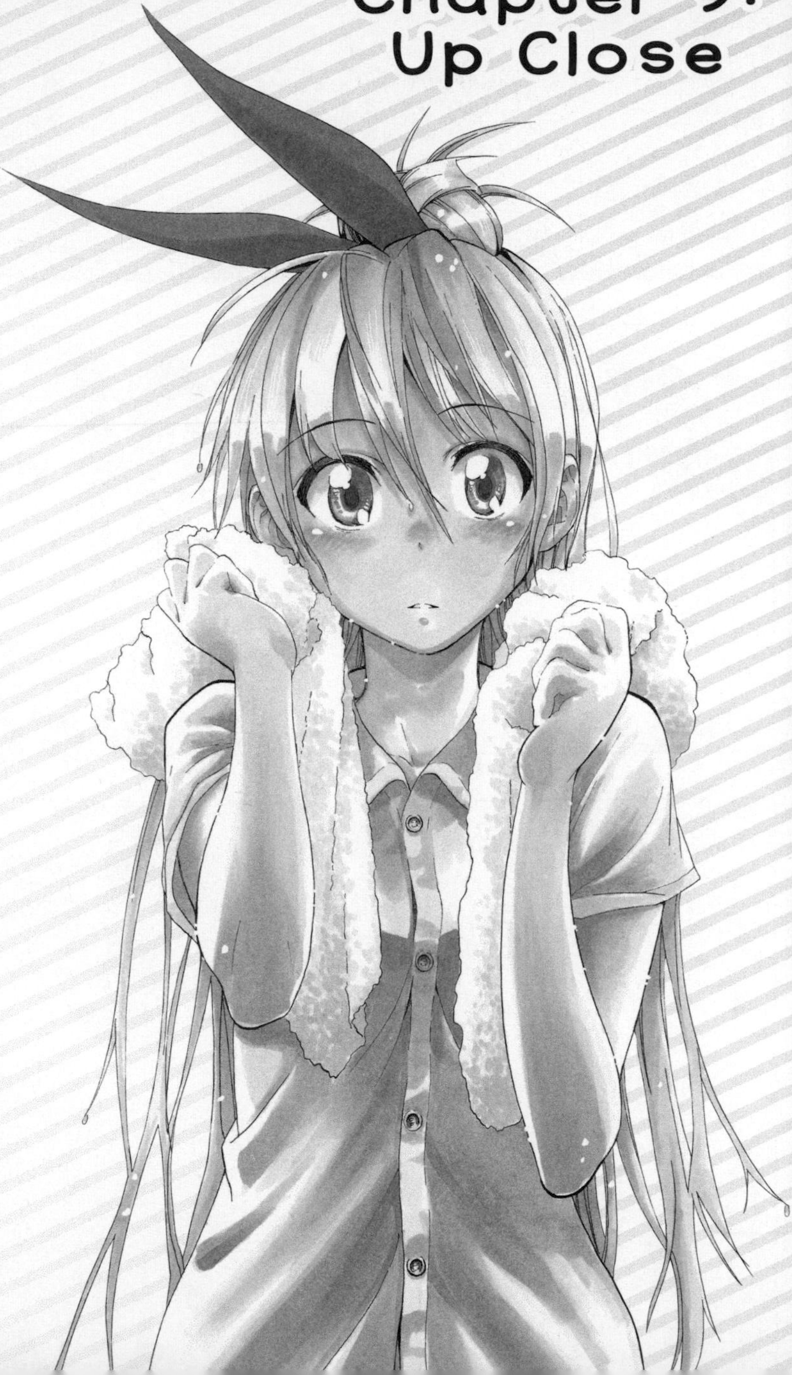

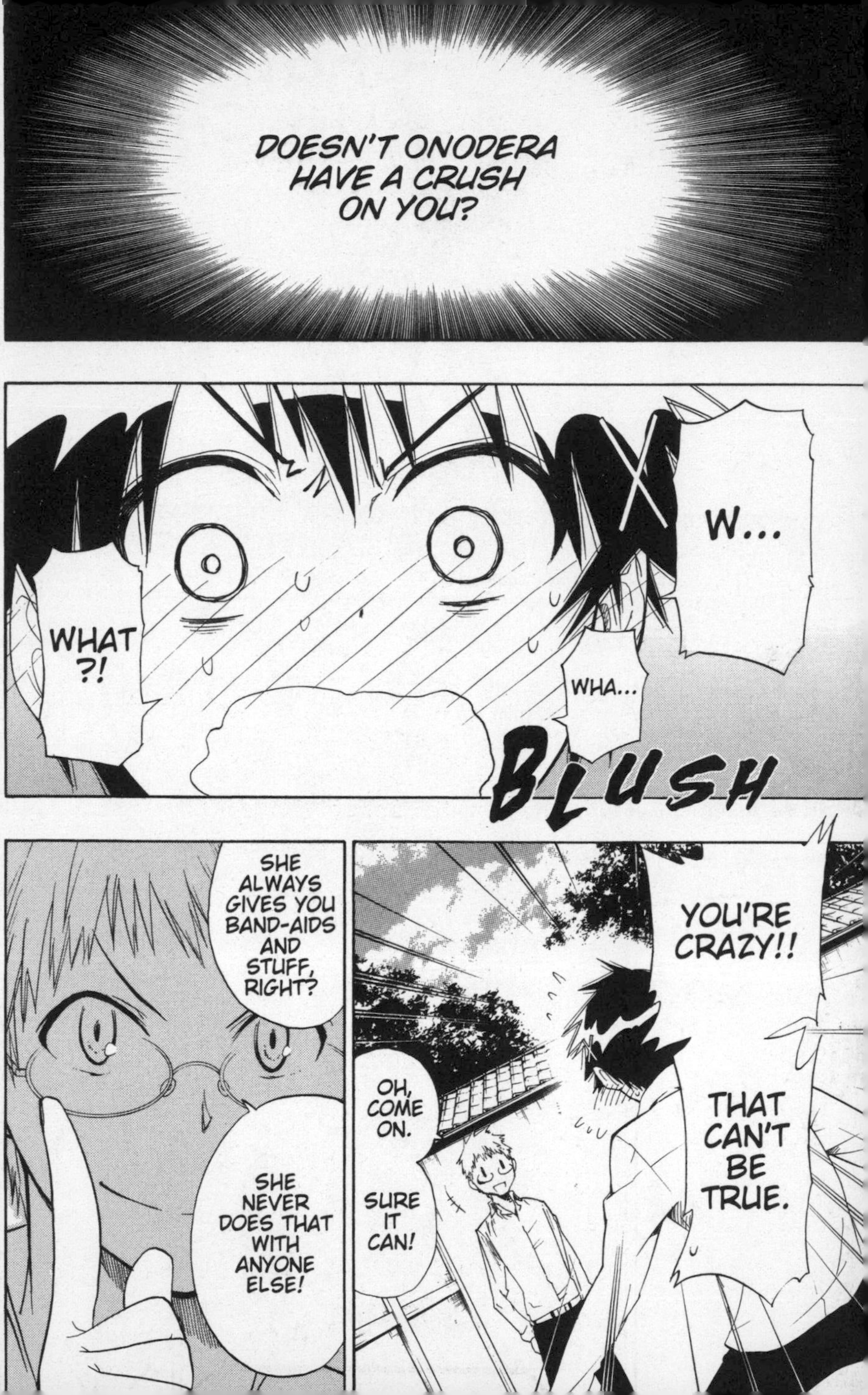
DOESN'T ONODERA HAVE A CRUSH ON YOU?
W...
WHA...
WHAT ?!
BLUSH
YOU'RE CRAZY!!
THAT CAN'T BE TRUE.
OH, COME ON.
SURE IT CAN!
SHE ALWAYS GIVES YOU BAND-AIDS AND STUFF, RIGHT?
SHE NEVER DOES THAT WITH ANYONE ELSE!

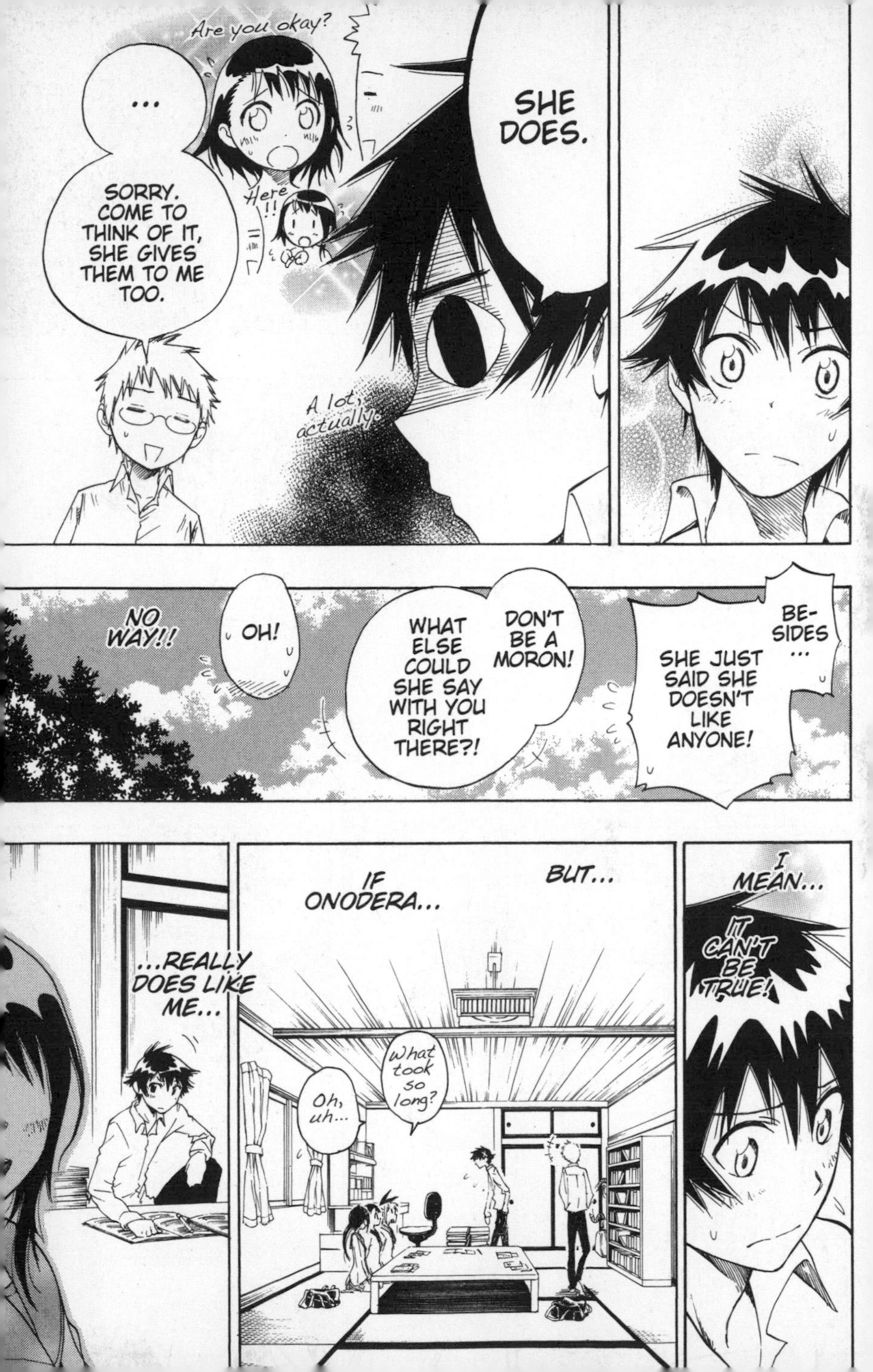
SHE DOES.
Are you okay?
...
SORRY. COME TO THINK OF IT, SHE GIVES THEM TO ME TOO.
Here!!
A lot, actually.
BE-SIDES... SHE JUST SAID SHE DOESN'T LIKE ANYONE!
DON'T BE A MORON!
WHAT ELSE COULD SHE SAY WITH YOU RIGHT THERE?!
OH!
NO WAY!!
I MEAN...
IT CAN'T BE TRUE!
BUT...
IF ONODERA...
What took so long?
Oh, uh...
...REALLY DOES LIKE ME...

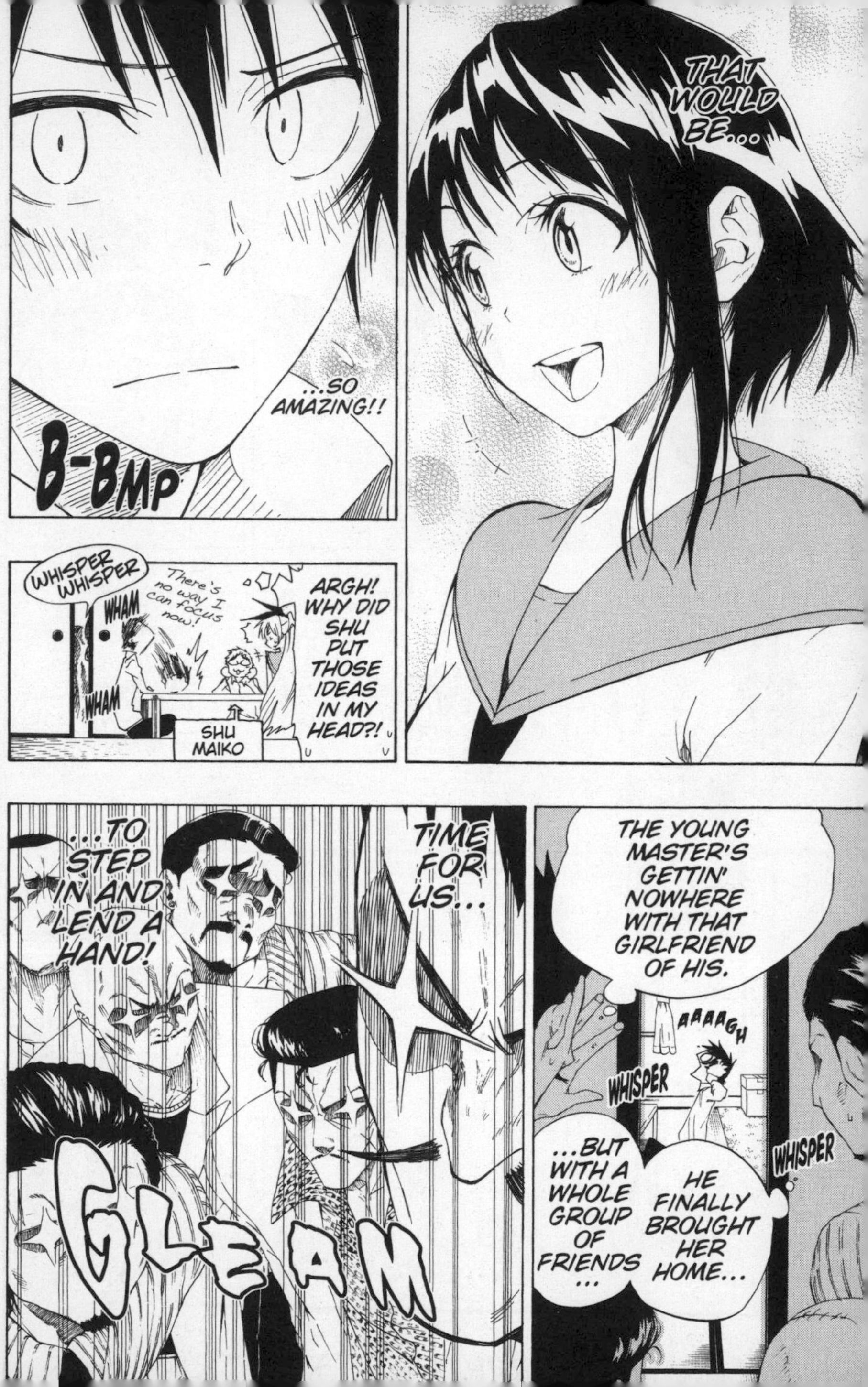
THAT WOULD BE...
...SO AMAZING!!
B-BMP
ARGH! WHY DID SHU PUT THOSE IDEAS IN MY HEAD?!
There's no way I can focus now!
WHISPER WHISPER
WHAM
WHAM
SHU MAIKO
THE YOUNG MASTER'S GETTIN' NOWHERE WITH THAT GIRLFRIEND OF HIS.
AAAAGH
WHISPER
WHISPER
HE FINALLY BROUGHT HER HOME...
...BUT WITH A WHOLE GROUP OF FRIENDS...
TIME FOR US...
...TO STEP IN AND LEND A HAND!
GLEAM

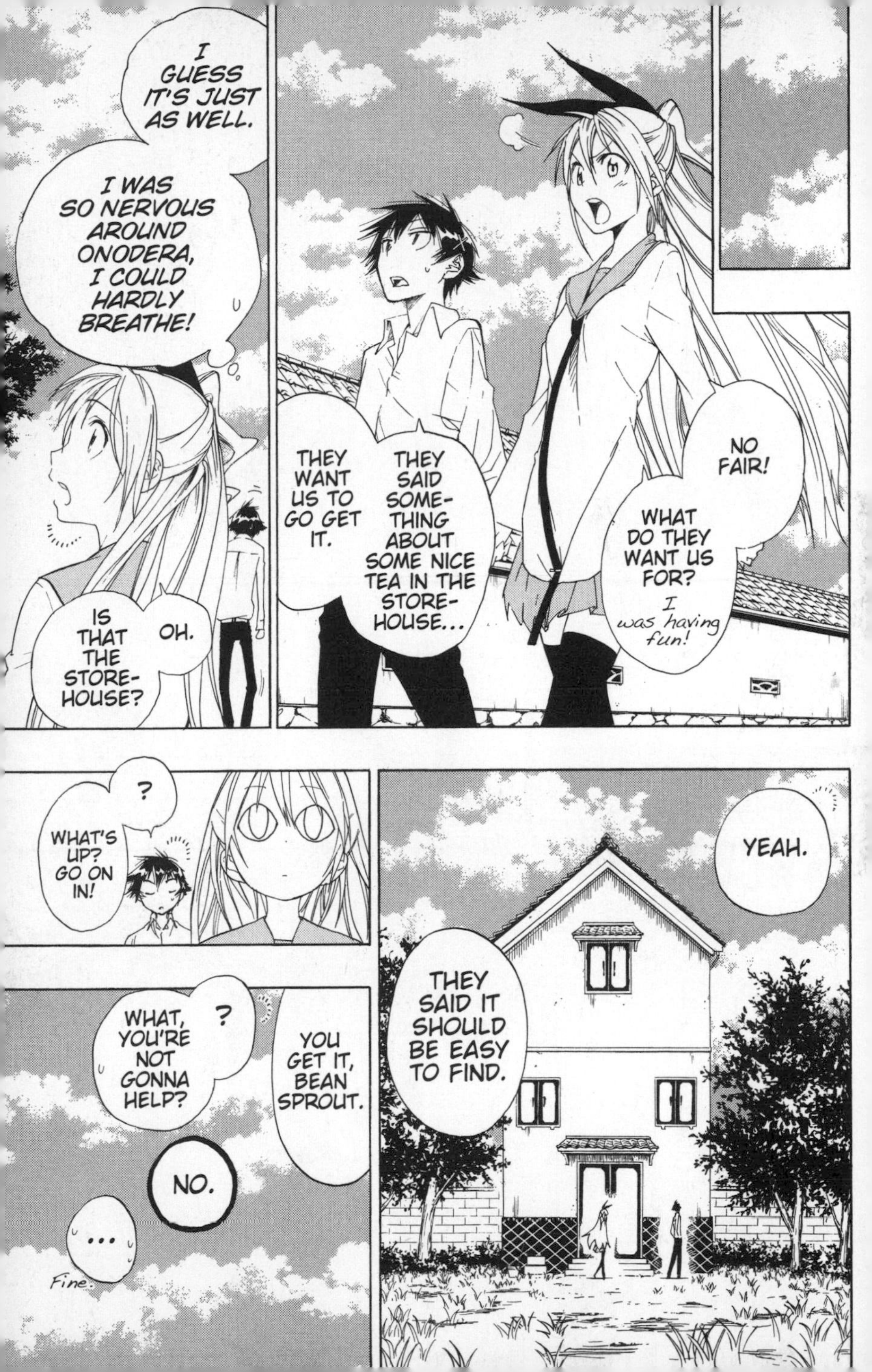

NO FAIR!
WHAT DO THEY WANT US FOR?
I was having fun!
THEY SAID SOME-THING ABOUT SOME NICE TEA IN THE STORE-HOUSE...
THEY WANT US TO GO GET IT.
I GUESS IT'S JUST AS WELL.
I WAS SO NERVOUS AROUND ONODERA, I COULD HARDLY BREATHE!
OH.
IS THAT THE STORE-HOUSE?
YEAH.
THEY SAID IT SHOULD BE EASY TO FIND.
?
WHAT'S UP? GO ON IN!
YOU GET IT, BEAN SPROUT.
?
WHAT, YOU'RE NOT GONNA HELP?
NO.
...
Fine.

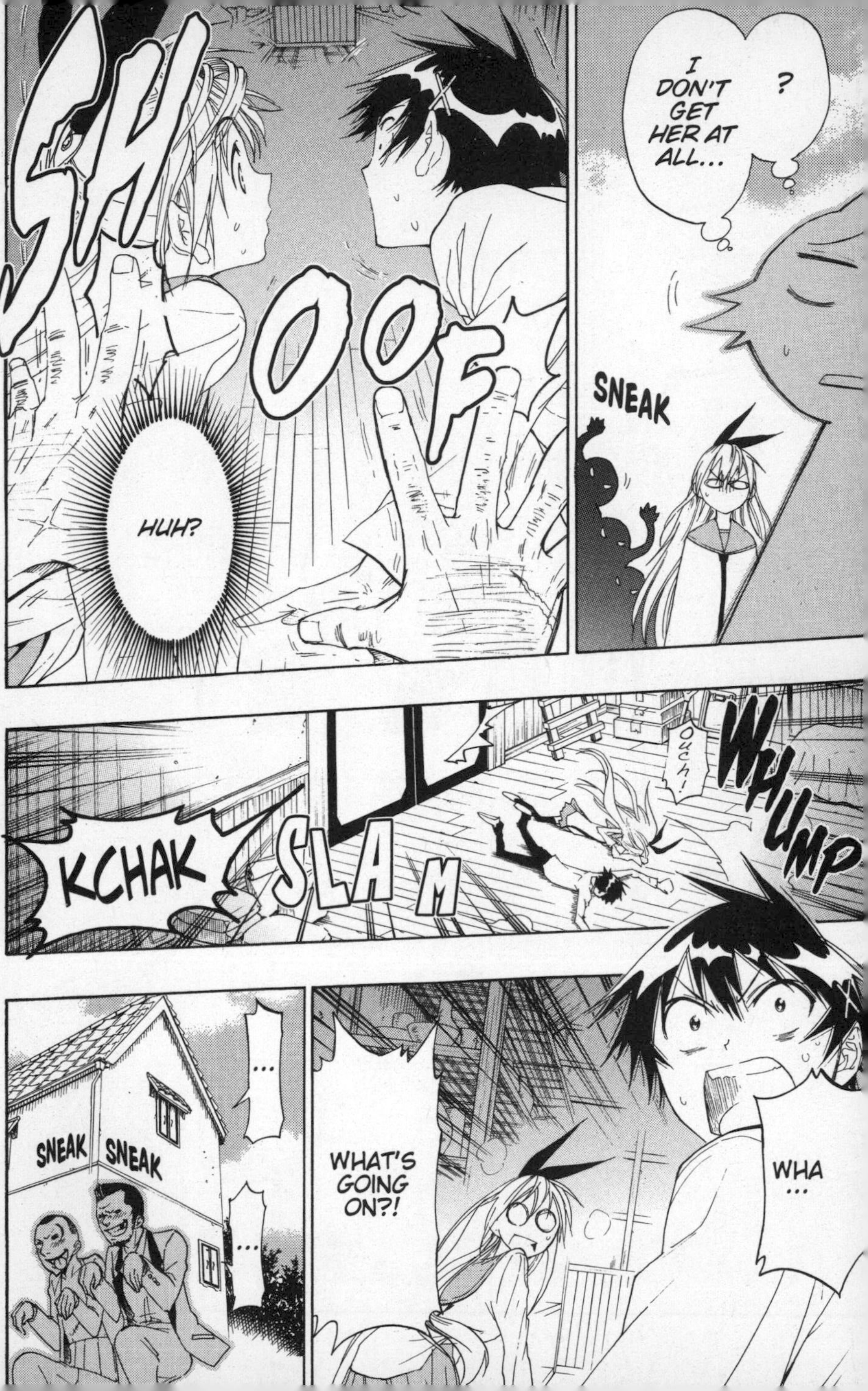
I DON'T GET HER AT ALL... ?
SNEAK
SH
OOF
HUH?
WHUMP
OUCH!
SLAM
KCHAK
WHA ...
WHAT'S GOING ON?!
...
...
SNEAK SNEAK

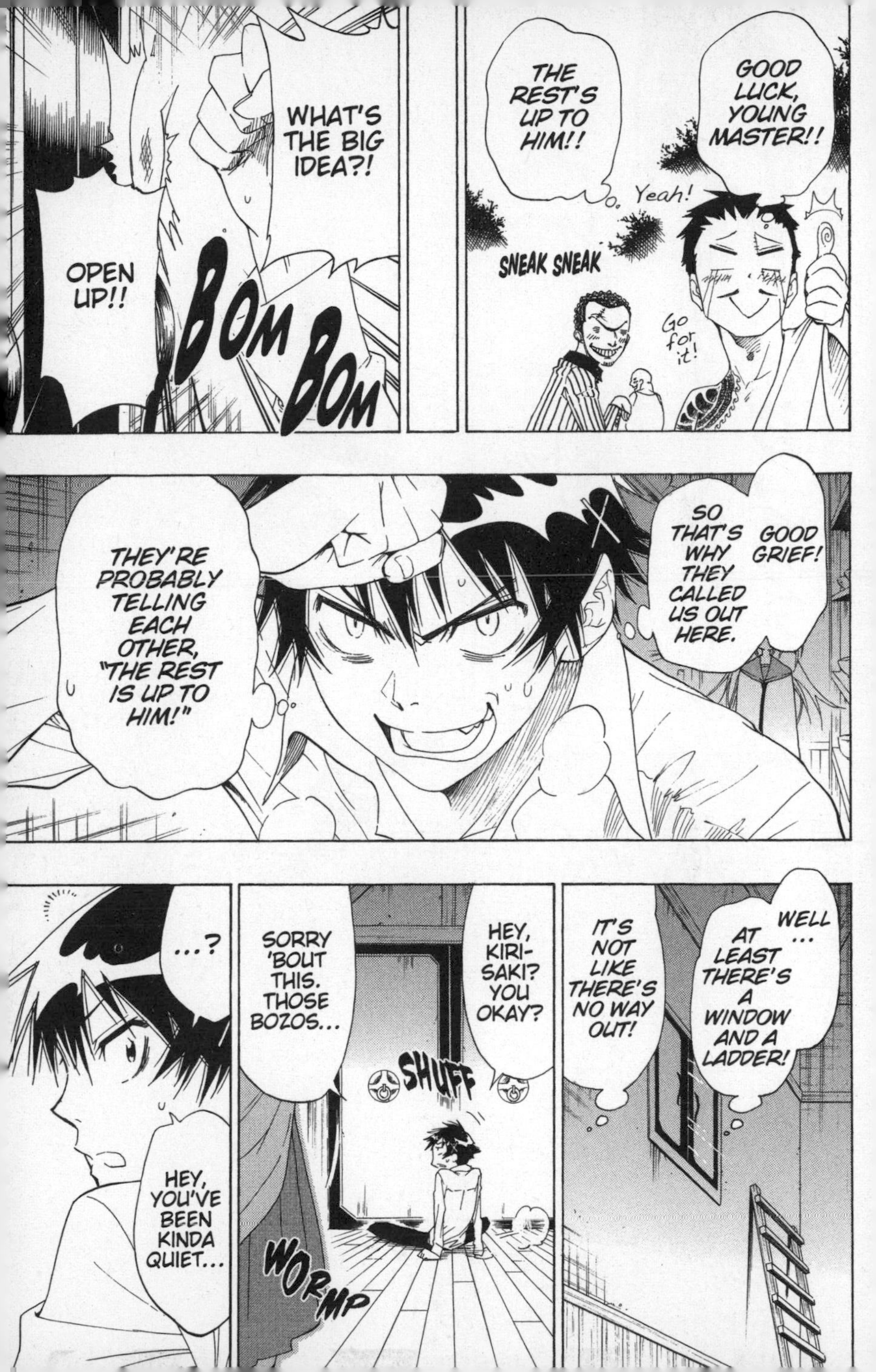
GOOD LUCK, YOUNG MASTER!!
THE REST'S UP TO HIM!!
Yeah!
Go for it!
SNEAK SNEAK
WHAT'S THE BIG IDEA?!
OPEN UP!!
BOM BOM BOM
GOOD GRIEF!
SO THAT'S WHY THEY CALLED US OUT HERE.
THEY'RE PROBABLY TELLING EACH OTHER, "THE REST IS UP TO HIM!"
WELL... AT LEAST THERE'S A WINDOW AND A LADDER!
IT'S NOT LIKE THERE'S NO WAY OUT!
HEY, KIRI-SAKI? YOU OKAY?
SORRY 'BOUT THIS. THOSE BOZOS...
SHUFF
WORMP
...?
HEY, YOU'VE BEEN KINDA QUIET...

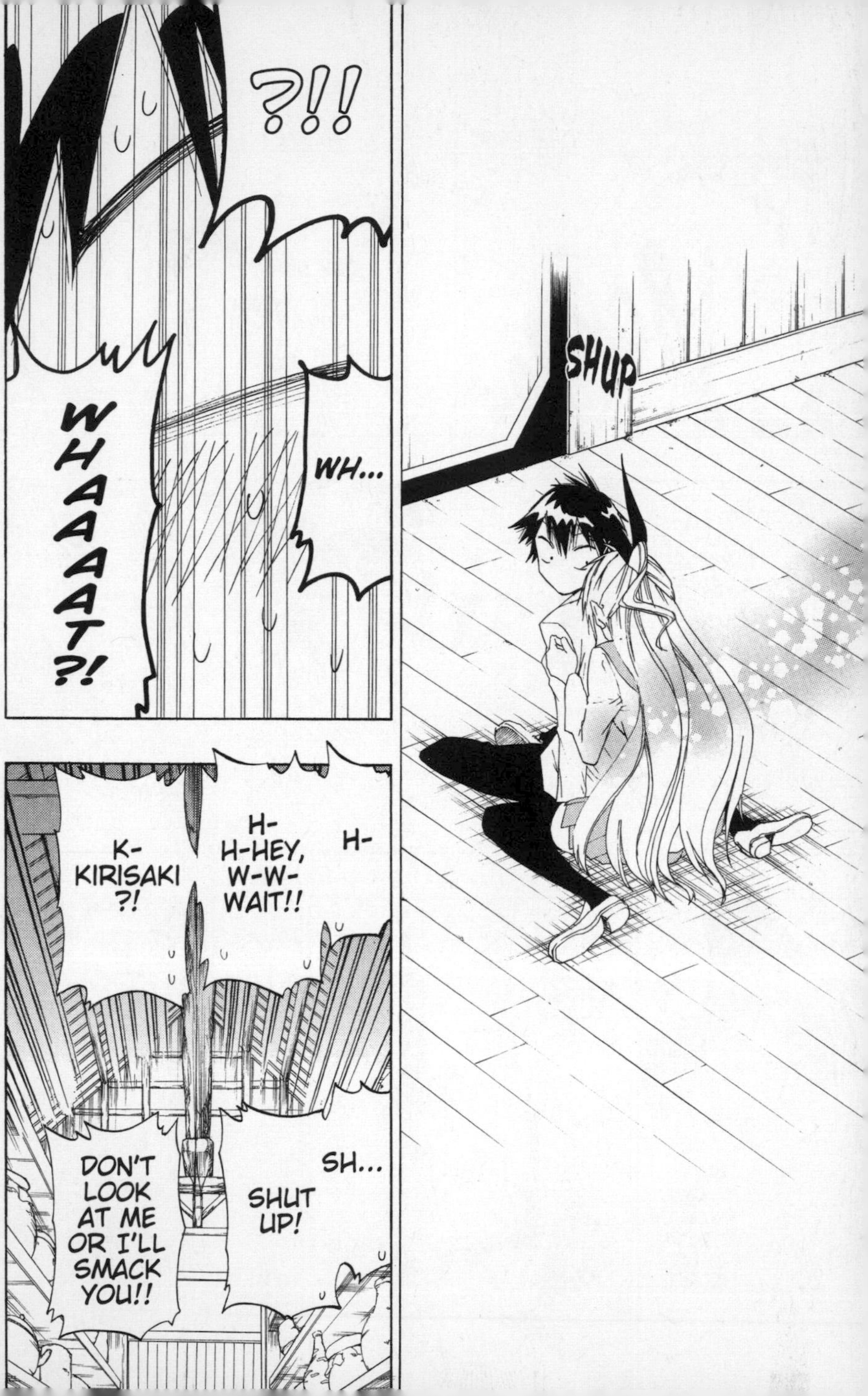
SHUP
?!!
WH...
WHAAAAAT?!
H-
H-H-HEY, W-W-WAIT!!
K-KIRISAKI?!
SH...
SHUT UP!
DON'T LOOK AT ME OR I'LL SMACK YOU!!

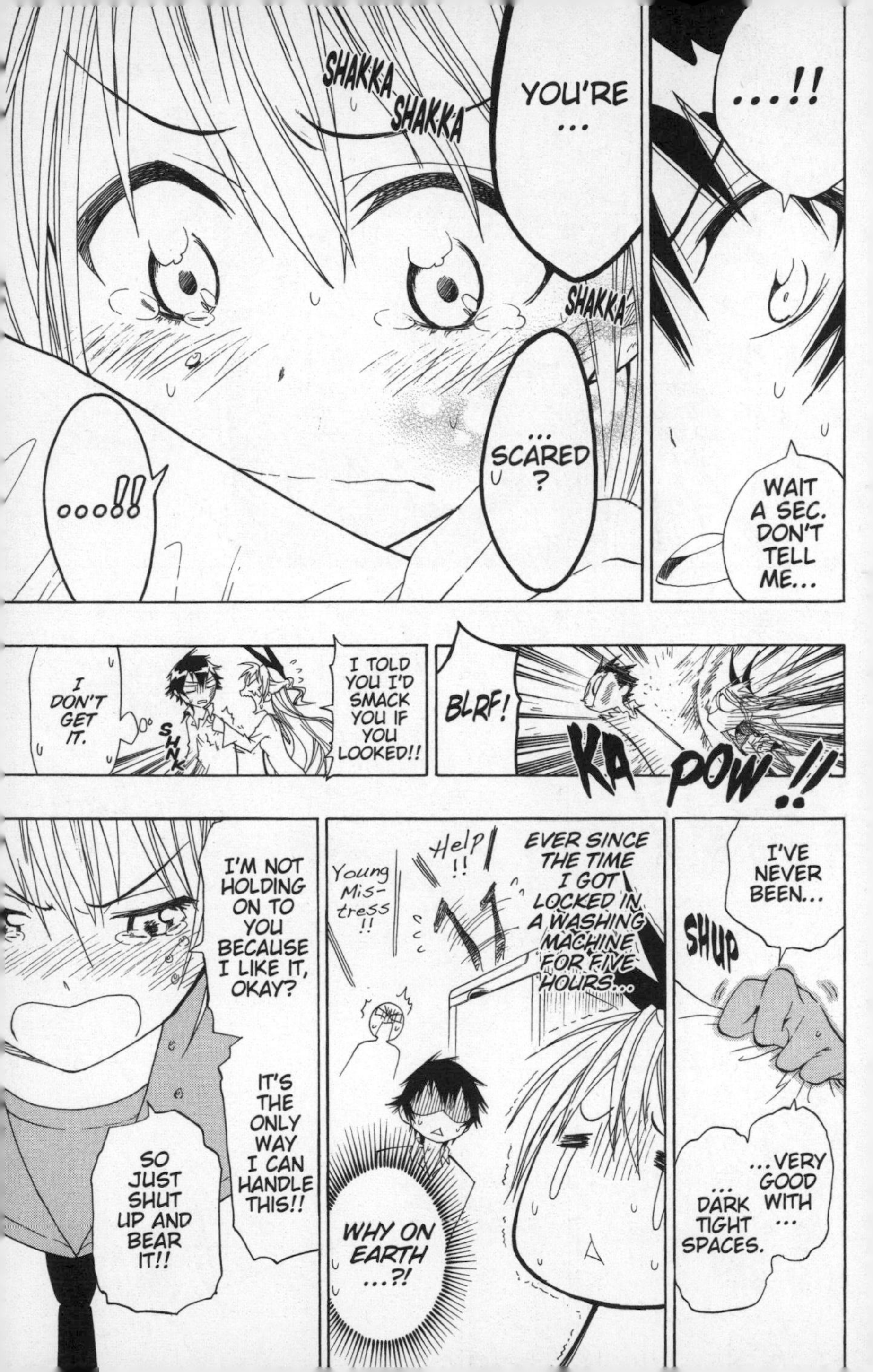
...!!
WAIT A SEC. DON'T TELL ME...
YOU'RE ...
SHAKKA SHAKKA
SHAKKA
... SCARED?
OOOO!!
BLRF!
KA POW!!
I TOLD YOU I'D SMACK YOU IF YOU LOOKED!!
SHNK
I DON'T GET IT.
I'VE NEVER BEEN...
SHUP
...VERY GOOD WITH...
... DARK TIGHT SPACES.
EVER SINCE THE TIME I GOT LOCKED IN A WASHING MACHINE FOR FIVE HOURS...
Help!!
Young Mis-tress!!
WHY ON EARTH ...?!
I'M NOT HOLDING ON TO YOU BECAUSE I LIKE IT, OKAY?
IT'S THE ONLY WAY I CAN HANDLE THIS!!
SO JUST SHUT UP AND BEAR IT!!

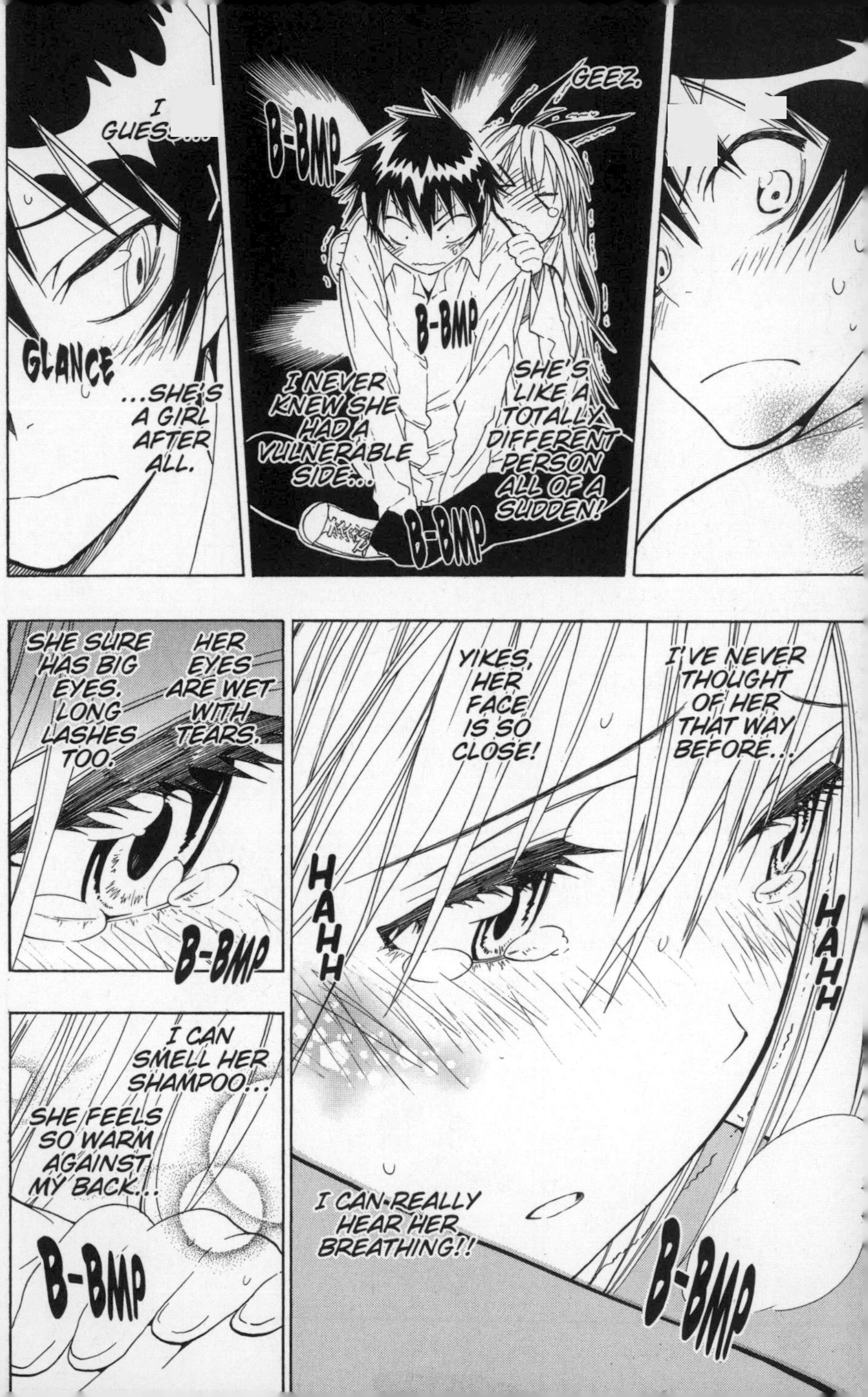
GEEZ.
B-BMP
B-BMP
SHE'S LIKE A TOTALLY DIFFERENT PERSON ALL OF A SUDDEN!
I NEVER KNEW SHE HAD A VULNERABLE SIDE...
B-BMP
I GUESS...
GLANCE
...SHE'S A GIRL AFTER ALL.
I'VE NEVER THOUGHT OF HER THAT WAY BEFORE...
YIKES, HER FACE IS SO CLOSE!
HAHH
HAHH
I CAN REALLY HEAR HER BREATHING!!
B-BMP
HER EYES ARE WET WITH TEARS.
SHE SURE HAS BIG EYES. LONG LASHES TOO.
B-BMP
I CAN SMELL HER SHAMPOO...
SHE FEELS SO WARM AGAINST MY BACK...
B-BMP

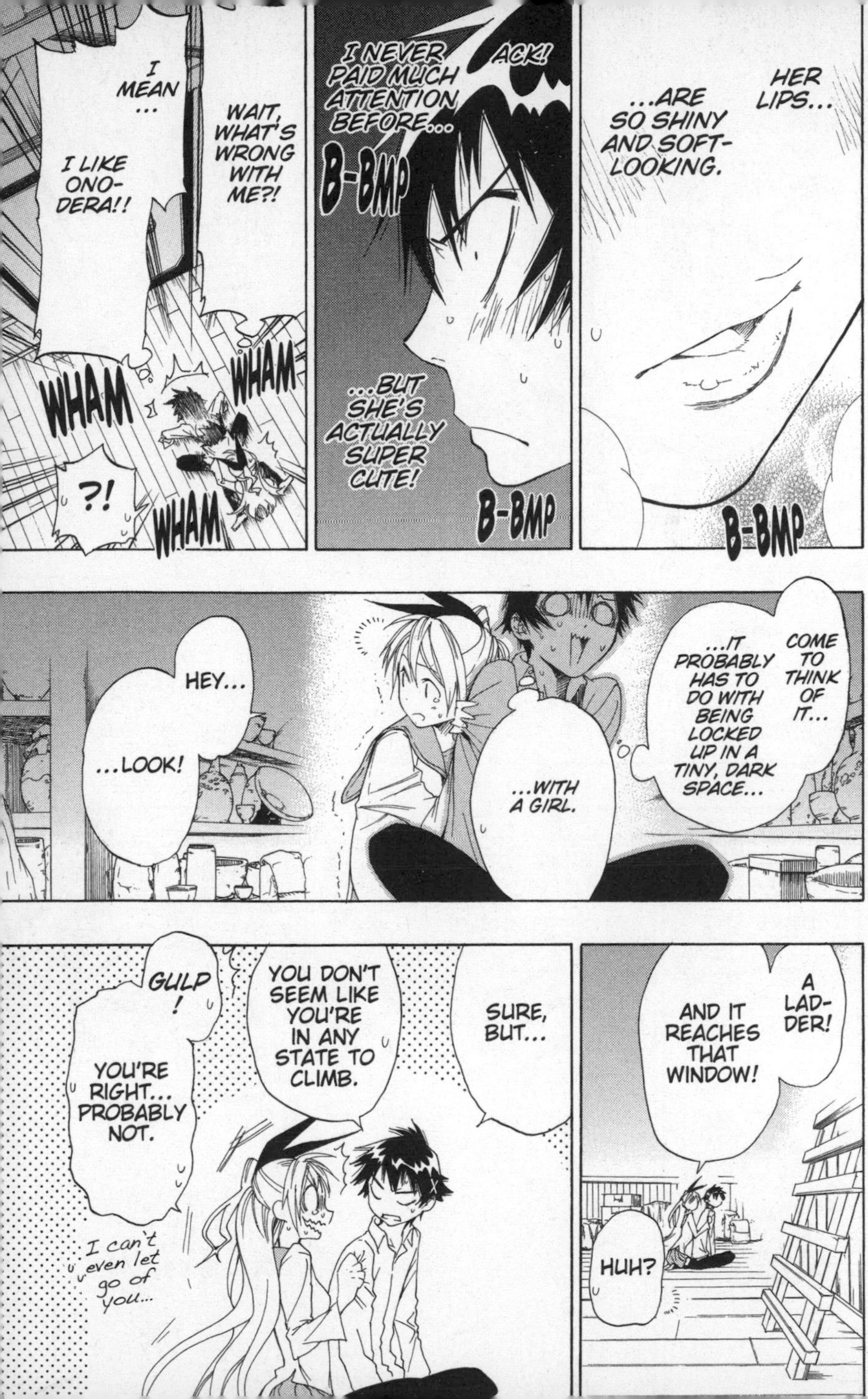
HER LIPS...
...ARE SO SHINY AND SOFT-LOOKING.
B-BMP
ACK!
I NEVER PAID MUCH ATTENTION BEFORE...
B-BMP
...BUT SHE'S ACTUALLY SUPER CUTE!
B-BMP
WAIT, WHAT'S WRONG WITH ME?!
I MEAN... I LIKE ONO-DERA!!
WHAM
WHAM
WHAM
?!
COME TO THINK OF IT...
...IT PROBABLY HAS TO DO WITH BEING LOCKED UP IN A TINY, DARK SPACE...
...WITH A GIRL.
HEY...
...LOOK!
A LAD-DER!
AND IT REACHES THAT WINDOW!
HUH?
SURE, BUT...
YOU DON'T SEEM LIKE YOU'RE IN ANY STATE TO CLIMB.
GULP!
YOU'RE RIGHT... PROBABLY NOT.
I can't even let go of you...

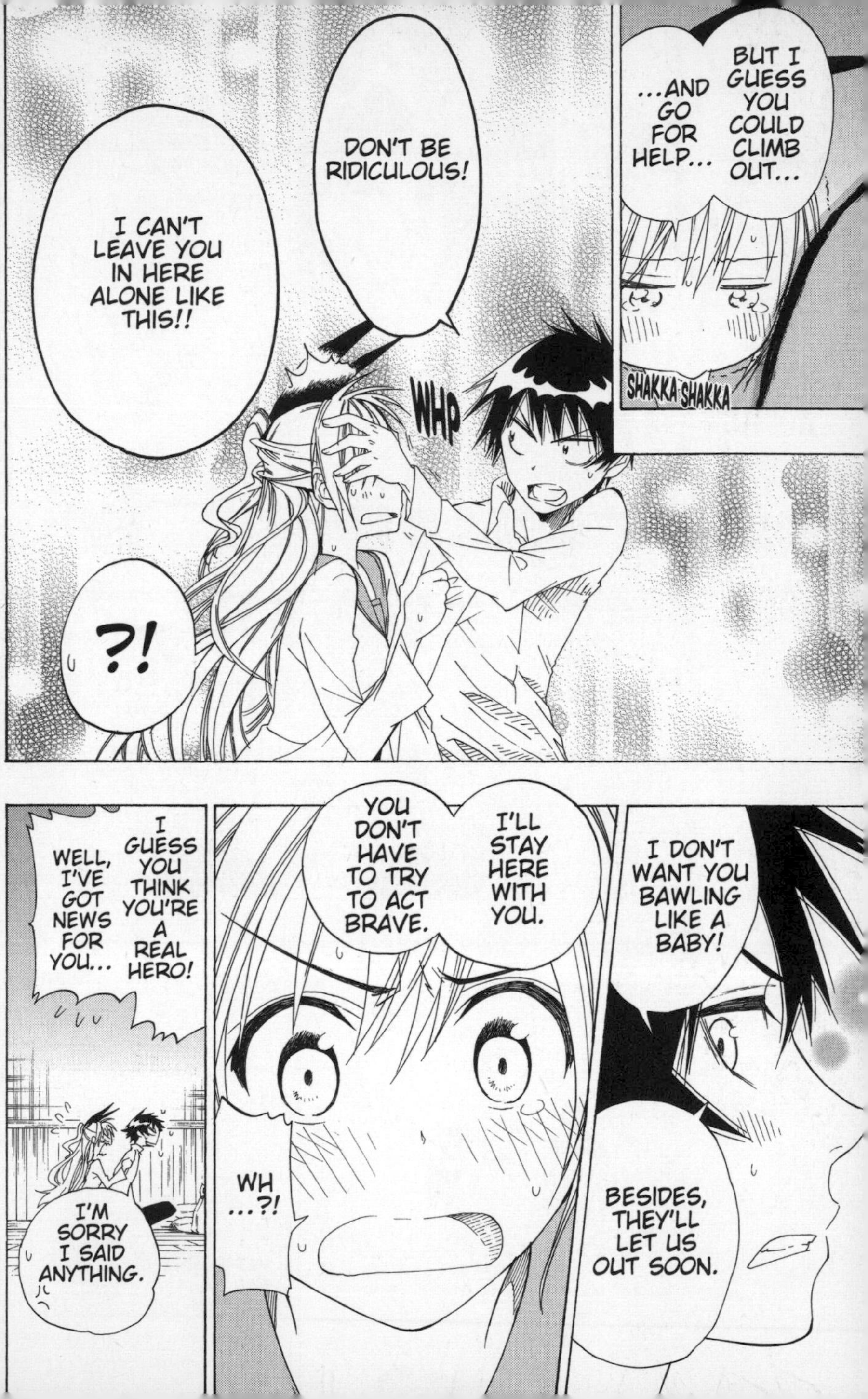
BUT I GUESS YOU COULD CLIMB OUT...
...AND GO FOR HELP...
SHAKKA SHAKKA
DON'T BE RIDICULOUS!
I CAN'T LEAVE YOU IN HERE ALONE LIKE THIS!!
WHP
?!
I DON'T WANT YOU BAWLING LIKE A BABY!
BESIDES, THEY'LL LET US OUT SOON.
I'LL STAY HERE WITH YOU.
YOU DON'T HAVE TO TRY TO ACT BRAVE.
WH...?!
I GUESS YOU THINK YOU'RE A REAL HERO!
WELL, I'VE GOT NEWS FOR YOU...
I'M SORRY I SAID ANYTHING.

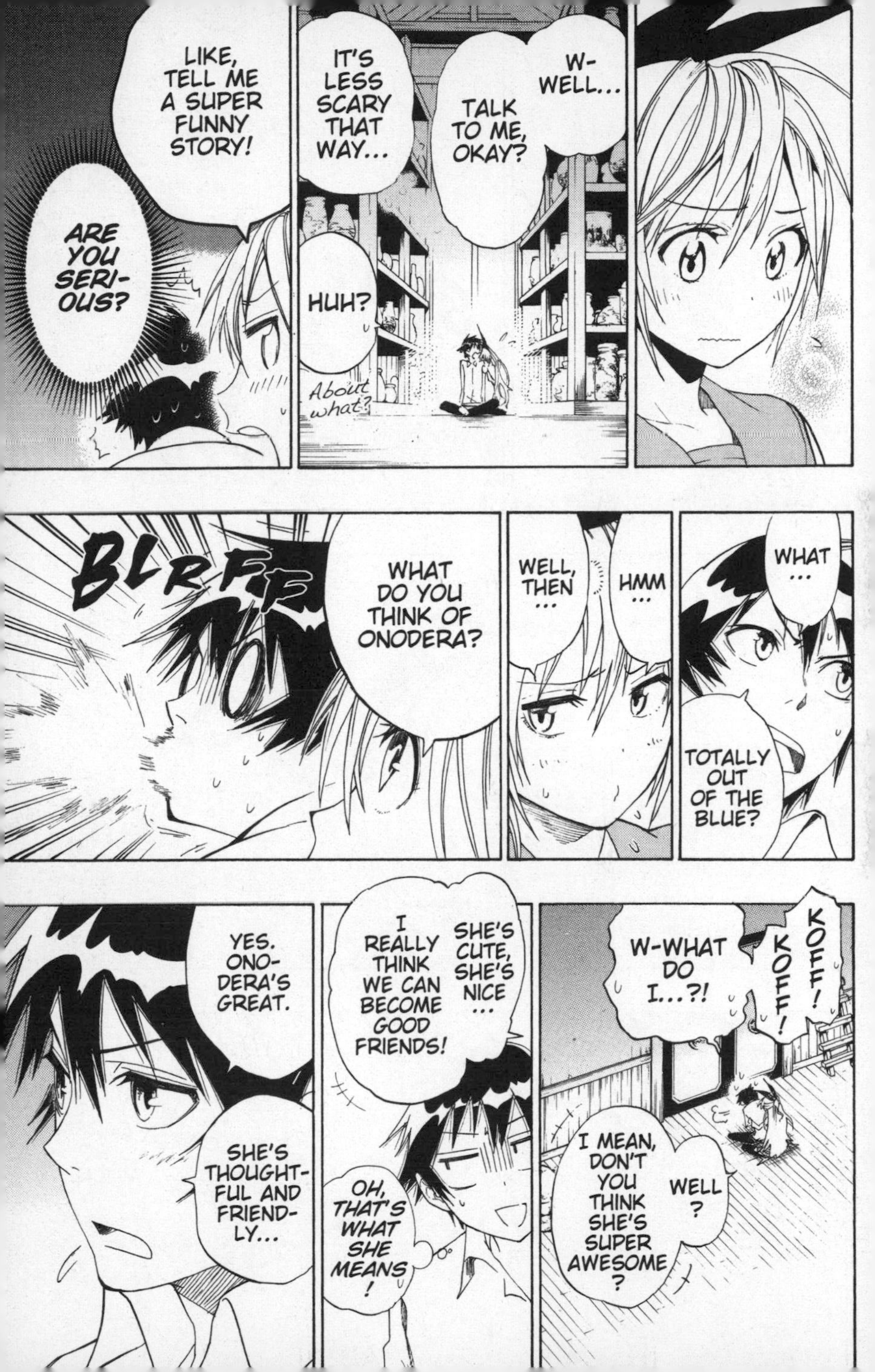
W-WELL...
TALK TO ME, OKAY?
IT'S LESS SCARY THAT WAY...
HUH?
About what?
LIKE, TELL ME A SUPER FUNNY STORY!
ARE YOU SERI-OUS?
WHAT...
TOTALLY OUT OF THE BLUE?
HMM...
WELL, THEN...
WHAT DO YOU THINK OF ONODERA?
BLRFF
KOFF! KOFF!
W-WHAT DO I...?!
WELL?
I MEAN, DON'T YOU THINK SHE'S SUPER AWESOME?
SHE'S CUTE, SHE'S NICE...
I REALLY THINK WE CAN BECOME GOOD FRIENDS!
OH, THAT'S WHAT SHE MEANS!
YES. ONO-DERA'S GREAT.
SHE'S THOUGHT-FUL AND FRIEND-LY...

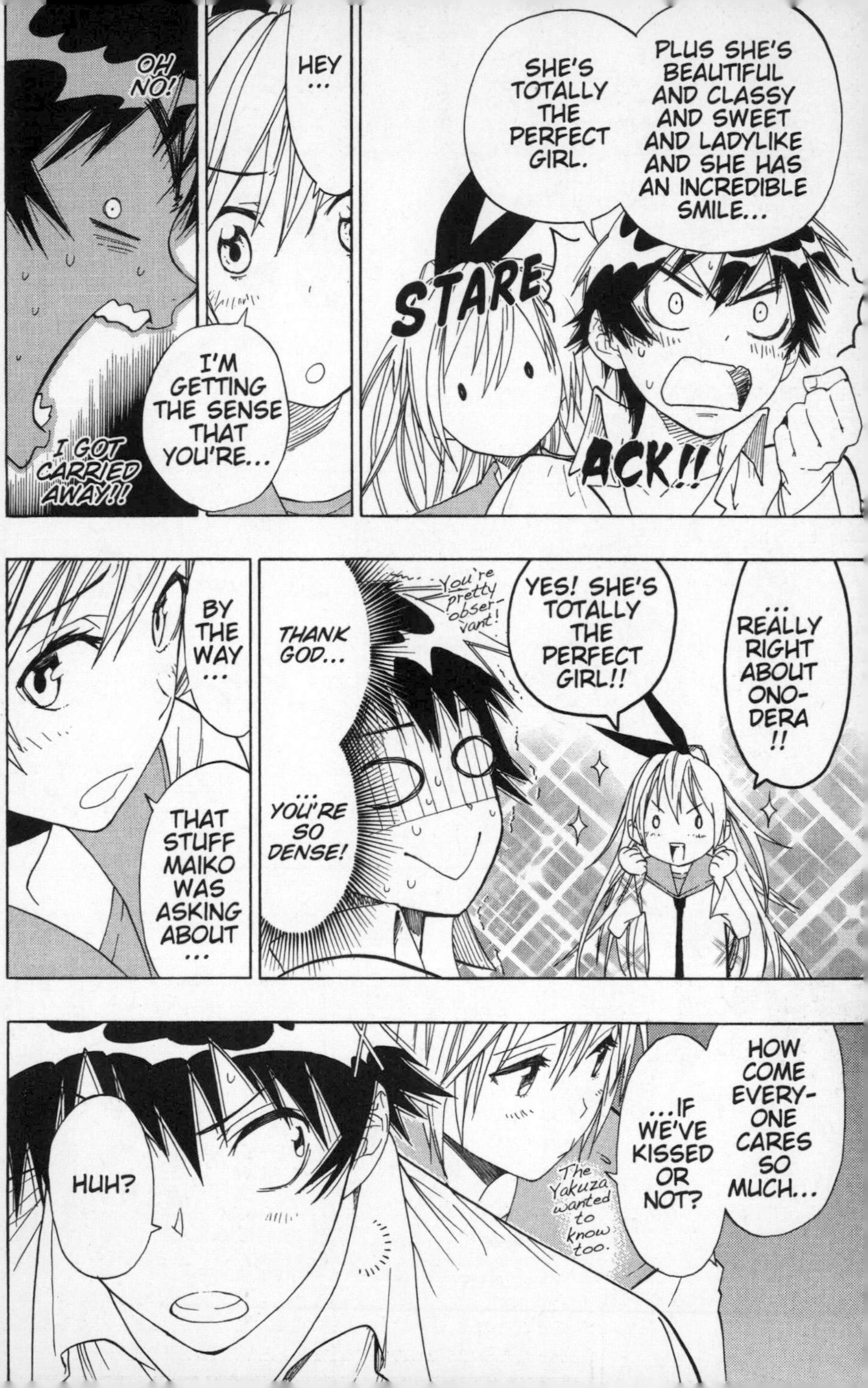
PLUS SHE'S BEAUTIFUL AND CLASSY AND SWEET AND LADYLIKE AND SHE HAS AN INCREDIBLE SMILE...
SHE'S TOTALLY THE PERFECT GIRL.
STARE
ACK!!
HEY...
I'M GETTING THE SENSE THAT YOU'RE...
OH NO!
I GOT CARRIED AWAY!!
...REALLY RIGHT ABOUT ONO-DERA!!
YES! SHE'S TOTALLY THE PERFECT GIRL!!
You're pretty obser-vant!
THANK GOD...
...YOU'RE SO DENSE!
BY THE WAY...
THAT STUFF MAIKO WAS ASKING ABOUT...
HOW COME EVERY-ONE CARES SO MUCH...
...IF WE'VE KISSED OR NOT?
The Yakuza wanted to know too.
HUH?

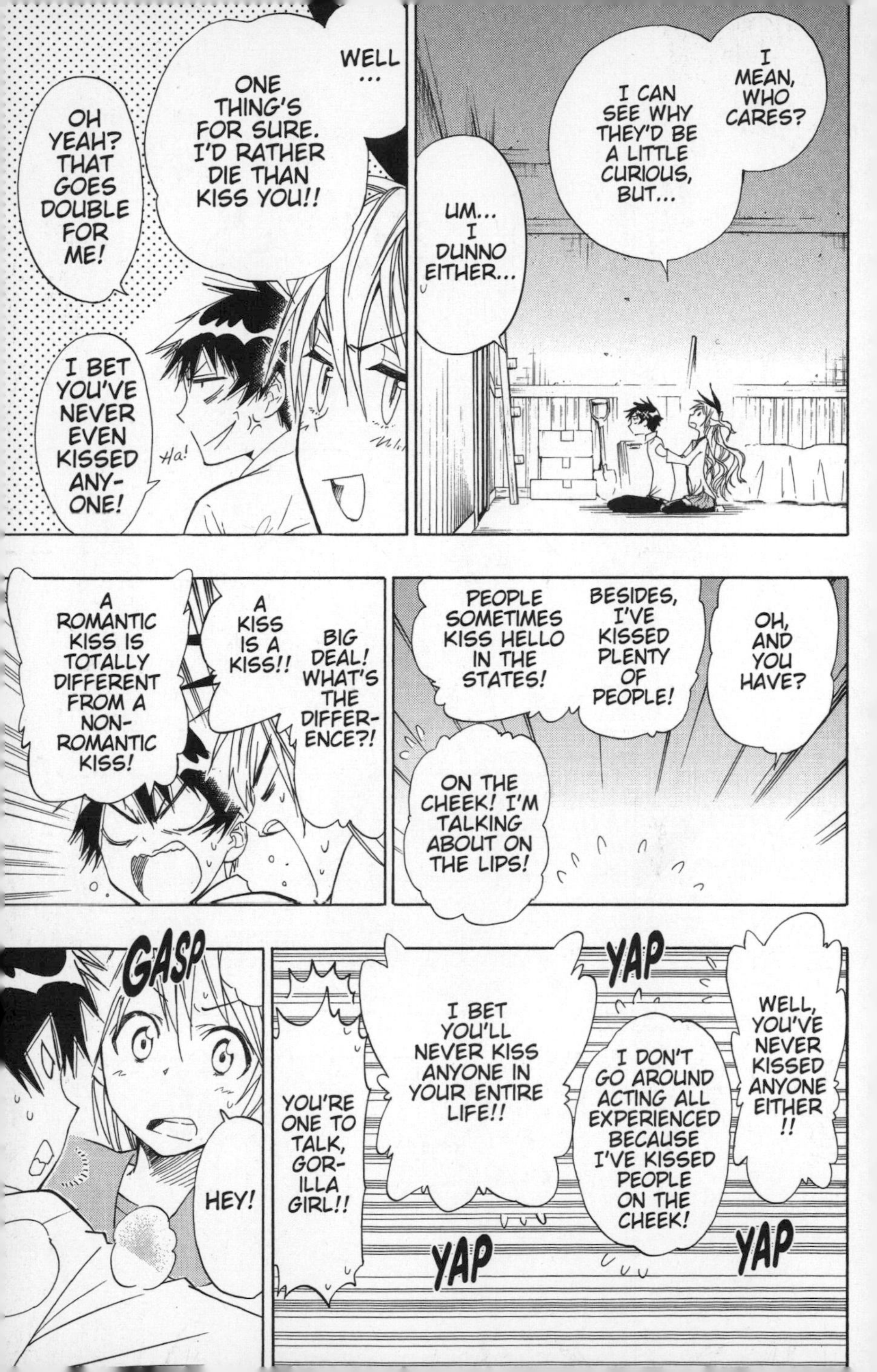
I MEAN, WHO CARES?
I CAN SEE WHY THEY'D BE A LITTLE CURIOUS, BUT...
UM... I DUNNO EITHER...
WELL...
ONE THING'S FOR SURE. I'D RATHER DIE THAN KISS YOU!!
OH YEAH? THAT GOES DOUBLE FOR ME!
I BET YOU'VE NEVER EVEN KISSED ANY-ONE!
Ha!
OH, AND YOU HAVE?
BESIDES, I'VE KISSED PLENTY OF PEOPLE!
PEOPLE SOMETIMES KISS HELLO IN THE STATES!
ON THE CHEEK! I'M TALKING ABOUT ON THE LIPS!
BIG DEAL! WHAT'S THE DIFFER-ENCE?!
A KISS IS A KISS!!
A ROMANTIC KISS IS TOTALLY DIFFERENT FROM A NON-ROMANTIC KISS!
WELL, YOU'VE NEVER KISSED ANYONE EITHER!!
YAP
I DON'T GO AROUND ACTING ALL EXPERIENCED BECAUSE I'VE KISSED PEOPLE ON THE CHEEK!
I BET YOU'LL NEVER KISS ANYONE IN YOUR ENTIRE LIFE!!
YOU'RE ONE TO TALK, GOR-ILLA GIRL!!
YAP
YAP
GASP
HEY!

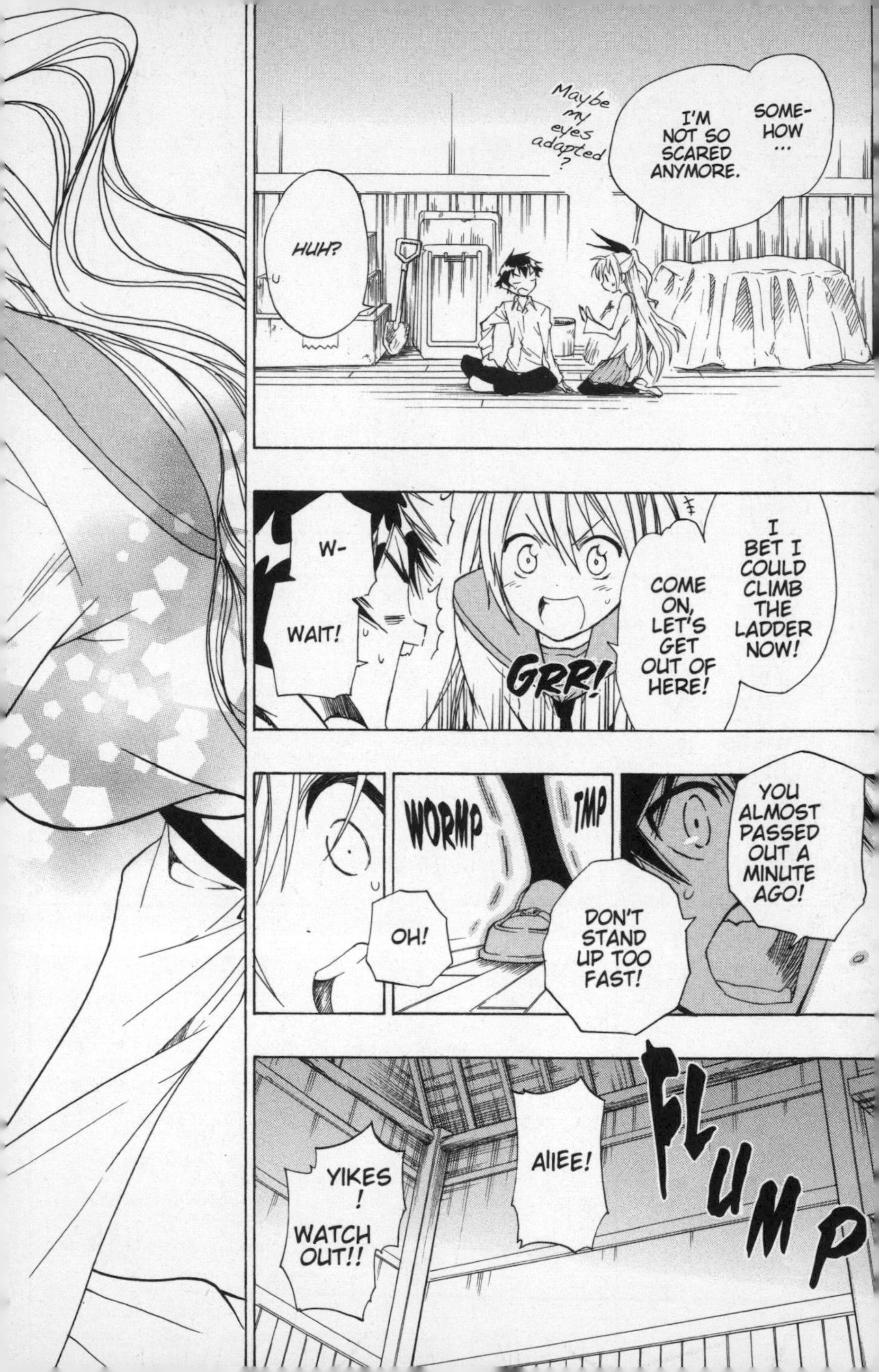
SOME-HOW... I'M NOT SO SCARED ANYMORE.
Maybe my eyes adapted?
HUH?
I BET I COULD CLIMB THE LADDER NOW!
COME ON, LET'S GET OUT OF HERE!
GRR!
W- WAIT!
YOU ALMOST PASSED OUT A MINUTE AGO!
DON'T STAND UP TOO FAST!
TMP
WORMP
OH!
FLUMP
AIIEE!
YIKES! WATCH OUT!!

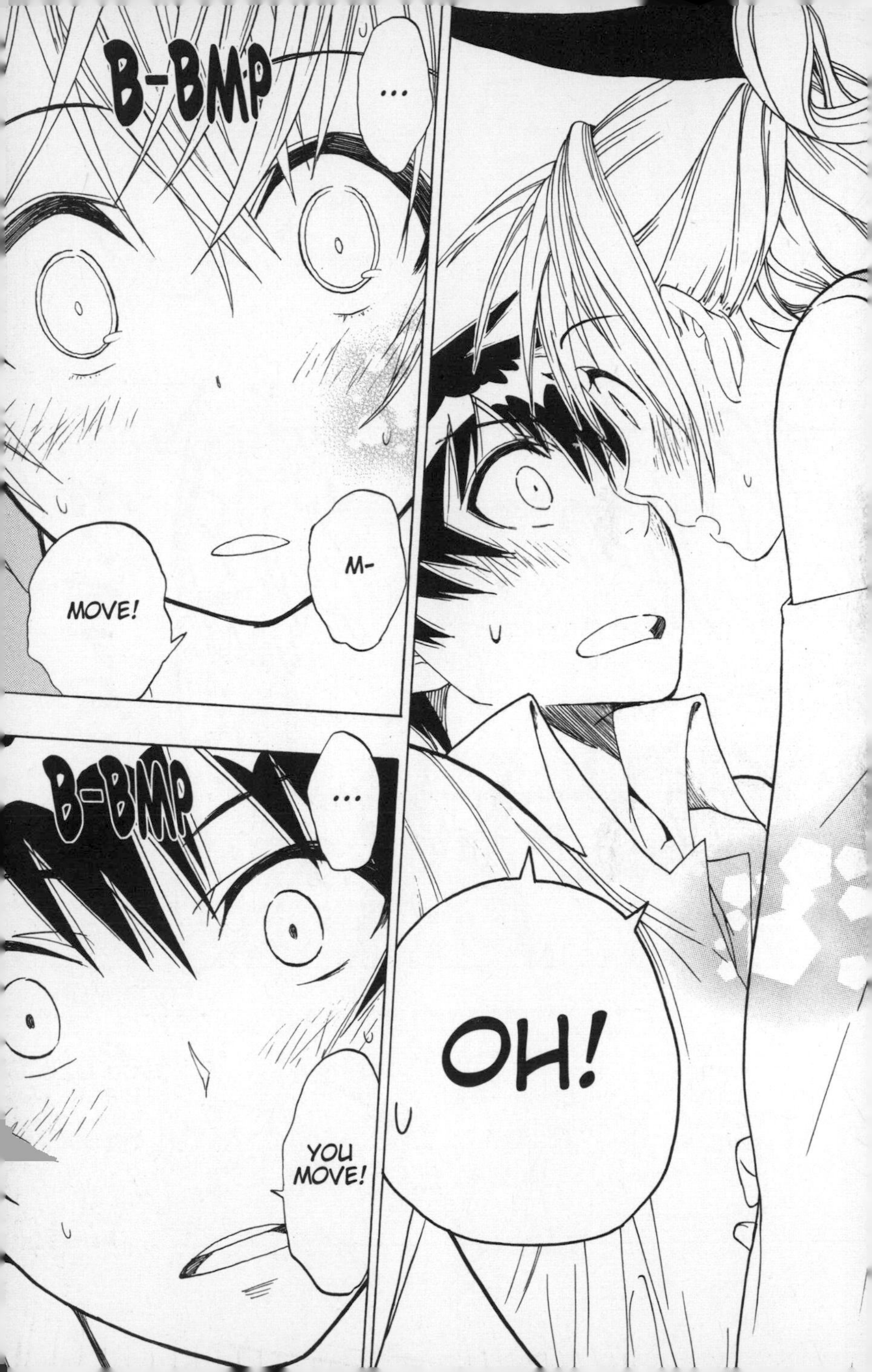
OH!
...
B-BMP
M-
MOVE!
...
B-BMP
YOU MOVE!

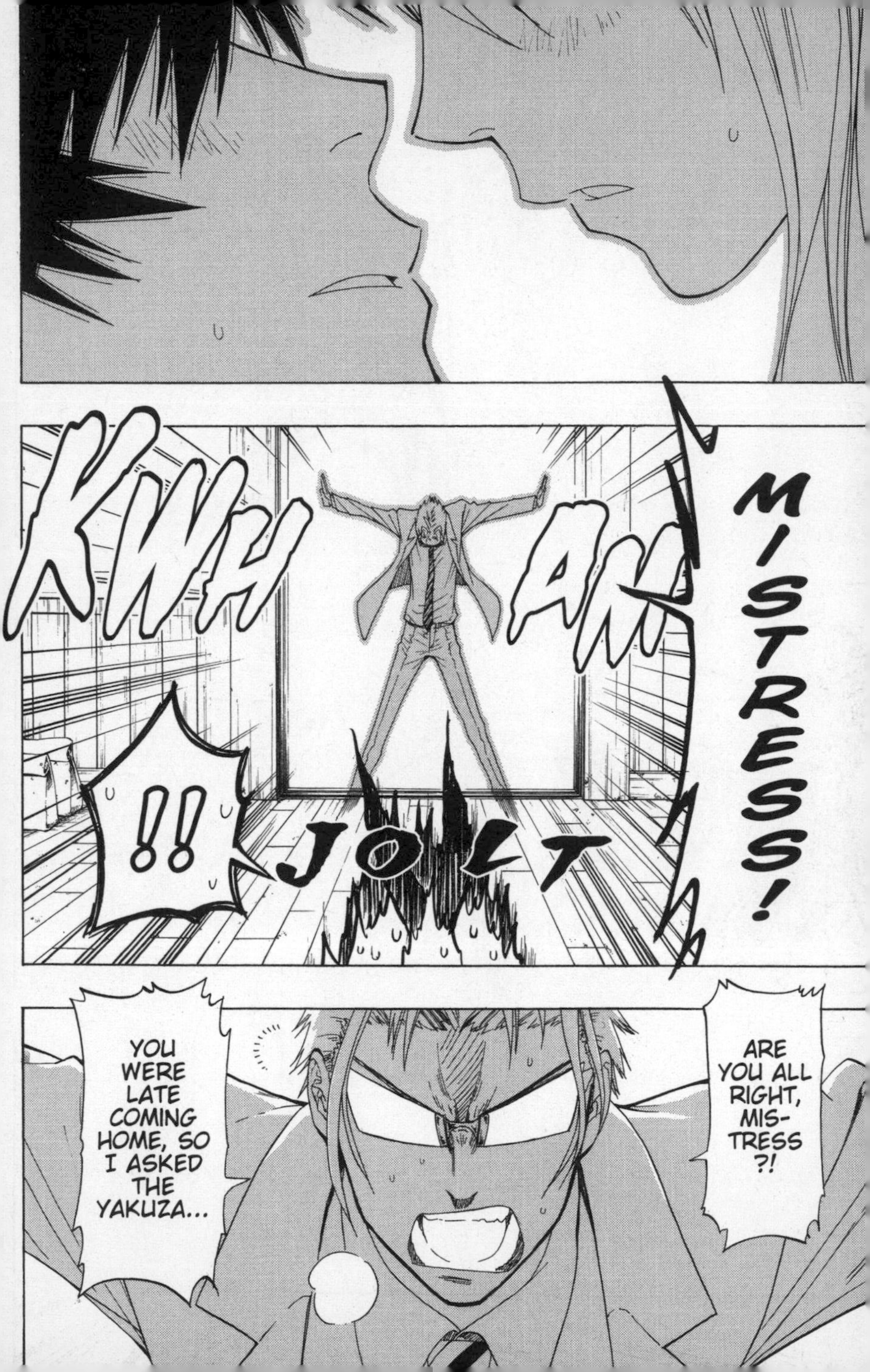
MISTRESS!
KWHAM
JOLT
!!
ARE YOU ALL RIGHT, MIS-TRESS?!
YOU WERE LATE COMING HOME, SO I ASKED THE YAKUZA...

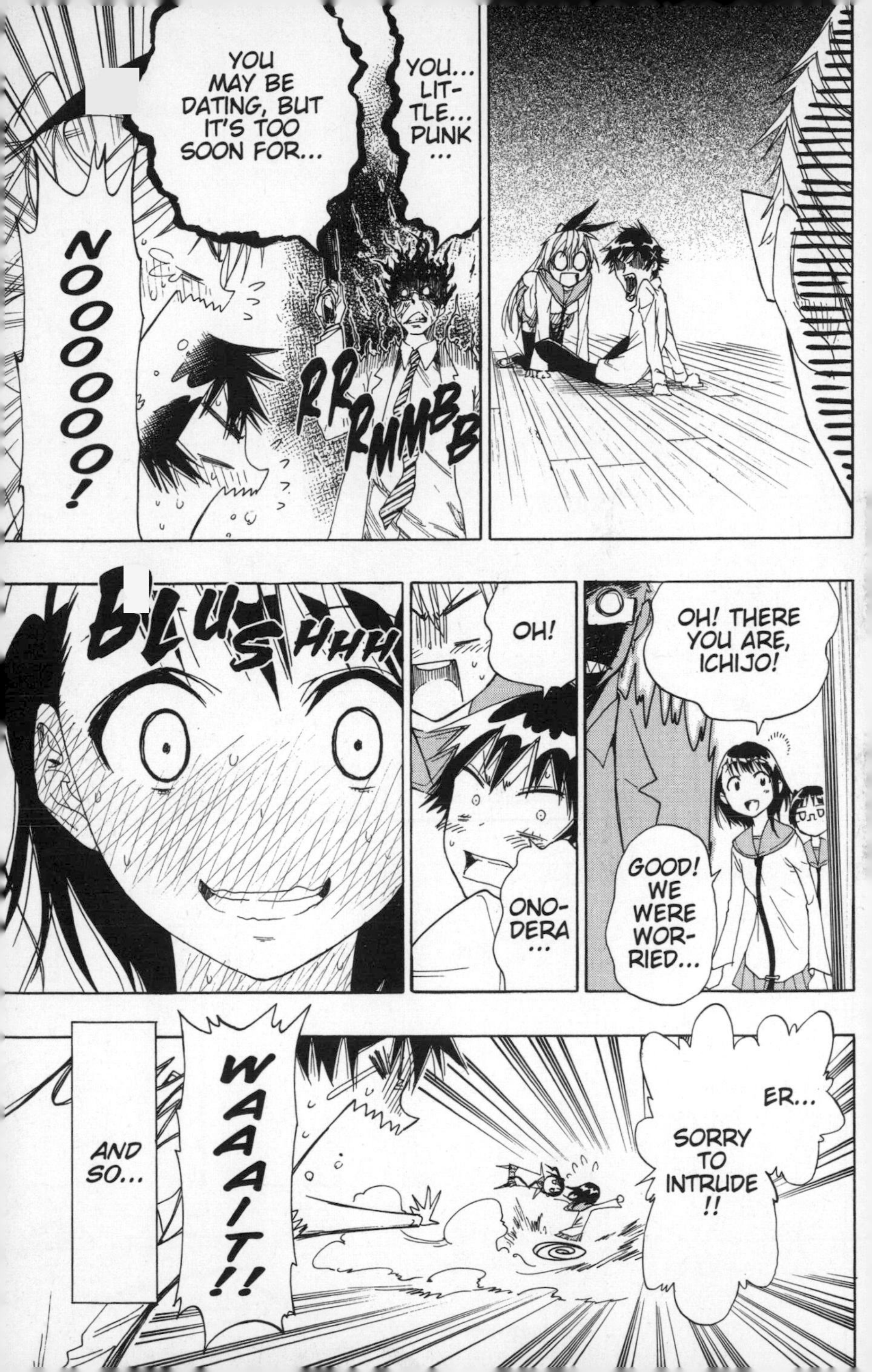
YOU... LIT-TLE... PUNK...
YOU MAY BE DATING, BUT IT'S TOO SOON FOR...
RRRMMBB
NOOOOOOO!
OH! THERE YOU ARE, ICHIJO!
GOOD! WE WERE WOR-RIED...
OH!
ONO-DERA...
BLUSHHH
ER...
SORRY TO INTRUDE!!
WAAAIT!!
AND SO...

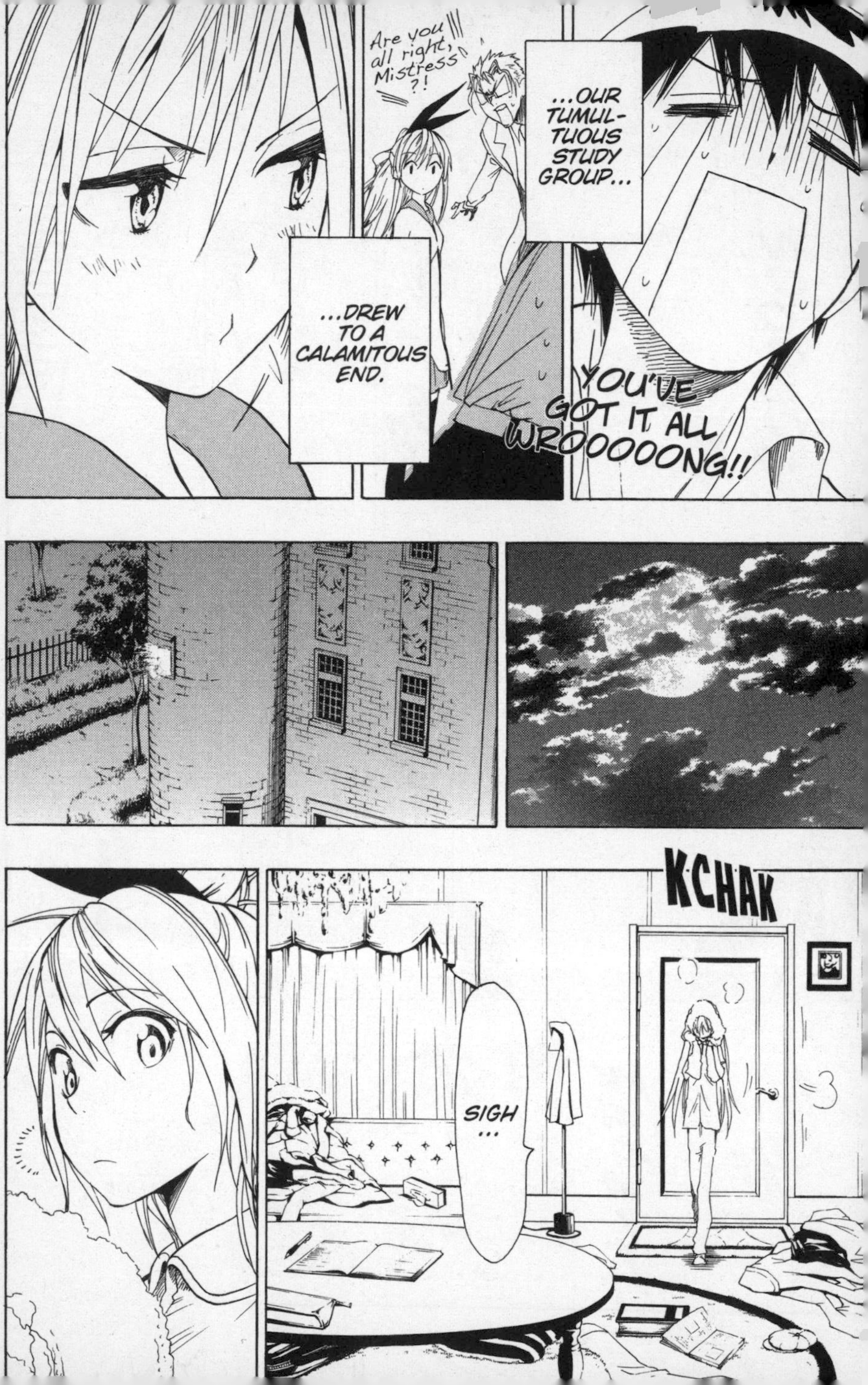
...OUR TUMULTUOUS STUDY GROUP...
YOU'VE GOT IT ALL WROOOOOONG!!
Are you all right, Mistress?!
...DREW TO A CALAMITOUS END.
KCHAK
SIGH...

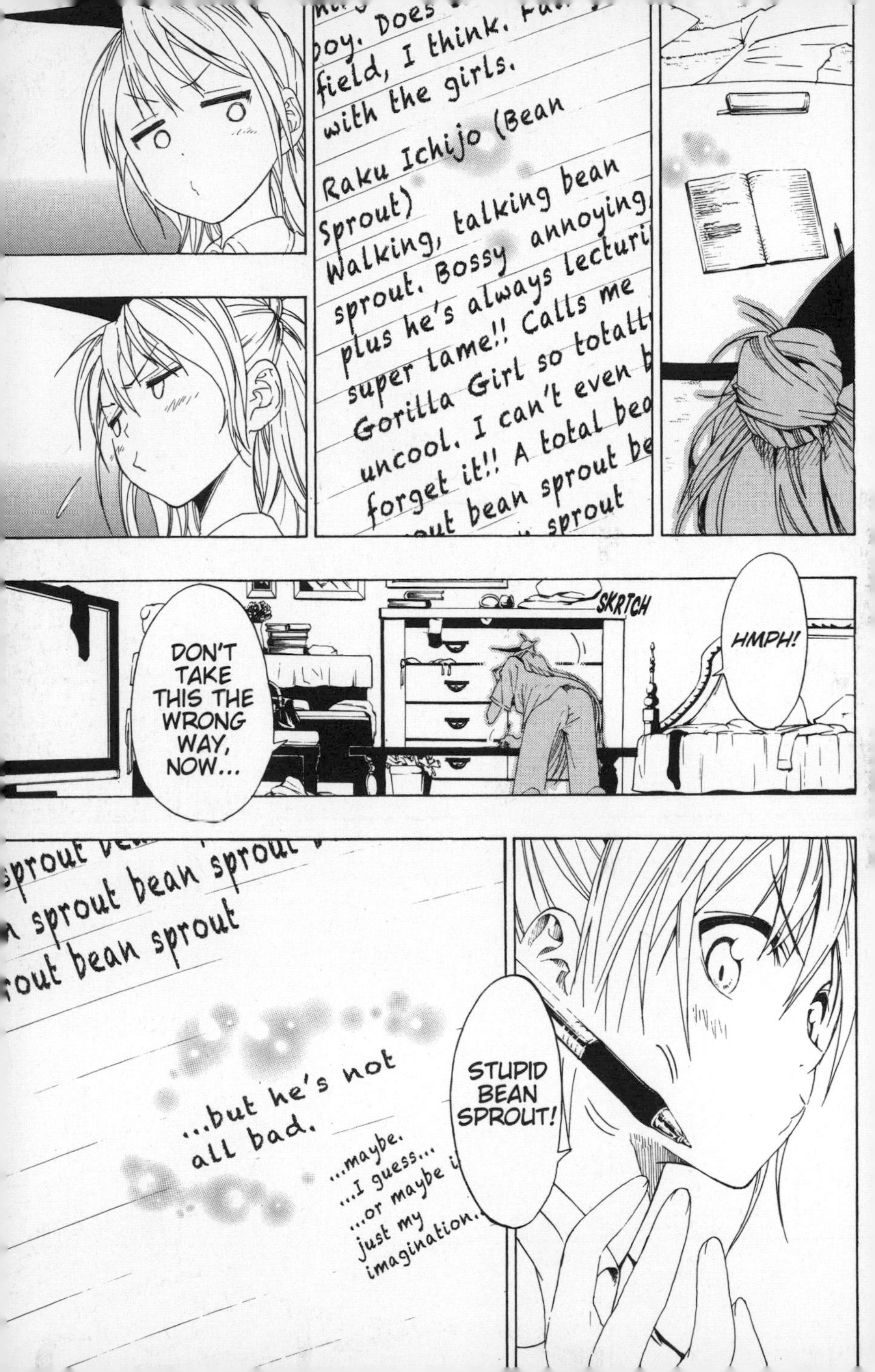

boy. Does
field, I think.
with the girls.
Raku Ichijo (Bean
Sprout)
Walking, talking bean
sprout. Bossy annoying,
plus he's always lecturi
super lame!! Calls me
Gorilla Girl so totall
uncool. I can't even b
forget it!! A total bea
out bean sprout be
sprout
HMPH!
SKRTCH
DON'T TAKE THIS THE WRONG WAY, NOW...
STUPID BEAN SPROUT!
sprout
n sprout bean sprout
rout bean sprout
...but he's not all bad.
...maybe.
...I guess...
...or maybe i
just my
imagination...

PAT
PAT

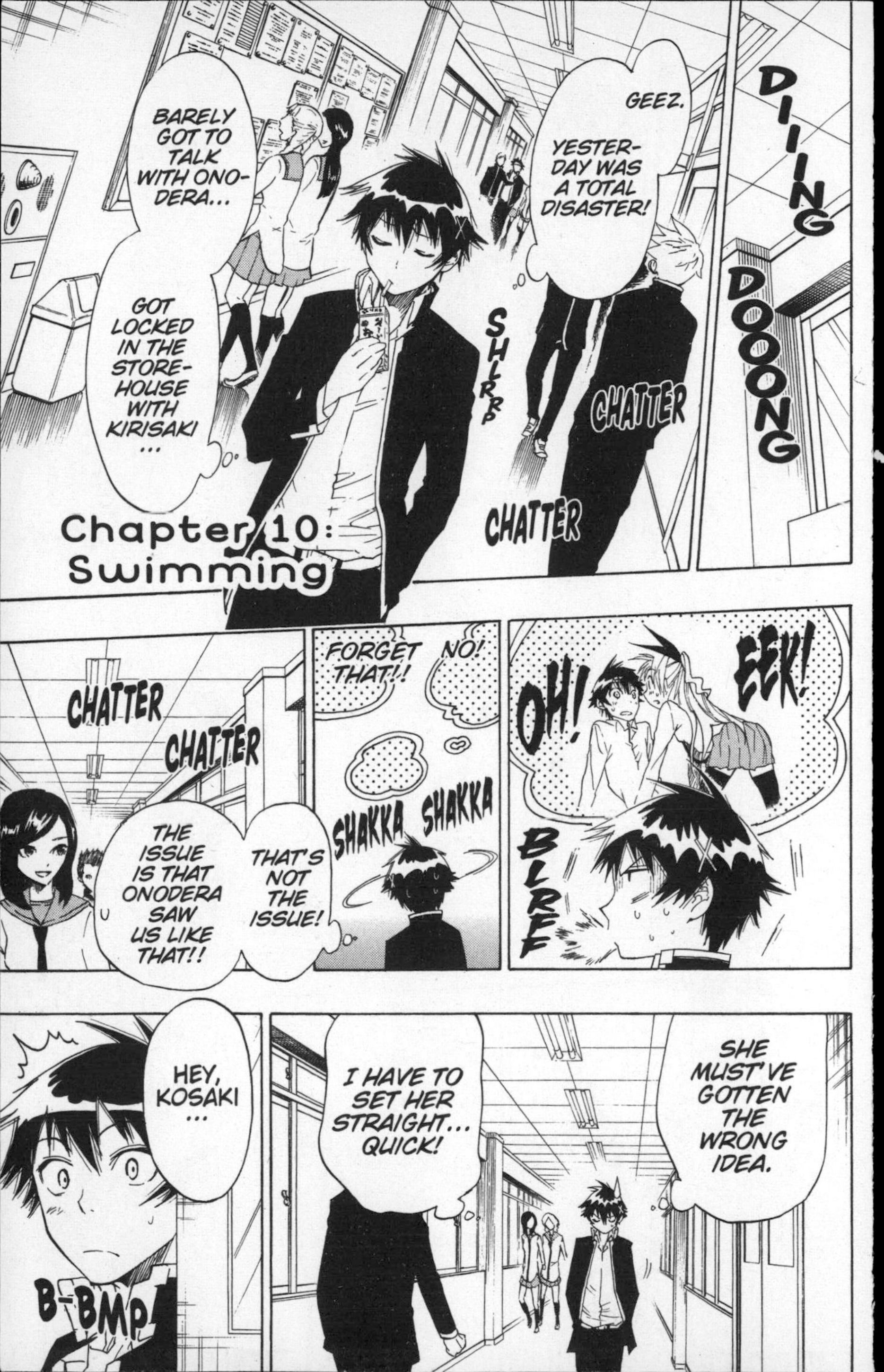
DIIING
DOOONG
GEEZ.
YESTER-DAY WAS A TOTAL DISASTER!
SHLRP
CHATTER
CHATTER
BARELY GOT TO TALK WITH ONO-DERA...
GOT LOCKED IN THE STORE-HOUSE WITH KIRISAKI ...
Chapter 10: Swimming
OH!
EEK!
BLRFF
FORGET THAT!!
NO!
SHAKKA
SHAKKA
THAT'S NOT THE ISSUE!
THE ISSUE IS THAT ONODERA SAW US LIKE THAT!!
CHATTER
CHATTER
SHE MUST'VE GOTTEN THE WRONG IDEA.
I HAVE TO SET HER STRAIGHT... QUICK!
HEY, KOSAKI ...
B-BMP

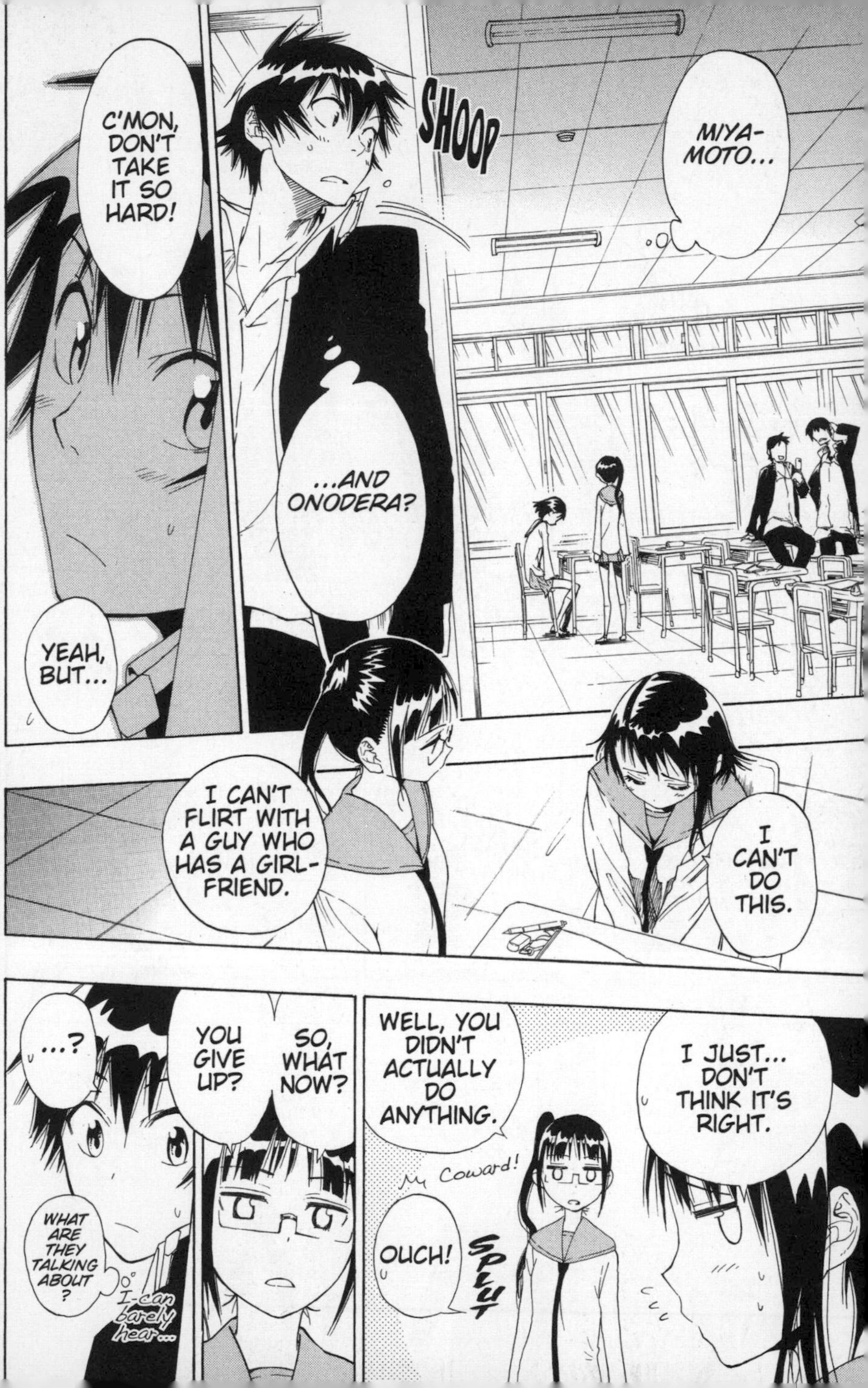
MIYA-MOTO...
SHOOP
...AND ONODERA?
C'MON, DON'T TAKE IT SO HARD!
YEAH, BUT...
I CAN'T DO THIS.
I CAN'T FLIRT WITH A GUY WHO HAS A GIRL-FRIEND.
I JUST... DON'T THINK IT'S RIGHT.
WELL, YOU DIDN'T ACTUALLY DO ANYTHING.
Coward!
OUCH!
SPLUT
SO, WHAT NOW?
YOU GIVE UP?
...?
WHAT ARE THEY TALKING ABOUT?
I can barely hear...

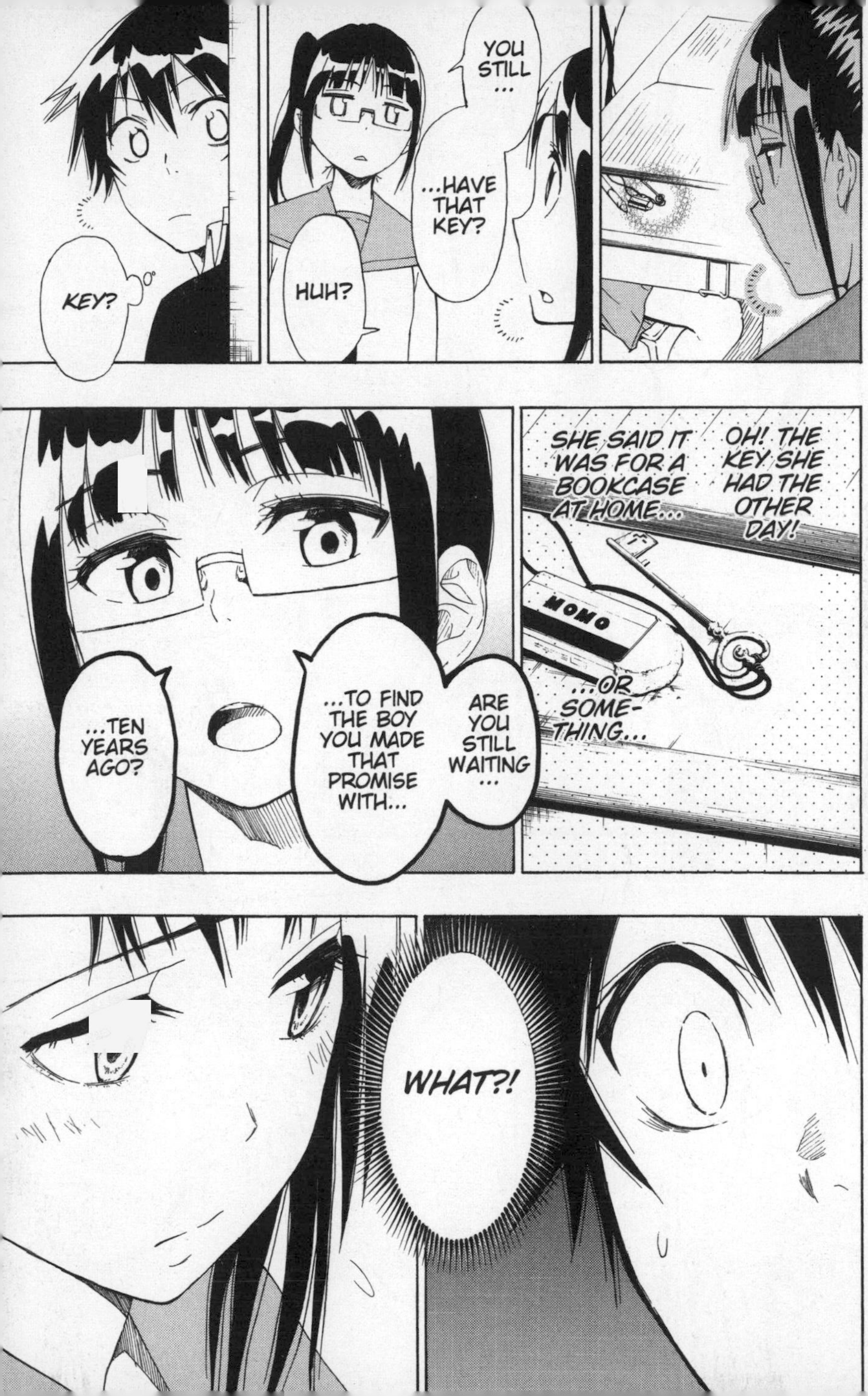
YOU STILL ...
...HAVE THAT KEY?
HUH?
KEY?
OH! THE KEY SHE HAD THE OTHER DAY!
SHE SAID IT WAS FOR A BOOKCASE AT HOME...
MOMO
...OR SOMETHING...
ARE YOU STILL WAITING ...
...TO FIND THE BOY YOU MADE THAT PROMISE WITH...
...TEN YEARS AGO?
WHAT?!

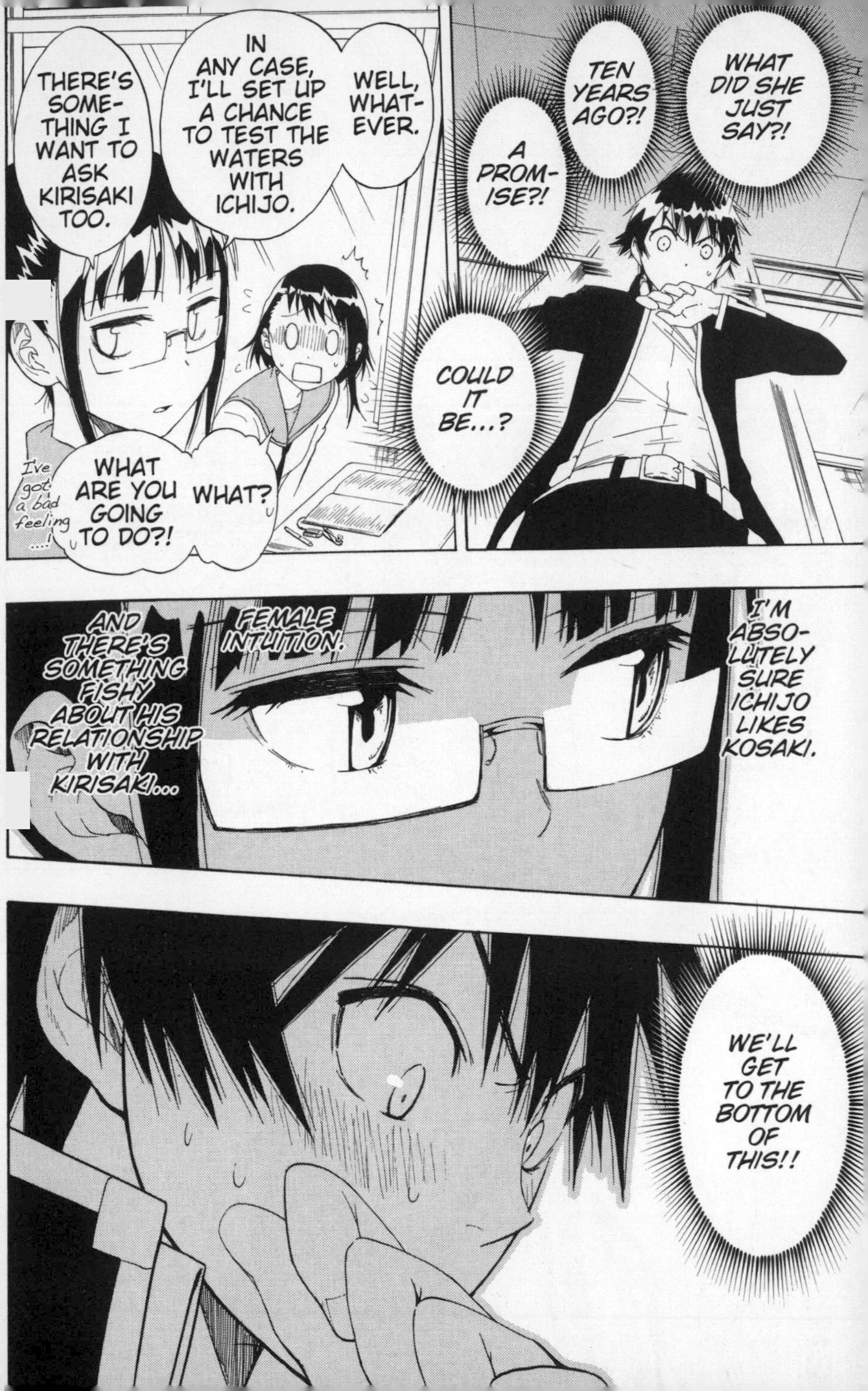
WHAT DID SHE JUST SAY?!
TEN YEARS AGO?!
A PROMISE?!
COULD IT BE...?
WELL, WHATEVER.
IN ANY CASE, I'LL SET UP A CHANCE TO TEST THE WATERS WITH ICHIJO.
THERE'S SOMETHING I WANT TO ASK KIRISAKI TOO.
WHAT?
WHAT ARE YOU GOING TO DO?!
I've got a bad feeling...!
I'M ABSOLUTELY SURE ICHIJO LIKES KOSAKI.
FEMALE INTUITION.
AND THERE'S SOMETHING FISHY ABOUT HIS RELATIONSHIP WITH KIRISAKI...
WE'LL GET TO THE BOTTOM OF THIS!!

Chapter 10: Swimming

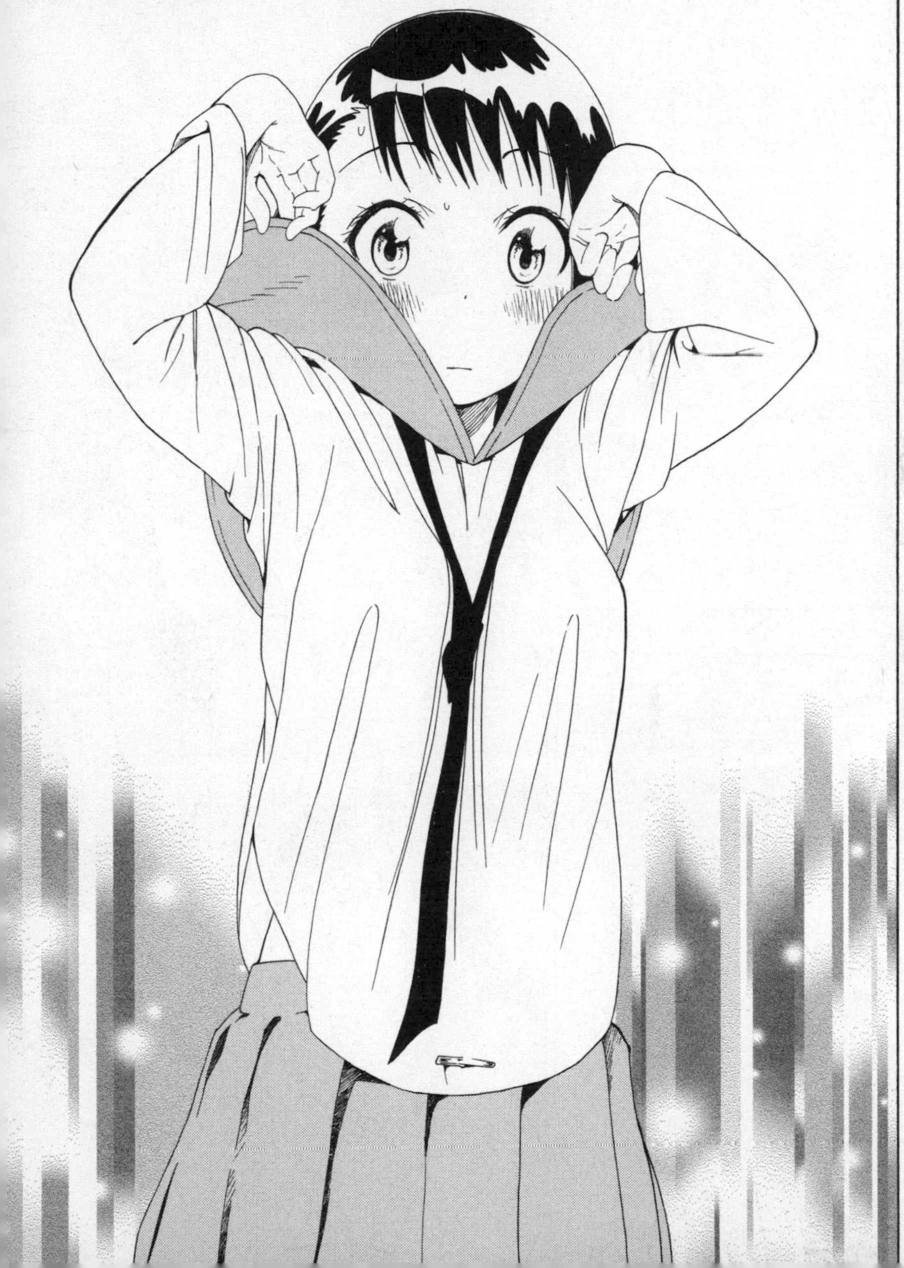

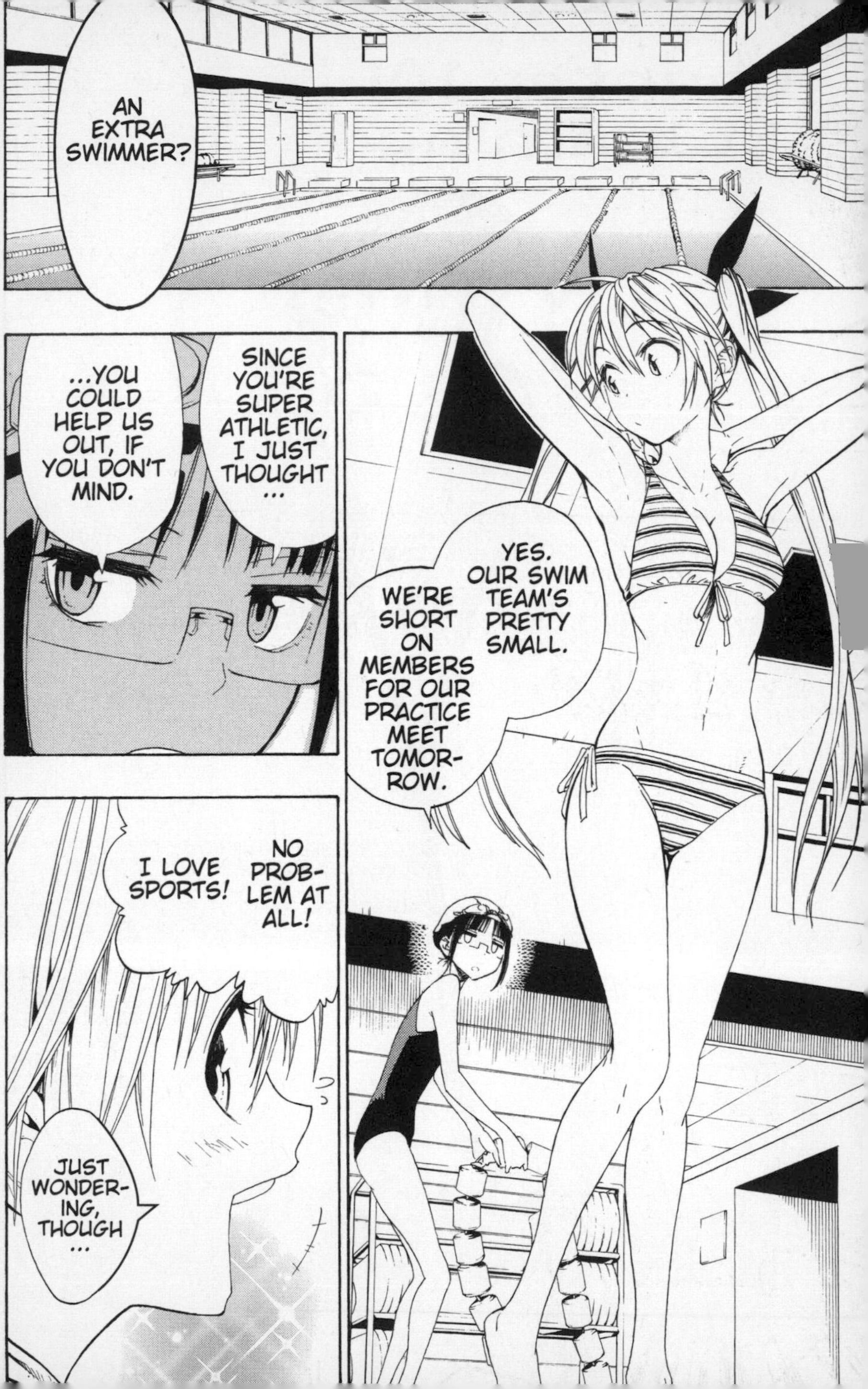
AN EXTRA SWIMMER?
YES. OUR SWIM TEAM'S PRETTY SMALL.
WE'RE SHORT ON MEMBERS FOR OUR PRACTICE MEET TOMOR-ROW.
SINCE YOU'RE SUPER ATHLETIC, I JUST THOUGHT...
...YOU COULD HELP US OUT, IF YOU DON'T MIND.
NO PROB-LEM AT ALL!
I LOVE SPORTS!
JUST WONDER-ING, THOUGH...

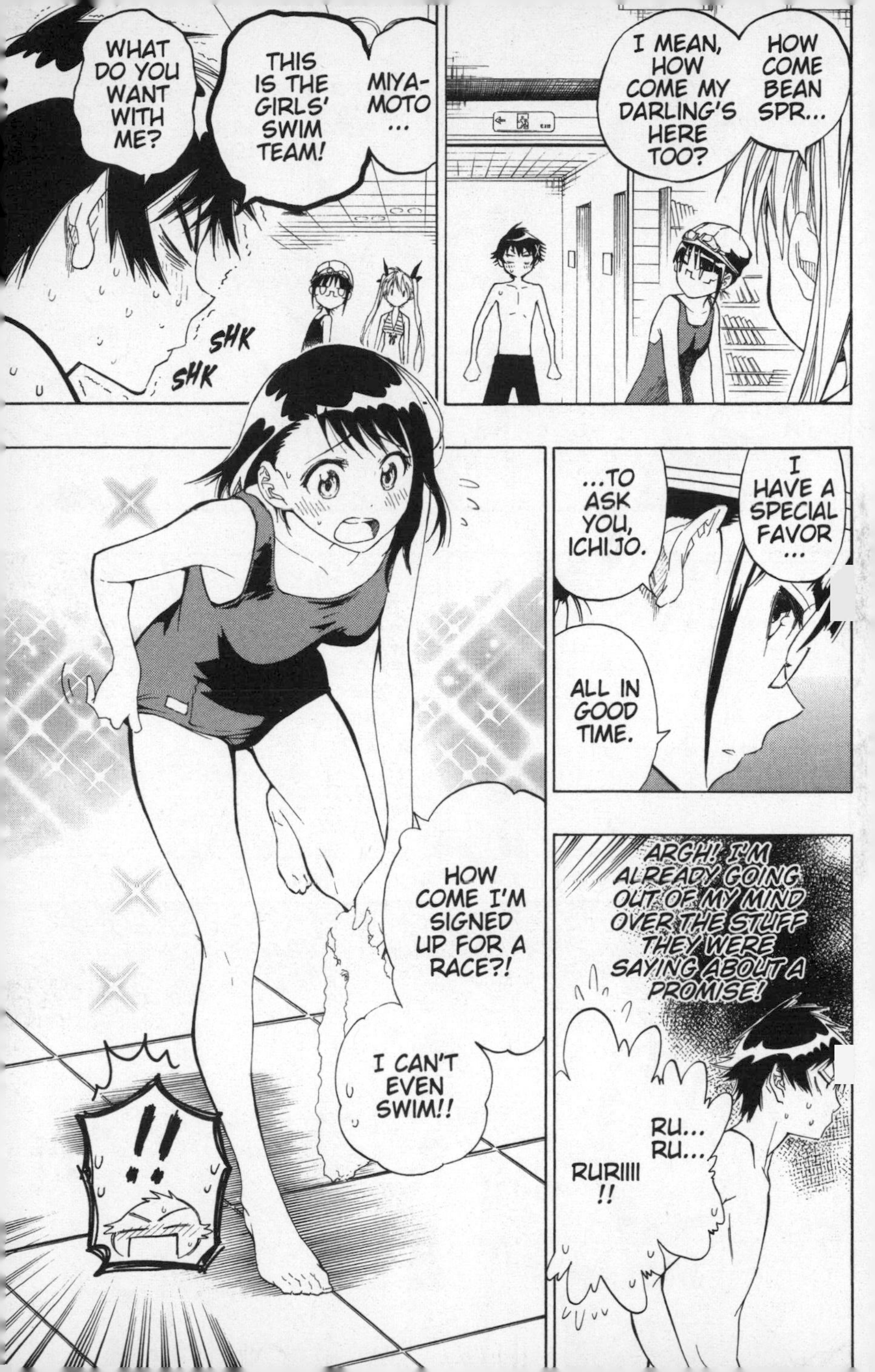
HOW COME BEAN SPR...
I MEAN, HOW COME MY DARLING'S HERE TOO?
MIYA-MOTO...
THIS IS THE GIRLS' SWIM TEAM!
WHAT DO YOU WANT WITH ME?
SHK
SHK
I HAVE A SPECIAL FAVOR...
...TO ASK YOU, ICHIJO.
ALL IN GOOD TIME.
ARGH! I'M ALREADY GOING OUT OF MY MIND OVER THE STUFF THEY WERE SAYING ABOUT A PROMISE!
RU... RU...
RURIIII!!
HOW COME I'M SIGNED UP FOR A RACE?!
I CAN'T EVEN SWIM!!
!!

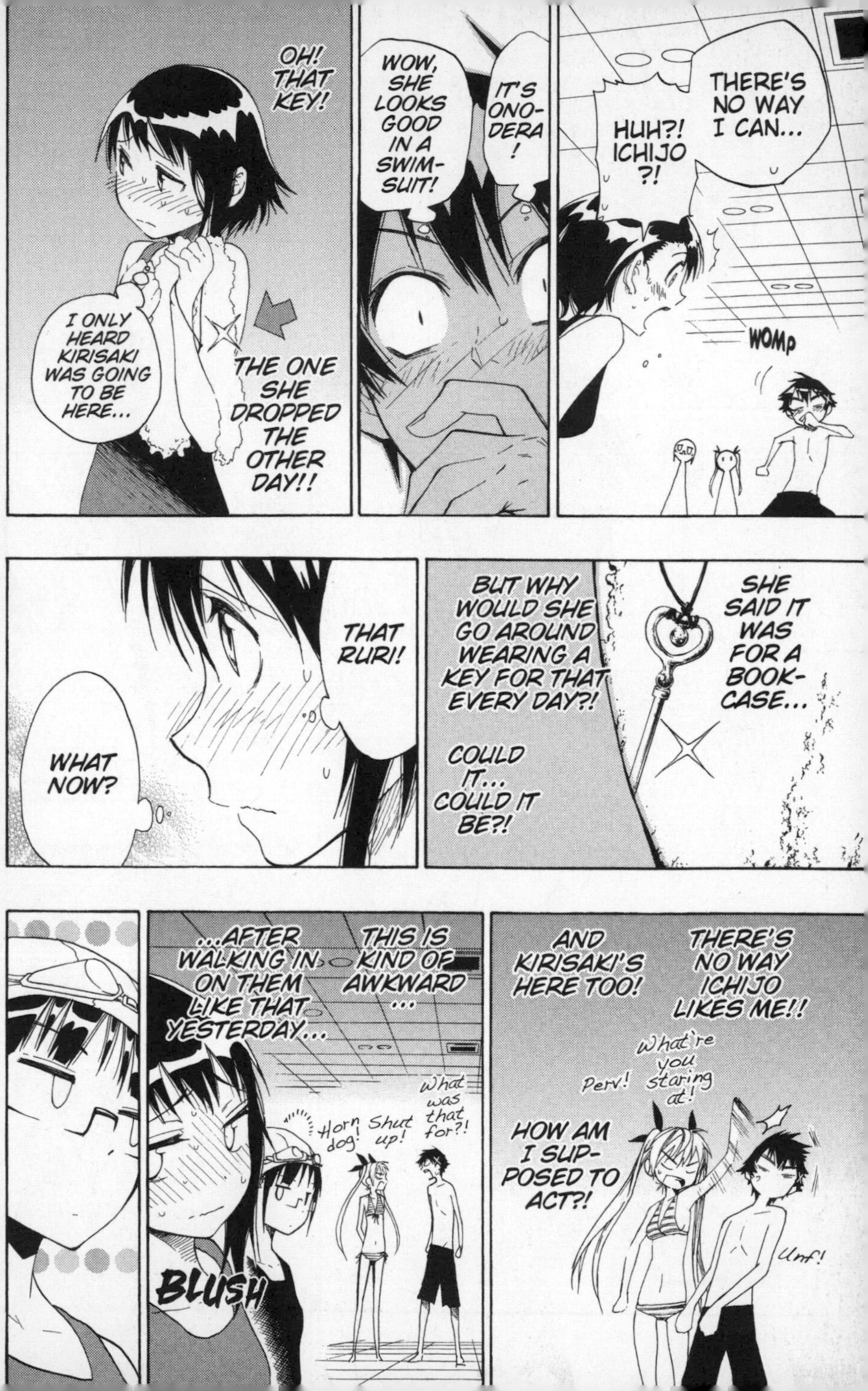
THERE'S NO WAY I CAN...
HUH?! ICHIJO?!
WOMp
IT'S ONO-DERA!
WOW, SHE LOOKS GOOD IN A SWIM-SUIT!
OH! THAT KEY!
THE ONE SHE DROPPED THE OTHER DAY!!
I ONLY HEARD KIRISAKI WAS GOING TO BE HERE...
SHE SAID IT WAS FOR A BOOK-CASE...
BUT WHY WOULD SHE GO AROUND WEARING A KEY FOR THAT EVERY DAY?!
COULD IT... COULD IT BE?!
THAT RURI!
WHAT NOW?
THERE'S NO WAY ICHIJO LIKES ME!!
AND KIRISAKI'S HERE TOO!
What're you staring at!
Perv!
HOW AM I SUP-POSED TO ACT?!
Unf!
THIS IS KIND OF AWKWARD...
...AFTER WALKING IN ON THEM LIKE THAT YESTERDAY...
What was that for?!
Shut up!
Horn dog!
BLUSH

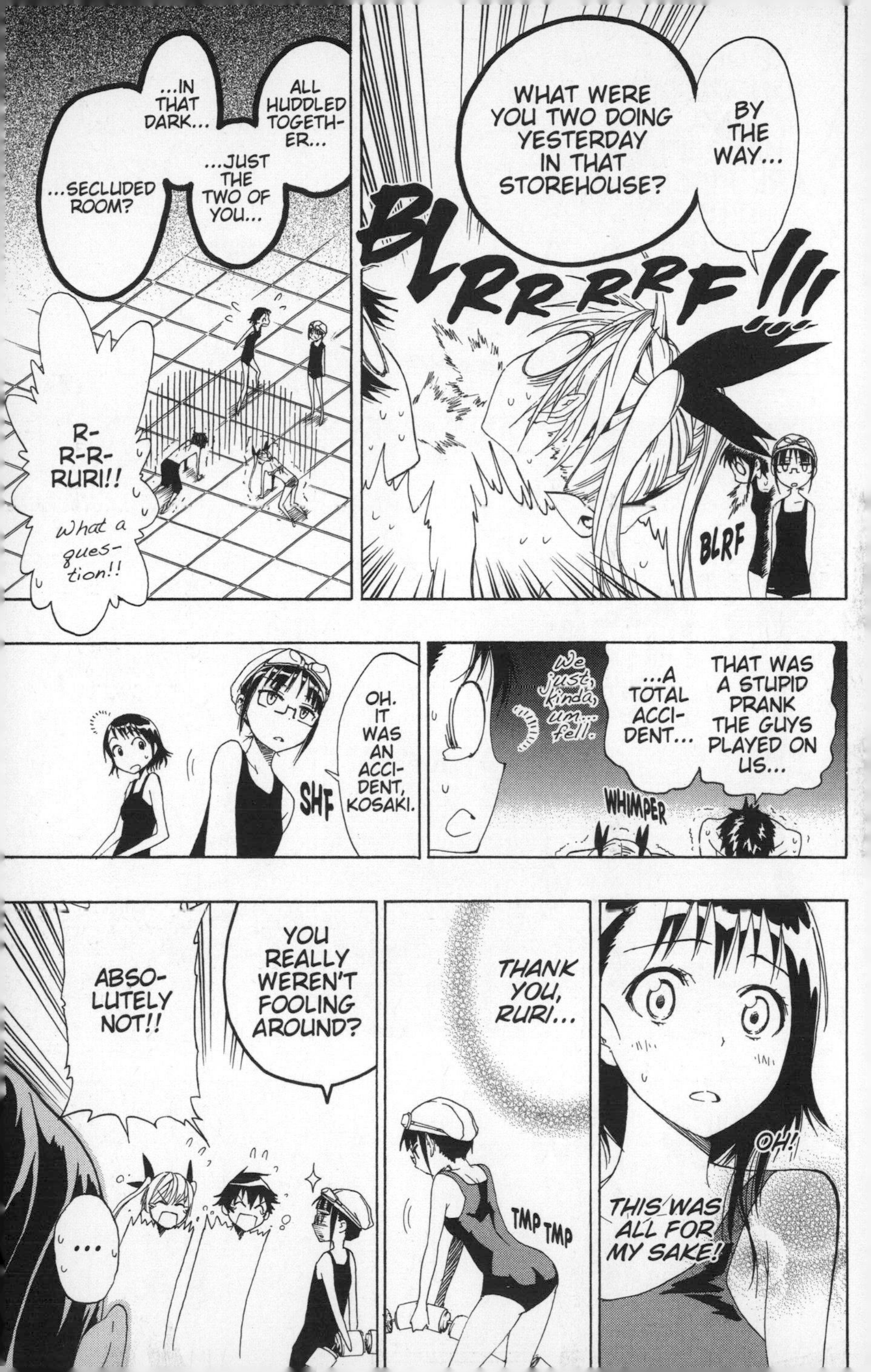
BY THE WAY...
WHAT WERE YOU TWO DOING YESTERDAY IN THAT STOREHOUSE?
BLRRRRRF!!
BLRF
ALL HUDDLED TOGETH-ER...
...IN THAT DARK...
...JUST THE TWO OF YOU...
...SECLUDED ROOM?
R-R-R-RURI!!
What a ques-tion!!
THAT WAS A STUPID PRANK THE GUYS PLAYED ON US...
...A TOTAL ACCI-DENT...
We just, kinda, um... fell.
WHIMPER
OH. IT WAS AN ACCI-DENT, KOSAKI.
SHF
OH!
THIS WAS ALL FOR MY SAKE!
THANK YOU, RURI...
TMP TMP
YOU REALLY WEREN'T FOOLING AROUND?
ABSO-LUTELY NOT!!
...

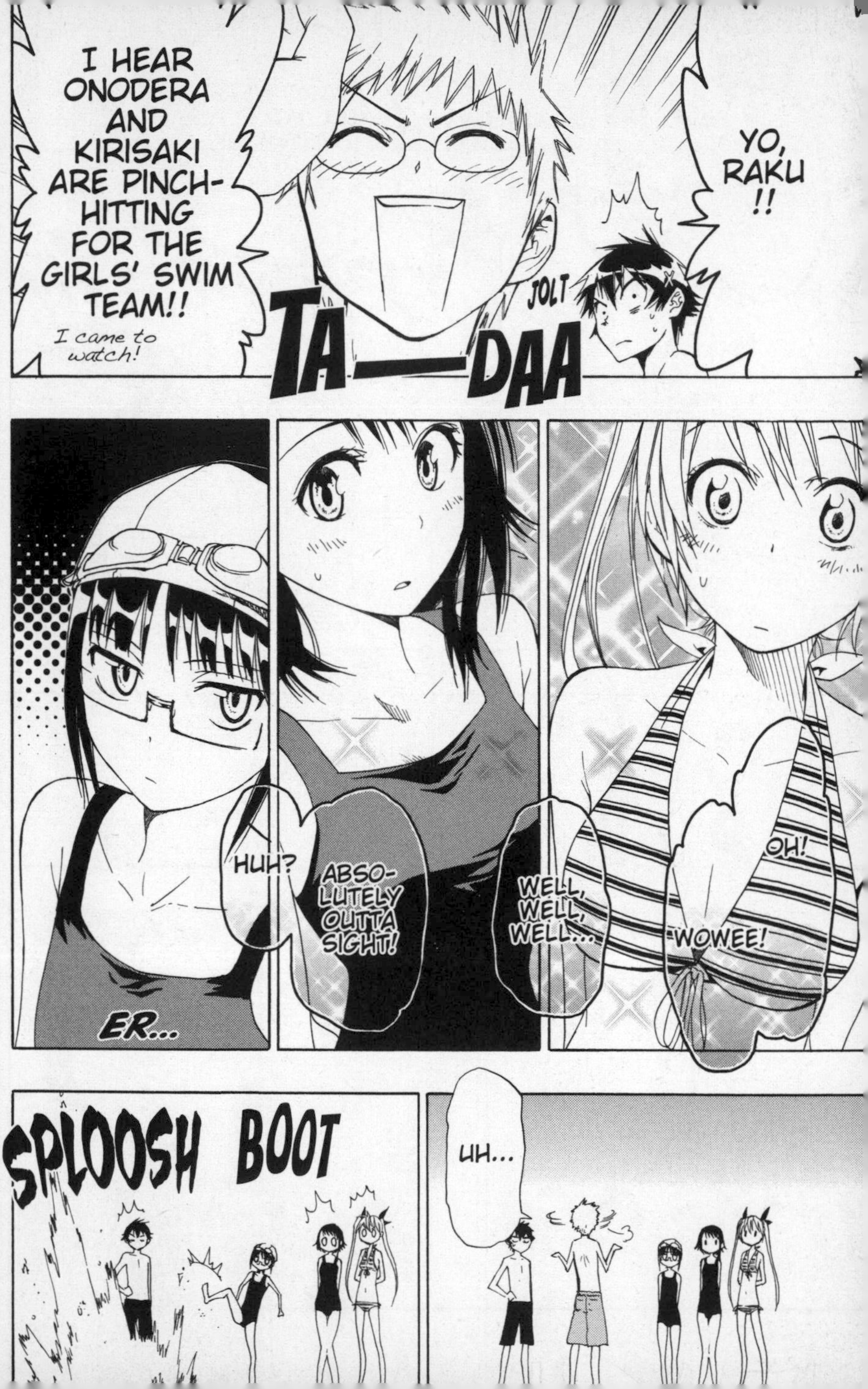
YO, RAKU!!
JOLT
TA—DAA
I HEAR ONODERA AND KIRISAKI ARE PINCH-HITTING FOR THE GIRLS' SWIM TEAM!!
I came to watch!
OH!
WOWEE!
WELL, WELL, WELL...
ABSO-LUTELY OUTTA SIGHT!
HUH?
ER...
UH...
BOOT
SPLOOSH

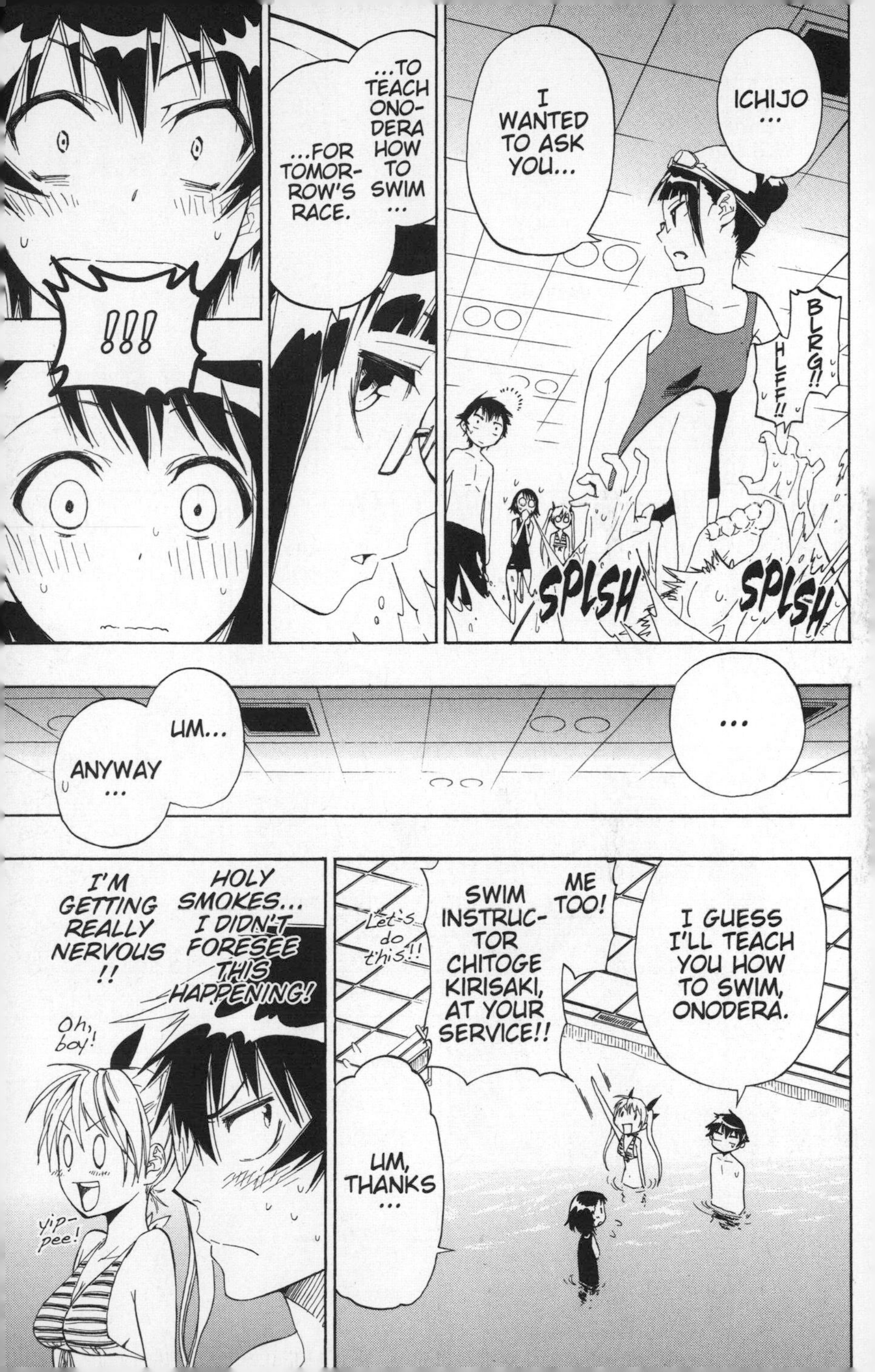
ICHIJO ...
I WANTED TO ASK YOU...
BLRG!!
HLFF!!
SPLSH
SPLSH
...TO TEACH ONODERA HOW TO SWIM ...
...FOR TOMORROW'S RACE.
!!!
...
UM... ANYWAY ...
I GUESS I'LL TEACH YOU HOW TO SWIM, ONODERA.
ME TOO!
SWIM INSTRUCTOR CHITOGE KIRISAKI, AT YOUR SERVICE!!
Let's do this!!
UM, THANKS ...
HOLY SMOKES... I DIDN'T FORESEE THIS HAPPENING!
I'M GETTING REALLY NERVOUS !!
Oh, boy!
yip-pee!

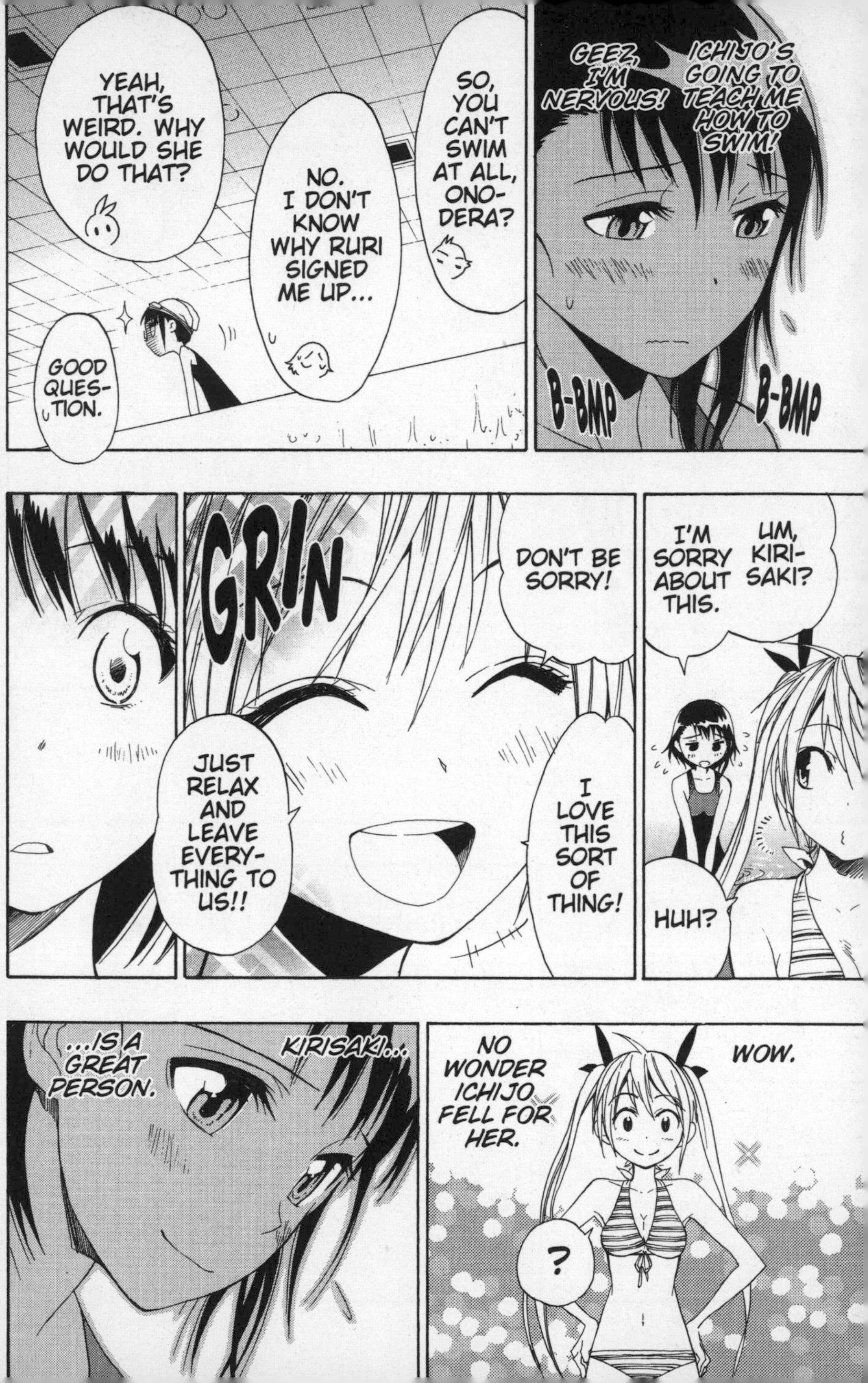
ICHIJO'S GOING TO TEACH ME HOW TO SWIM!
GEEZ, I'M NERVOUS!
B-BMP
B-BMP
SO, YOU CAN'T SWIM AT ALL, ONO-DERA?
NO. I DON'T KNOW WHY RURI SIGNED ME UP...
YEAH, THAT'S WEIRD. WHY WOULD SHE DO THAT?
GOOD QUES-TION.
UM, KIRI-SAKI?
I'M SORRY ABOUT THIS.
HUH?
DON'T BE SORRY!
GRIN
I LOVE THIS SORT OF THING!
JUST RELAX AND LEAVE EVERY-THING TO US!!
WOW.
NO WONDER ICHIJO FELL FOR HER.
?
KIRISAKI...
...IS A GREAT PERSON.

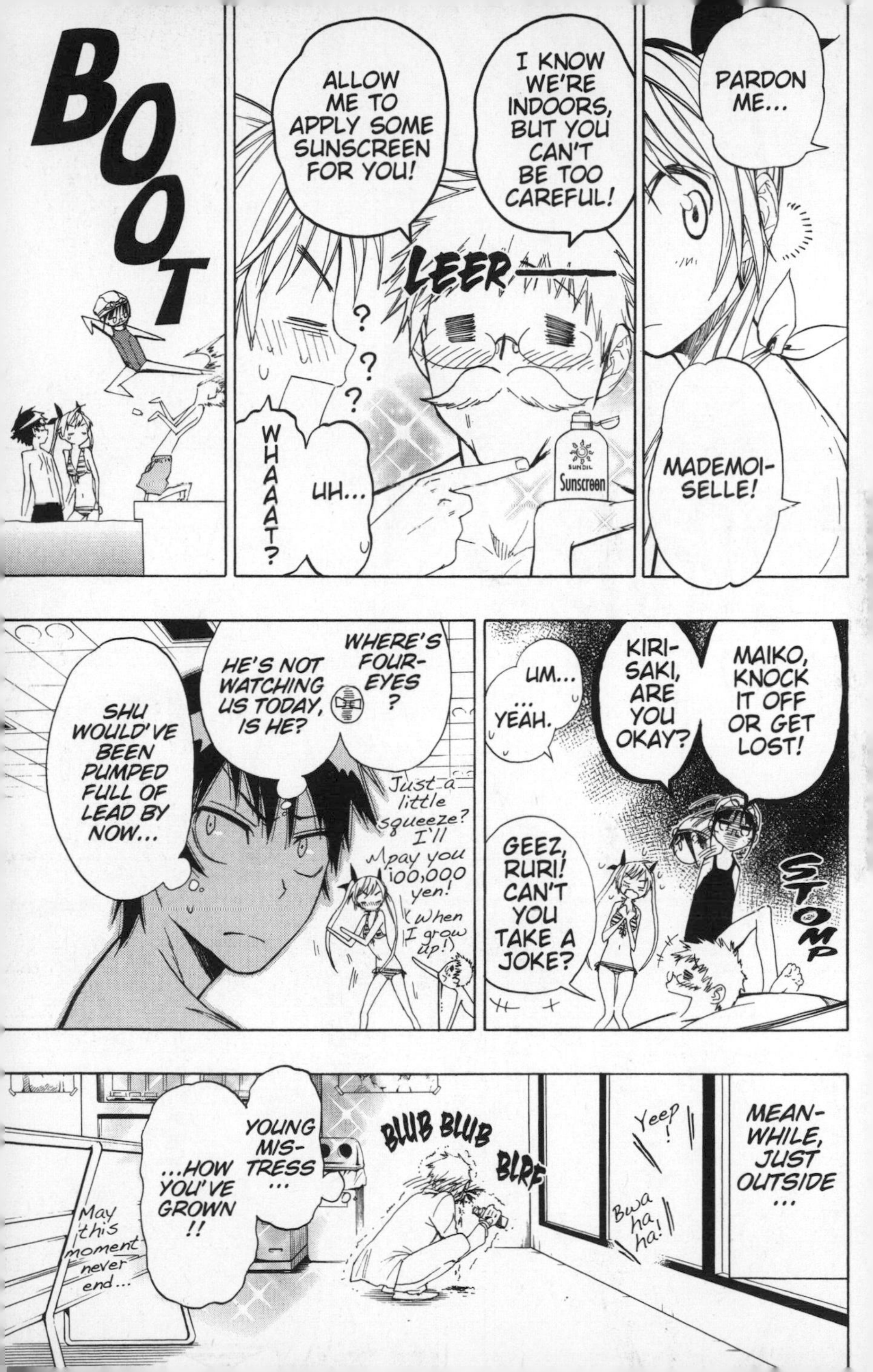
PARDON ME...
MADEMOI-SELLE!
I KNOW WE'RE INDOORS, BUT YOU CAN'T BE TOO CAREFUL!
ALLOW ME TO APPLY SOME SUNSCREEN FOR YOU!
LEER
SUNDIL
Sunscreen
???
UH...
WHAAAT?
BOOT
MAIKO, KNOCK IT OFF OR GET LOST!
KIRI-SAKI, ARE YOU OKAY?
UM...
...YEAH.
STOMP
GEEZ, RURI! CAN'T YOU TAKE A JOKE?
WHERE'S FOUR-EYES?
HE'S NOT WATCHING US TODAY, IS HE?
SHU WOULD'VE BEEN PUMPED FULL OF LEAD BY NOW...
Just a little squeeze? I'll pay you 100,000 yen! (When I grow up!)
MEAN-WHILE, JUST OUTSIDE...
Yeep!
Bwa ha ha!
BLUB BLUB
BLRF
YOUNG MIS-TRESS...
...HOW YOU'VE GROWN!!
May this moment never end...

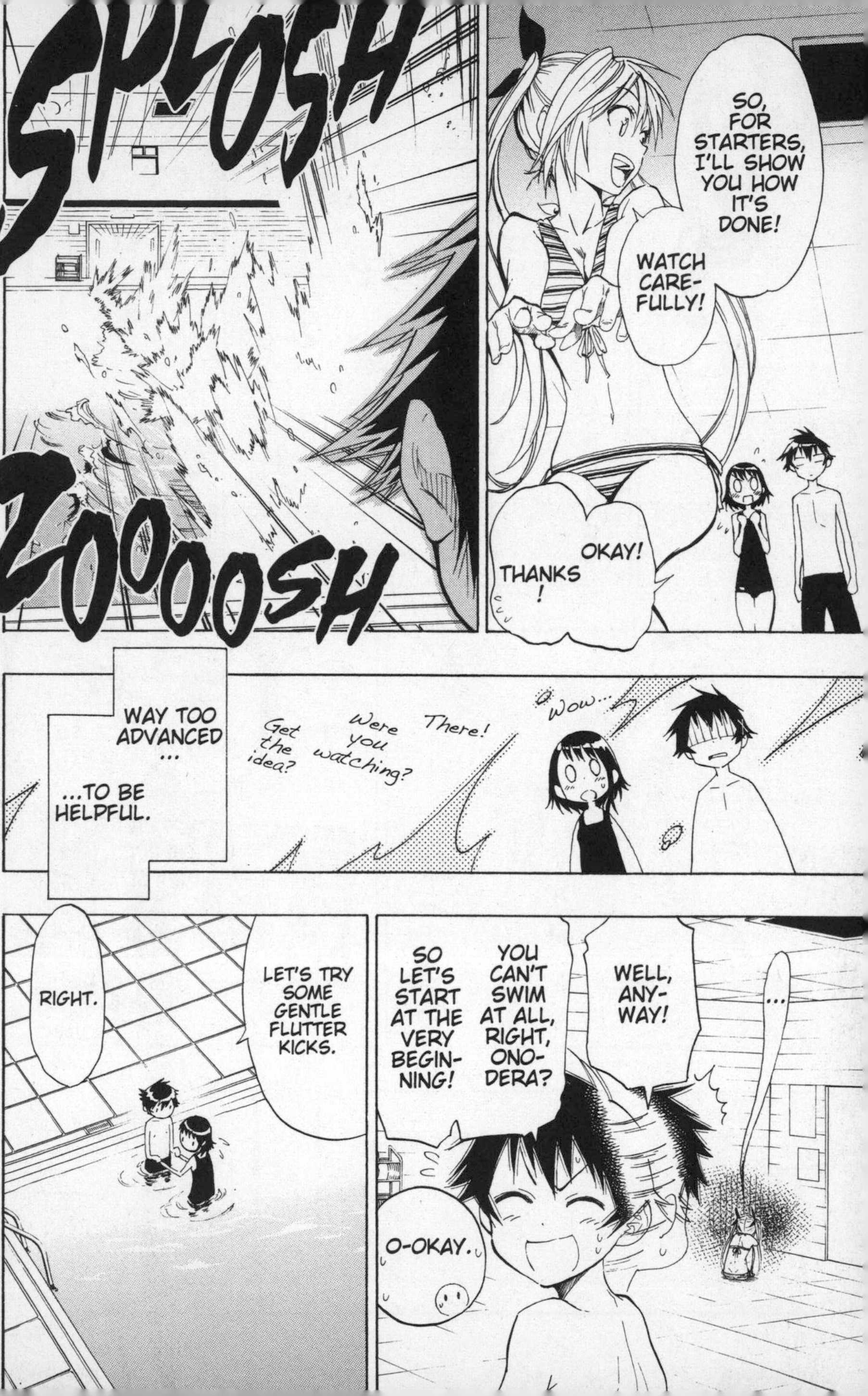
SO, FOR STARTERS, I'LL SHOW YOU HOW IT'S DONE!
WATCH CARE-FULLY!
OKAY!
THANKS!
SPLOSH
ZOOOOSH
Wow...
There!
Were you watching?
Get the idea?
WAY TOO ADVANCED...
...TO BE HELPFUL.
...
WELL, ANY-WAY!
YOU CAN'T SWIM AT ALL, RIGHT, ONO-DERA?
SO LET'S START AT THE VERY BEGIN-NING!
O-OKAY.
LET'S TRY SOME GENTLE FLUTTER KICKS.
RIGHT.

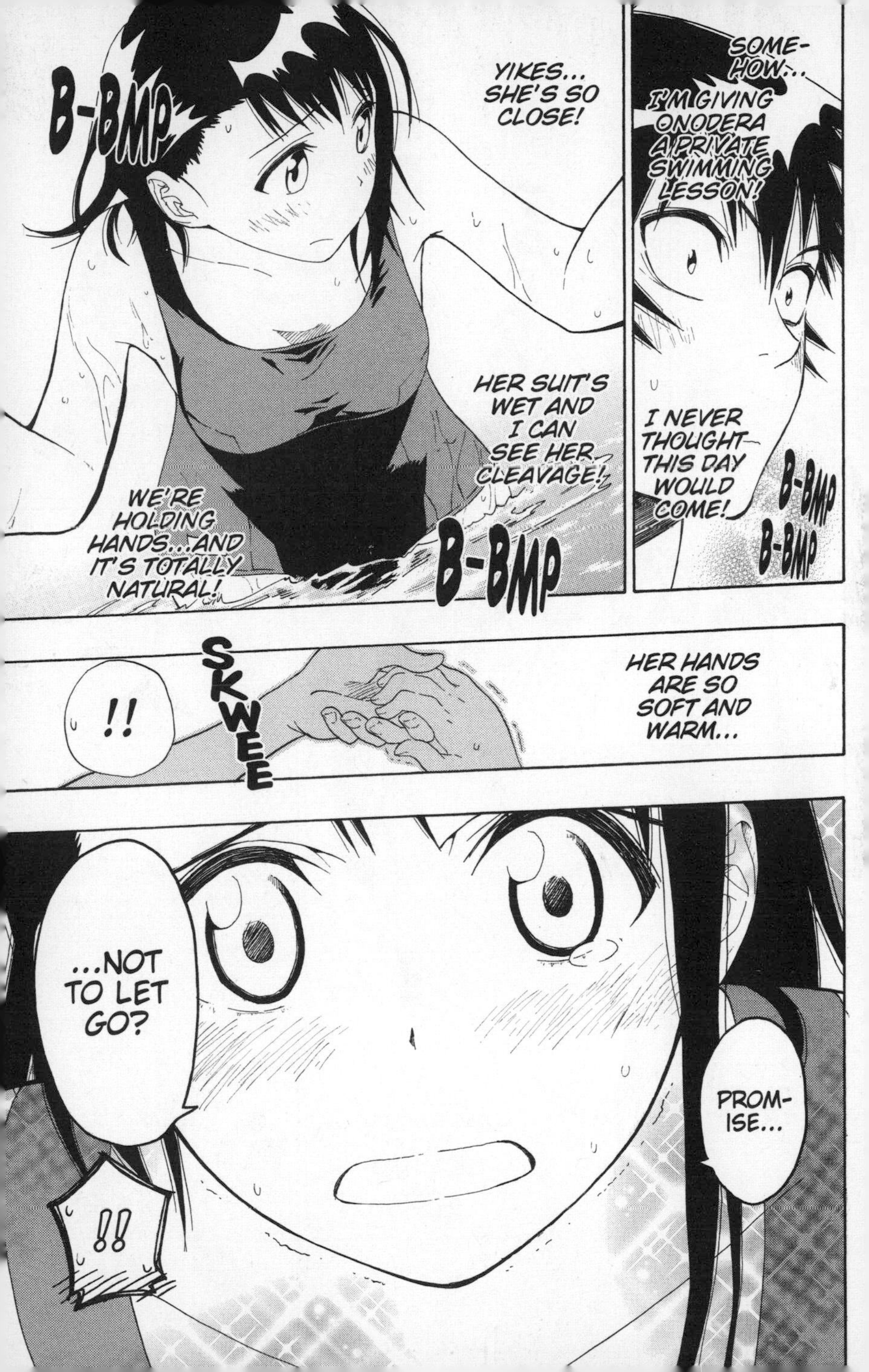
SOME-HOW... I'M GIVING ONODERA A PRIVATE SWIMMING LESSON!
I NEVER THOUGHT THIS DAY WOULD COME!
B-BMP
B-BMP
YIKES... SHE'S SO CLOSE!
B-BMP
HER SUIT'S WET AND I CAN SEE HER CLEAVAGE!
WE'RE HOLDING HANDS...AND IT'S TOTALLY NATURAL!
B-BMP
HER HANDS ARE SO SOFT AND WARM...
SKWEE
!!
PROMISE...
...NOT TO LET GO?
!!

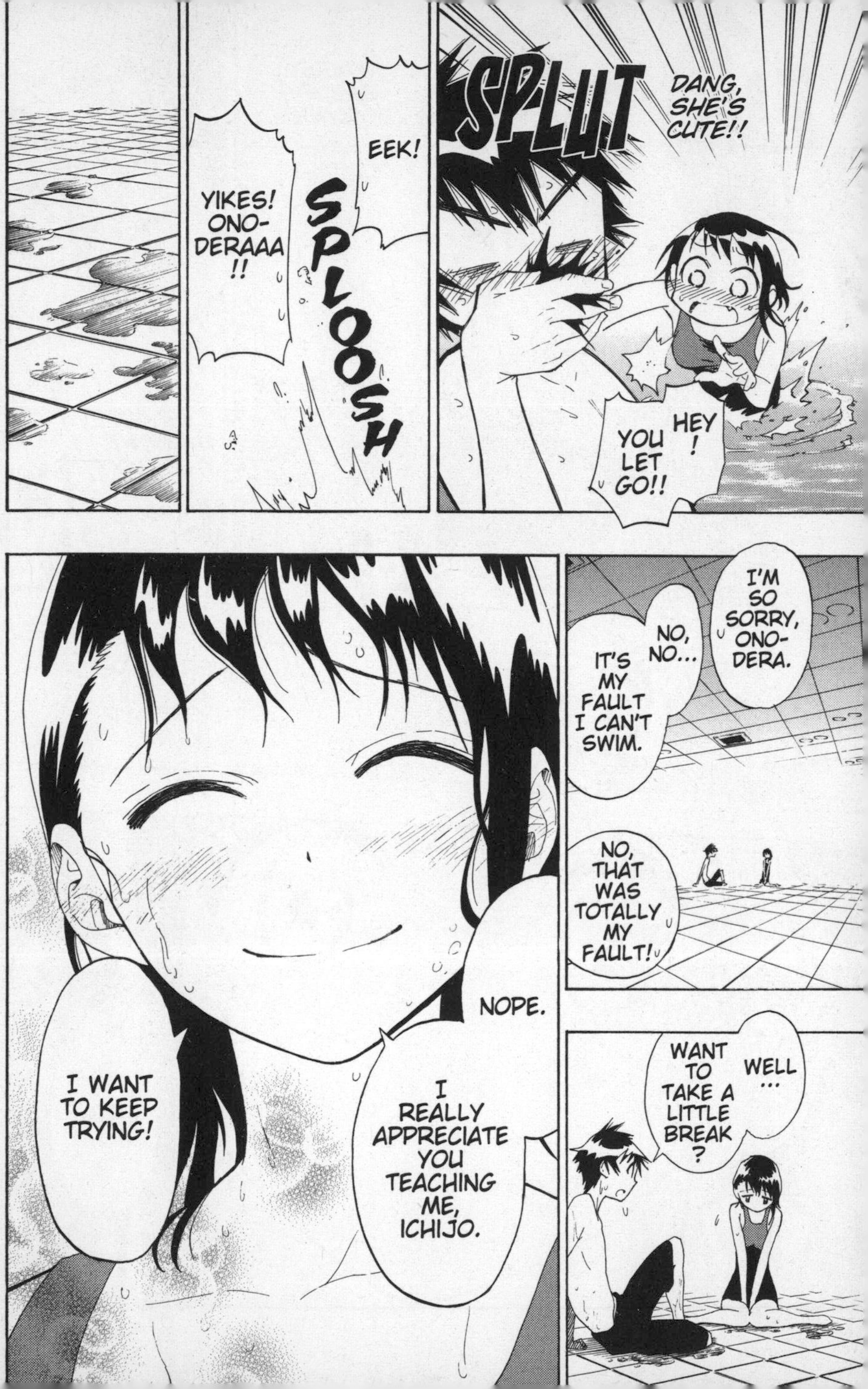
DANG, SHE'S CUTE!!
SPLUT
HEY! YOU LET GO!!
EEK!
SPLOOSH
YIKES! ONO-DERAAA!!
I'M SO SORRY, ONO-DERA.
NO, NO...
IT'S MY FAULT I CAN'T SWIM.
NO, THAT WAS TOTALLY MY FAULT!
WELL...
WANT TO TAKE A LITTLE BREAK?
NOPE.
I REALLY APPRECIATE YOU TEACHING ME, ICHIJO.
I WANT TO KEEP TRYING!

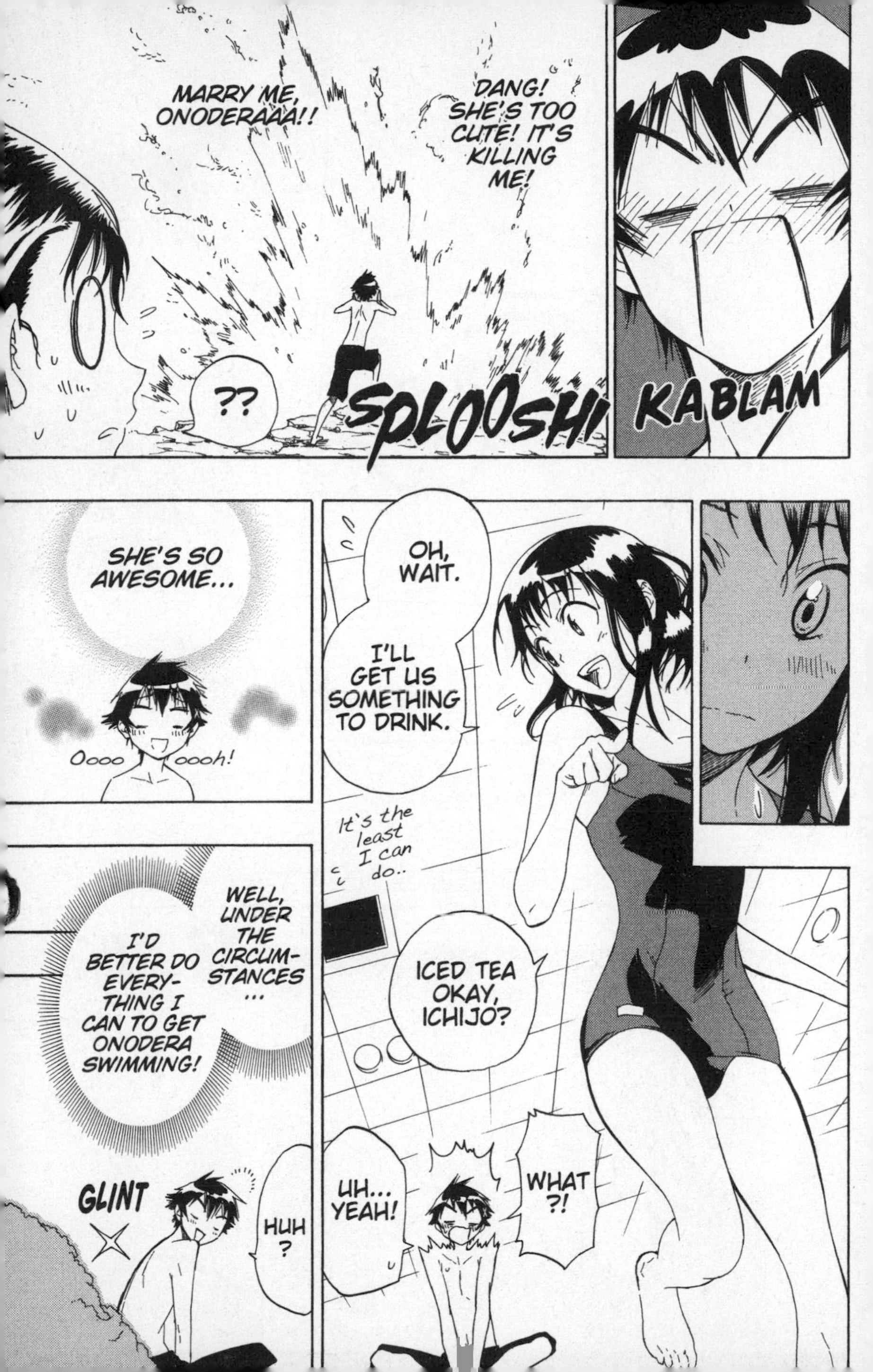
KABLAM
DANG! SHE'S TOO CUTE! IT'S KILLING ME!
MARRY ME, ONODERAAA!!
SPLOOSH!
??
OH, WAIT.
I'LL GET US SOMETHING TO DRINK.
It's the least I can do..
ICED TEA OKAY, ICHIJO?
WHAT?!
UH... YEAH!
SHE'S SO AWESOME...
Oooo oooh!
WELL, UNDER THE CIRCUMSTANCES...
I'D BETTER DO EVERYTHING I CAN TO GET ONODERA SWIMMING!
HUH?
GLINT

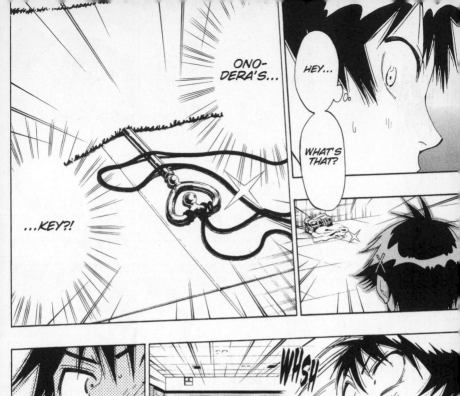

HEY...
WHAT'S THAT?
ONO-DERA'S...
...KEY?!
WHSH
B-BMP
COULD IT BE...
...THAT ONODERA'S THE GIRL...
...I MADE THAT PROMISE WITH TEN YEARS AGO?
WHEN WE'RE ALL GROWN UP, WE'LL MEET AGAIN!
...

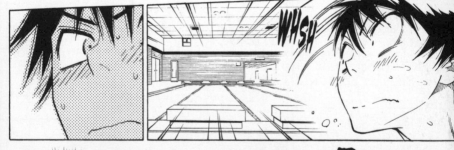

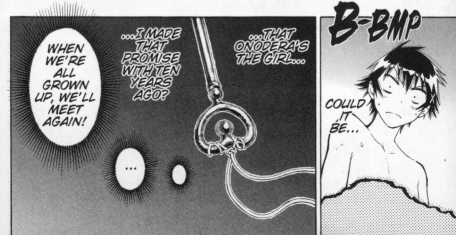

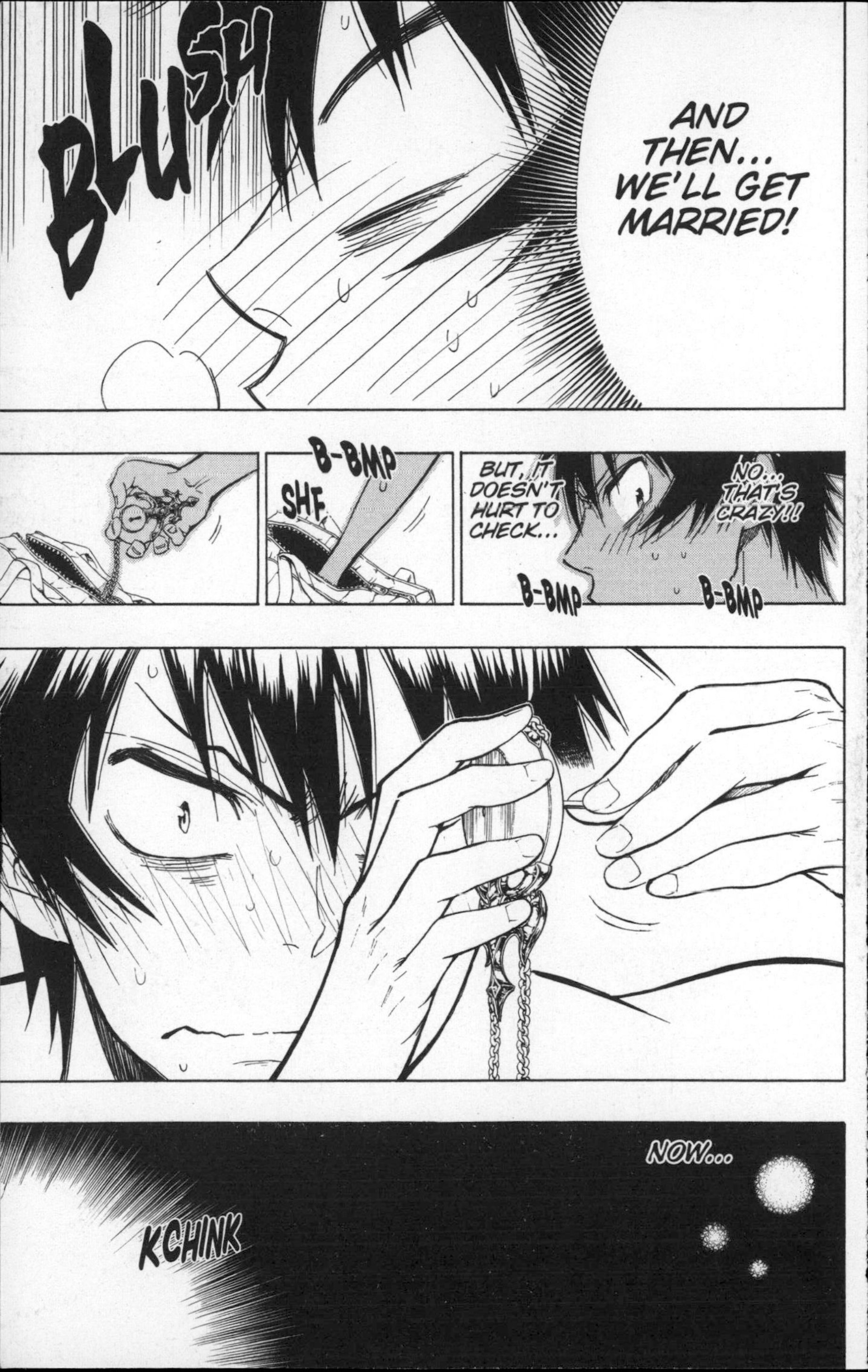
AND THEN... WE'LL GET MARRIED!
BLUSH
NO... THAT'S CRAZY!!
BUT, IT DOESN'T HURT TO CHECK...
B-BMP
B-BMP
B-BMP
SHF
NOW...
KCHINK

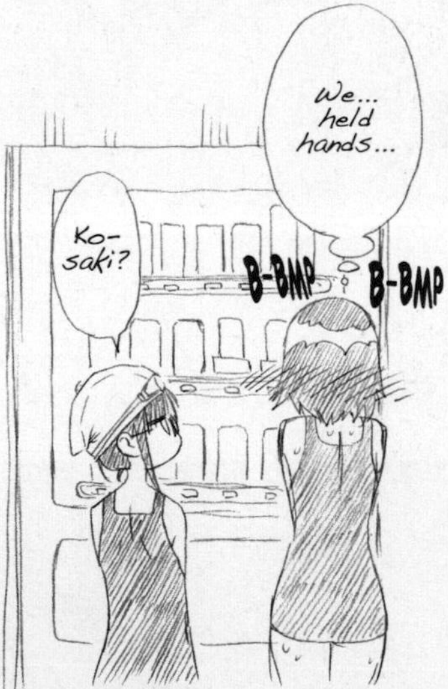
We... held hands...
B-BMP
B-BMP
Ko-saki?

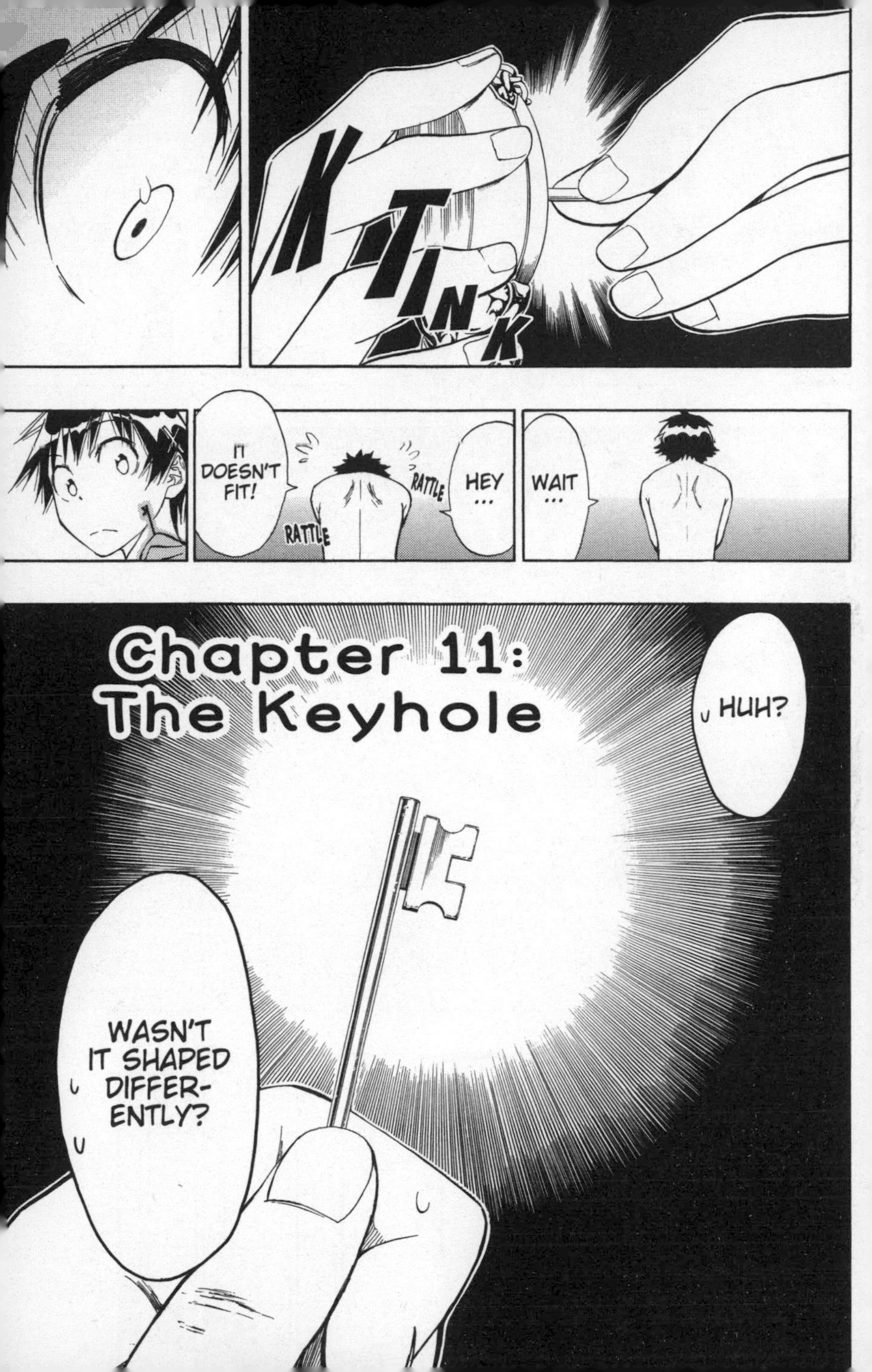
KTINK
WAIT ...
HEY ...
RATTLE
IT DOESN'T FIT!
RATTLE
HUH?
Chapter 11: The Keyhole
WASN'T IT SHAPED DIFFER-ENTLY?

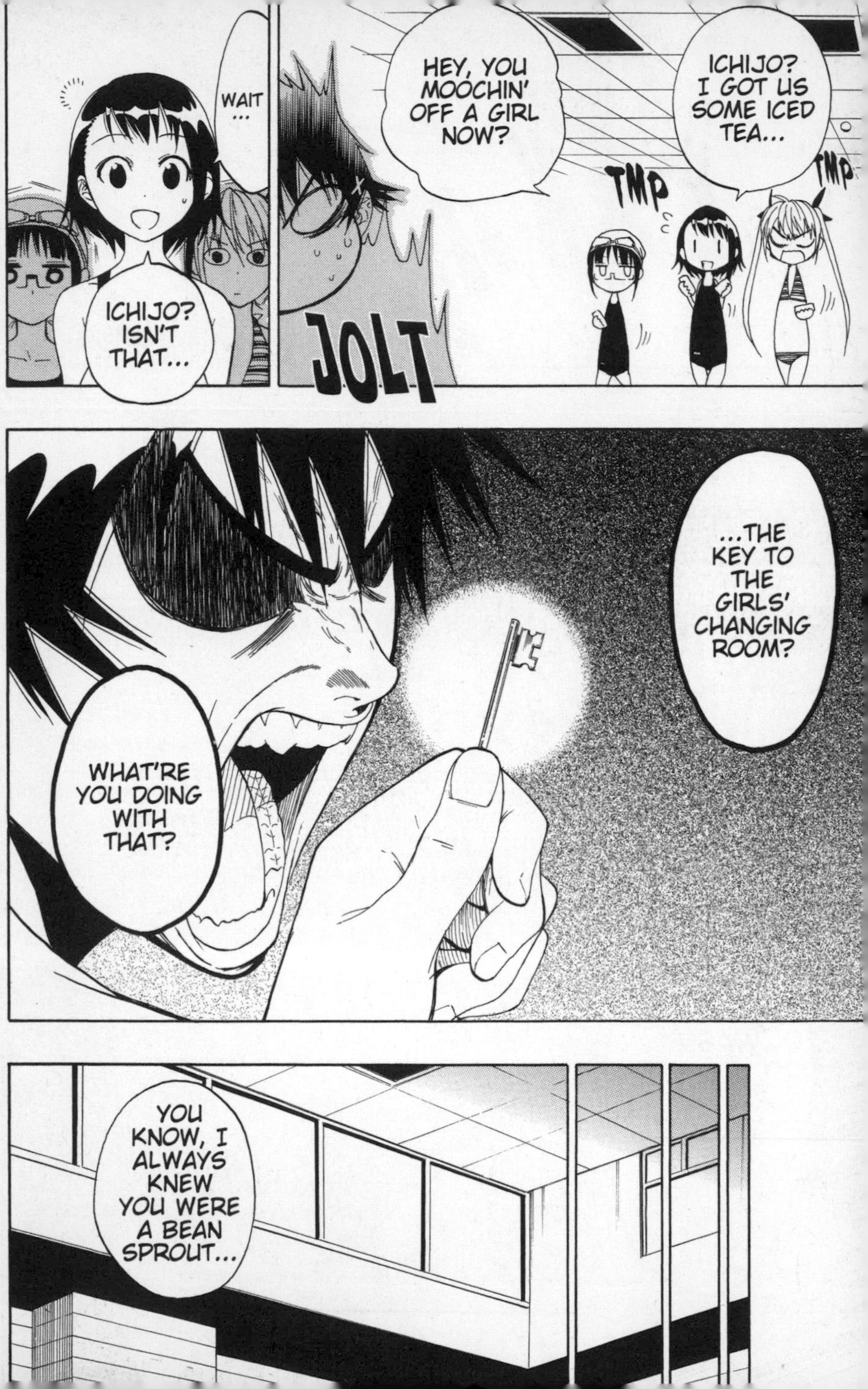
ICHIJO? I GOT US SOME ICED TEA...
TMP
TMP
HEY, YOU MOOCHIN' OFF A GIRL NOW?
JOLT
WAIT ...
ICHIJO? ISN'T THAT...
...THE KEY TO THE GIRLS' CHANGING ROOM?
WHAT'RE YOU DOING WITH THAT?
YOU KNOW, I ALWAYS KNEW YOU WERE A BEAN SPROUT...

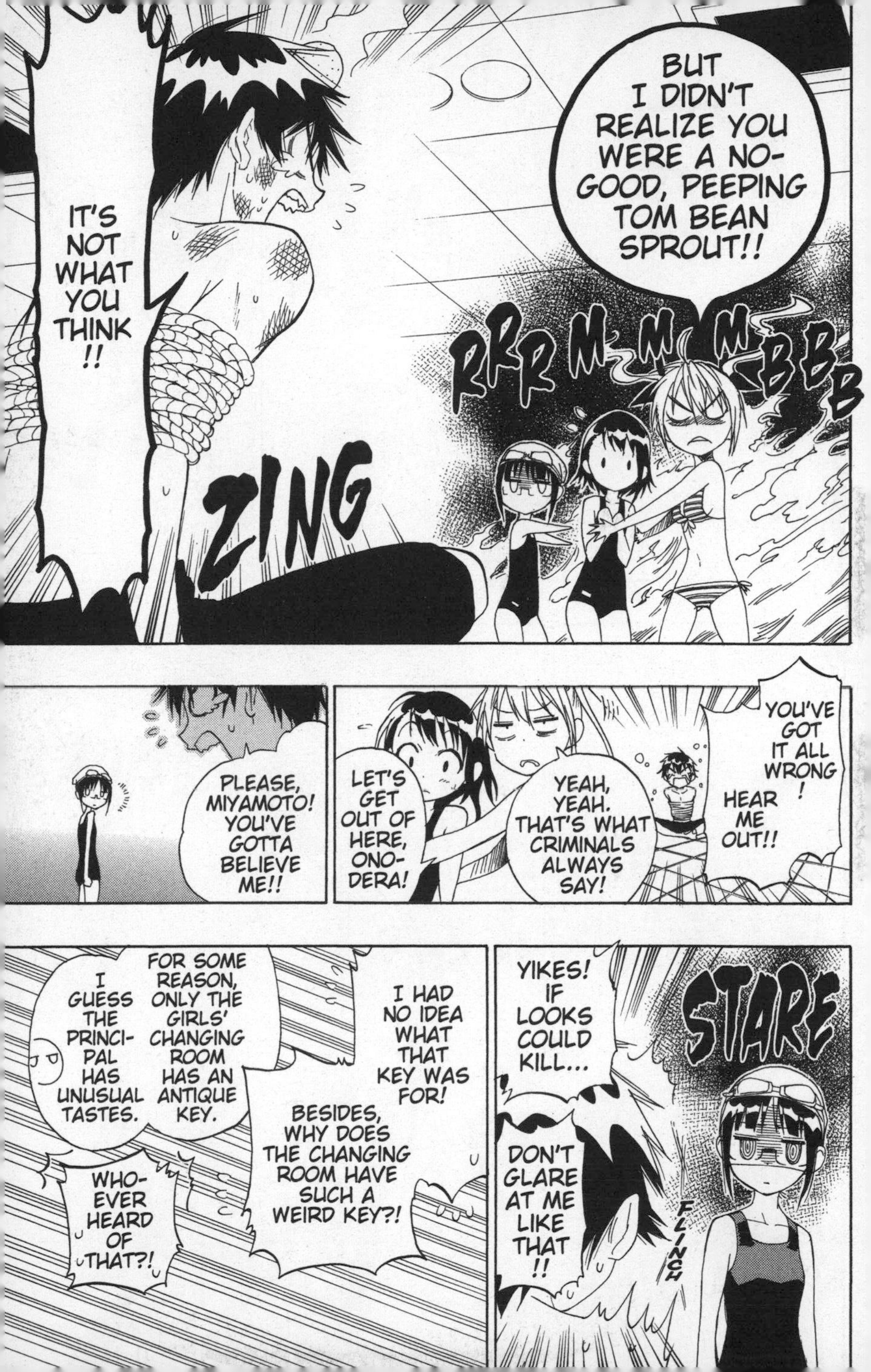
BUT I DIDN'T REALIZE YOU WERE A NO-GOOD, PEEPING TOM BEAN SPROUT!!
RRRMMMMBBB
IT'S NOT WHAT YOU THINK!!
ZING
YOU'VE GOT IT ALL WRONG!
HEAR ME OUT!!
YEAH, YEAH. THAT'S WHAT CRIMINALS ALWAYS SAY!
LET'S GET OUT OF HERE, ONO-DERA!
PLEASE, MIYAMOTO! YOU'VE GOTTA BELIEVE ME!!
STARE
YIKES! IF LOOKS COULD KILL...
DON'T GLARE AT ME LIKE THAT!!
FLINCH
I HAD NO IDEA WHAT THAT KEY WAS FOR!
BESIDES, WHY DOES THE CHANGING ROOM HAVE SUCH A WEIRD KEY?!
FOR SOME REASON, ONLY THE GIRLS' CHANGING ROOM HAS AN ANTIQUE KEY.
I GUESS THE PRINCI-PAL HAS UNUSUAL TASTES.
WHO-EVER HEARD OF THAT?!

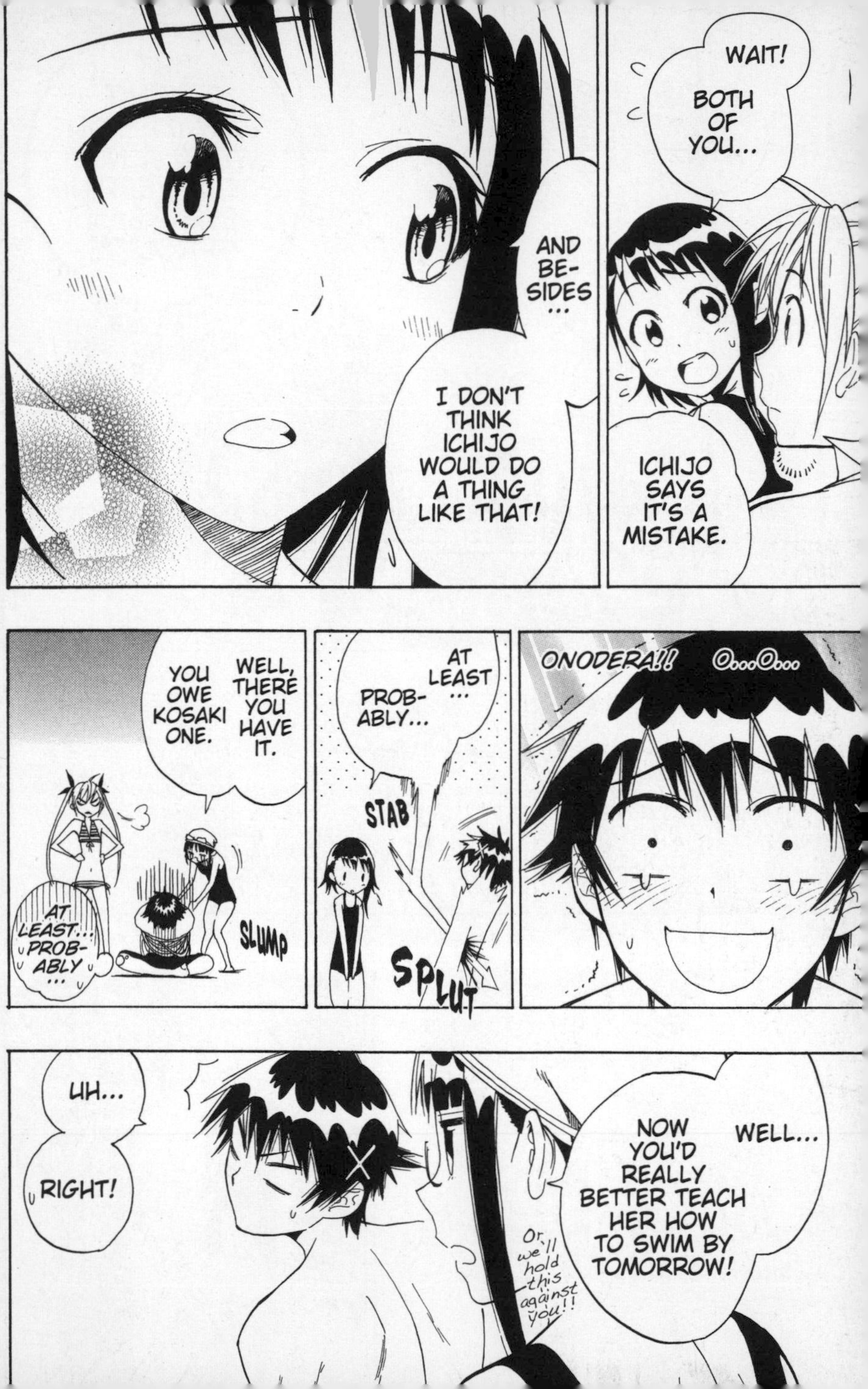
WAIT!
BOTH OF YOU...
ICHIJO SAYS IT'S A MISTAKE.
AND BE-SIDES...
I DON'T THINK ICHIJO WOULD DO A THING LIKE THAT!
ONODERA!!
O...O...
AT LEAST...
PROB-ABLY...
STAB
SPLUT
WELL, THERE YOU HAVE IT.
YOU OWE KOSAKI ONE.
AT LEAST... PROB-ABLY...
SLUMP
WELL...
NOW YOU'D REALLY BETTER TEACH HER HOW TO SWIM BY TOMORROW!
Or we'll hold this against you!!
UH...
RIGHT!

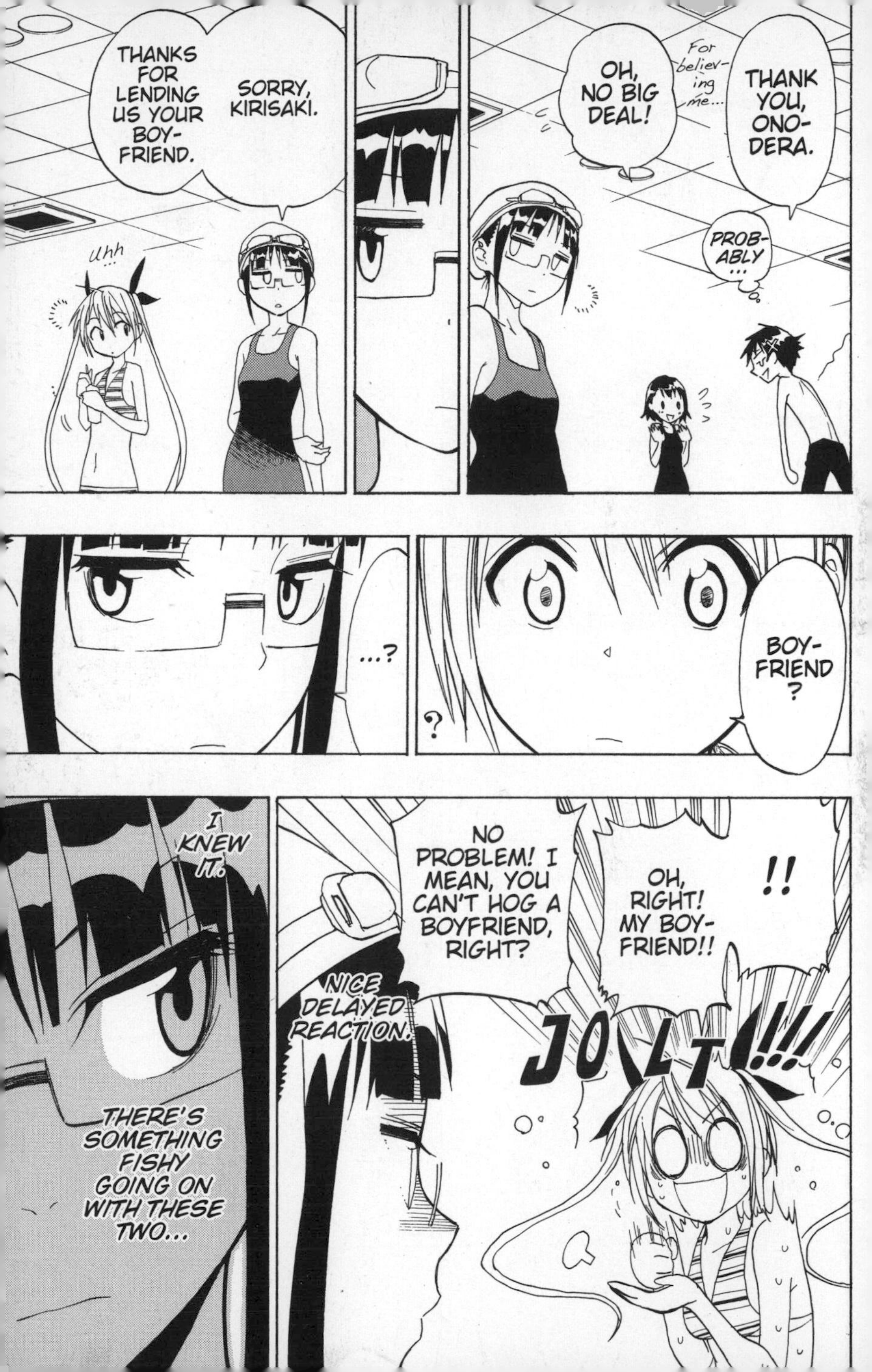
THANK YOU, ONODERA.
For believing me...
OH, NO BIG DEAL!
PROBABLY...
SORRY, KIRISAKI.
THANKS FOR LENDING US YOUR BOYFRIEND.
Uhh...
BOYFRIEND?
...?
!!
OH, RIGHT! MY BOYFRIEND!!
NO PROBLEM! I MEAN, YOU CAN'T HOG A BOYFRIEND, RIGHT?
JOLT!!!!
NICE DELAYED REACTION.
I KNEW IT.
THERE'S SOMETHING FISHY GOING ON WITH THESE TWO...

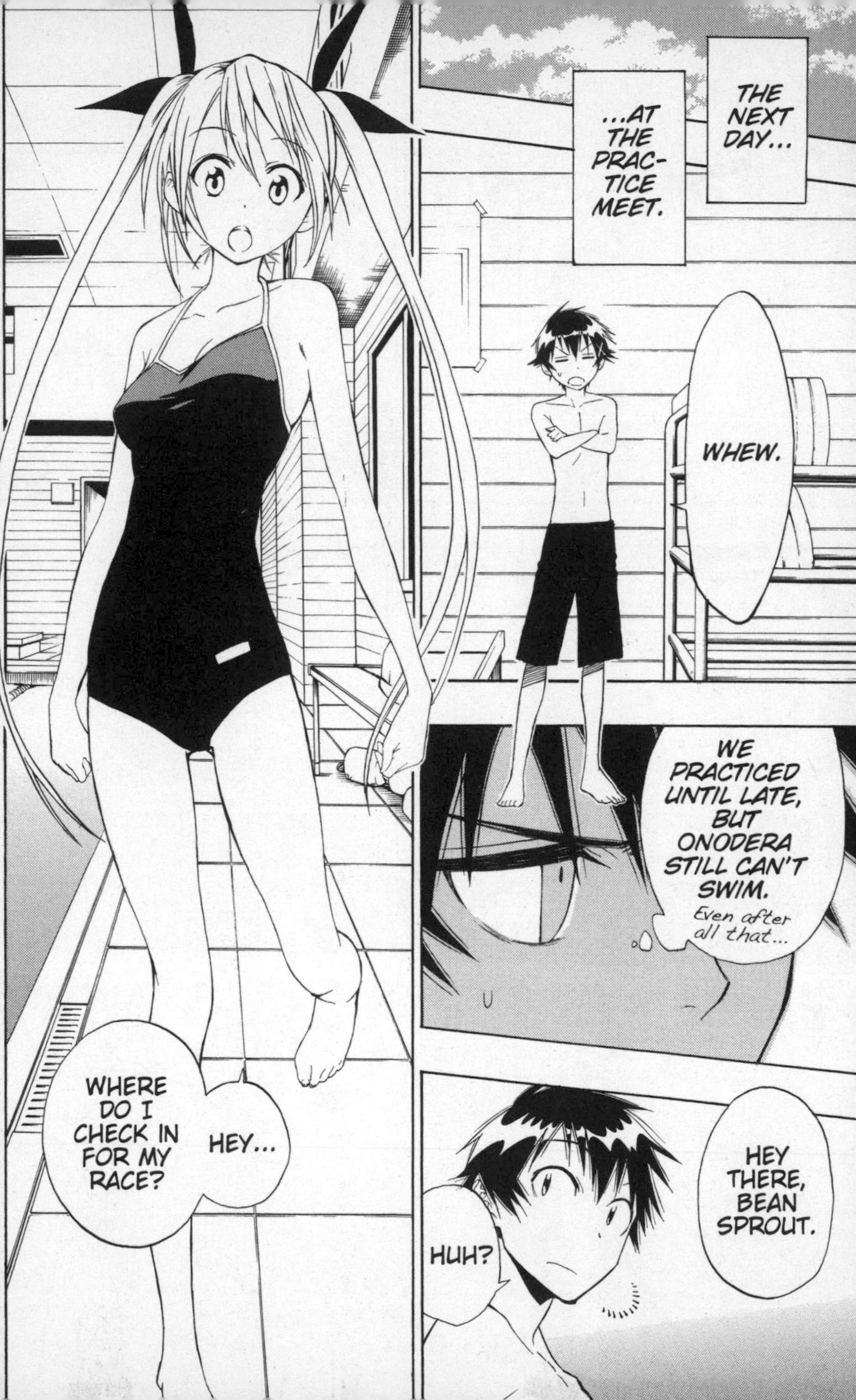
THE NEXT DAY...
...AT THE PRAC-TICE MEET.
WHEW.
WE PRACTICED UNTIL LATE, BUT ONODERA STILL CAN'T SWIM.
Even after all that...
HEY THERE, BEAN SPROUT.
HUH?
HEY...
WHERE DO I CHECK IN FOR MY RACE?

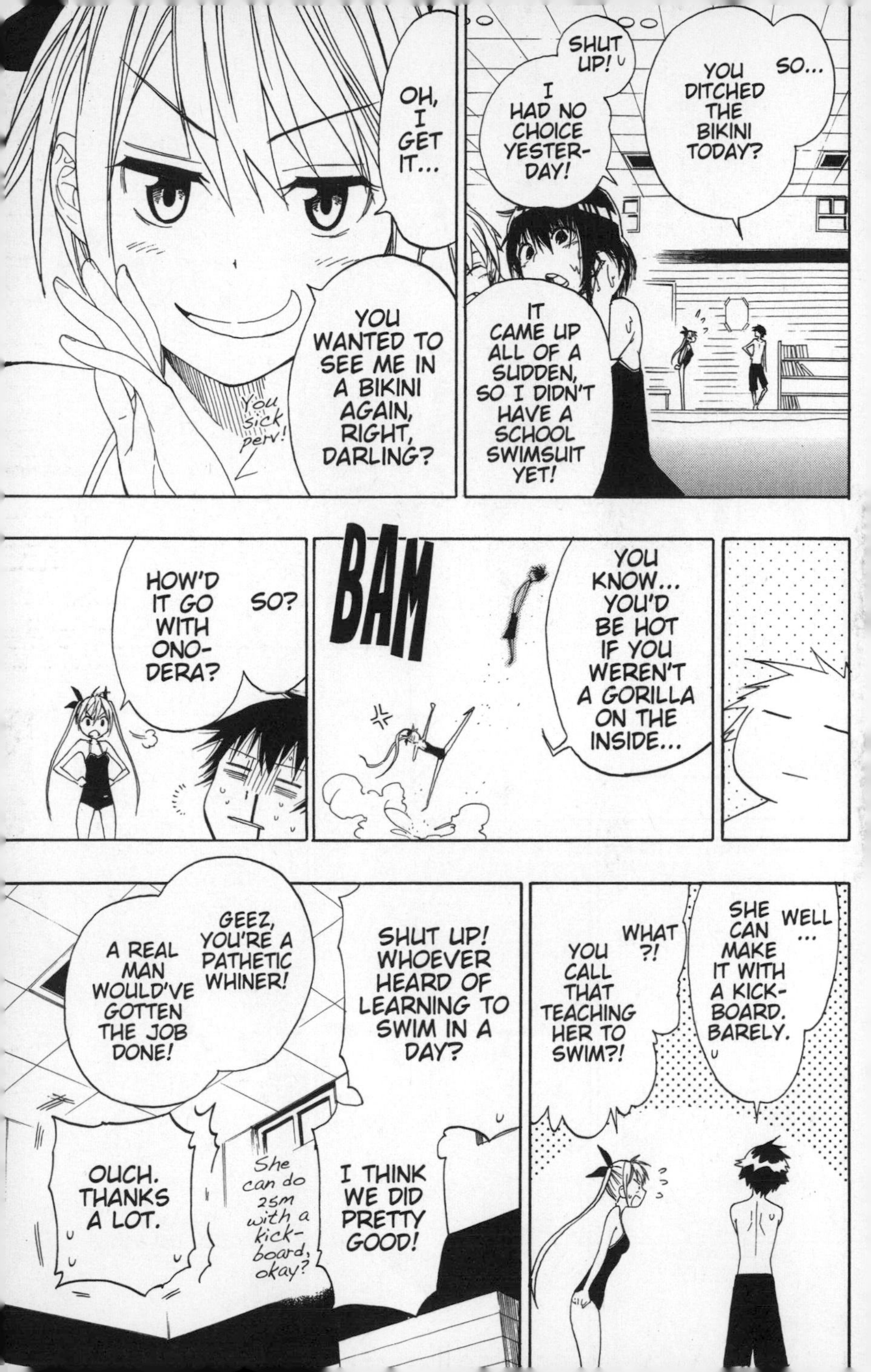
SO... YOU DITCHED THE BIKINI TODAY?
SHUT UP!
I HAD NO CHOICE YESTERDAY!
IT CAME UP ALL OF A SUDDEN, SO I DIDN'T HAVE A SCHOOL SWIMSUIT YET!
OH, I GET IT...
YOU WANTED TO SEE ME IN A BIKINI AGAIN, RIGHT, DARLING?
You sick perv!
YOU KNOW... YOU'D BE HOT IF YOU WEREN'T A GORILLA ON THE INSIDE...
BAM
SO?
HOW'D IT GO WITH ONODERA?
WELL...
SHE CAN MAKE IT WITH A KICKBOARD. BARELY.
WHAT?!
YOU CALL THAT TEACHING HER TO SWIM?!
SHUT UP! WHOEVER HEARD OF LEARNING TO SWIM IN A DAY?
GEEZ, YOU'RE A PATHETIC WHINER!
A REAL MAN WOULD'VE GOTTEN THE JOB DONE!
I THINK WE DID PRETTY GOOD!
She can do 25m with a kickboard, okay?
OUCH. THANKS A LOT.

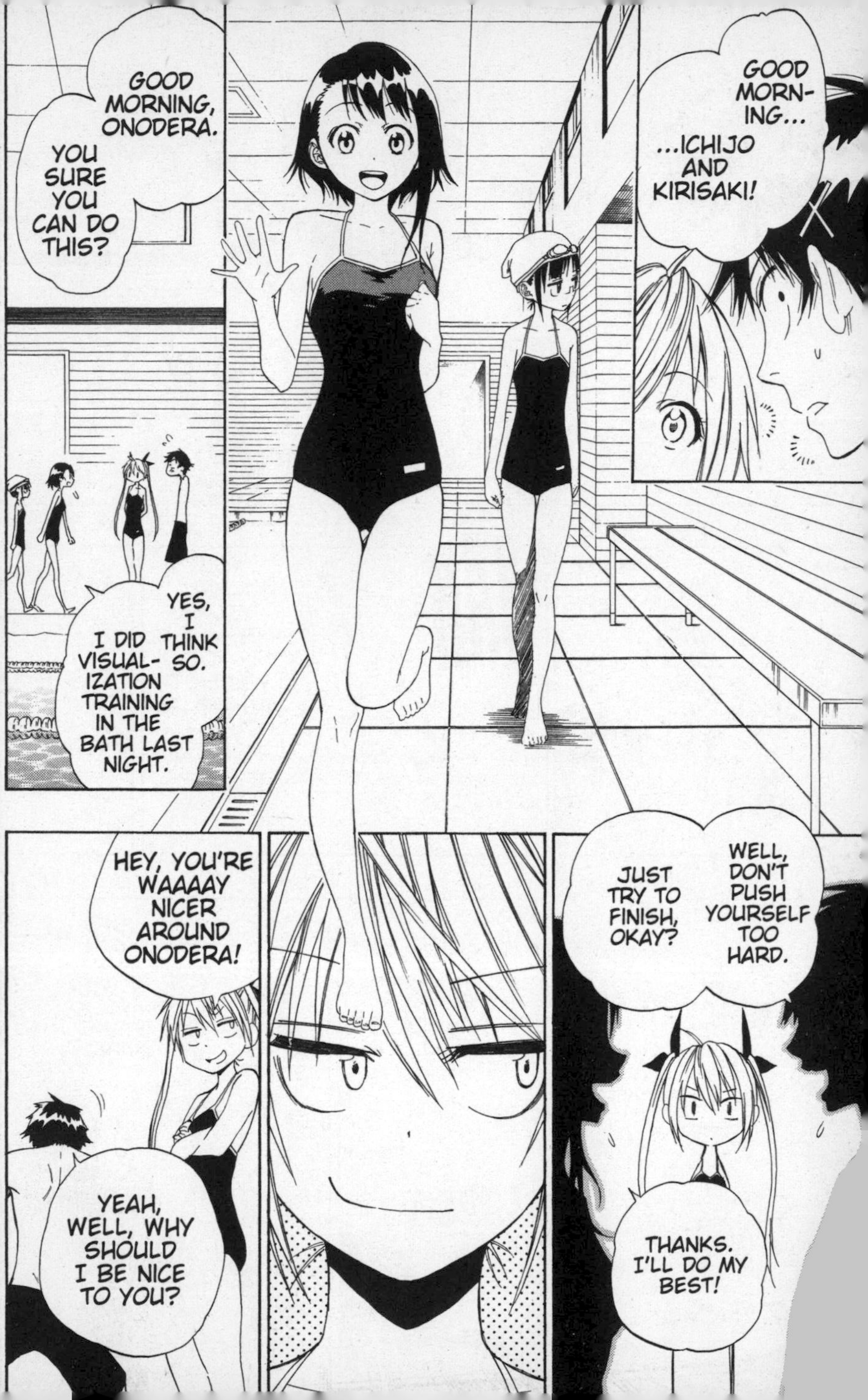
GOOD MORNING...
...ICHIJO AND KIRISAKI!
GOOD MORNING, ONODERA.
YOU SURE YOU CAN DO THIS?
YES, I THINK SO.
I DID VISUALIZATION TRAINING IN THE BATH LAST NIGHT.
WELL, DON'T PUSH YOURSELF TOO HARD.
JUST TRY TO FINISH, OKAY?
THANKS. I'LL DO MY BEST!
HEY, YOU'RE WAAAAY NICER AROUND ONODERA!
YEAH, WELL, WHY SHOULD I BE NICE TO YOU?

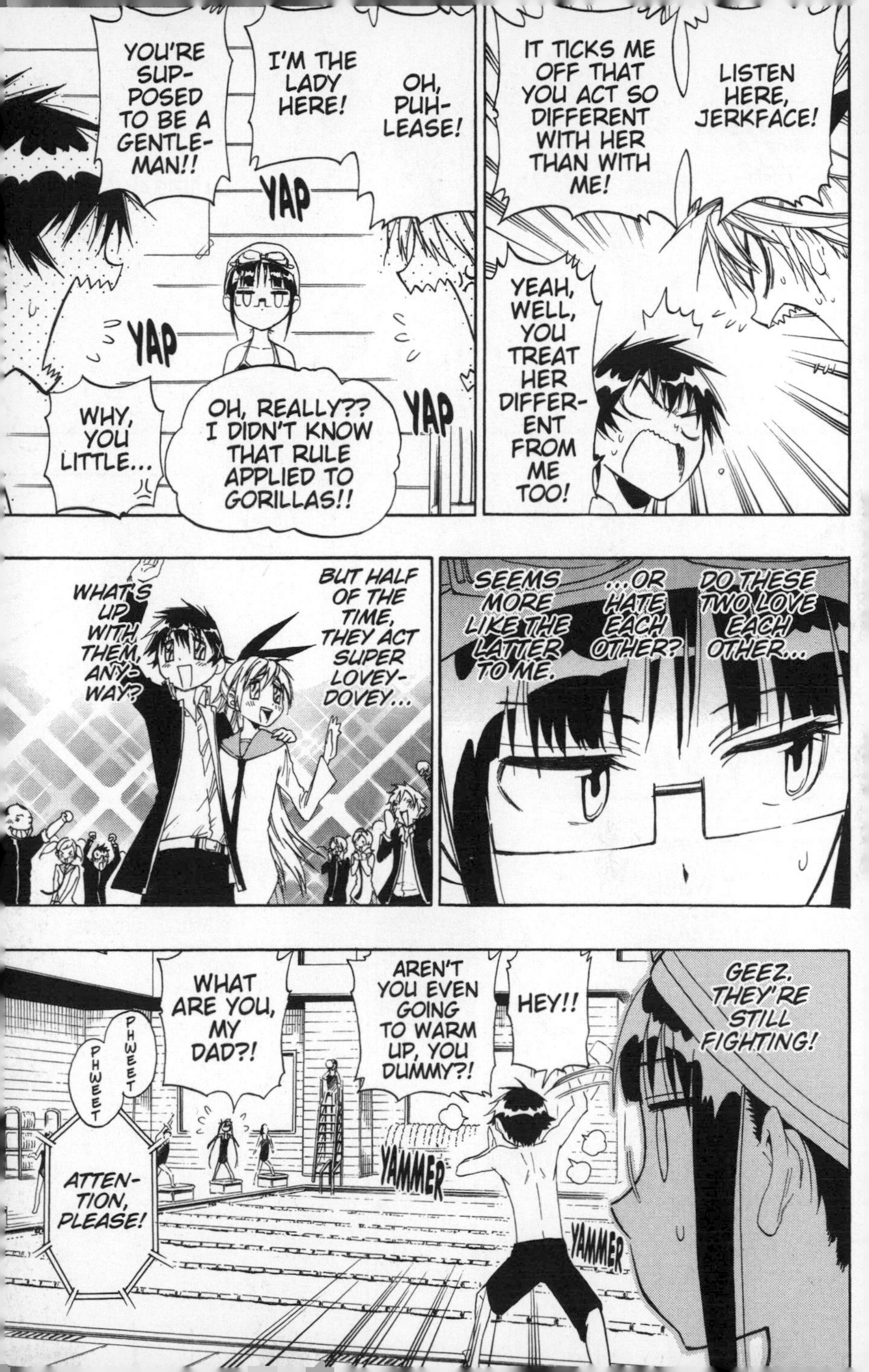
LISTEN HERE, JERKFACE!
IT TICKS ME OFF THAT YOU ACT SO DIFFERENT WITH HER THAN WITH ME!
YEAH, WELL, YOU TREAT HER DIFFERENT FROM ME TOO!
OH, PUH-LEASE!
I'M THE LADY HERE!
YOU'RE SUPPOSED TO BE A GENTLEMAN!!
YAP
YAP
YAP
OH, REALLY?? I DIDN'T KNOW THAT RULE APPLIED TO GORILLAS!!
WHY, YOU LITTLE...
DO THESE TWO LOVE EACH OTHER...
...OR HATE EACH OTHER?
SEEMS MORE LIKE THE LATTER TO ME.
BUT HALF OF THE TIME, THEY ACT SUPER LOVEY-DOVEY...
WHAT'S UP WITH THEM, ANYWAY?
GEEZ. THEY'RE STILL FIGHTING!
HEY!!
AREN'T YOU EVEN GOING TO WARM UP, YOU DUMMY?!
WHAT ARE YOU, MY DAD?!
YAMMER
YAMMER
PHWEET
PHWEET
ATTENTION, PLEASE!

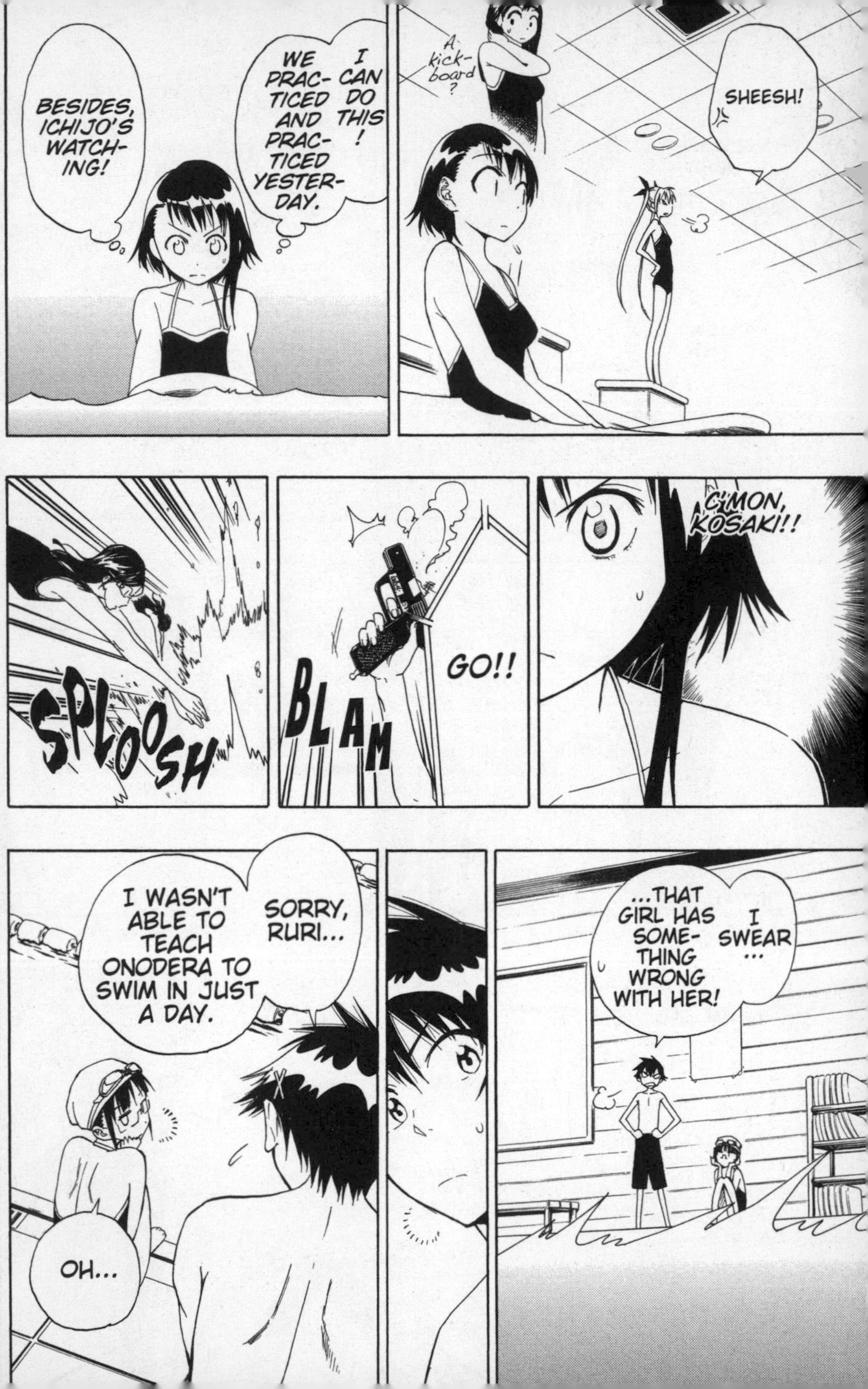
SHEESH!
A kick-board?
I CAN DO THIS! WE PRACTICED AND PRACTICED YESTERDAY.
BESIDES, ICHIJO'S WATCHING!
C'MON, KOSAKI!!
GO!!
BLAM
SPLOOSH
I SWEAR... ...THAT GIRL HAS SOMETHING WRONG WITH HER!
SORRY, RURI... I WASN'T ABLE TO TEACH ONODERA TO SWIM IN JUST A DAY.
OH...

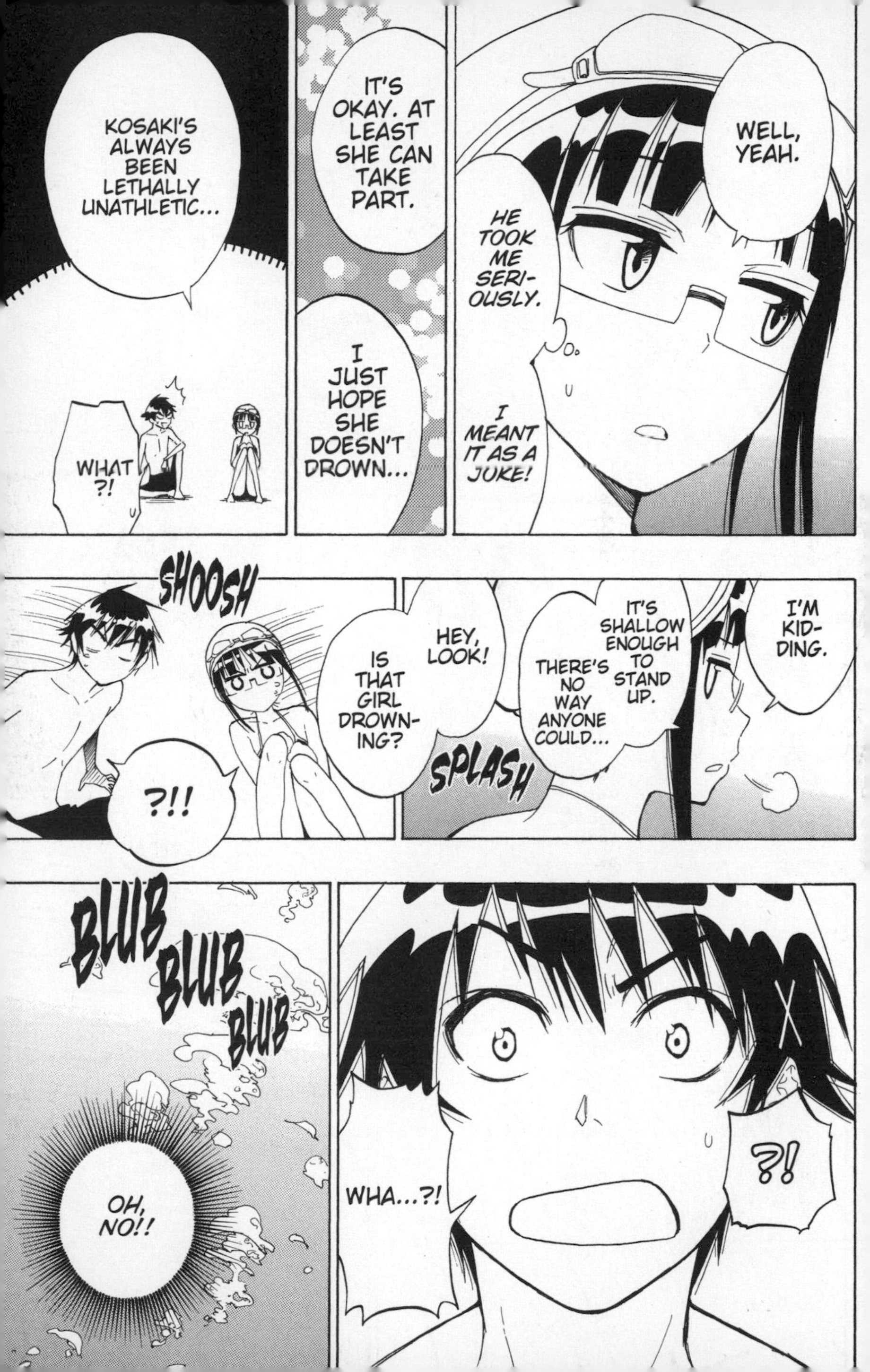
WELL, YEAH.
HE TOOK ME SERIOUSLY.
I MEANT IT AS A JOKE!
IT'S OKAY. AT LEAST SHE CAN TAKE PART.
I JUST HOPE SHE DOESN'T DROWN...
KOSAKI'S ALWAYS BEEN LETHALLY UNATHLETIC...
WHAT?!
I'M KIDDING.
IT'S SHALLOW ENOUGH TO STAND UP.
THERE'S NO WAY ANYONE COULD...
SPLASH
HEY, LOOK!
IS THAT GIRL DROWNING?
SHOOSH
?!!
?!
WHA...?!
BLUB
BLUB
BLUB
OH, NO!!

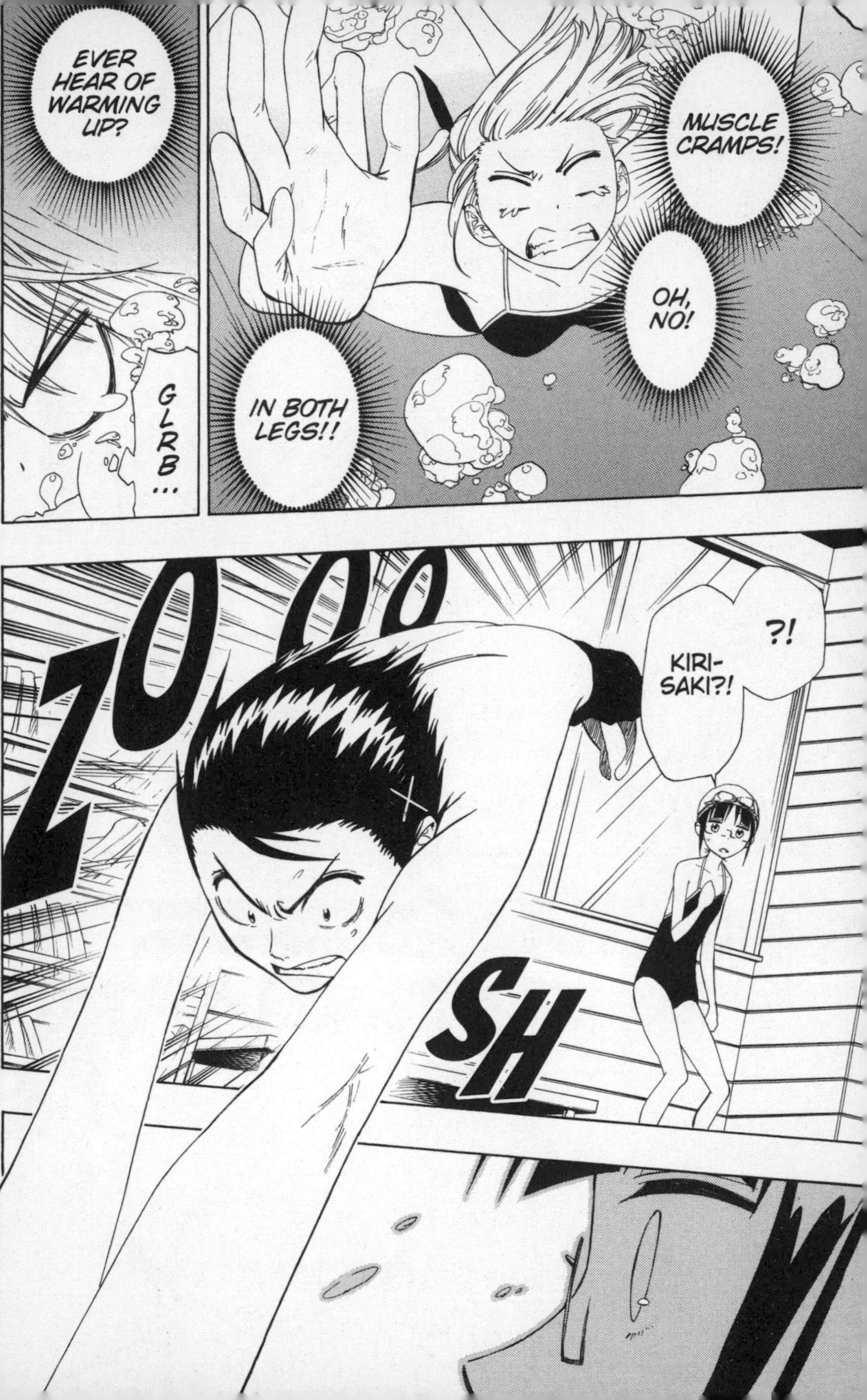
MUSCLE CRAMPS!
OH, NO!
IN BOTH LEGS!!
EVER HEAR OF WARMING UP?
GLRB...
?!
KIRI-SAKI?!
ZOOO
SH

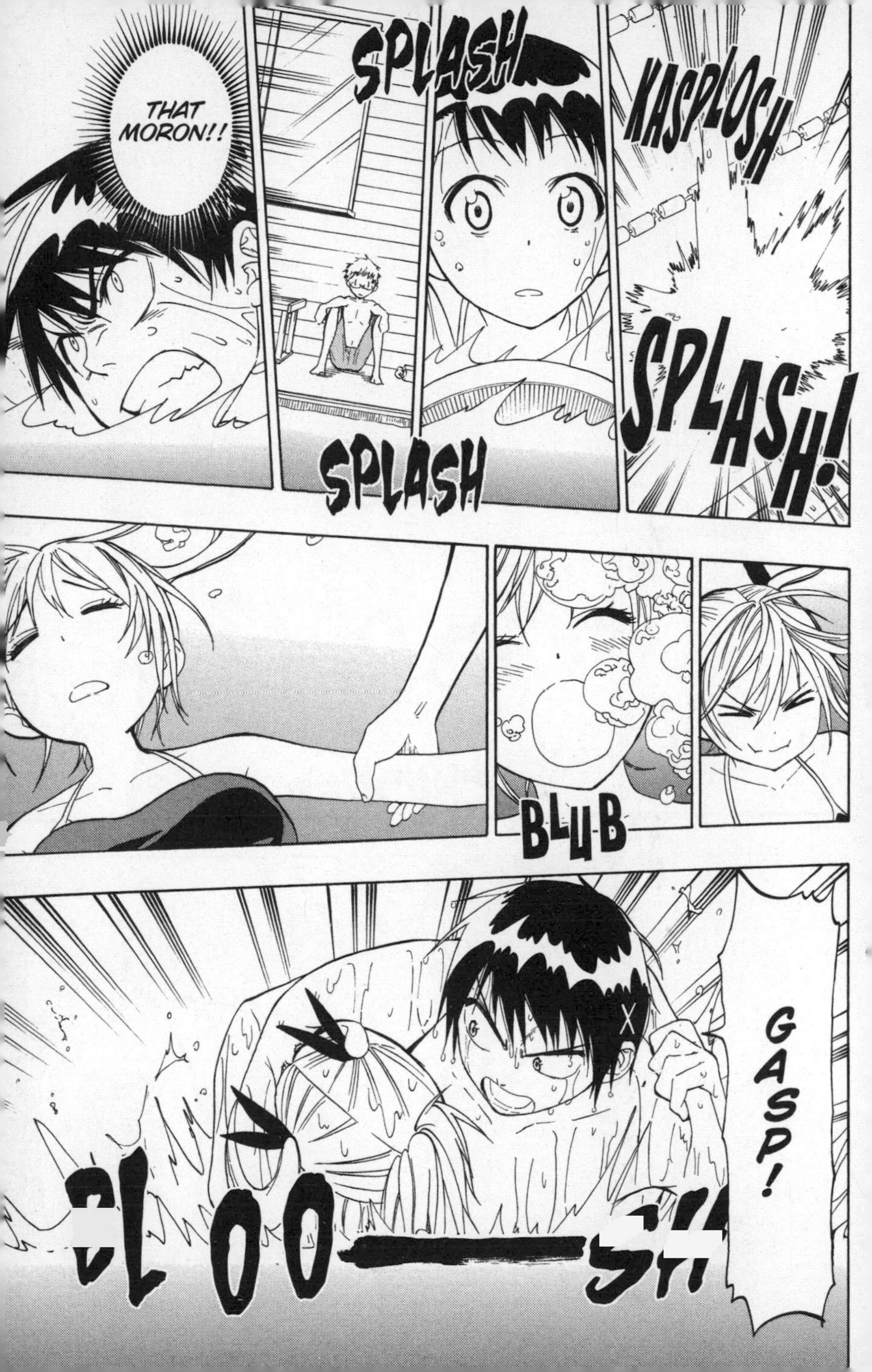
KASPLOSH
SPLASH!
SPLASH
SPLASH
THAT MORON!!
BLUB
GASP!
LOO—SH

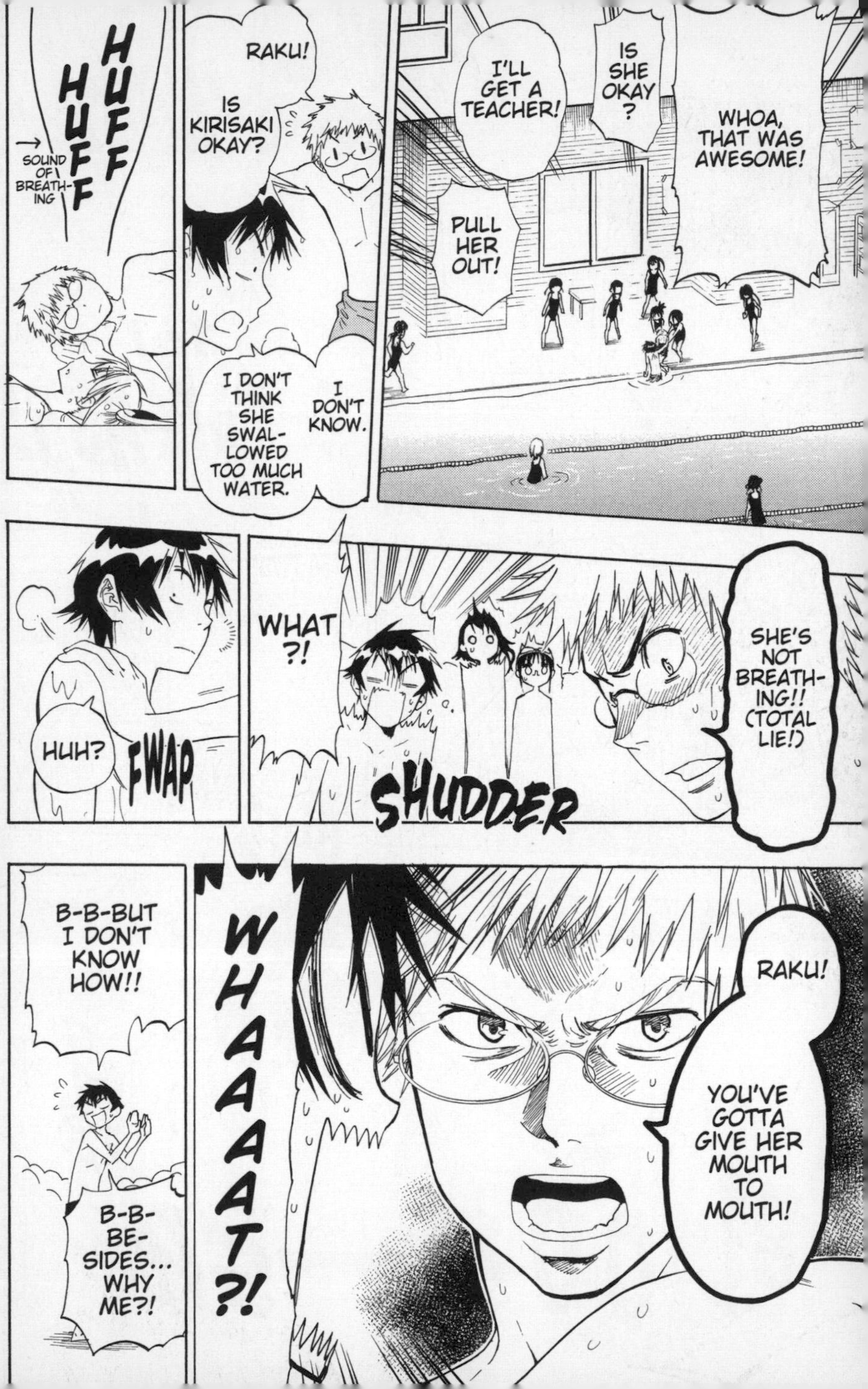
WHOA, THAT WAS AWESOME!
IS SHE OKAY?
I'LL GET A TEACHER!
PULL HER OUT!
RAKU!
IS KIRISAKI OKAY?
I DON'T KNOW.
I DON'T THINK SHE SWALLOWED TOO MUCH WATER.
HUFF HUFF
SOUND OF BREATHING
SHE'S NOT BREATHING!! (TOTAL LIE!)
SHUDDER
WHAT?!
HUH?
FWAP
RAKU!
YOU'VE GOTTA GIVE HER MOUTH TO MOUTH!
WHAAAAAT?!
B-B-BUT I DON'T KNOW HOW!!
B-B-BESIDES... WHY ME?!

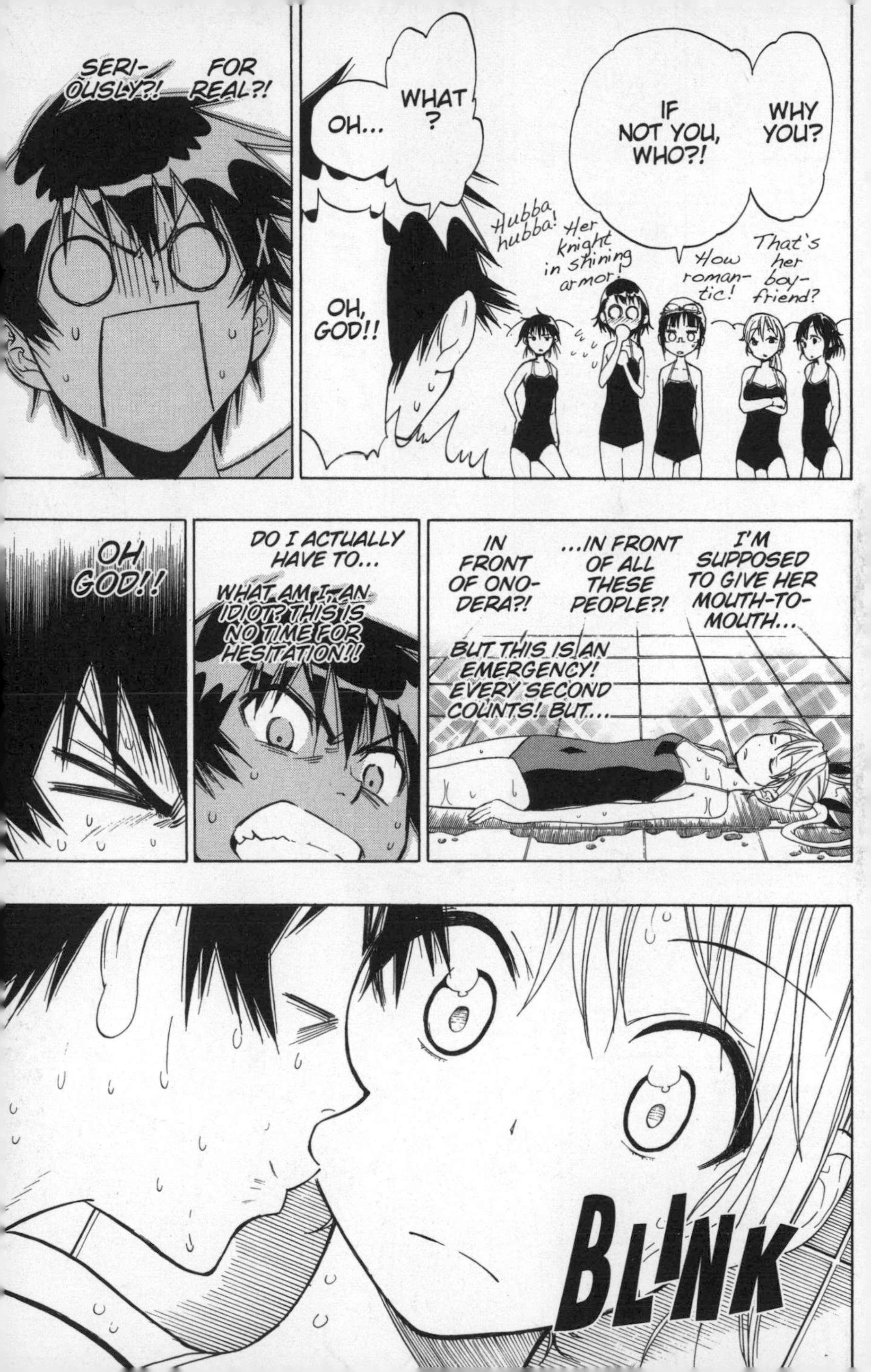
WHY YOU?
IF NOT YOU, WHO?!
That's her boy-friend?
How roman-tic!
Her knight in shining armor!
Hubba hubba!
WHAT?
OH...
OH, GOD!!
FOR REAL?!
SERI-OUSLY?!
I'M SUPPOSED TO GIVE HER MOUTH-TO-MOUTH...
...IN FRONT OF ALL THESE PEOPLE?!
IN FRONT OF ONO-DERA?!
BUT THIS IS AN EMERGENCY! EVERY SECOND COUNTS! BUT....
DO I ACTUALLY HAVE TO...
WHAT AM I, AN IDIOT? THIS IS NO TIME FOR HESITATION!!
OH GOD!!
BLINK

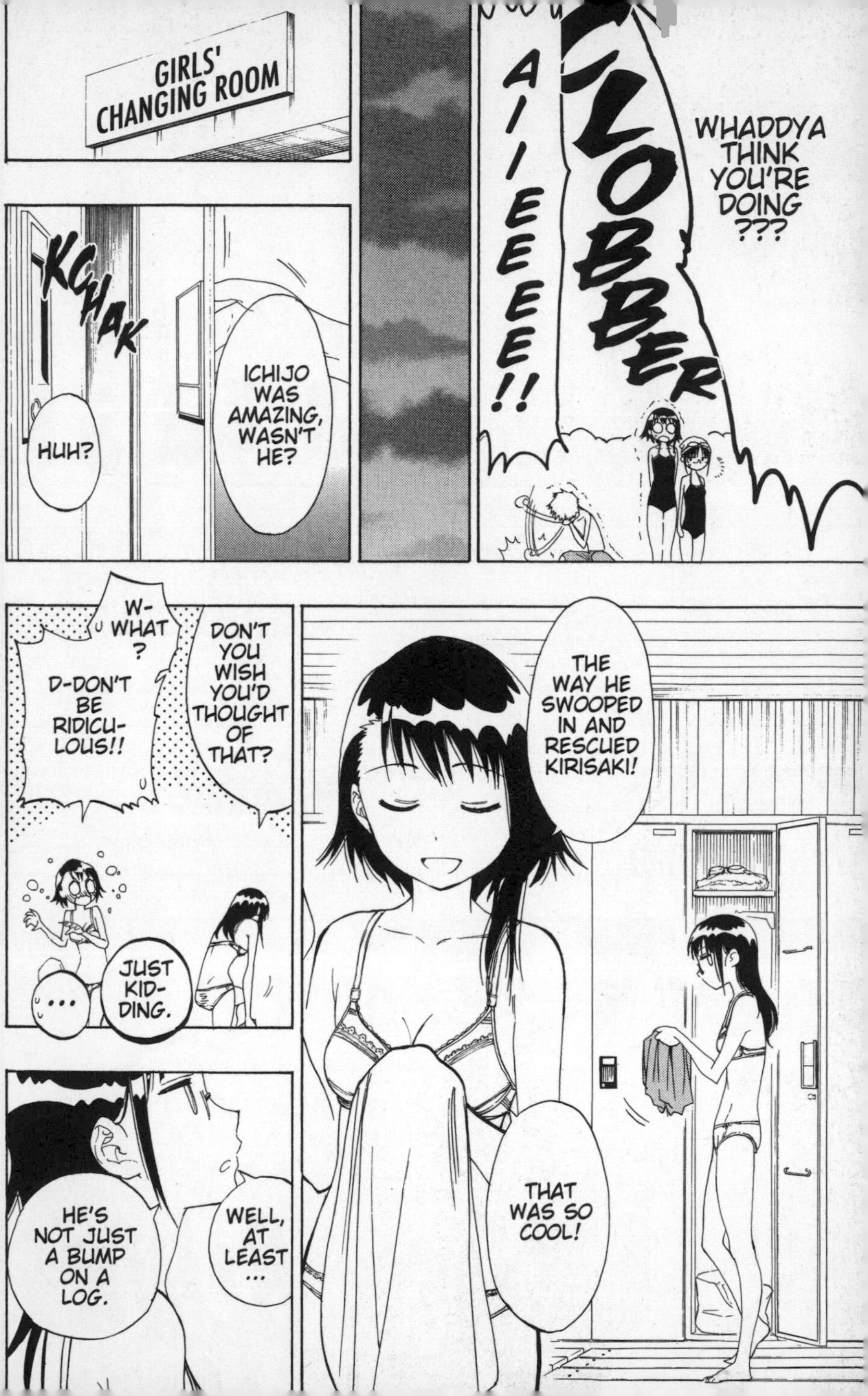
CLOBBER
AIIEEEEE!!
WHADDYA THINK YOU'RE DOING???
GIRLS' CHANGING ROOM
KCHAK
ICHIJO WAS AMAZING, WASN'T HE?
HUH?
THE WAY HE SWOOPED IN AND RESCUED KIRISAKI!
THAT WAS SO COOL!
DON'T YOU WISH YOU'D THOUGHT OF THAT?
W-WHAT?
D-DON'T BE RIDICULOUS!!
JUST KID-DING.
...
WELL, AT LEAST...
HE'S NOT JUST A BUMP ON A LOG.

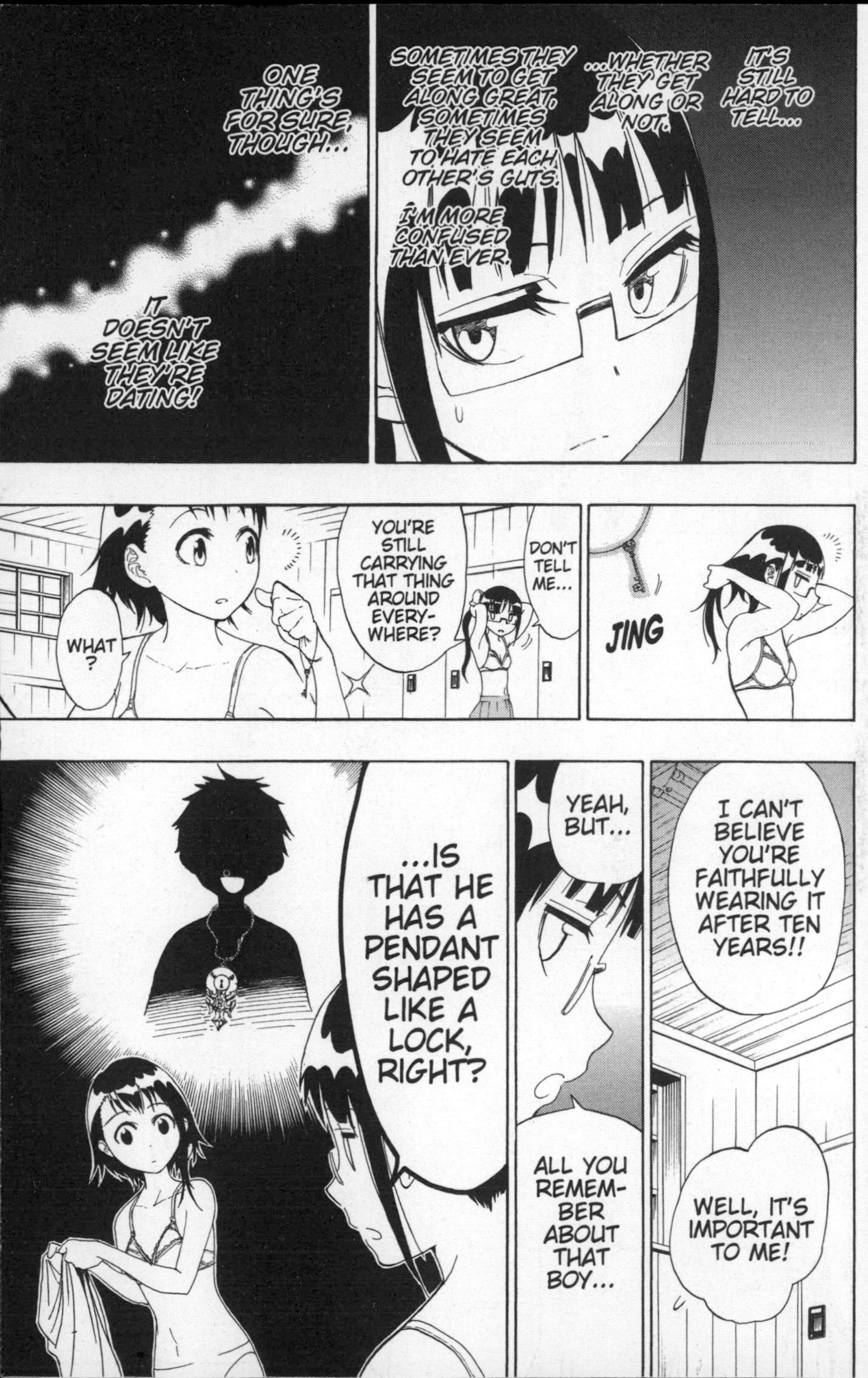
IT'S STILL HARD TO TELL...
...WHETHER THEY GET ALONG OR NOT.
SOMETIMES THEY SEEM TO GET ALONG GREAT, SOMETIMES THEY SEEM TO HATE EACH OTHER'S GUTS.
I'M MORE CONFUSED THAN EVER.
ONE THING'S FOR SURE, THOUGH...
IT DOESN'T SEEM LIKE THEY'RE DATING!
JING
DON'T TELL ME...
YOU'RE STILL CARRYING THAT THING AROUND EVERY-WHERE?
WHAT?
I CAN'T BELIEVE YOU'RE FAITHFULLY WEARING IT AFTER TEN YEARS!!
WELL, IT'S IMPORTANT TO ME!
YEAH, BUT...
ALL YOU REMEM-BER ABOUT THAT BOY...
...IS THAT HE HAS A PENDANT SHAPED LIKE A LOCK, RIGHT?

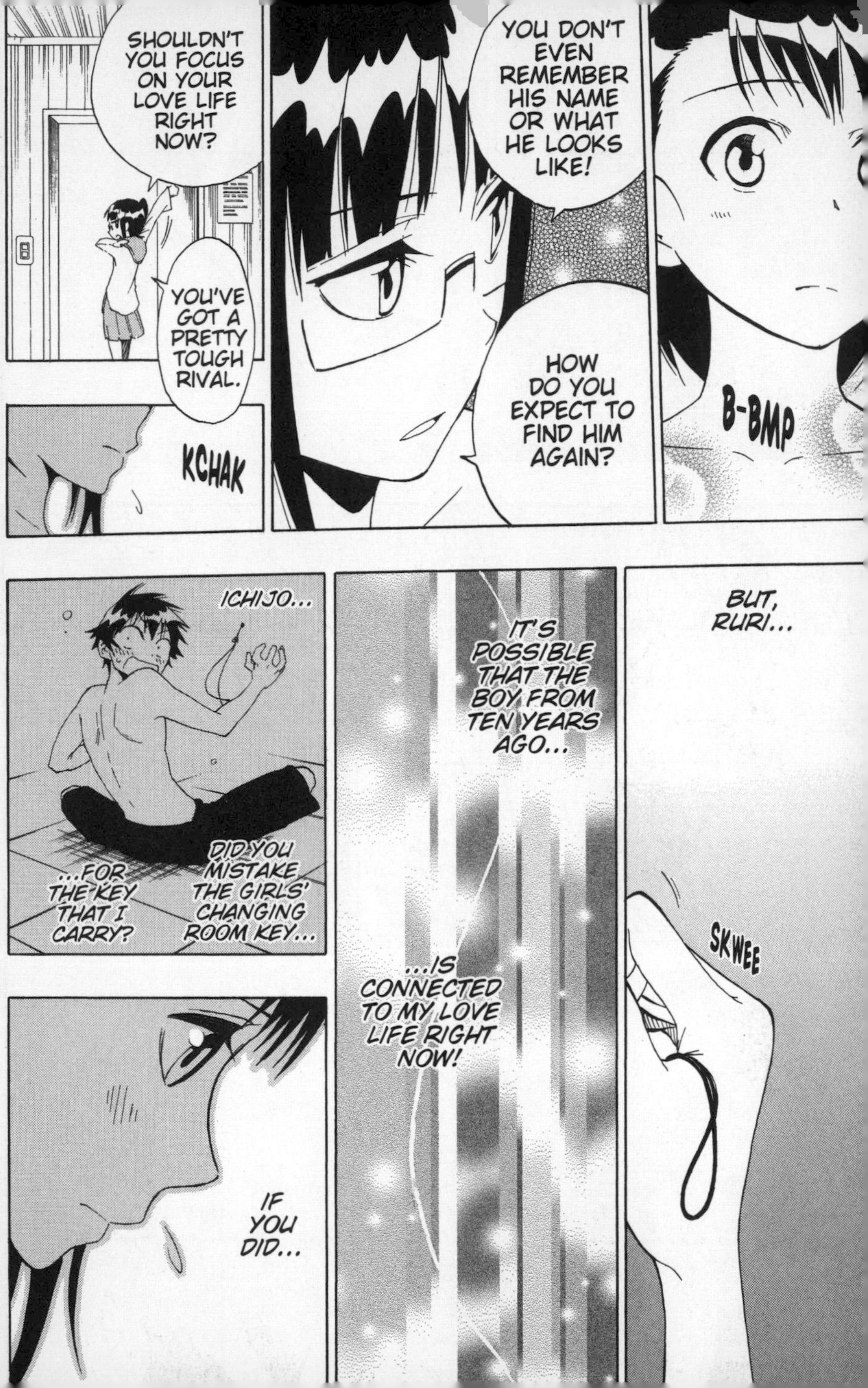
B-BMP
YOU DON'T EVEN REMEMBER HIS NAME OR WHAT HE LOOKS LIKE!
HOW DO YOU EXPECT TO FIND HIM AGAIN?
SHOULDN'T YOU FOCUS ON YOUR LOVE LIFE RIGHT NOW?
YOU'VE GOT A PRETTY TOUGH RIVAL.
KCHAK
BUT, RURI...
SKWEE
IT'S POSSIBLE THAT THE BOY FROM TEN YEARS AGO...
...IS CONNECTED TO MY LOVE LIFE RIGHT NOW!
ICHIJO...
DID YOU MISTAKE THE GIRLS' CHANGING ROOM KEY...
...FOR THE KEY THAT I CARRY?
IF YOU DID...

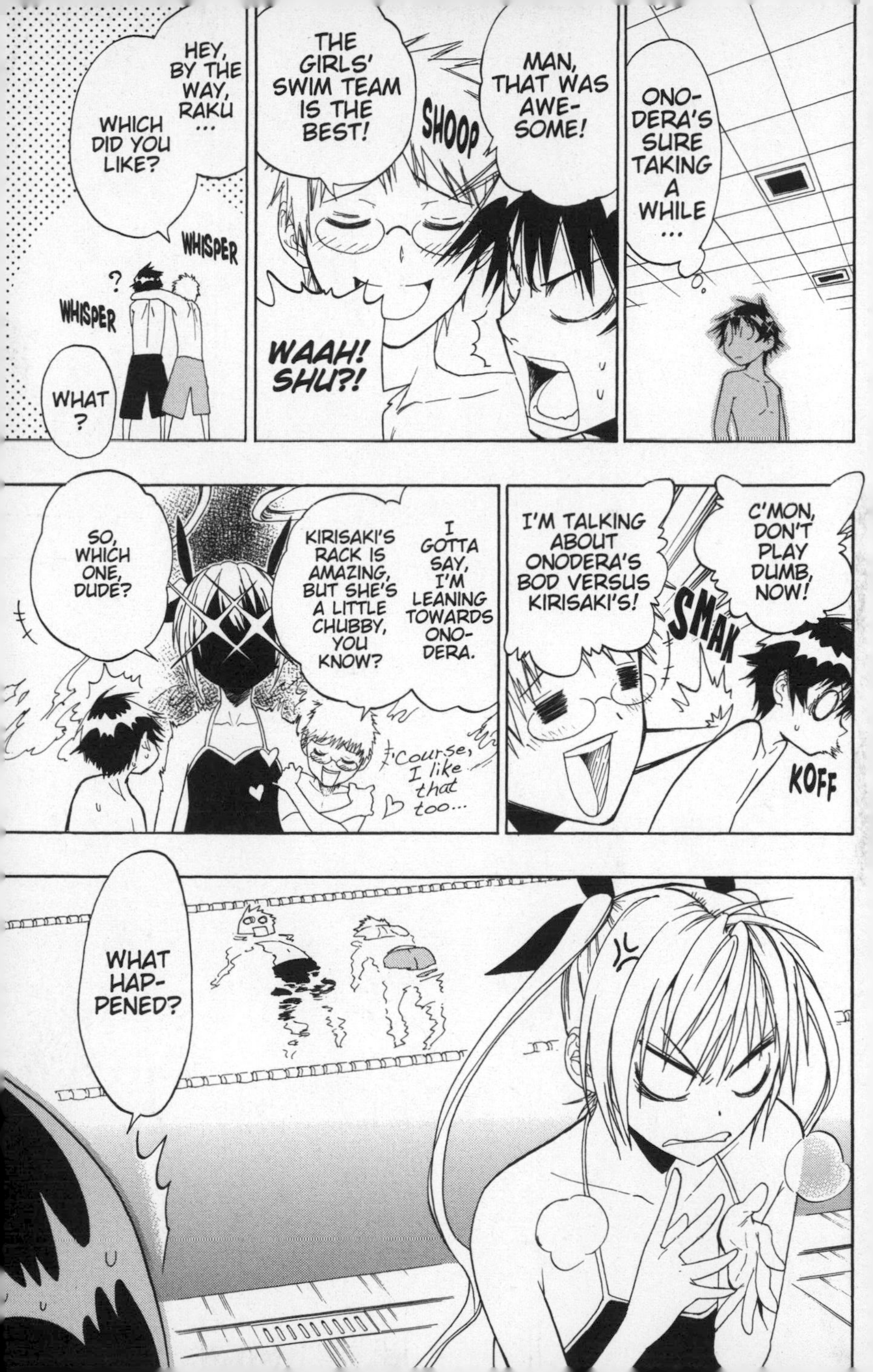
ONODERA'S SURE TAKING A WHILE...
MAN, THAT WAS AWESOME!
SHOOP
THE GIRLS' SWIM TEAM IS THE BEST!
WAAH! SHU?!
HEY, BY THE WAY, RAKU...
WHICH DID YOU LIKE?
WHISPER
WHISPER
WHAT?
C'MON, DON'T PLAY DUMB, NOW!
SMAK
I'M TALKING ABOUT ONODERA'S BOD VERSUS KIRISAKI'S!
KOFF
I GOTTA SAY, I'M LEANING TOWARDS ONODERA.
KIRISAKI'S RACK IS AMAZING, BUT SHE'S A LITTLE CHUBBY, YOU KNOW?
'Course, I like that too...
SO, WHICH ONE, DUDE?
WHAT HAPPENED?

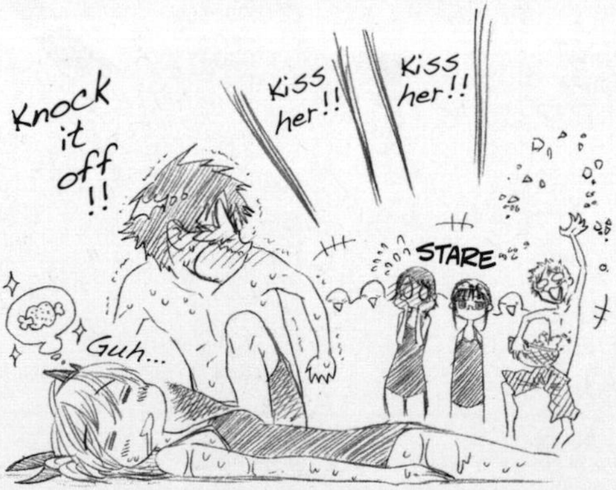
Kiss her!!
Kiss her!!
Knock it off!!
STARE
Guh...

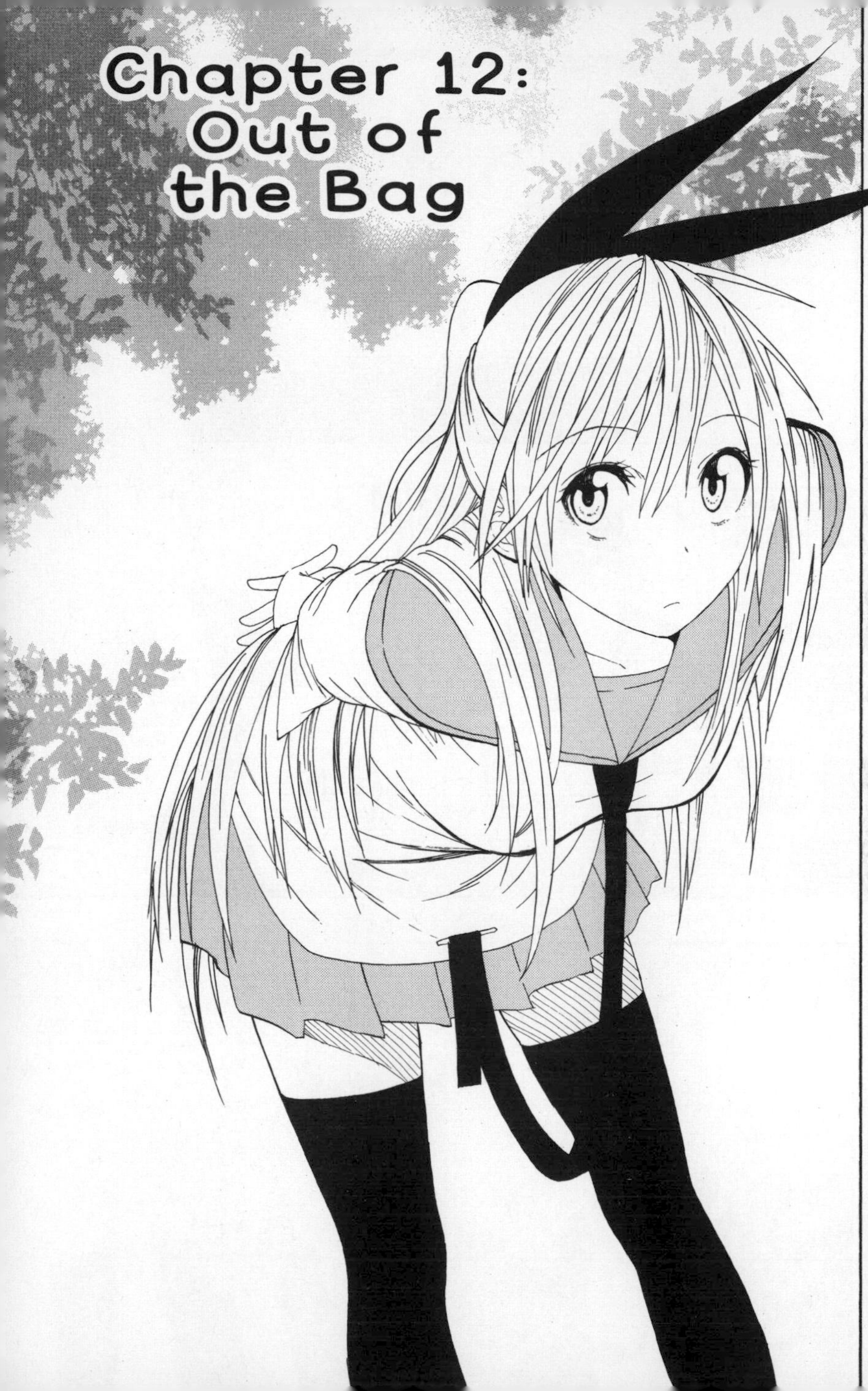
Chapter 12:
Out of
the Bag

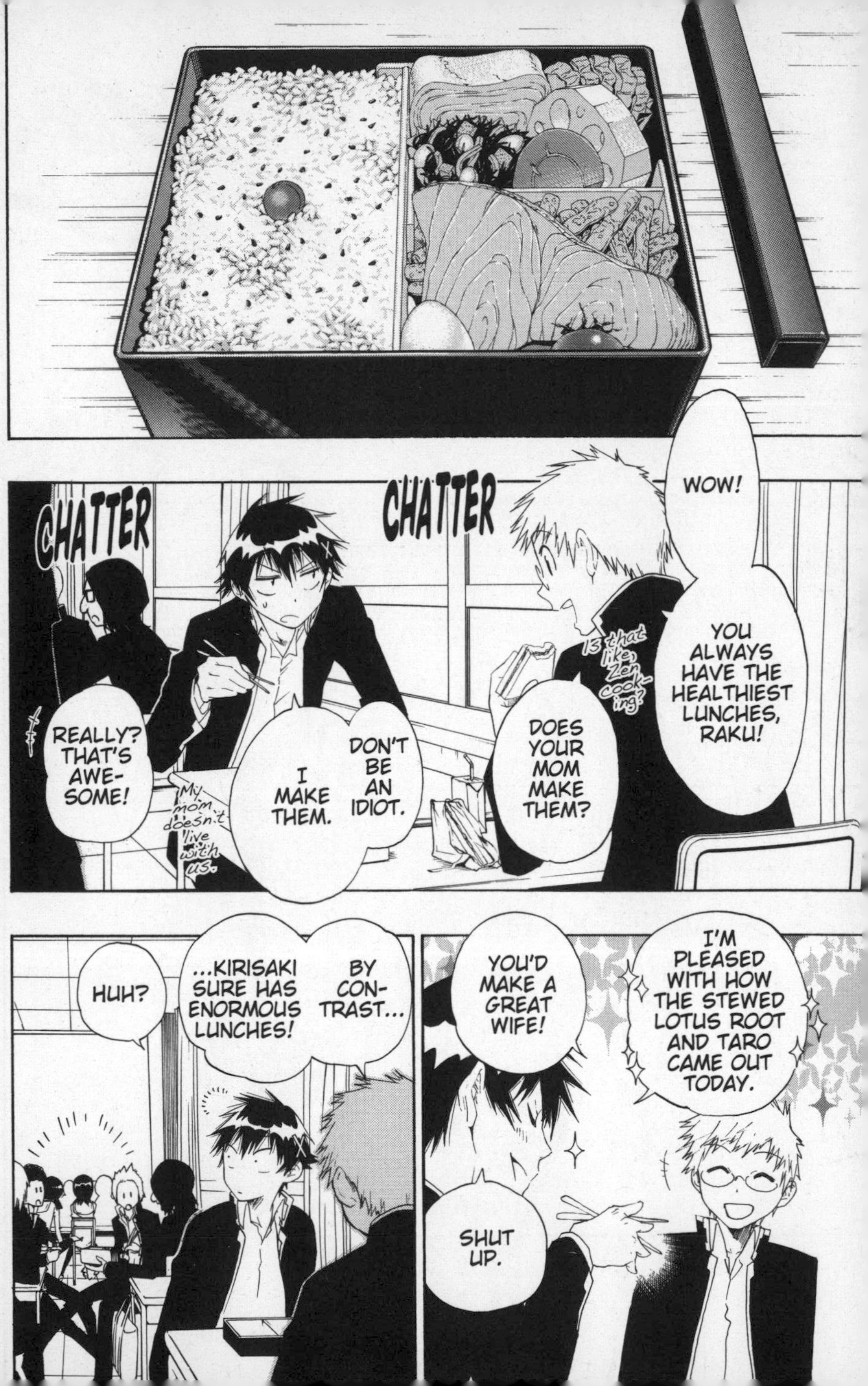
WOW!
YOU ALWAYS HAVE THE HEALTHIEST LUNCHES, RAKU!
Is that like, Zen cooking?
CHATTER
DOES YOUR MOM MAKE THEM?
DON'T BE AN IDIOT.
I MAKE THEM.
My mom doesn't live with us.
REALLY? THAT'S AWE-SOME!
CHATTER
I'M PLEASED WITH HOW THE STEWED LOTUS ROOT AND TARO CAME OUT TODAY.
YOU'D MAKE A GREAT WIFE!
SHUT UP.
BY CON-TRAST...
...KIRISAKI SURE HAS ENORMOUS LUNCHES!
HUH?

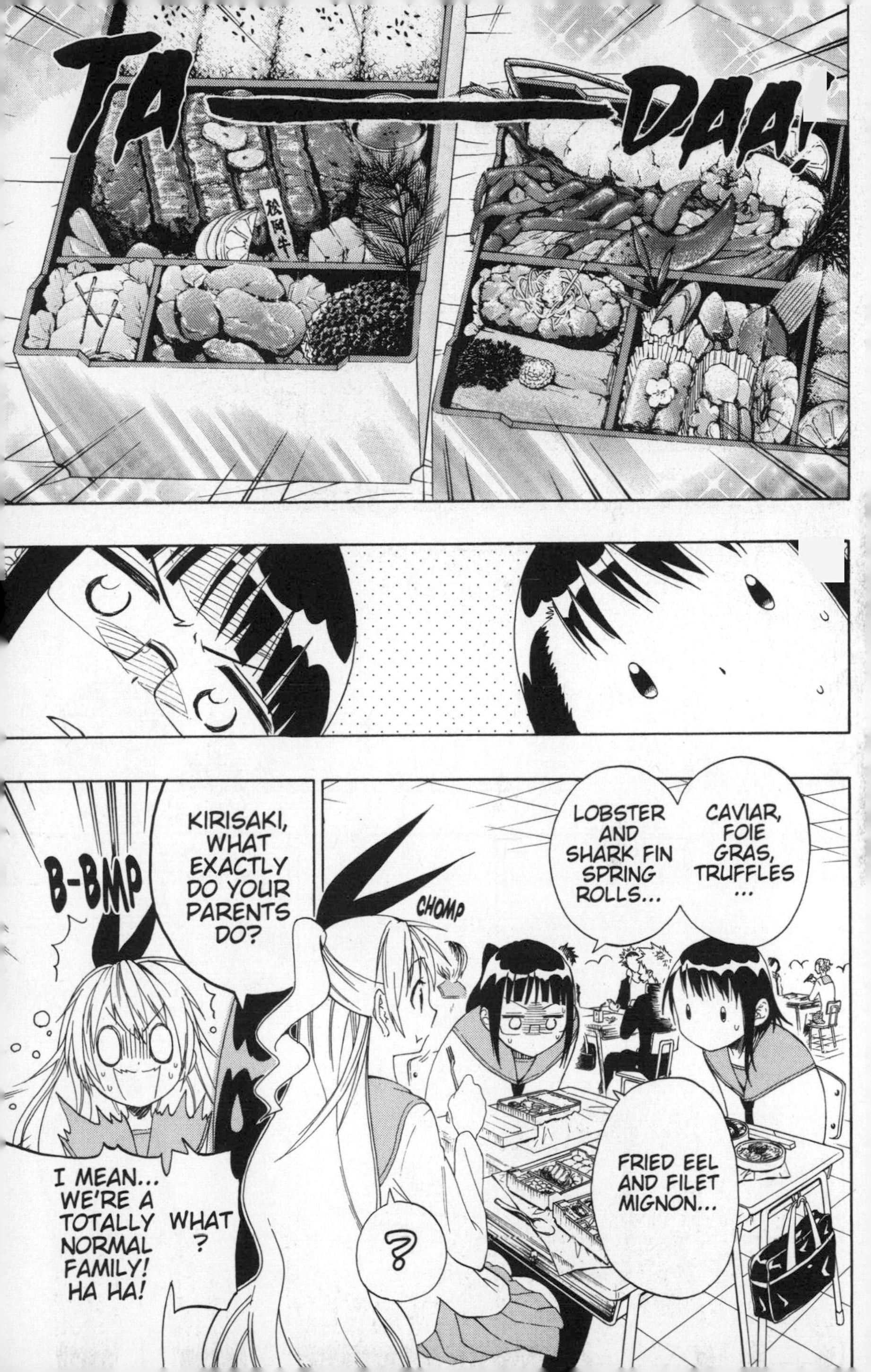
TA—DAA!
CAVIAR, FOIE GRAS, TRUFFLES...
LOBSTER AND SHARK FIN SPRING ROLLS...
CHOMP
FRIED EEL AND FILET MIGNON...
?
KIRISAKI, WHAT EXACTLY DO YOUR PARENTS DO?
B-BMP
WHAT?
I MEAN... WE'RE A TOTALLY NORMAL FAMILY! HA HA!

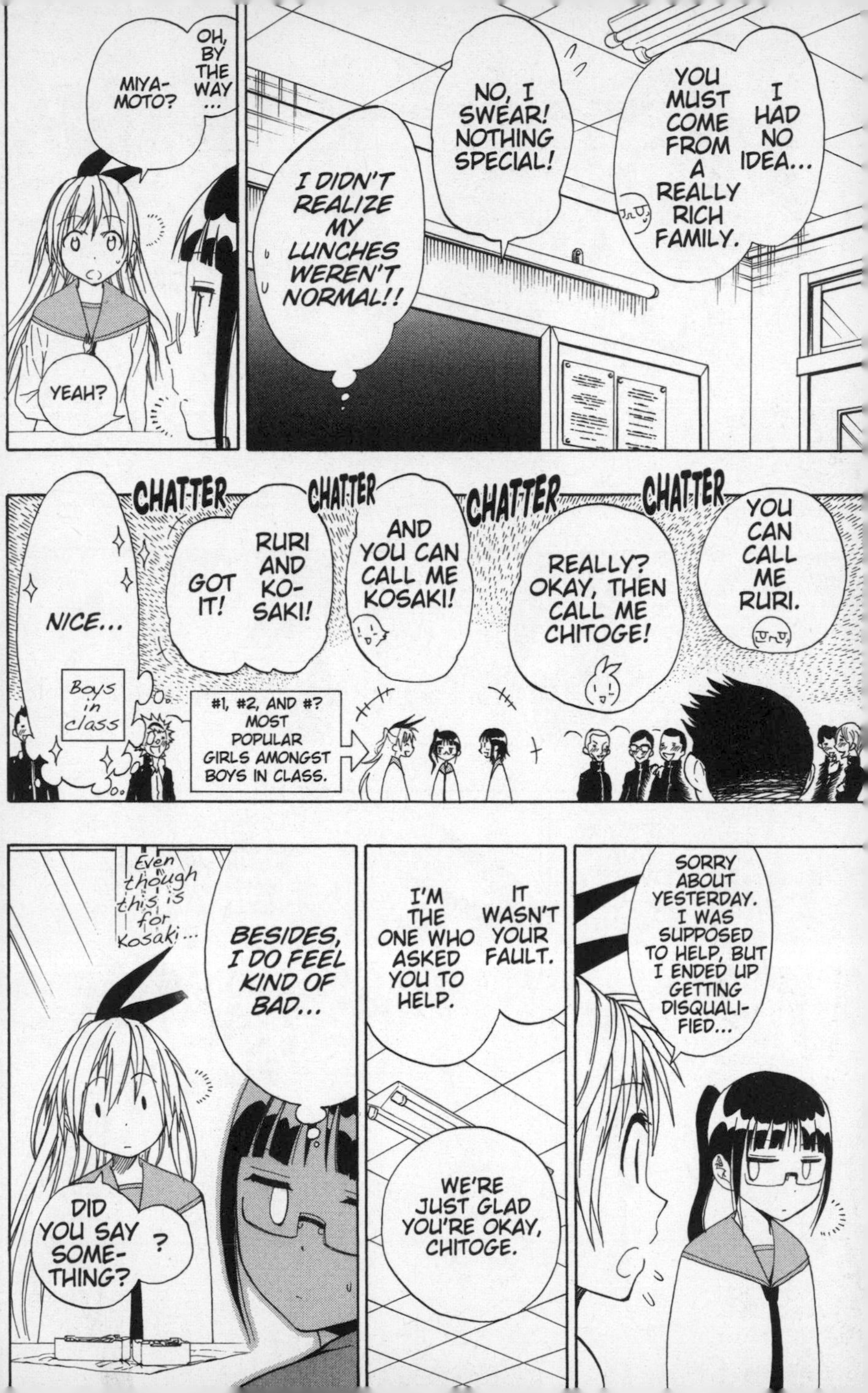
I HAD NO IDEA...
YOU MUST COME FROM A REALLY RICH FAMILY.
NO, I SWEAR! NOTHING SPECIAL!
I DIDN'T REALIZE MY LUNCHES WEREN'T NORMAL!!
OH, BY THE WAY...
MIYAMOTO?
YEAH?
YOU CAN CALL ME RURI.
CHATTER
CHATTER
CHATTER
CHATTER
REALLY? OKAY, THEN CALL ME CHITOGE!
AND YOU CAN CALL ME KOSAKI!
RURI AND KOSAKI!
GOT IT!
NICE...
#1, #2, AND #? MOST POPULAR GIRLS AMONGST BOYS IN CLASS.
Boys in class
SORRY ABOUT YESTERDAY. I WAS SUPPOSED TO HELP, BUT I ENDED UP GETTING DISQUALIFIED...
IT WASN'T YOUR FAULT.
I'M THE ONE WHO ASKED YOU TO HELP.
WE'RE JUST GLAD YOU'RE OKAY, CHITOGE.
Even though this is for Kosaki...
BESIDES, I DO FEEL KIND OF BAD...
DID YOU SAY SOMETHING?
?

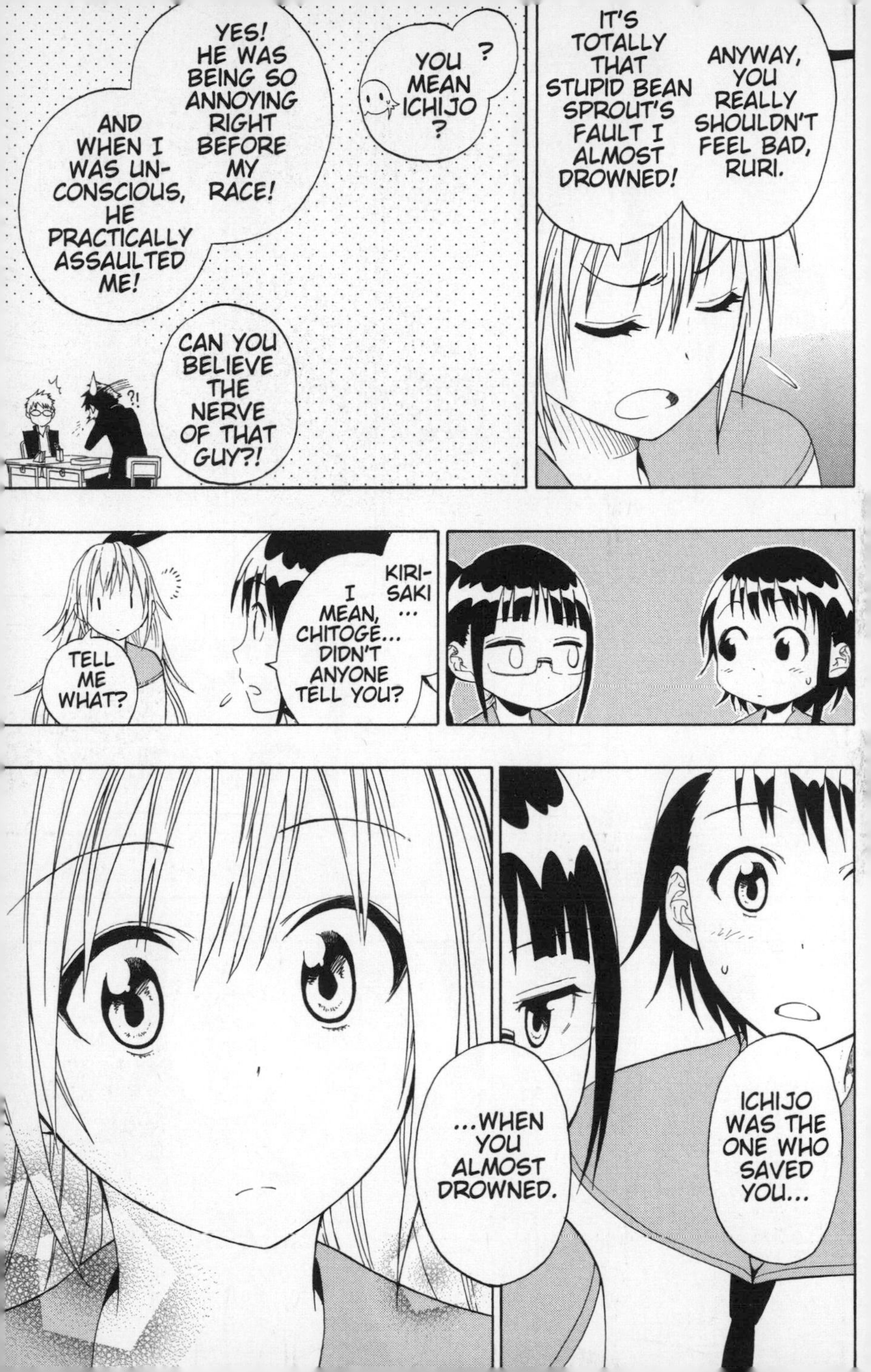
ANYWAY, YOU REALLY SHOULDN'T FEEL BAD, RURI.
IT'S TOTALLY THAT STUPID BEAN SPROUT'S FAULT I ALMOST DROWNED!
YOU MEAN ICHIJO?
YES! HE WAS BEING SO ANNOYING RIGHT BEFORE MY RACE!
AND WHEN I WAS UN-CONSCIOUS, HE PRACTICALLY ASSAULTED ME!
CAN YOU BELIEVE THE NERVE OF THAT GUY?!
KIRI-SAKI...
I MEAN, CHITOGE... DIDN'T ANYONE TELL YOU?
TELL ME WHAT?
ICHIJO WAS THE ONE WHO SAVED YOU...
...WHEN YOU ALMOST DROWNED.

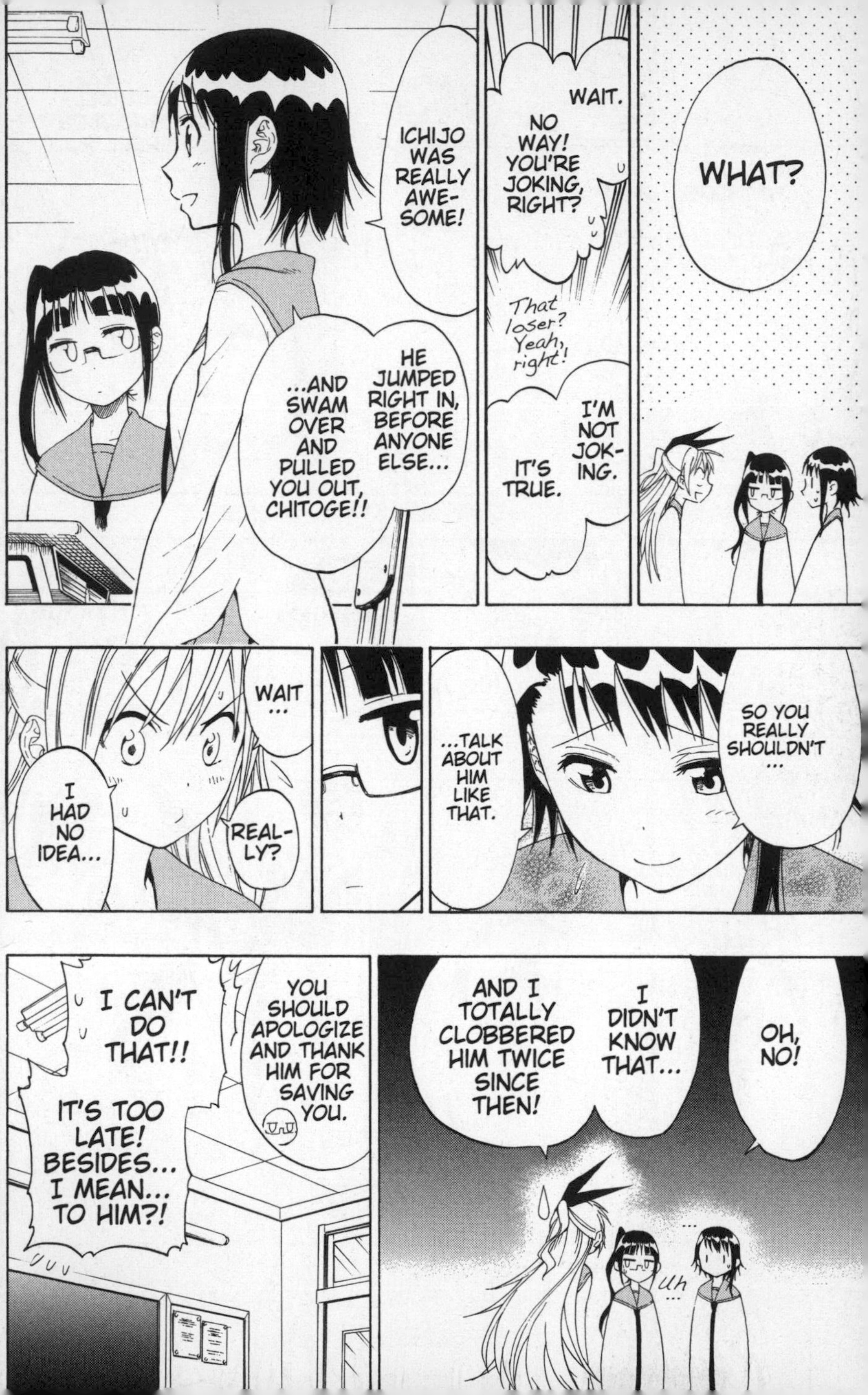
WHAT?
WAIT.
NO WAY! YOU'RE JOKING, RIGHT?
That loser? Yeah, right!
I'M NOT JOKING.
IT'S TRUE.
ICHIJO WAS REALLY AWESOME!
HE JUMPED RIGHT IN, BEFORE ANYONE ELSE...
...AND SWAM OVER AND PULLED YOU OUT, CHITOGE!!
SO YOU REALLY SHOULDN'T ...
...TALK ABOUT HIM LIKE THAT.
WAIT ...
REALLY?
I HAD NO IDEA...
OH, NO!
I DIDN'T KNOW THAT...
AND I TOTALLY CLOBBERED HIM TWICE SINCE THEN!
...
Uh ...
YOU SHOULD APOLOGIZE AND THANK HIM FOR SAVING YOU.
I CAN'T DO THAT!!
IT'S TOO LATE! BESIDES... I MEAN... TO HIM?!

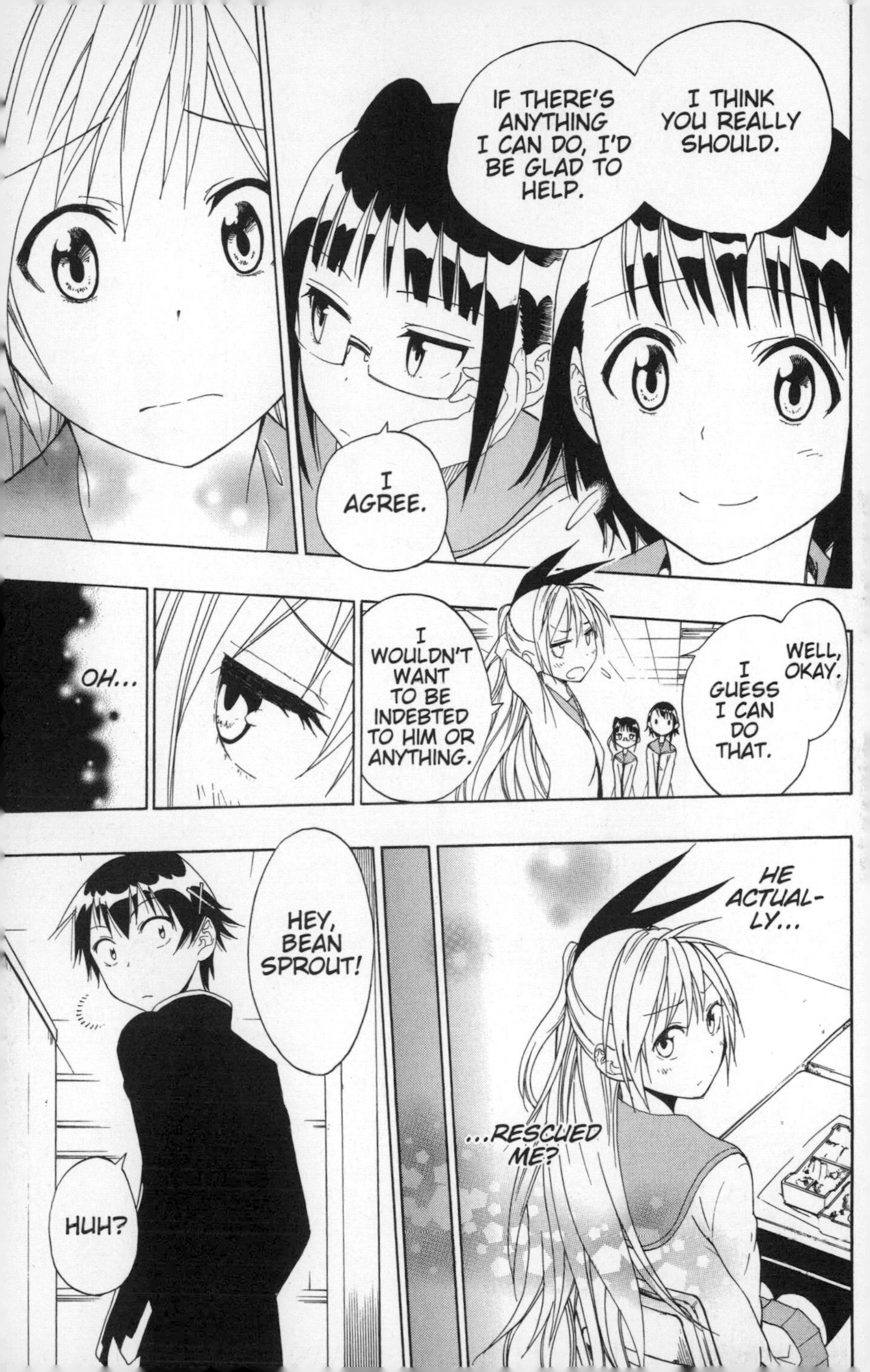
I THINK YOU REALLY SHOULD.
IF THERE'S ANYTHING I CAN DO, I'D BE GLAD TO HELP.
I AGREE.
WELL, OKAY.
I GUESS I CAN DO THAT.
I WOULDN'T WANT TO BE INDEBTED TO HIM OR ANYTHING.
OH...
HE ACTUAL-LY...
...RESCUED ME?
HEY, BEAN SPROUT!
HUH?

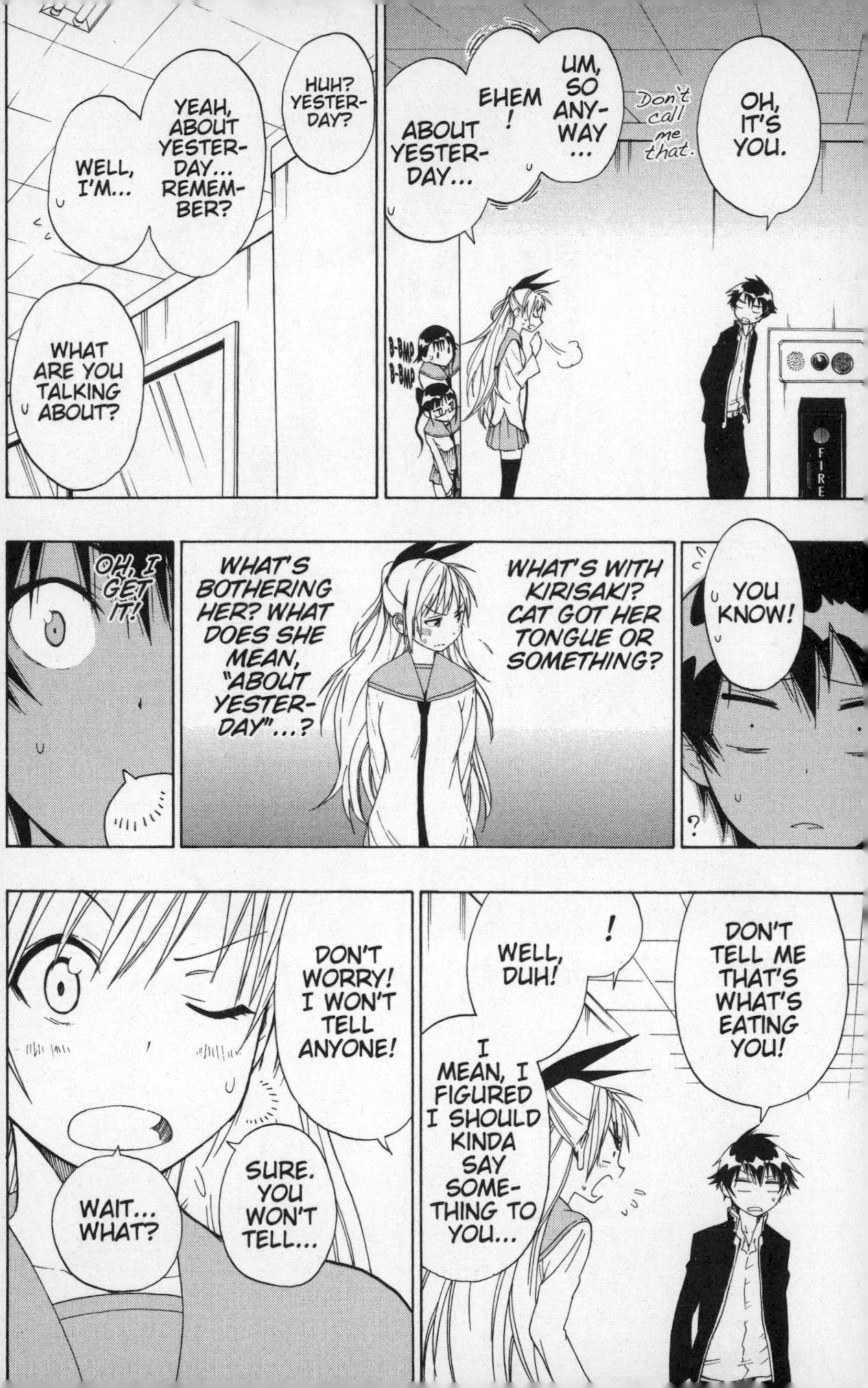
OH, IT'S YOU.
Don't call me that.
UM, SO ANYWAY...
EHEM!
ABOUT YESTERDAY...
B-BMP B-BMP
HUH? YESTERDAY?
YEAH, ABOUT YESTERDAY... REMEMBER?
WELL, I'M...
WHAT ARE YOU TALKING ABOUT?
YOU KNOW!
?
WHAT'S WITH KIRISAKI? CAT GOT HER TONGUE OR SOMETHING?
WHAT'S BOTHERING HER? WHAT DOES SHE MEAN, "ABOUT YESTERDAY"...?
OH, I GET IT!
DON'T TELL ME THAT'S WHAT'S EATING YOU!
!
WELL, DUH!
I MEAN, I FIGURED I SHOULD KINDA SAY SOMETHING TO YOU...
DON'T WORRY! I WON'T TELL ANYONE!
SURE. YOU WON'T TELL...
WAIT... WHAT?

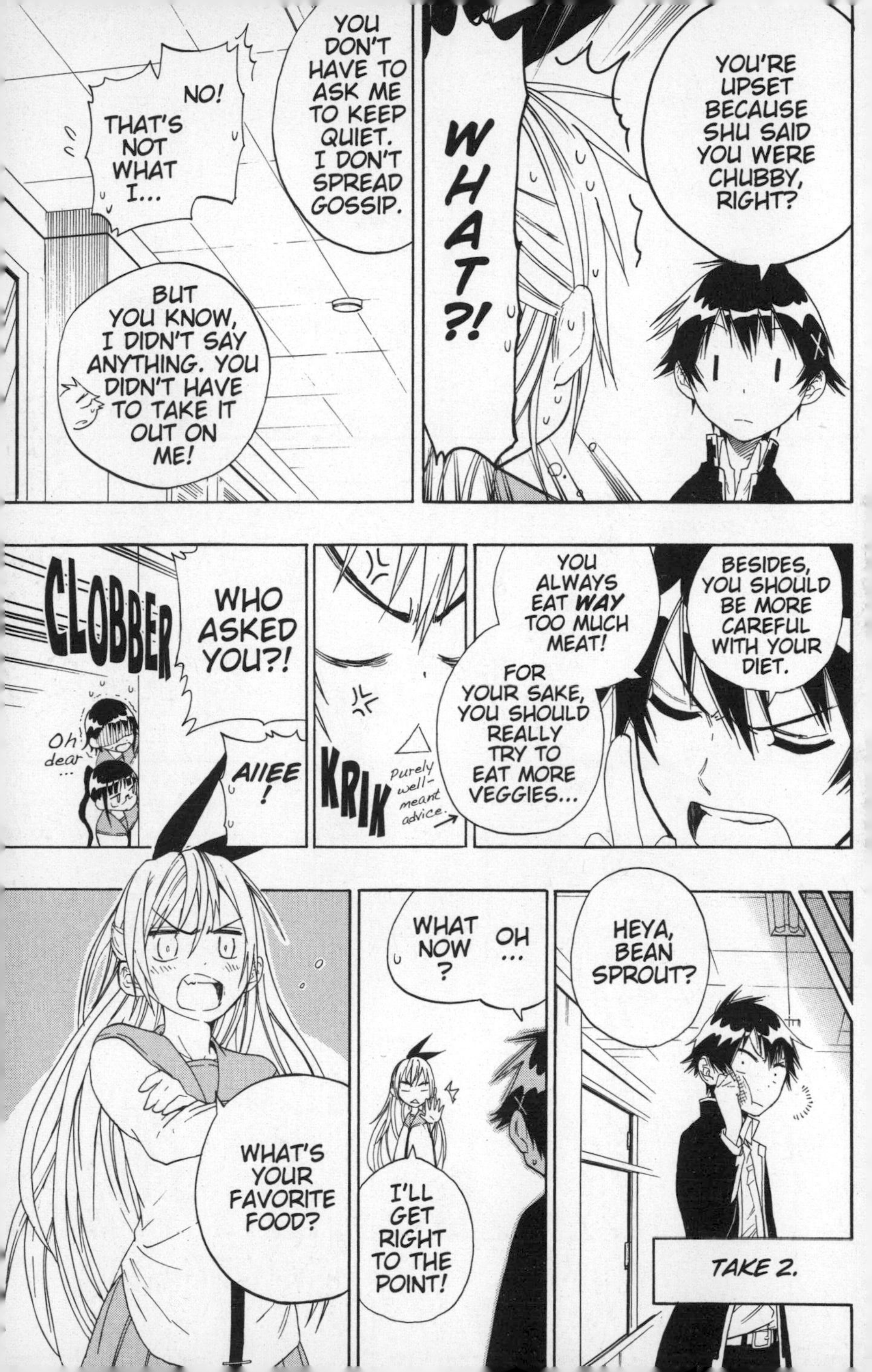
YOU'RE UPSET BECAUSE SHU SAID YOU WERE CHUBBY, RIGHT?
WHAT?!
YOU DON'T HAVE TO ASK ME TO KEEP QUIET. I DON'T SPREAD GOSSIP.
NO! THAT'S NOT WHAT I...
BUT YOU KNOW, I DIDN'T SAY ANYTHING. YOU DIDN'T HAVE TO TAKE IT OUT ON ME!
BESIDES, YOU SHOULD BE MORE CAREFUL WITH YOUR DIET.
YOU ALWAYS EAT WAY TOO MUCH MEAT!
FOR YOUR SAKE, YOU SHOULD REALLY TRY TO EAT MORE VEGGIES...
Purely well-meant advice.
KRIK
WHO ASKED YOU?!
CLOBBER
AIIEE!
Oh dear...
TAKE 2.
HEYA, BEAN SPROUT?
OH...
WHAT NOW?
I'LL GET RIGHT TO THE POINT!
WHAT'S YOUR FAVORITE FOOD?

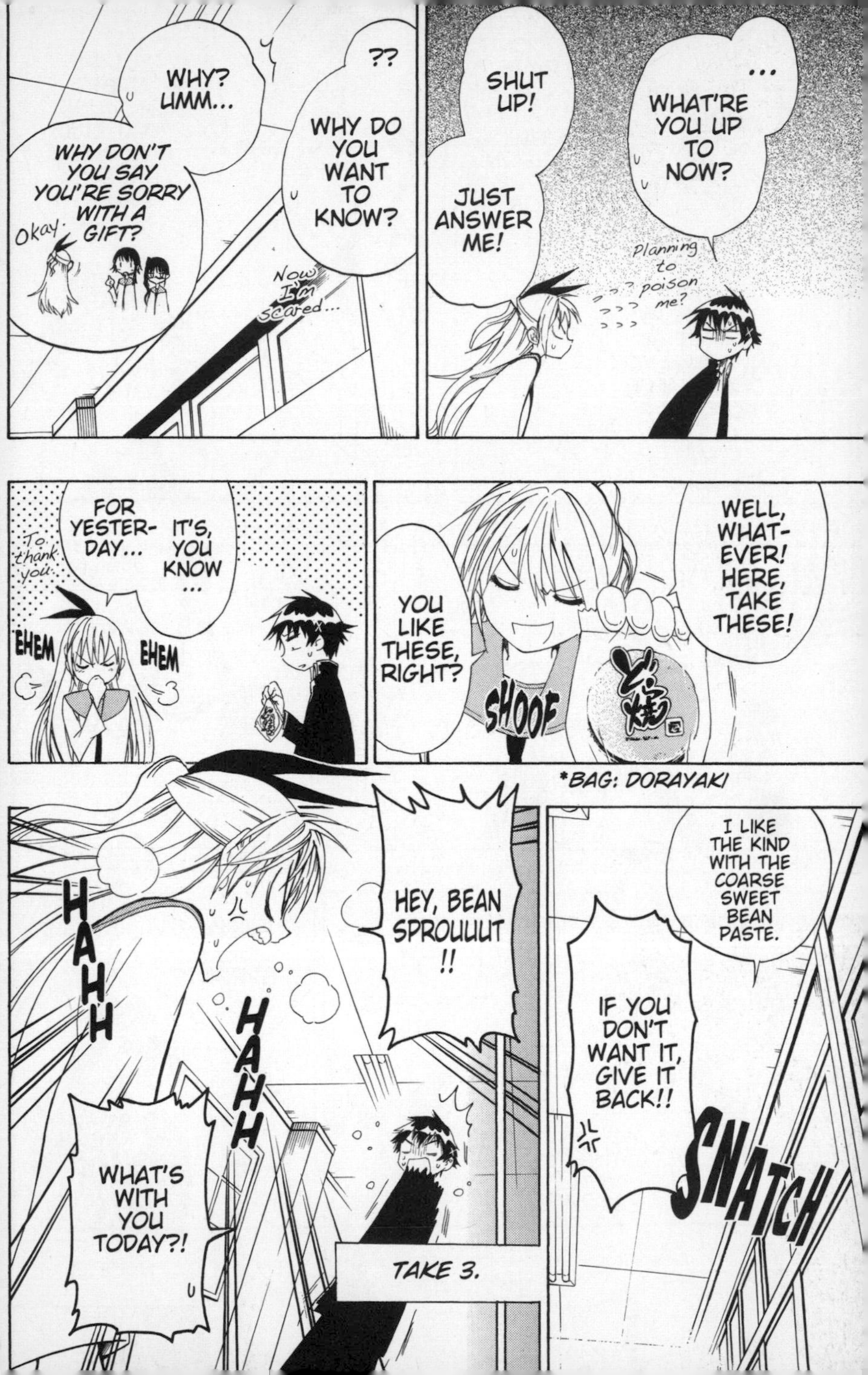
...
WHAT'RE YOU UP TO NOW?
Planning to poison me?
SHUT UP!
JUST ANSWER ME!
??
WHY DO YOU WANT TO KNOW?
Now I'm scared...
WHY? UMM...
WHY DON'T YOU SAY YOU'RE SORRY WITH A GIFT?
Okay.
WELL, WHATEVER! HERE, TAKE THESE!
YOU LIKE THESE, RIGHT?
SHOOF
*BAG: DORAYAKI
IT'S, YOU KNOW...
FOR YESTERDAY...
To thank you.
EHEM
EHEM
I LIKE THE KIND WITH THE COARSE SWEET BEAN PASTE.
IF YOU DON'T WANT IT, GIVE IT BACK!!
SNATCH
HEY, BEAN SPROUUUT!!
HAHH
HAHH
WHAT'S WITH YOU TODAY?!
TAKE 3.

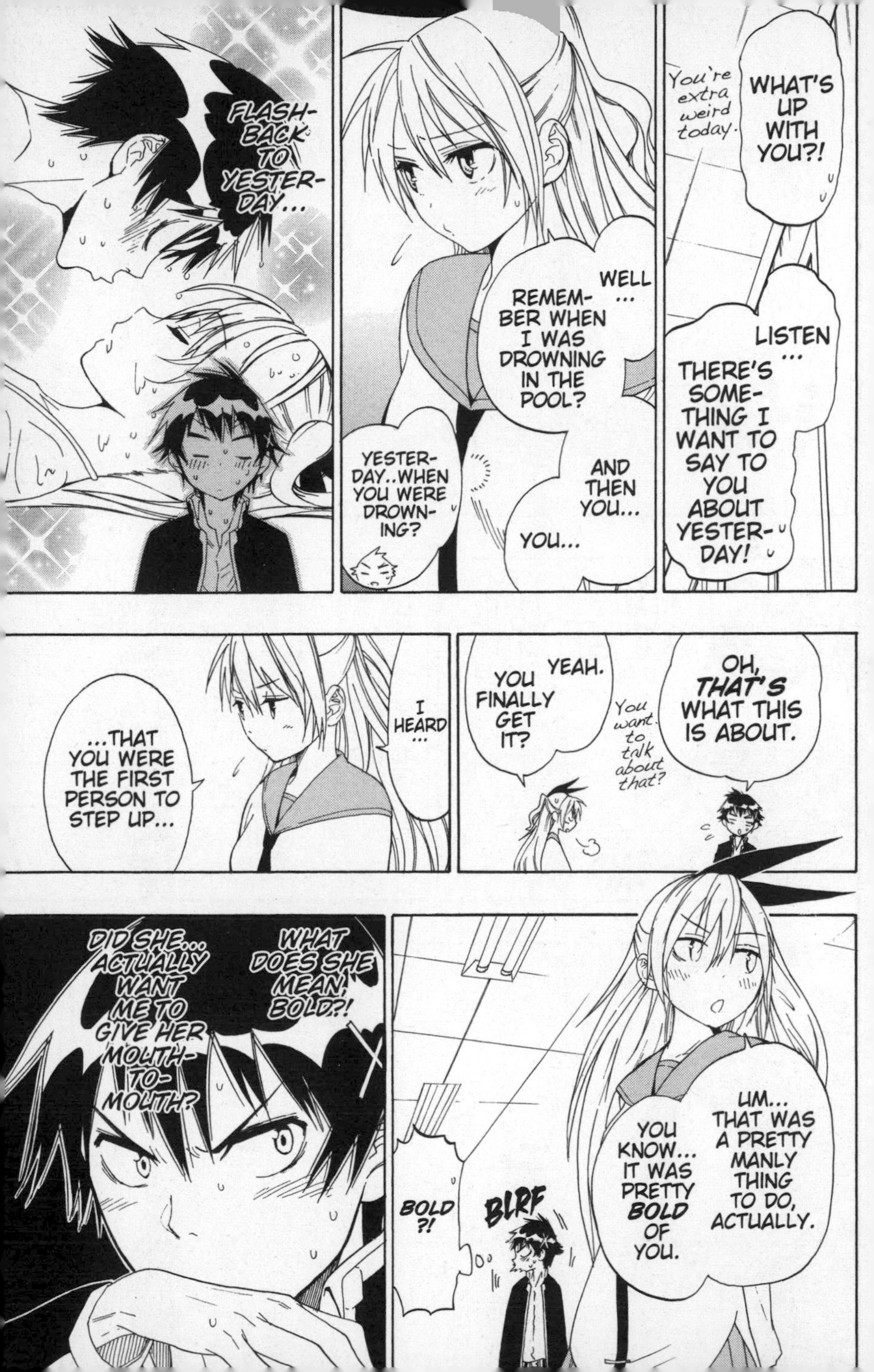
WHAT'S UP WITH YOU?!
You're extra weird today.
LISTEN... THERE'S SOMETHING I WANT TO SAY TO YOU ABOUT YESTERDAY!
WELL... REMEMBER WHEN I WAS DROWNING IN THE POOL?
AND THEN YOU... YOU...
YESTERDAY..WHEN YOU WERE DROWNING?
FLASHBACK TO YESTERDAY...
OH, THAT'S WHAT THIS IS ABOUT.
You want to talk about that?
YEAH. YOU FINALLY GET IT?
I HEARD...
...THAT YOU WERE THE FIRST PERSON TO STEP UP...
UM... THAT WAS A PRETTY MANLY THING TO DO, ACTUALLY.
YOU KNOW... IT WAS PRETTY BOLD OF YOU.
BLRF
BOLD?!
WHAT DOES SHE MEAN, BOLD?!
DID SHE... ACTUALLY WANT ME TO GIVE HER MOUTH-TO-MOUTH?

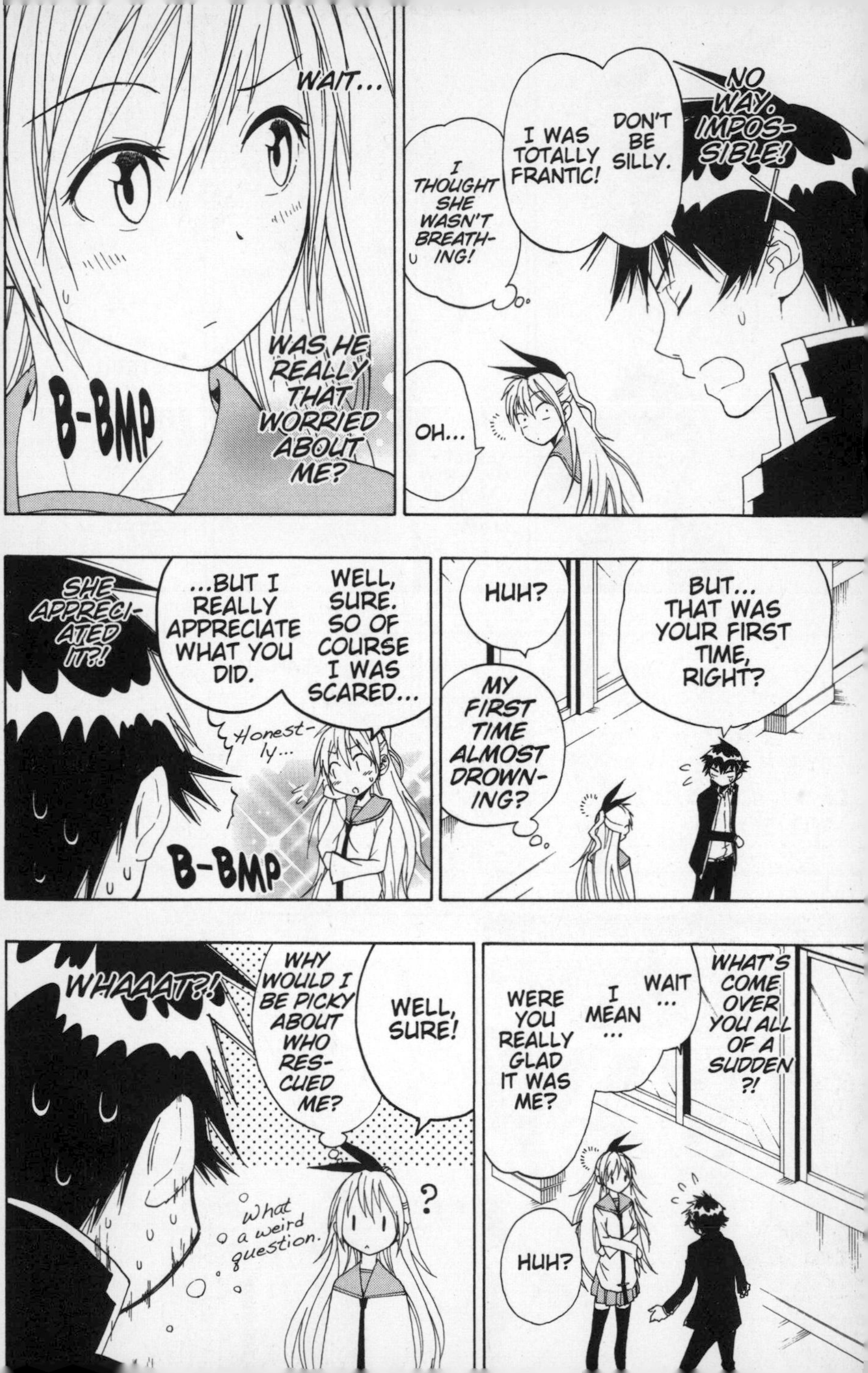
NO WAY. IMPOSSIBLE!
DON'T BE SILLY.
I WAS TOTALLY FRANTIC!
I THOUGHT SHE WASN'T BREATHING!
OH...
WAIT...
WAS HE REALLY THAT WORRIED ABOUT ME?
B-BMP
BUT... THAT WAS YOUR FIRST TIME, RIGHT?
HUH?
MY FIRST TIME ALMOST DROWNING?
WELL, SURE. SO OF COURSE I WAS SCARED...
...BUT I REALLY APPRECIATE WHAT YOU DID.
SHE APPRECIATED IT?!
Honestly...
B-BMP
WHAT'S COME OVER YOU ALL OF A SUDDEN?!
WAIT...
I MEAN...
WERE YOU REALLY GLAD IT WAS ME?
HUH?
WELL, SURE!
WHY WOULD I BE PICKY ABOUT WHO RESCUED ME?
WHAAAT?!
?
What a weird question.

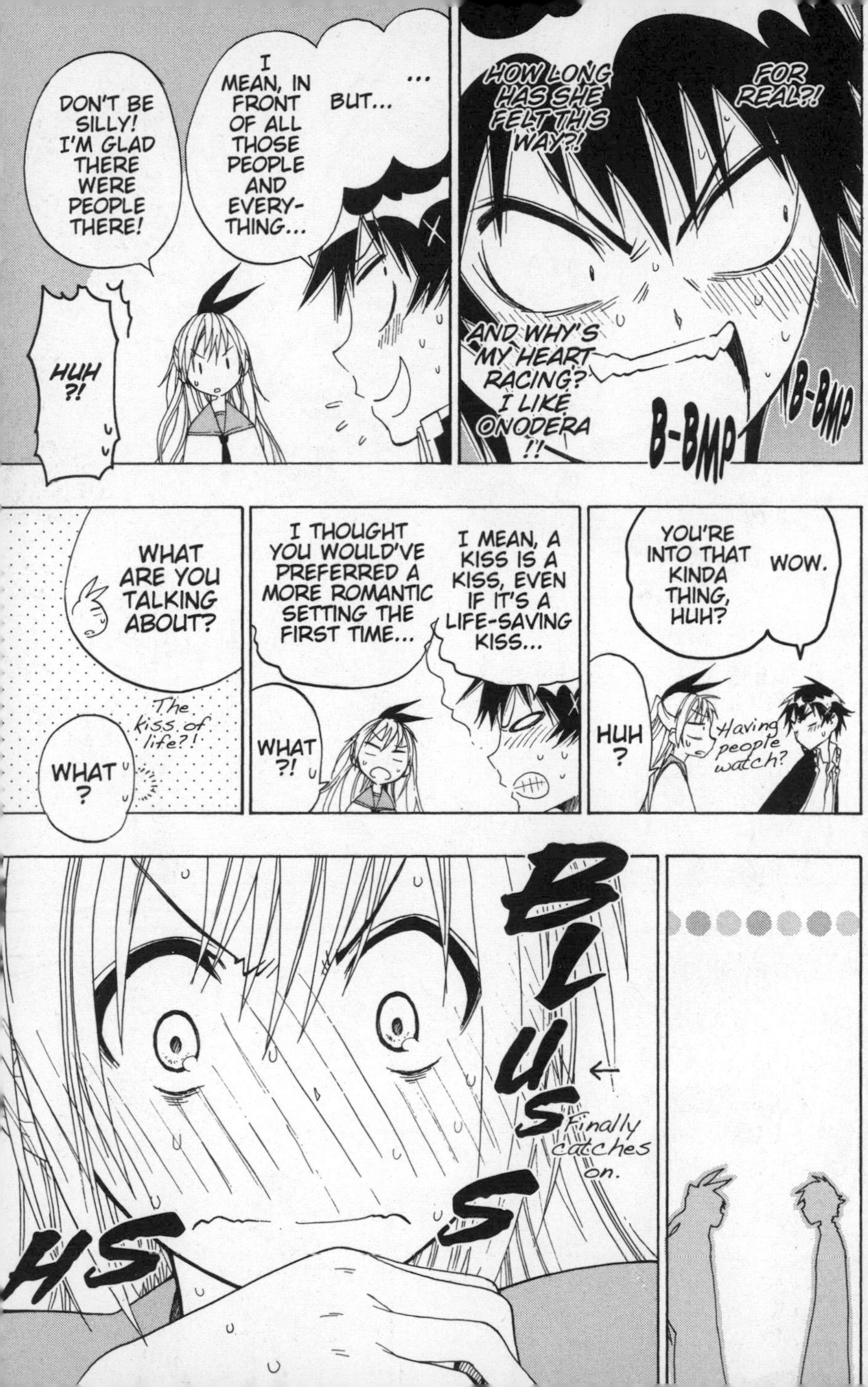
FOR REAL?!
HOW LONG HAS SHE FELT THIS WAY?!
AND WHY'S MY HEART RACING? I LIKE ONODERA!!
B-BMP
B-BMP
...BUT...
I MEAN, IN FRONT OF ALL THOSE PEOPLE AND EVERYTHING...
DON'T BE SILLY! I'M GLAD THERE WERE PEOPLE THERE!
HUH?!
WOW.
YOU'RE INTO THAT KINDA THING, HUH?
Having people watch?
HUH?
I MEAN, A KISS IS A KISS, EVEN IF IT'S A LIFE-SAVING KISS...
I THOUGHT YOU WOULD'VE PREFERRED A MORE ROMANTIC SETTING THE FIRST TIME...
WHAT?!
WHAT ARE YOU TALKING ABOUT?
The kiss of life?!
WHAT?
BLUSH
Finally catches on.

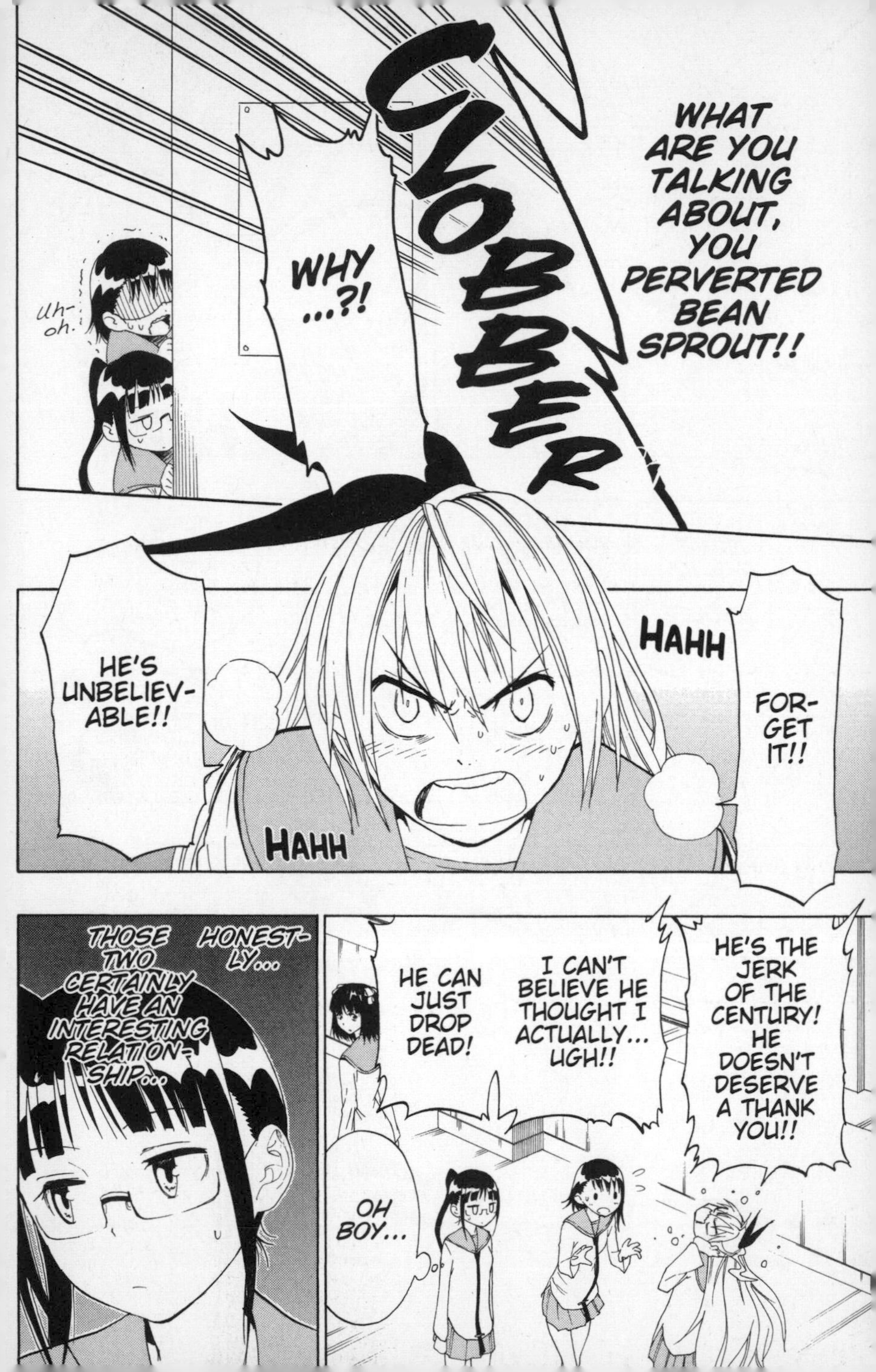
WHAT ARE YOU TALKING ABOUT, YOU PERVERTED BEAN SPROUT!!
CLOBBER
WHY ...?!
Uh-oh.
FOR-GET IT!!
HAHH
HE'S UNBELIEV-ABLE!!
HAHH
HE'S THE JERK OF THE CENTURY! HE DOESN'T DESERVE A THANK YOU!!
I CAN'T BELIEVE HE THOUGHT I ACTUALLY... UGH!!
HE CAN JUST DROP DEAD!
OH BOY...
HONEST-LY...
THOSE TWO CERTAINLY HAVE AN INTERESTING RELATION-SHIP...

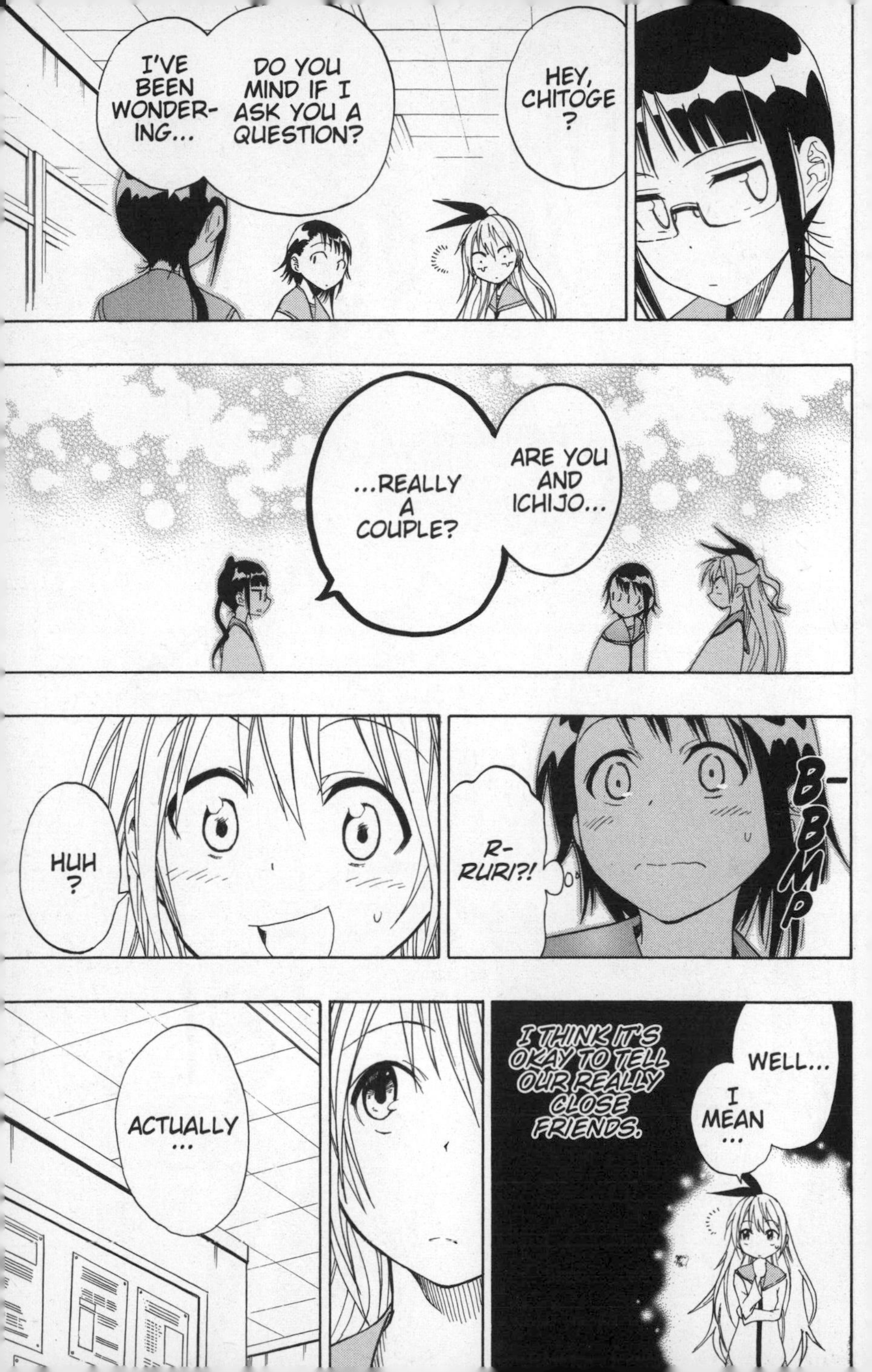
HEY, CHITOGE?
DO YOU MIND IF I ASK YOU A QUESTION?
I'VE BEEN WONDER-ING...
ARE YOU AND ICHIJO...
...REALLY A COUPLE?
B-BUMP
R-RURI?!
HUH?
WELL...
I MEAN...
I THINK IT'S OKAY TO TELL OUR REALLY CLOSE FRIENDS.
ACTUALLY...

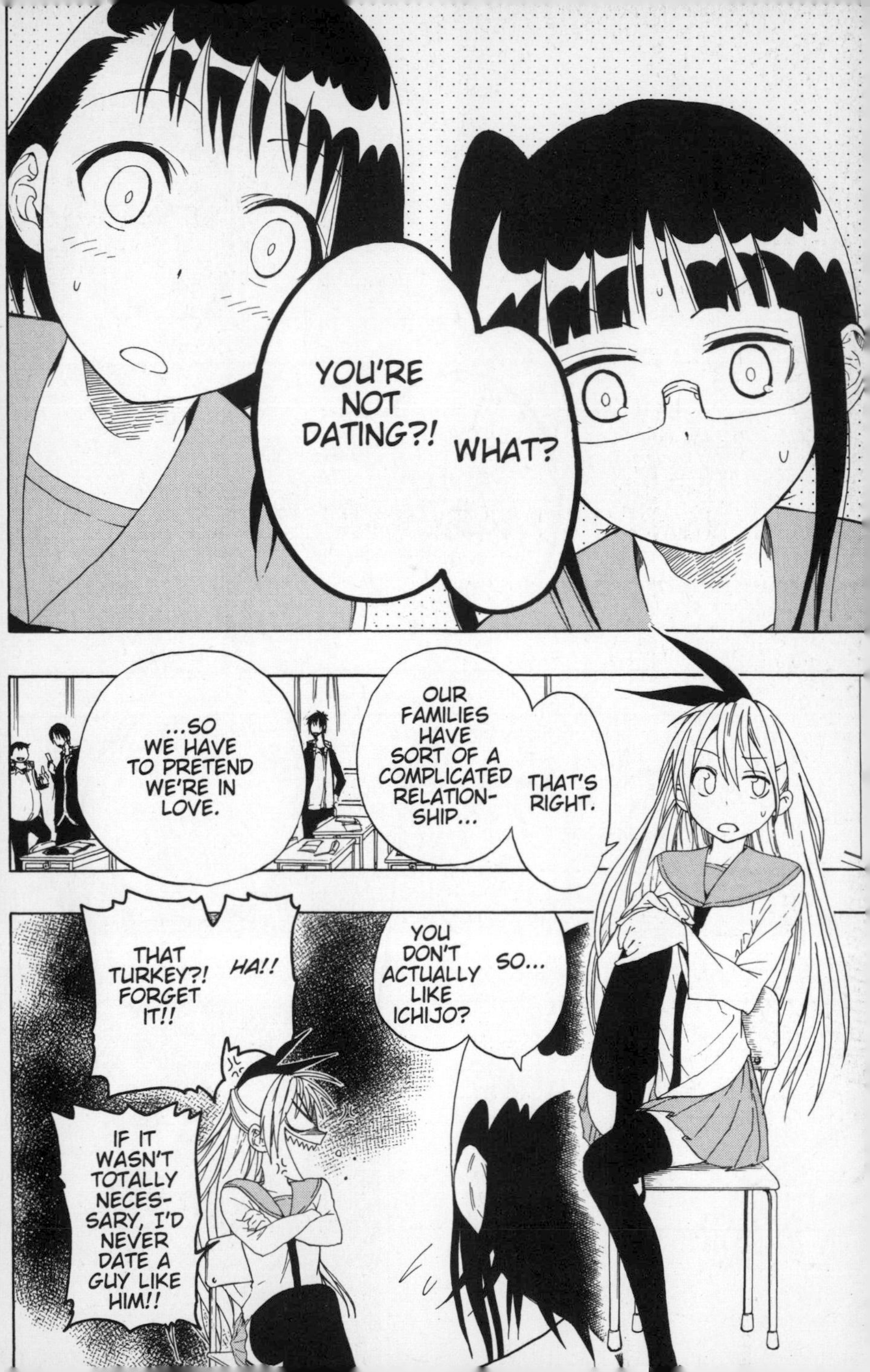
WHAT?
YOU'RE NOT DATING?!
THAT'S RIGHT.
OUR FAMILIES HAVE SORT OF A COMPLICATED RELATIONSHIP...
...SO WE HAVE TO PRETEND WE'RE IN LOVE.
SO...
YOU DON'T ACTUALLY LIKE ICHIJO?
HA!!
THAT TURKEY?! FORGET IT!!
IF IT WASN'T TOTALLY NECESSARY, I'D NEVER DATE A GUY LIKE HIM!!

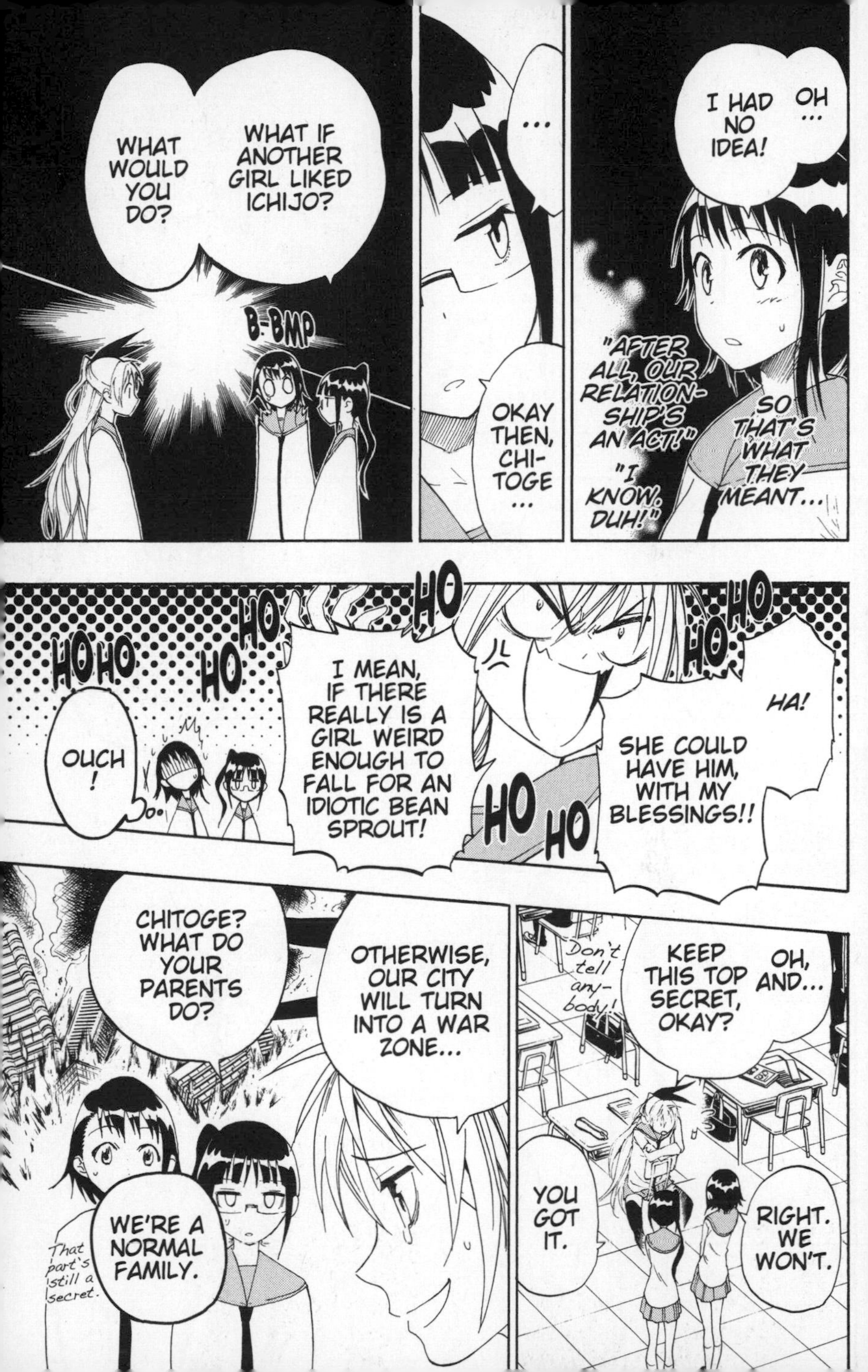
OH...
I HAD NO IDEA!
SO THAT'S WHAT THEY MEANT...
"AFTER ALL, OUR RELATIONSHIP'S AN ACT!"
"I KNOW. DUH!"
...
OKAY THEN, CHITOGE...
WHAT IF ANOTHER GIRL LIKED ICHIJO?
WHAT WOULD YOU DO?
B-BMP
HO HO HO HO HO HO HO HO HO
HA!
SHE COULD HAVE HIM, WITH MY BLESSINGS!!
I MEAN, IF THERE REALLY IS A GIRL WEIRD ENOUGH TO FALL FOR AN IDIOTIC BEAN SPROUT!
OUCH!
OH, AND...
KEEP THIS TOP SECRET, OKAY?
Don't tell anybody!
RIGHT. WE WON'T.
YOU GOT IT.
CHITOGE? WHAT DO YOUR PARENTS DO?
WE'RE A NORMAL FAMILY.
That part's still a secret.
OTHERWISE, OUR CITY WILL TURN INTO A WAR ZONE...

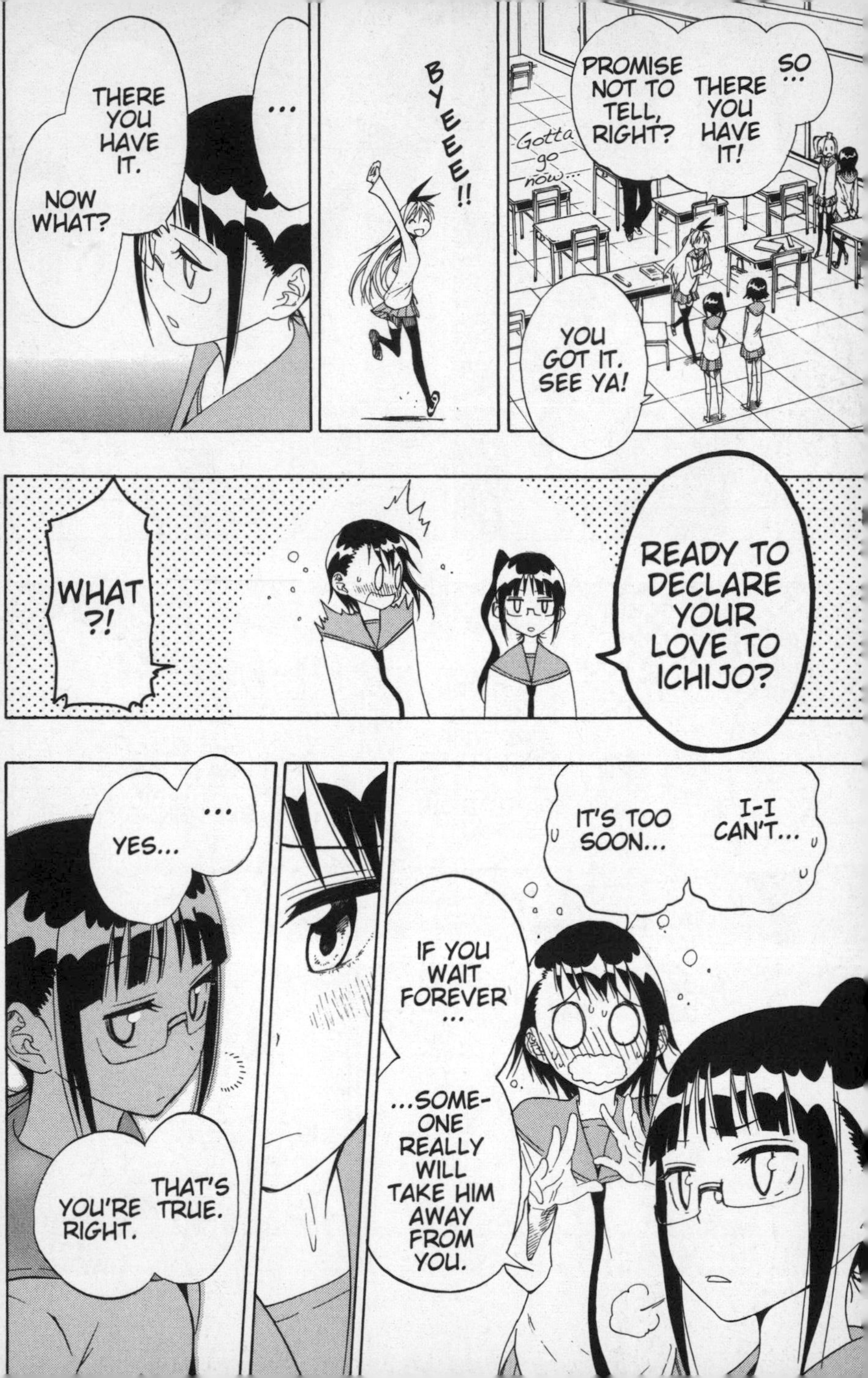
SO... THERE YOU HAVE IT!
PROMISE NOT TO TELL, RIGHT?
Gotta go now...
YOU GOT IT. SEE YA!
BYEEE!!
...
THERE YOU HAVE IT. NOW WHAT?
READY TO DECLARE YOUR LOVE TO ICHIJO?
WHAT?!
I-I CAN'T...
IT'S TOO SOON...
IF YOU WAIT FOREVER...
...SOMEONE REALLY WILL TAKE HIM AWAY FROM YOU.
...
YES...
THAT'S TRUE.
YOU'RE RIGHT.

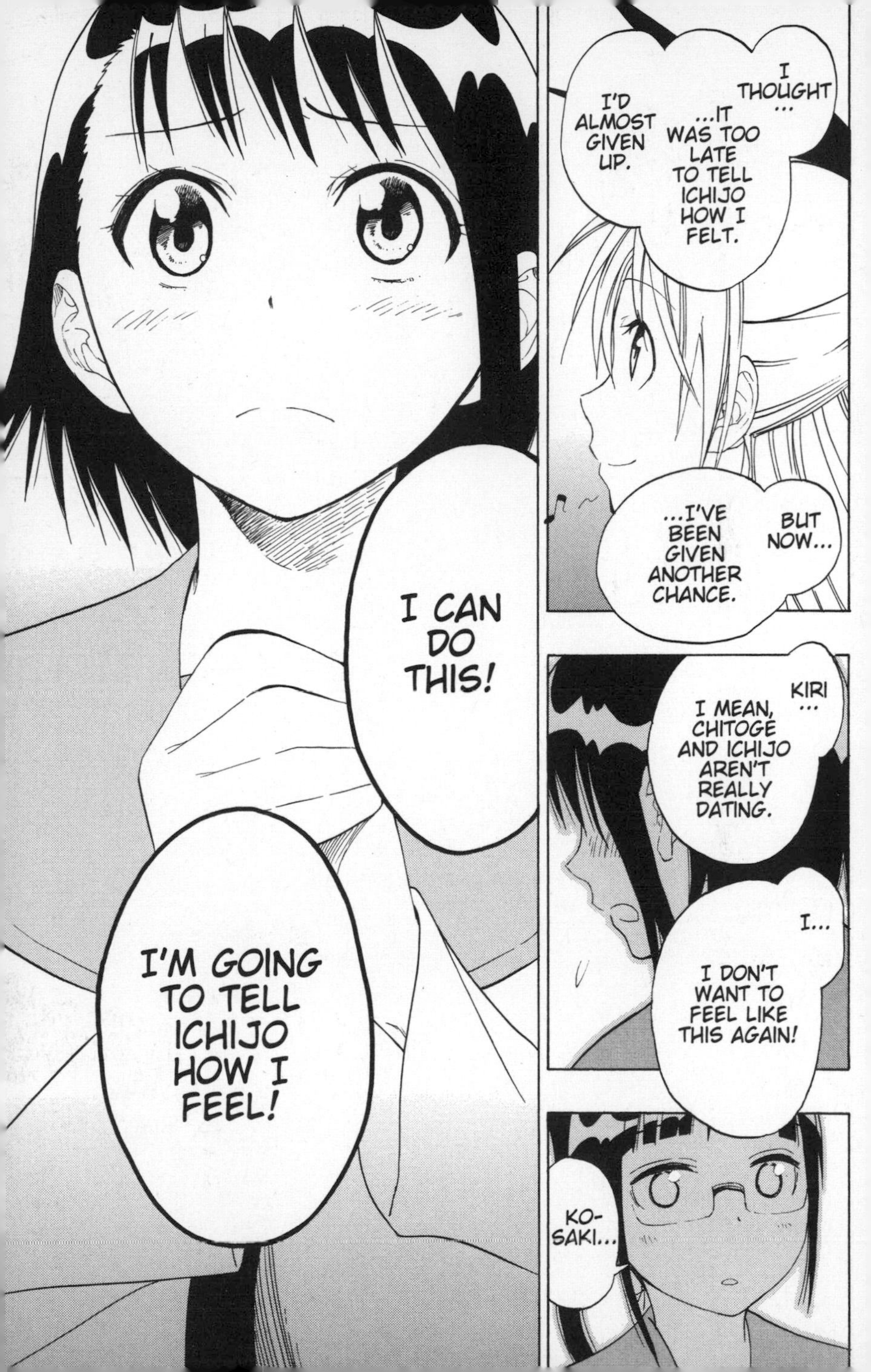
I THOUGHT... ...IT WAS TOO LATE TO TELL ICHIJO HOW I FELT. I'D ALMOST GIVEN UP.
BUT NOW... ...I'VE BEEN GIVEN ANOTHER CHANCE.
KIRI... I MEAN, CHITOGE AND ICHIJO AREN'T REALLY DATING.
I... I DON'T WANT TO FEEL LIKE THIS AGAIN!
KO-SAKI...
I CAN DO THIS!
I'M GOING TO TELL ICHIJO HOW I FEEL!

Tasting Chitoge's lunch

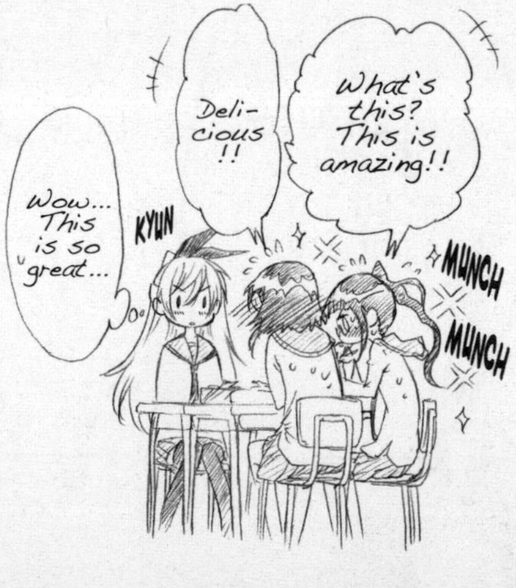
What's this? This is amazing!!
Deli-cious!!
MUNCH
MUNCH
KYUN
Wow... This is so great...

Chapter 13: Zawsze in Love

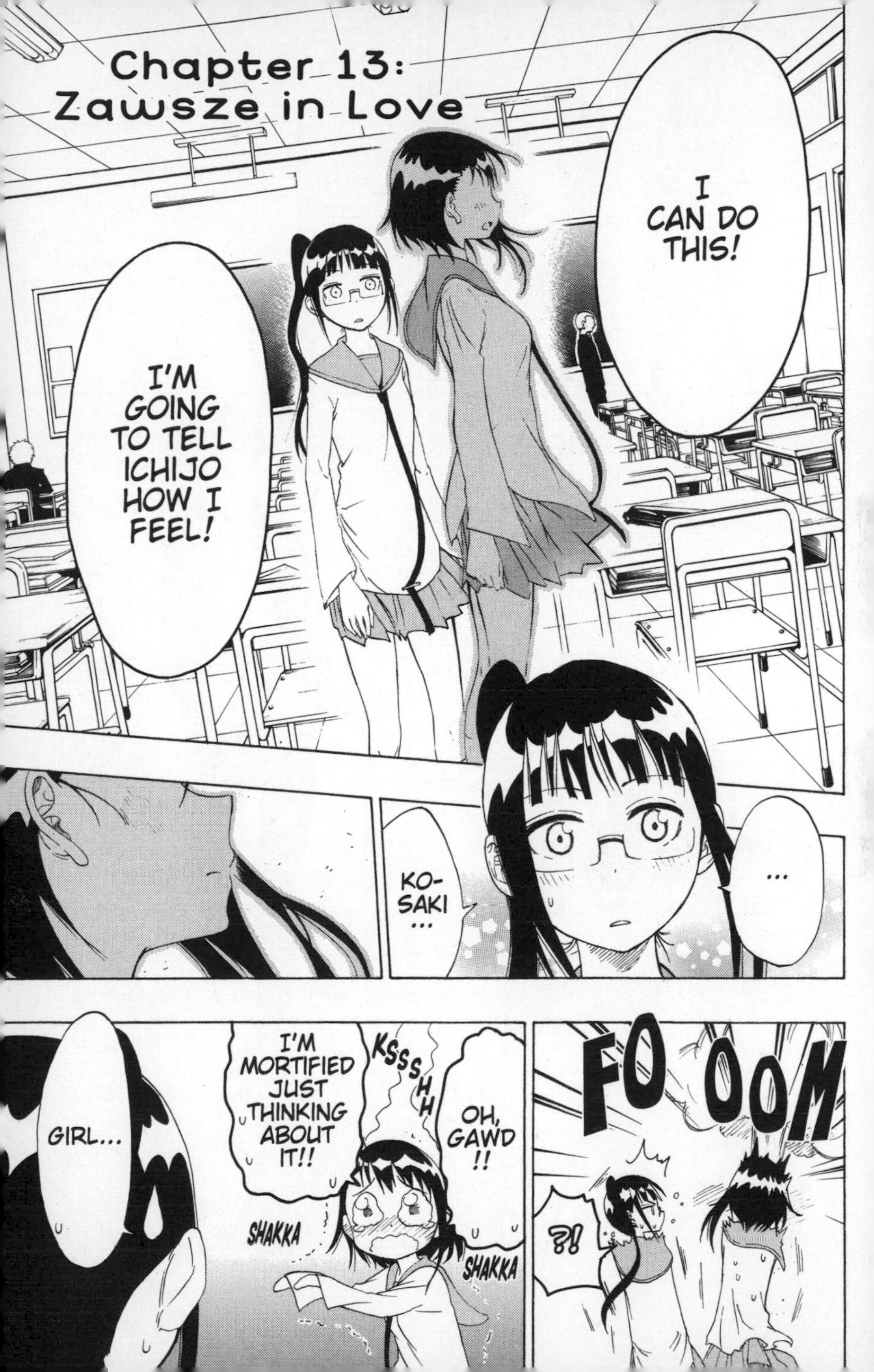
I CAN DO THIS!
I'M GOING TO TELL ICHIJO HOW I FEEL!
...
KO-SAKI ...
FO OOM
?!
OH, GAWD !!
KSSSHH
I'M MORTIFIED JUST THINKING ABOUT IT!!
SHAKKA
SHAKKA
GIRL...

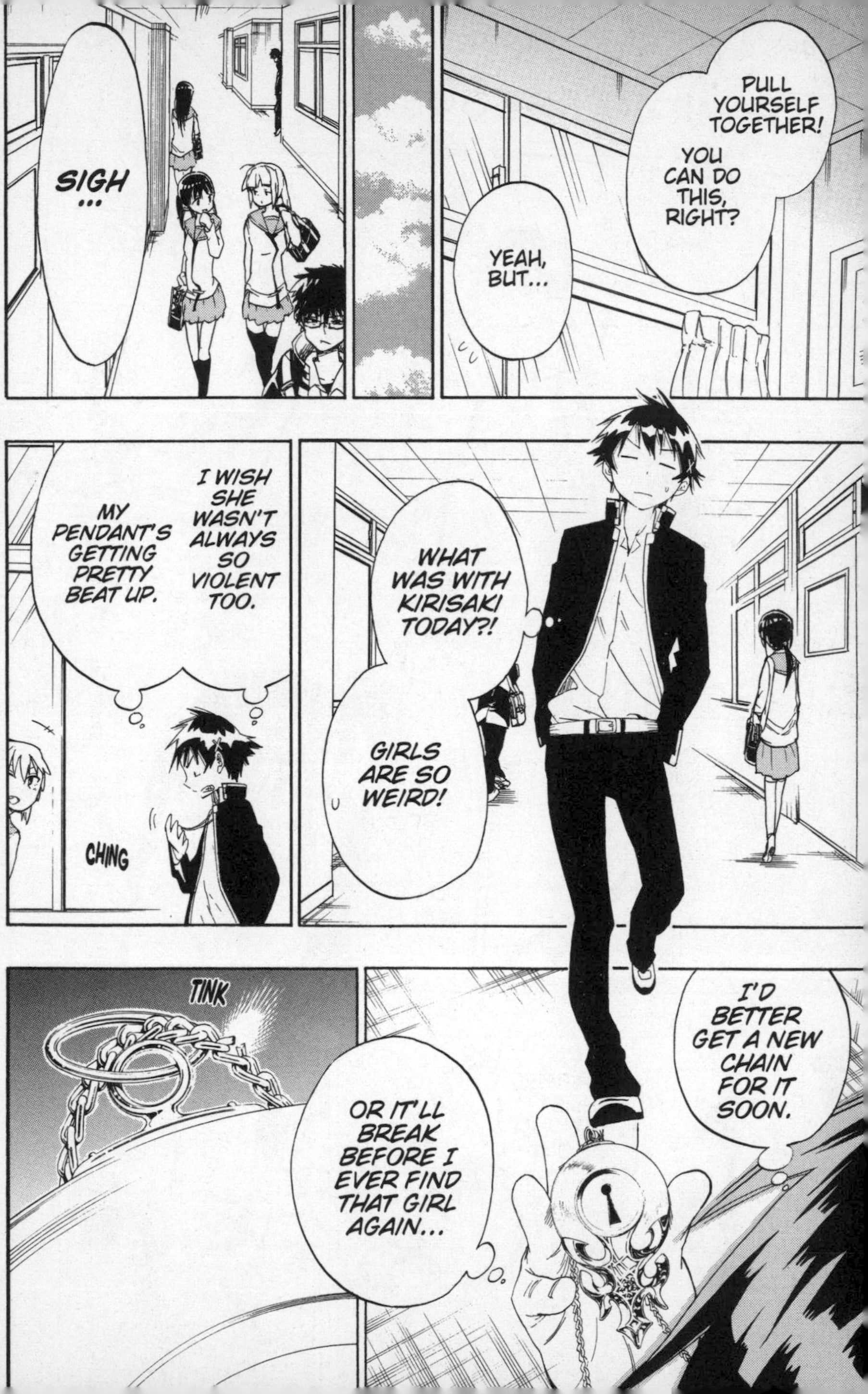
PULL YOURSELF TOGETHER!
YOU CAN DO THIS, RIGHT?
YEAH, BUT...
SIGH...
WHAT WAS WITH KIRISAKI TODAY?!
GIRLS ARE SO WEIRD!
I WISH SHE WASN'T ALWAYS SO VIOLENT TOO.
MY PENDANT'S GETTING PRETTY BEAT UP.
CHING
I'D BETTER GET A NEW CHAIN FOR IT SOON.
OR IT'LL BREAK BEFORE I EVER FIND THAT GIRL AGAIN...
TINK

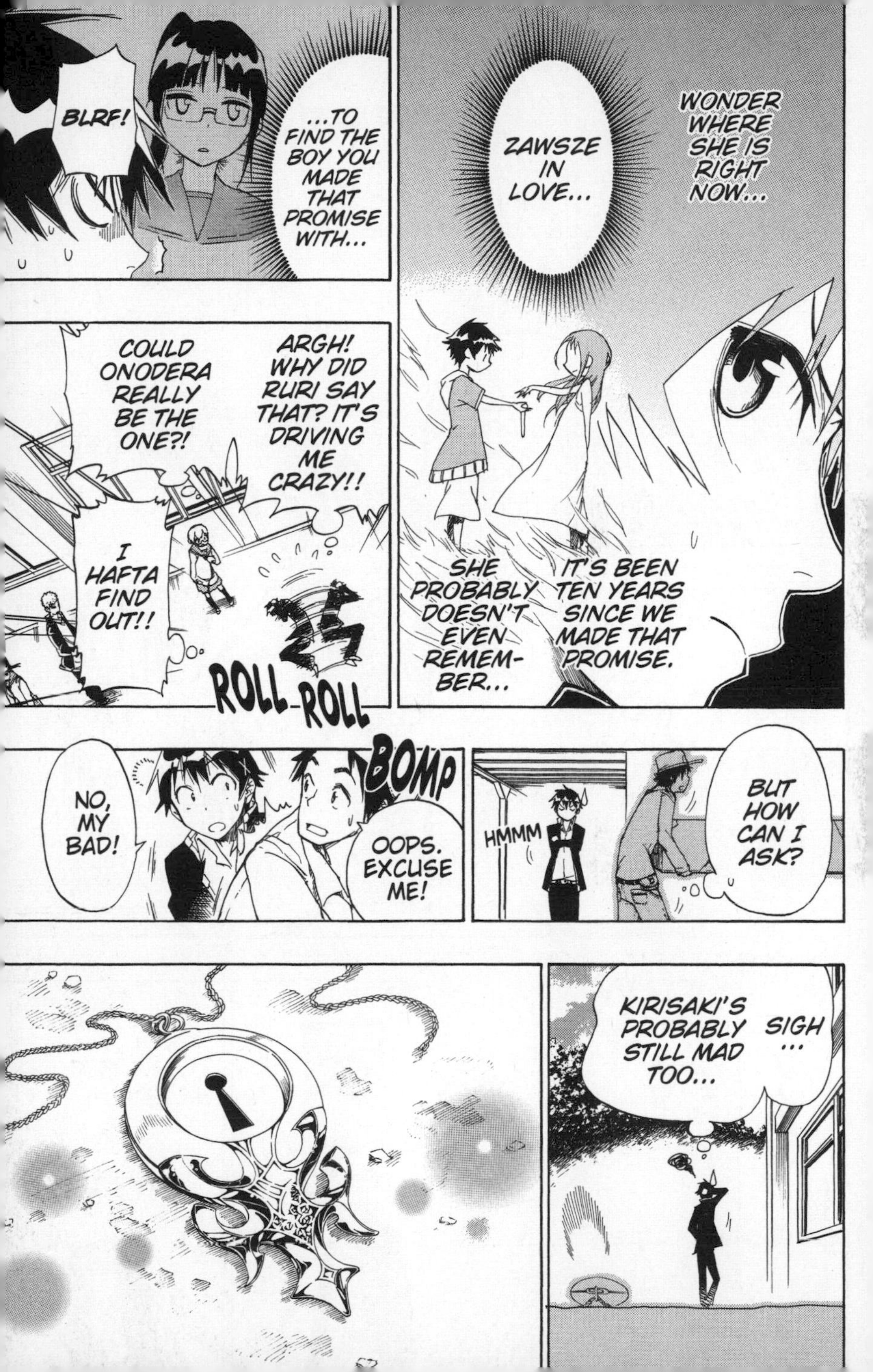
WONDER WHERE SHE IS RIGHT NOW...
ZAWSZE IN LOVE...
IT'S BEEN TEN YEARS SINCE WE MADE THAT PROMISE.
SHE PROBABLY DOESN'T EVEN REMEMBER...
...TO FIND THE BOY YOU MADE THAT PROMISE WITH...
BLRF!
ARGH! WHY DID RURI SAY THAT? IT'S DRIVING ME CRAZY!!
COULD ONODERA REALLY BE THE ONE?!
I HAFTA FIND OUT!!
ROLL-ROLL
BUT HOW CAN I ASK?
HMMM
BOMP
OOPS. EXCUSE ME!
NO, MY BAD!
SIGH...
KIRISAKI'S PROBABLY STILL MAD TOO...

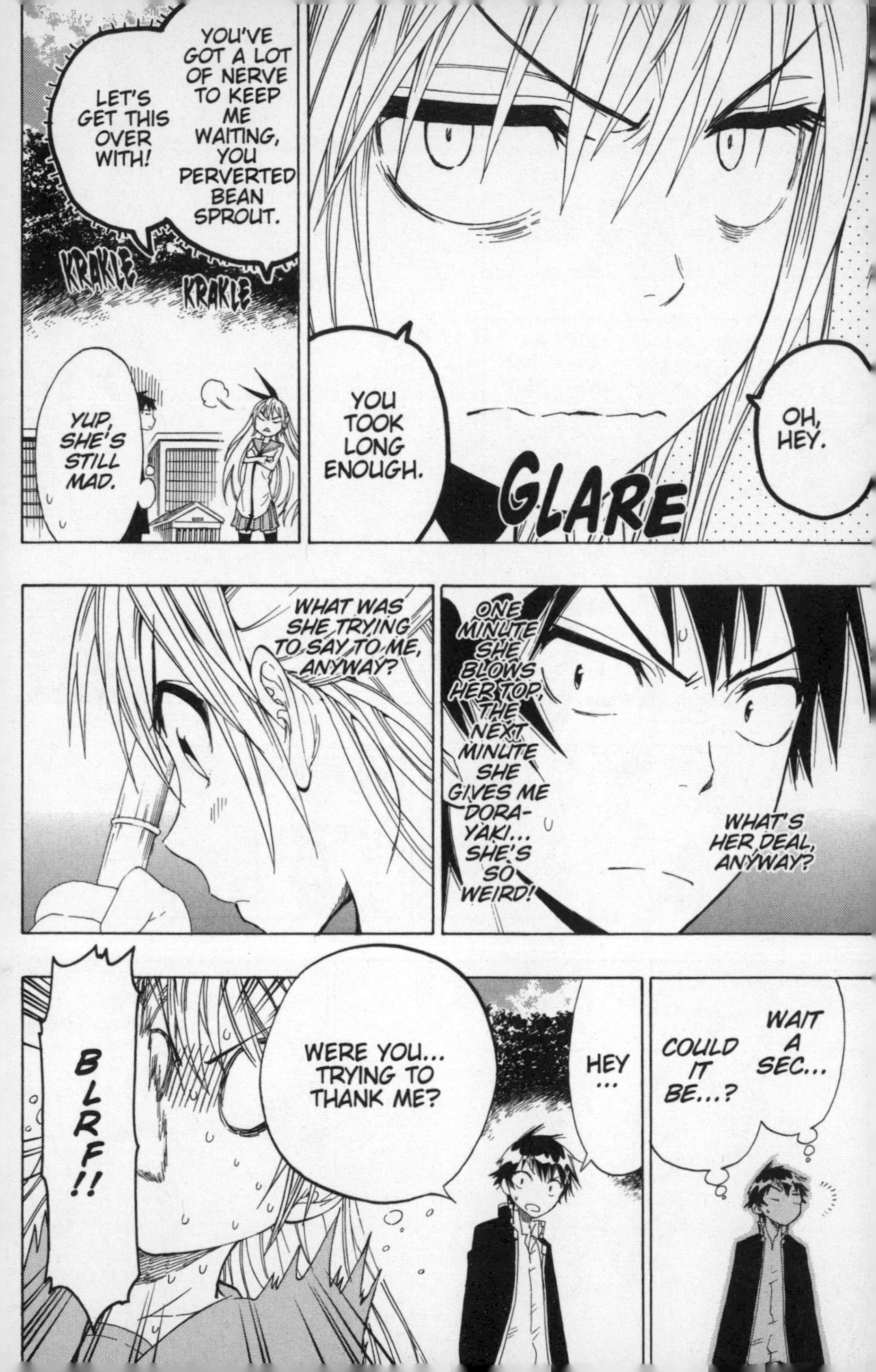
OH, HEY.
GLARE
YOU TOOK LONG ENOUGH.
YOU'VE GOT A LOT OF NERVE TO KEEP ME WAITING, YOU PERVERTED BEAN SPROUT.
LET'S GET THIS OVER WITH!
KRAKLE
KRAKLE
YUP, SHE'S STILL MAD.
WHAT'S HER DEAL, ANYWAY?
ONE MINUTE SHE BLOWS HER TOP, THE NEXT MINUTE SHE GIVES ME DORA-YAKI... SHE'S SO WEIRD!
WHAT WAS SHE TRYING TO SAY TO ME, ANYWAY?
WAIT A SEC...
COULD IT BE...?
HEY...
WERE YOU... TRYING TO THANK ME?
BLRF!!

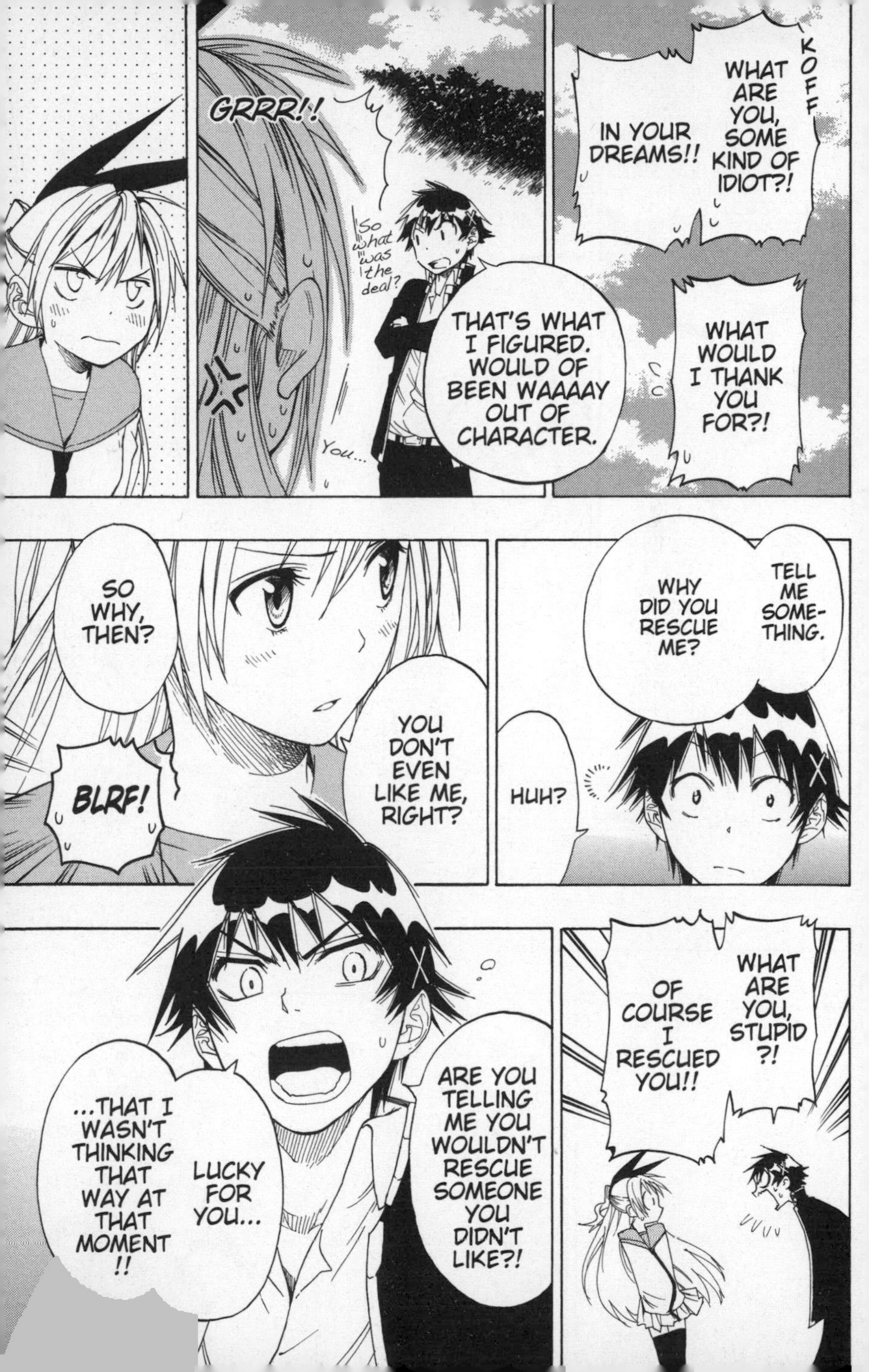
KOFF
WHAT ARE YOU, SOME KIND OF IDIOT?!
IN YOUR DREAMS!!
WHAT WOULD I THANK YOU FOR?!
So what was the deal?
GRRR!!
THAT'S WHAT I FIGURED. WOULD OF BEEN WAAAAY OUT OF CHARACTER.
You...
TELL ME SOMETHING.
WHY DID YOU RESCUE ME?
HUH?
YOU DON'T EVEN LIKE ME, RIGHT?
SO WHY, THEN?
BLRF!
WHAT ARE YOU, STUPID?!
OF COURSE I RESCUED YOU!!
ARE YOU TELLING ME YOU WOULDN'T RESCUE SOMEONE YOU DIDN'T LIKE?!
LUCKY FOR YOU...
...THAT I WASN'T THINKING THAT WAY AT THAT MOMENT!!

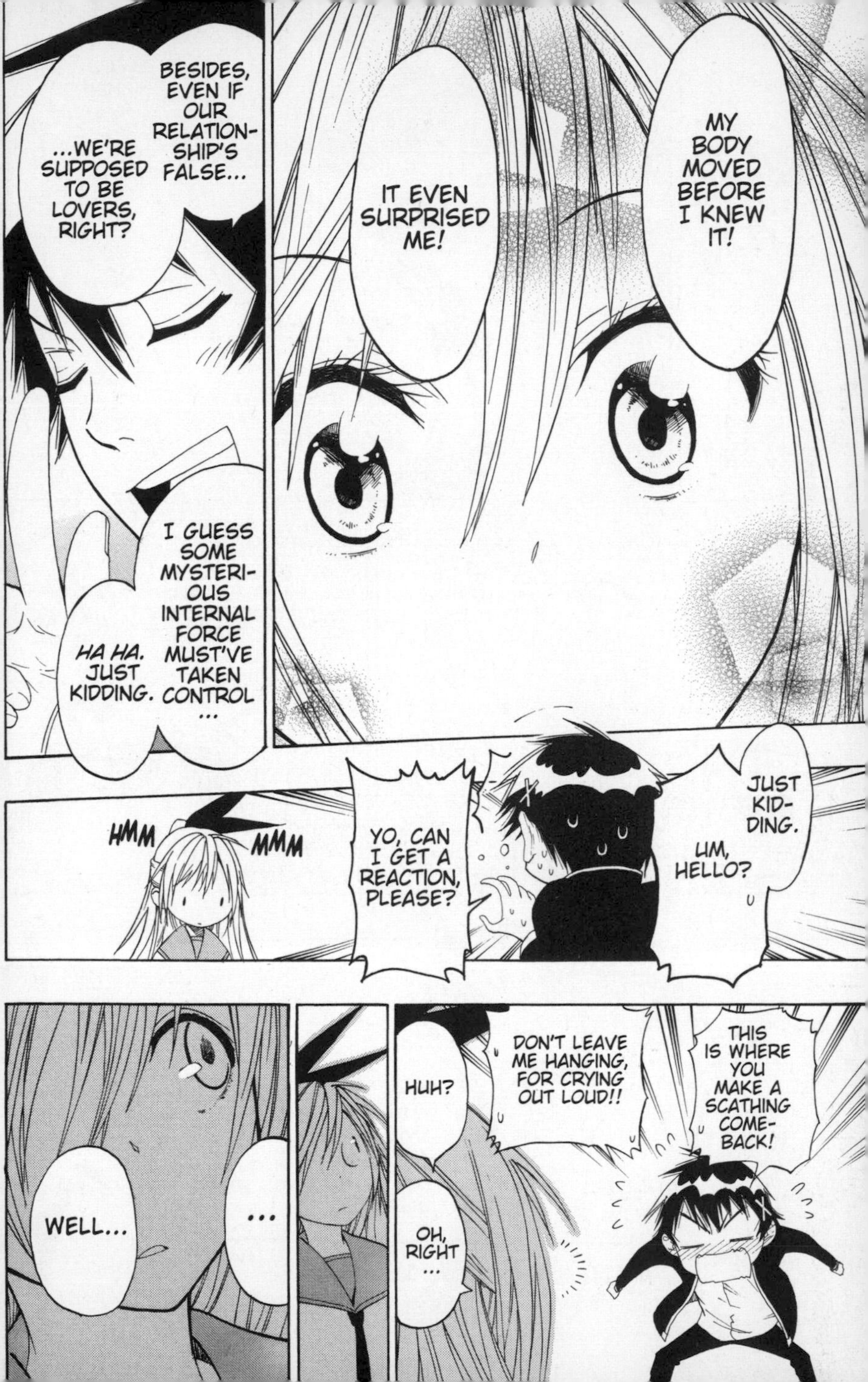
MY BODY MOVED BEFORE I KNEW IT!
IT EVEN SURPRISED ME!
BESIDES, EVEN IF OUR RELATIONSHIP'S FALSE...
...WE'RE SUPPOSED TO BE LOVERS, RIGHT?
I GUESS SOME MYSTERIOUS INTERNAL FORCE MUST'VE TAKEN CONTROL ...
HA HA. JUST KIDDING.
JUST KIDDING.
UM, HELLO?
YO, CAN I GET A REACTION, PLEASE?
HMM MMM
THIS IS WHERE YOU MAKE A SCATHING COMEBACK!
DON'T LEAVE ME HANGING, FOR CRYING OUT LOUD!!
HUH?
OH, RIGHT ...
...
WELL...

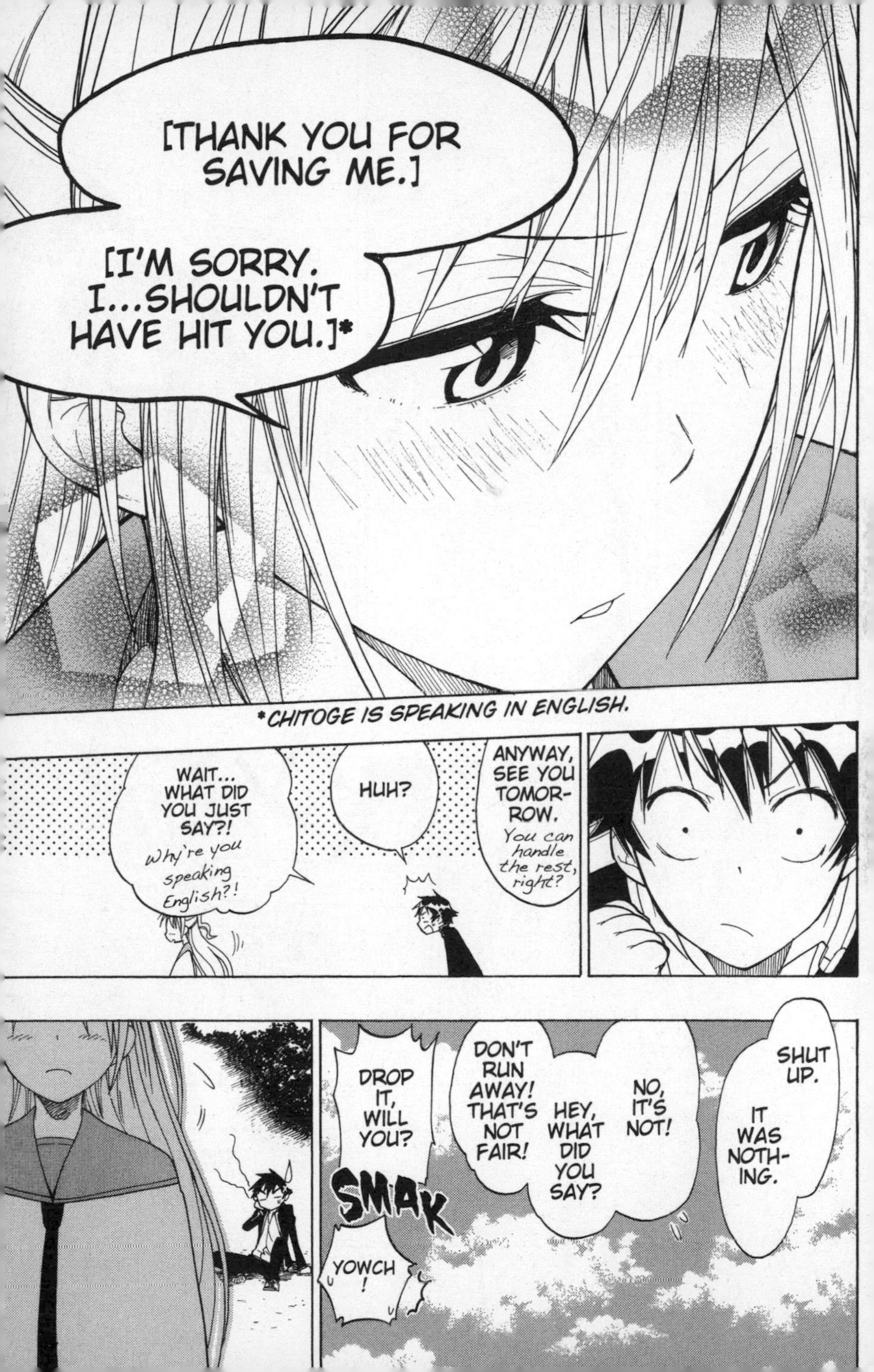
[THANK YOU FOR SAVING ME.]
[I'M SORRY. I...SHOULDN'T HAVE HIT YOU.]*
*CHITOGE IS SPEAKING IN ENGLISH.
ANYWAY, SEE YOU TOMOR-ROW. You can handle the rest, right?
HUH?
WAIT... WHAT DID YOU JUST SAY?! Why're you speaking English?!
SHUT UP.
IT WAS NOTH-ING.
NO, IT'S NOT!
HEY, WHAT DID YOU SAY?
DON'T RUN AWAY! THAT'S NOT FAIR!
DROP IT, WILL YOU?
SMAK
YOWCH!

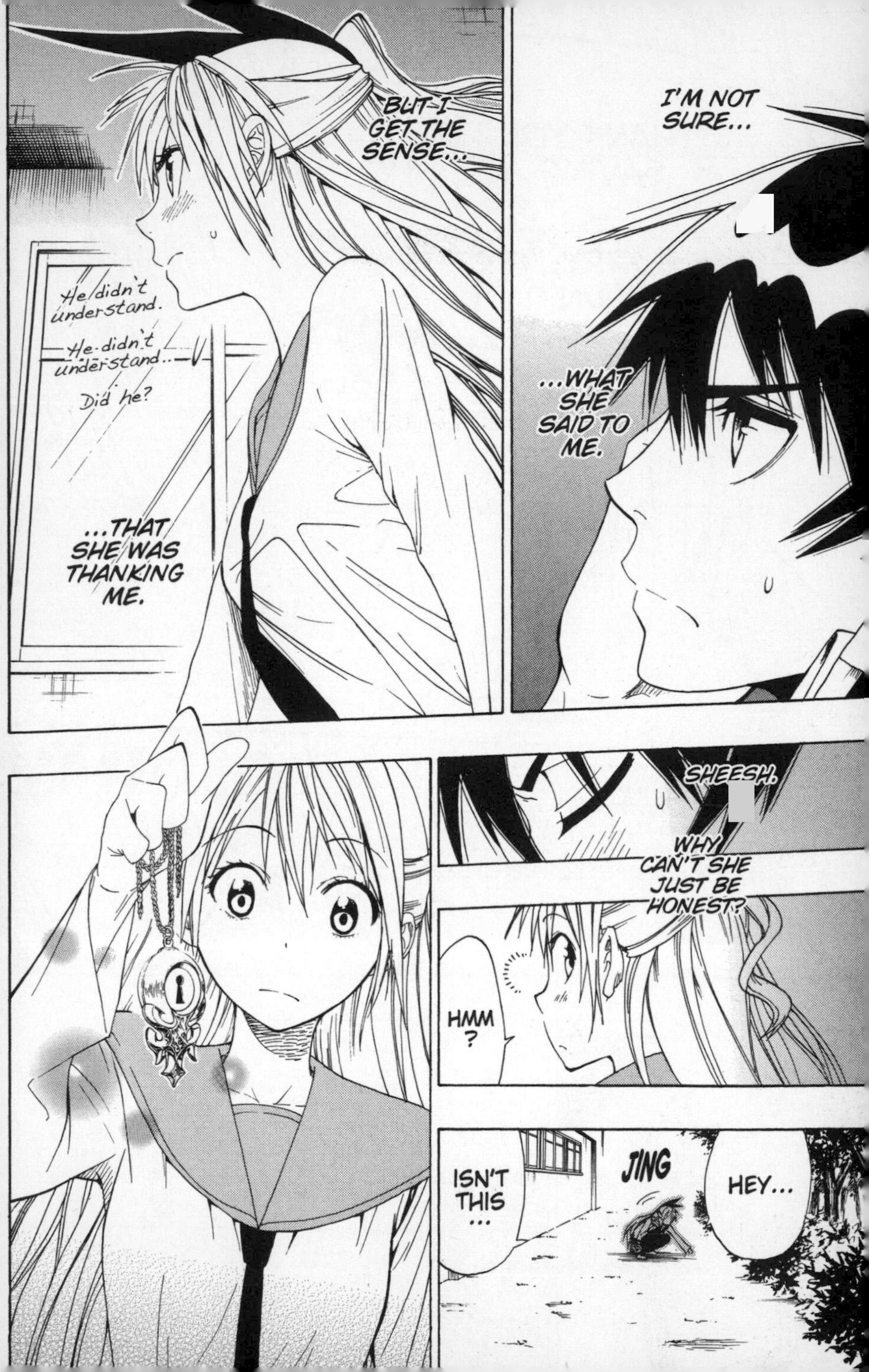
I'M NOT SURE...
...WHAT SHE SAID TO ME.
BUT I GET THE SENSE...
...THAT SHE WAS THANKING ME.
He didn't understand.
He didn't understand...
Did he?
SHEESH.
WHY CAN'T SHE JUST BE HONEST?
HMM?
HEY...
JING
ISN'T THIS...

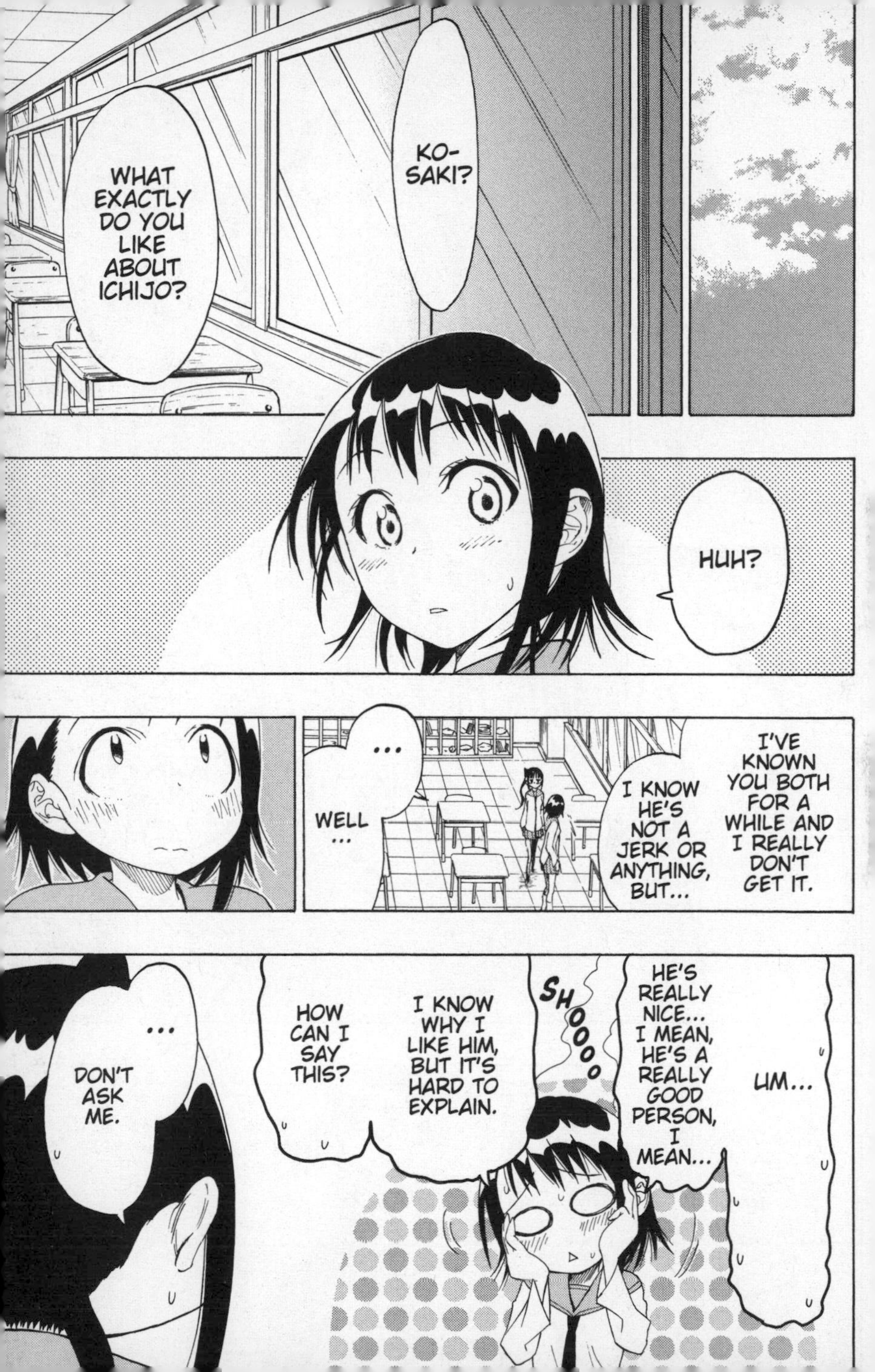
KO-SAKI?
WHAT EXACTLY DO YOU LIKE ABOUT ICHIJO?
HUH?
I'VE KNOWN YOU BOTH FOR A WHILE AND I REALLY DON'T GET IT.
I KNOW HE'S NOT A JERK OR ANYTHING, BUT...
...
WELL...
UM...
HE'S REALLY NICE... I MEAN, HE'S A REALLY GOOD PERSON, I MEAN...
SHOOOOO
I KNOW WHY I LIKE HIM, BUT IT'S HARD TO EXPLAIN.
HOW CAN I SAY THIS?
...
DON'T ASK ME.

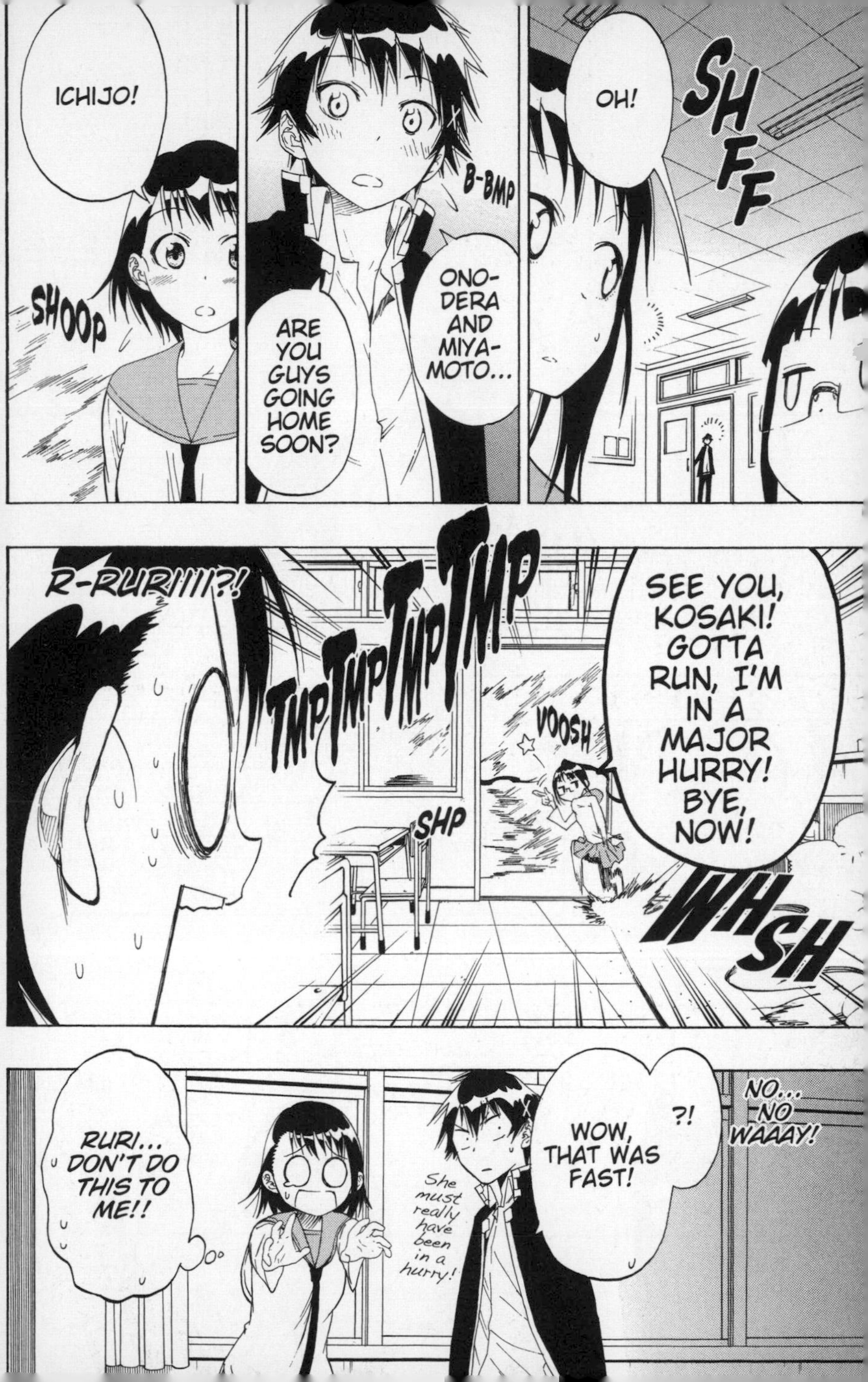

SHFF
OH!
B-BMP
ONO-DERA AND MIYA-MOTO...
ARE YOU GUYS GOING HOME SOON?
ICHIJO!
SHOOP
SEE YOU, KOSAKI! GOTTA RUN, I'M IN A MAJOR HURRY! BYE, NOW!
WHSH
VOOSH
SHP
TMP TMP TMP TMP
R-RURI!!!?!
NO... NO WAAAY!
?!
WOW, THAT WAS FAST!
She must really have been in a hurry!
RURI... DON'T DO THIS TO ME!!

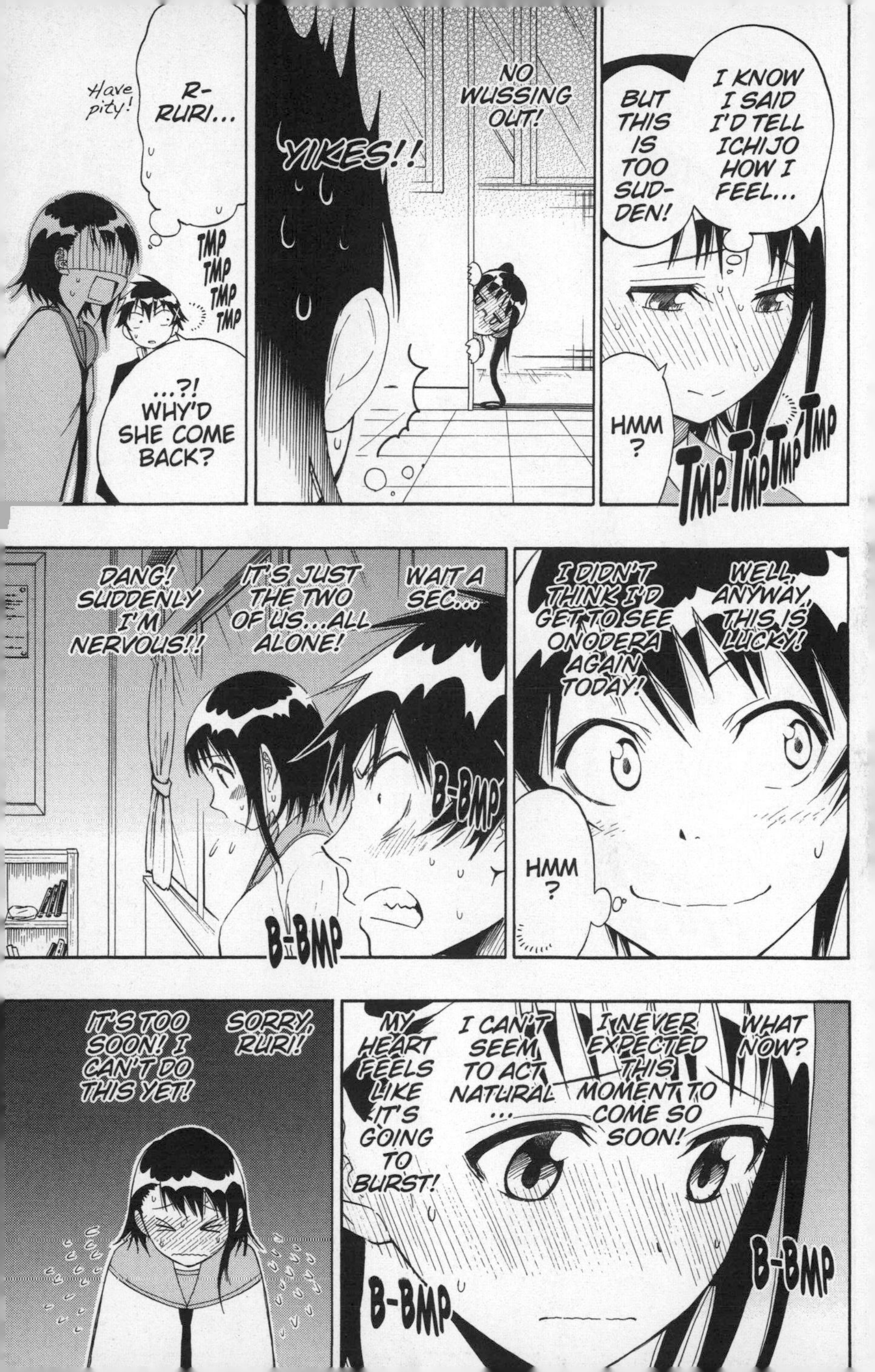
I KNOW I SAID I'D TELL ICHIJO HOW I FEEL...
BUT THIS IS TOO SUDDEN!
HMM ?
TMP TMP TMP TMP
NO WUSSING OUT!
YIKES!!
R-RURI...
Have pity!
TMP TMP TMP TMP
...?! WHY'D SHE COME BACK?
WELL, ANYWAY, THIS IS LUCKY!
I DIDN'T THINK I'D GET TO SEE ONODERA AGAIN TODAY!
HMM ?
WAIT A SEC...
IT'S JUST THE TWO OF US...ALL ALONE!
DANG! SUDDENLY I'M NERVOUS!!
B-BMP
B-BMP
WHAT NOW?
I NEVER EXPECTED THIS MOMENT TO COME SO SOON!
I CAN'T SEEM TO ACT NATURAL...
MY HEART FEELS LIKE IT'S GOING TO BURST!
B-BMP
B-BMP
SORRY, RURI!
IT'S TOO SOON! I CAN'T DO THIS YET!

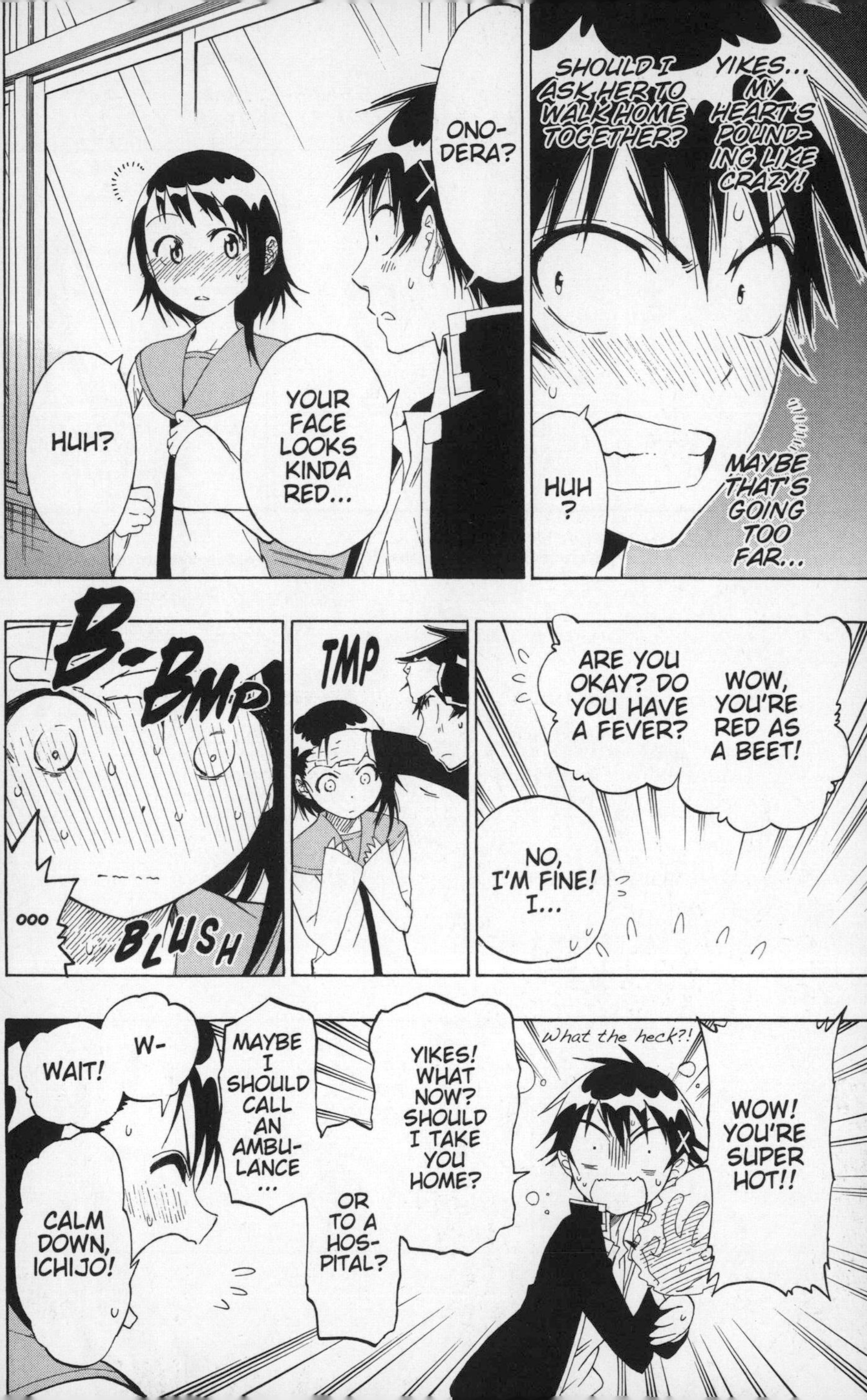
YIKES... MY HEART'S POUNDING LIKE CRAZY!
SHOULD I ASK HER TO WALK HOME TOGETHER?
MAYBE THAT'S GOING TOO FAR...
HUH?
ONO-DERA?
YOUR FACE LOOKS KINDA RED...
HUH?
WOW, YOU'RE RED AS A BEET!
ARE YOU OKAY? DO YOU HAVE A FEVER?
NO, I'M FINE! I...
TMP
B-BMP
ooo
BLUSH
What the heck?!
WOW! YOU'RE SUPER HOT!!
YIKES! WHAT NOW? SHOULD I TAKE YOU HOME?
OR TO A HOSPITAL?
MAYBE I SHOULD CALL AN AMBULANCE...
W-
WAIT!
CALM DOWN, ICHIJO!

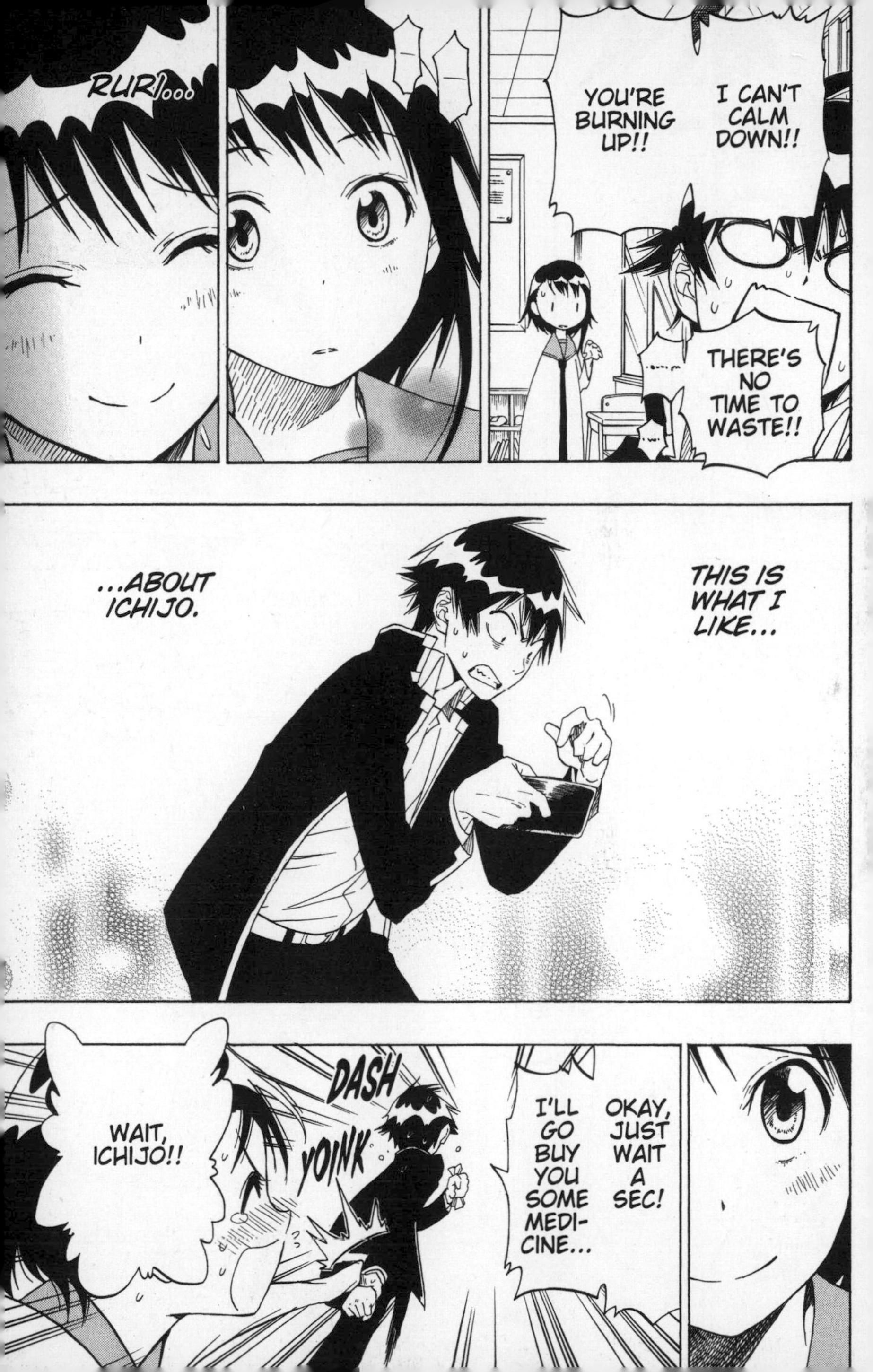
I CAN'T CALM DOWN!!
YOU'RE BURNING UP!!
THERE'S NO TIME TO WASTE!!
RURI...
THIS IS WHAT I LIKE...
...ABOUT ICHIJO.
OKAY, JUST WAIT A SEC!
I'LL GO BUY YOU SOME MEDI-CINE...
DASH
YOINK
WAIT, ICHIJO!!

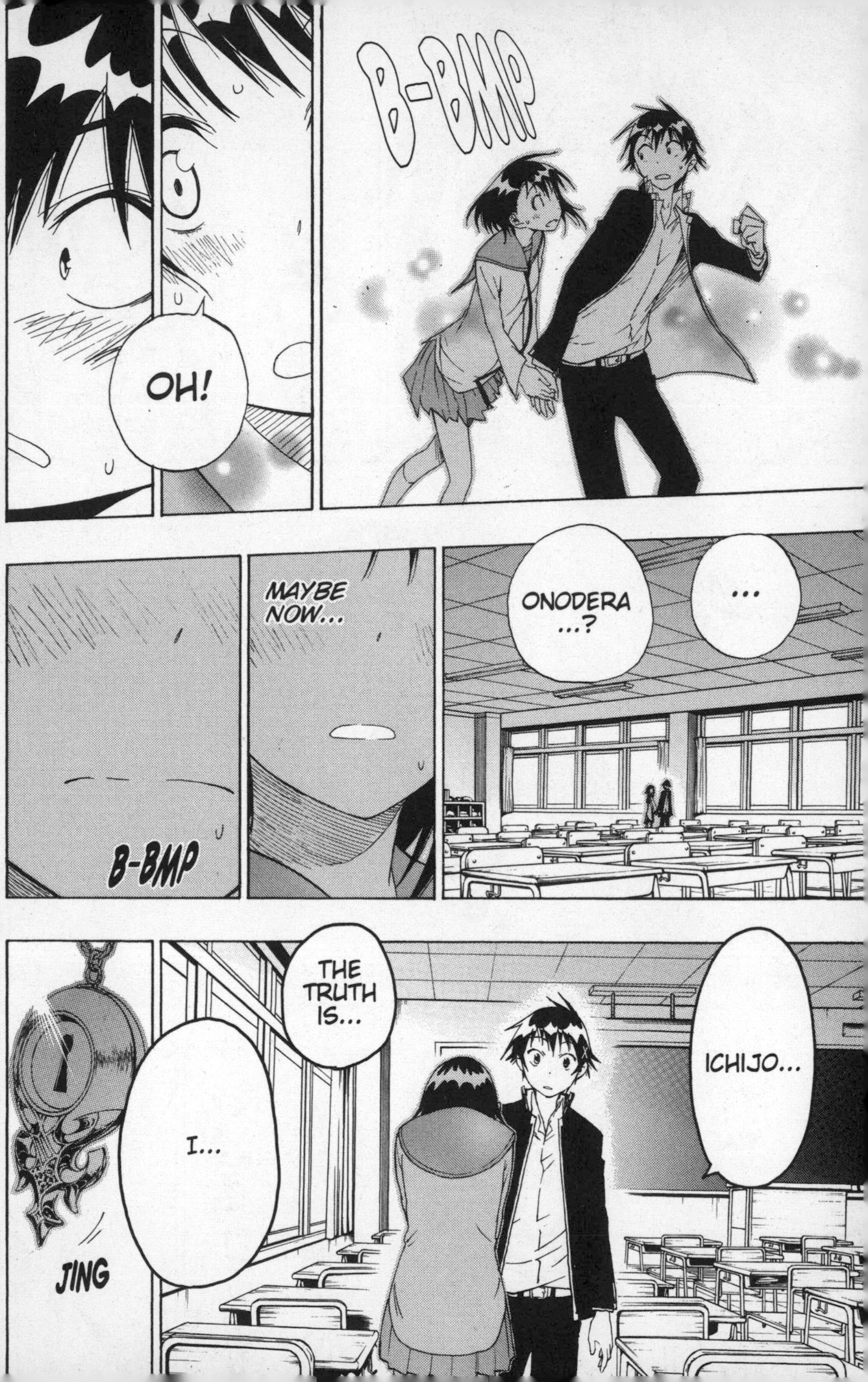
B-BMP
OH!
...
ONODERA ...?
MAYBE NOW...
B-BMP
ICHIJO...
THE TRUTH IS...
I...
JING

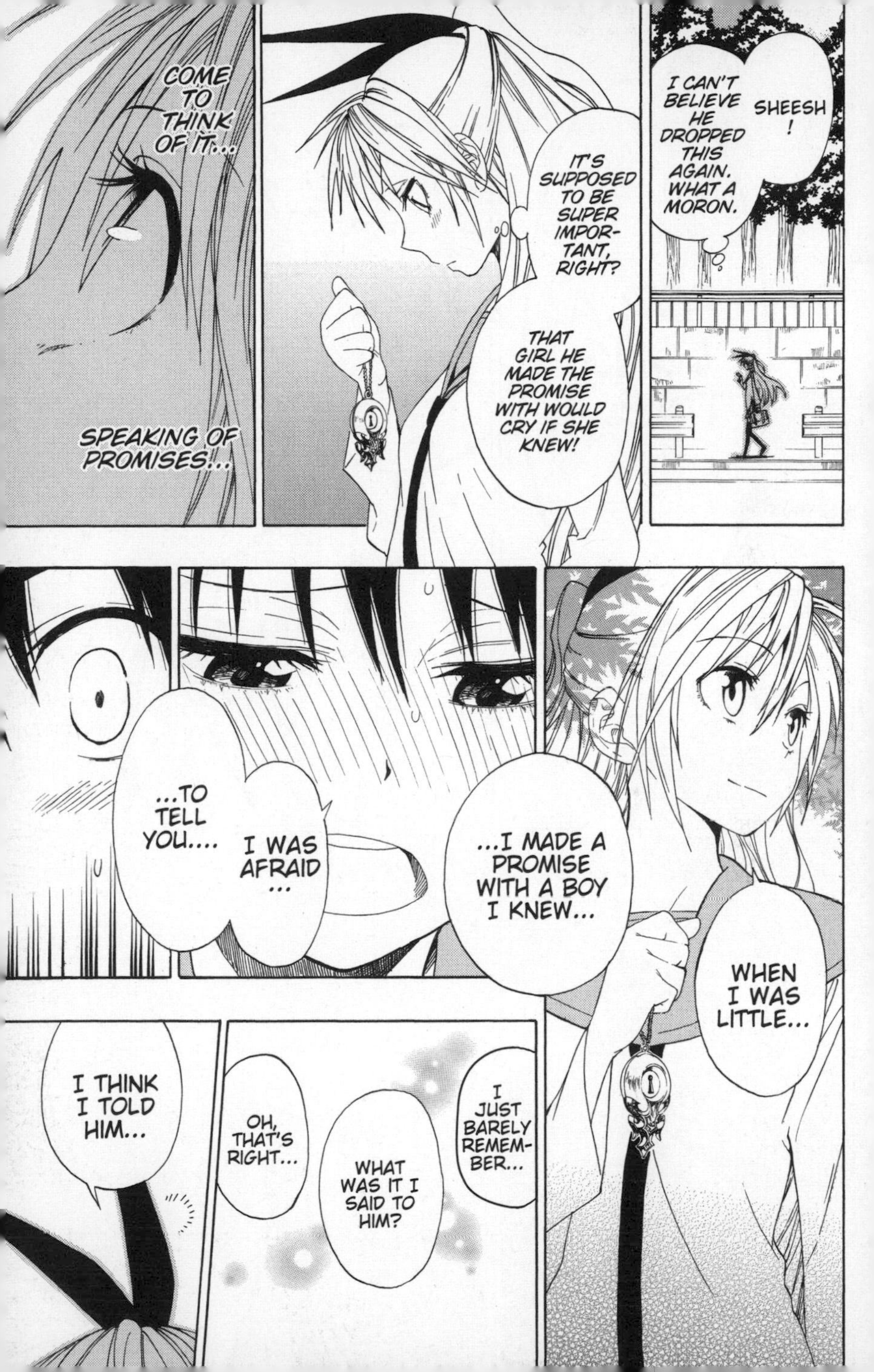
SHEESH!
I CAN'T BELIEVE HE DROPPED THIS AGAIN. WHAT A MORON.
IT'S SUPPOSED TO BE SUPER IMPORTANT, RIGHT?
THAT GIRL HE MADE THE PROMISE WITH WOULD CRY IF SHE KNEW!
COME TO THINK OF IT...
SPEAKING OF PROMISES...
WHEN I WAS LITTLE...
...I MADE A PROMISE WITH A BOY I KNEW...
I WAS AFRAID ...
...TO TELL YOU....
I JUST BARELY REMEMBER...
OH, THAT'S RIGHT...
WHAT WAS IT I SAID TO HIM?
I THINK I TOLD HIM...

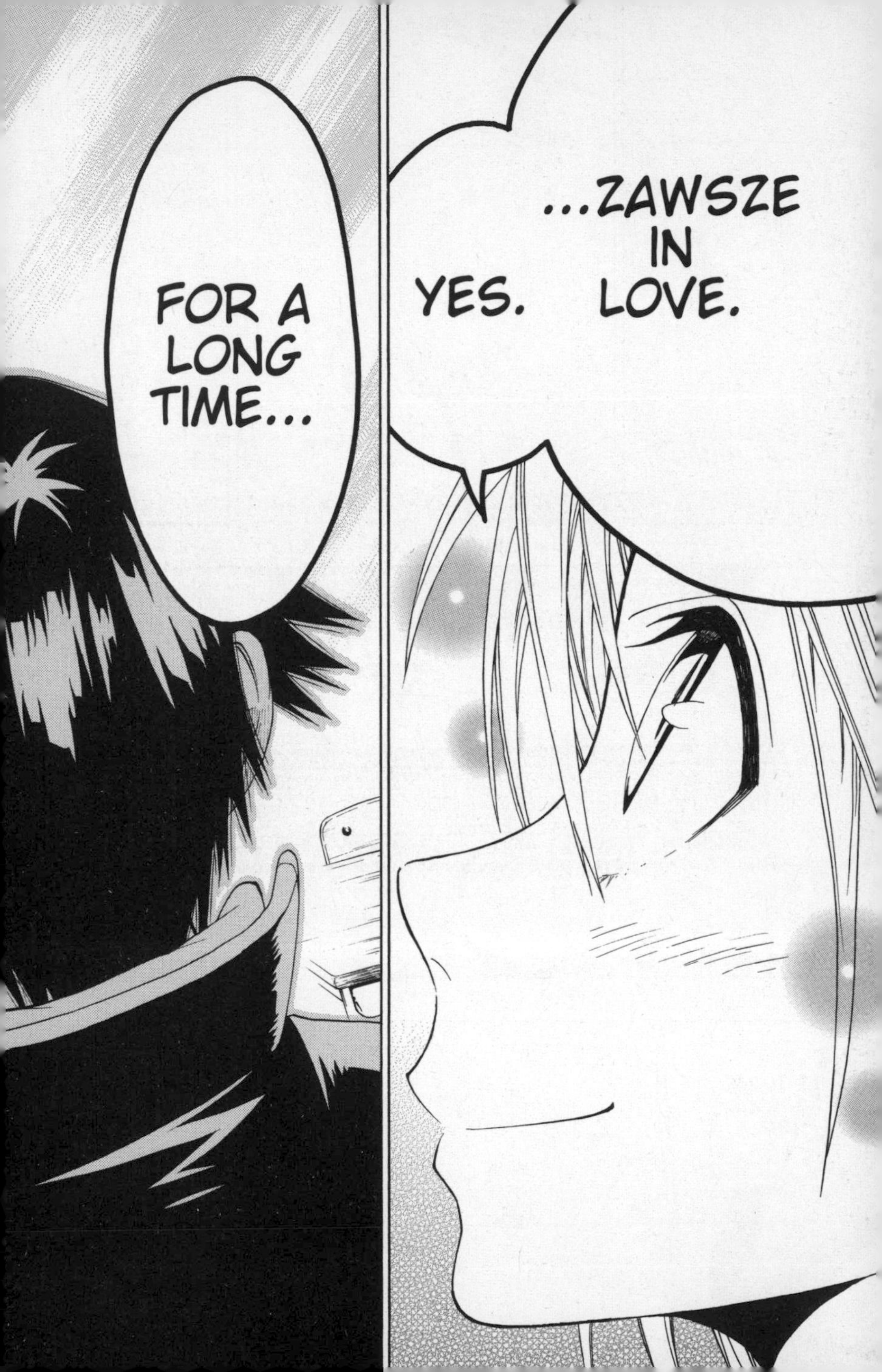
YES.
...ZAWSZE IN LOVE.
FOR A LONG TIME...

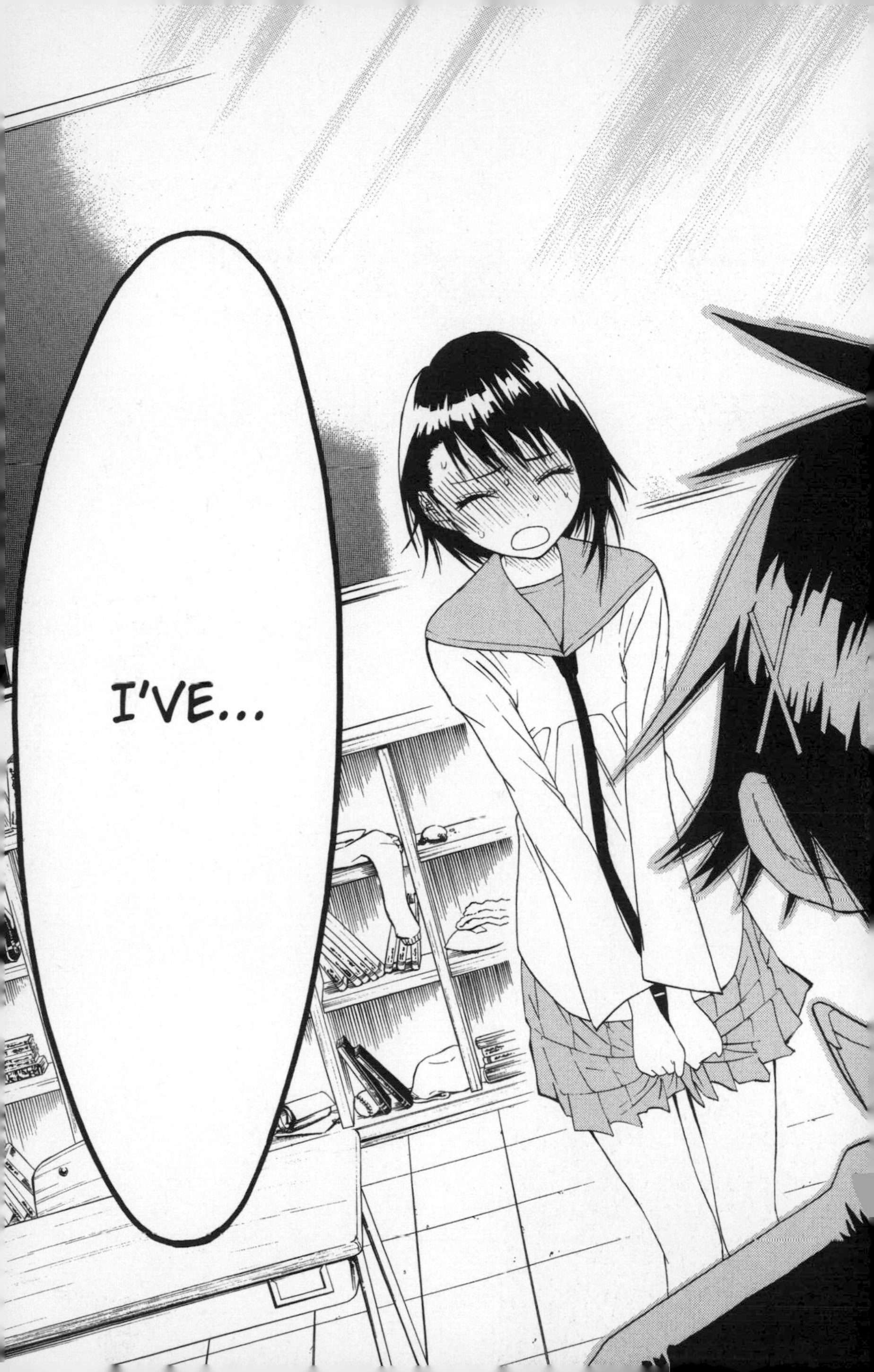
I'VE...

Good
luck,
Kosaki!

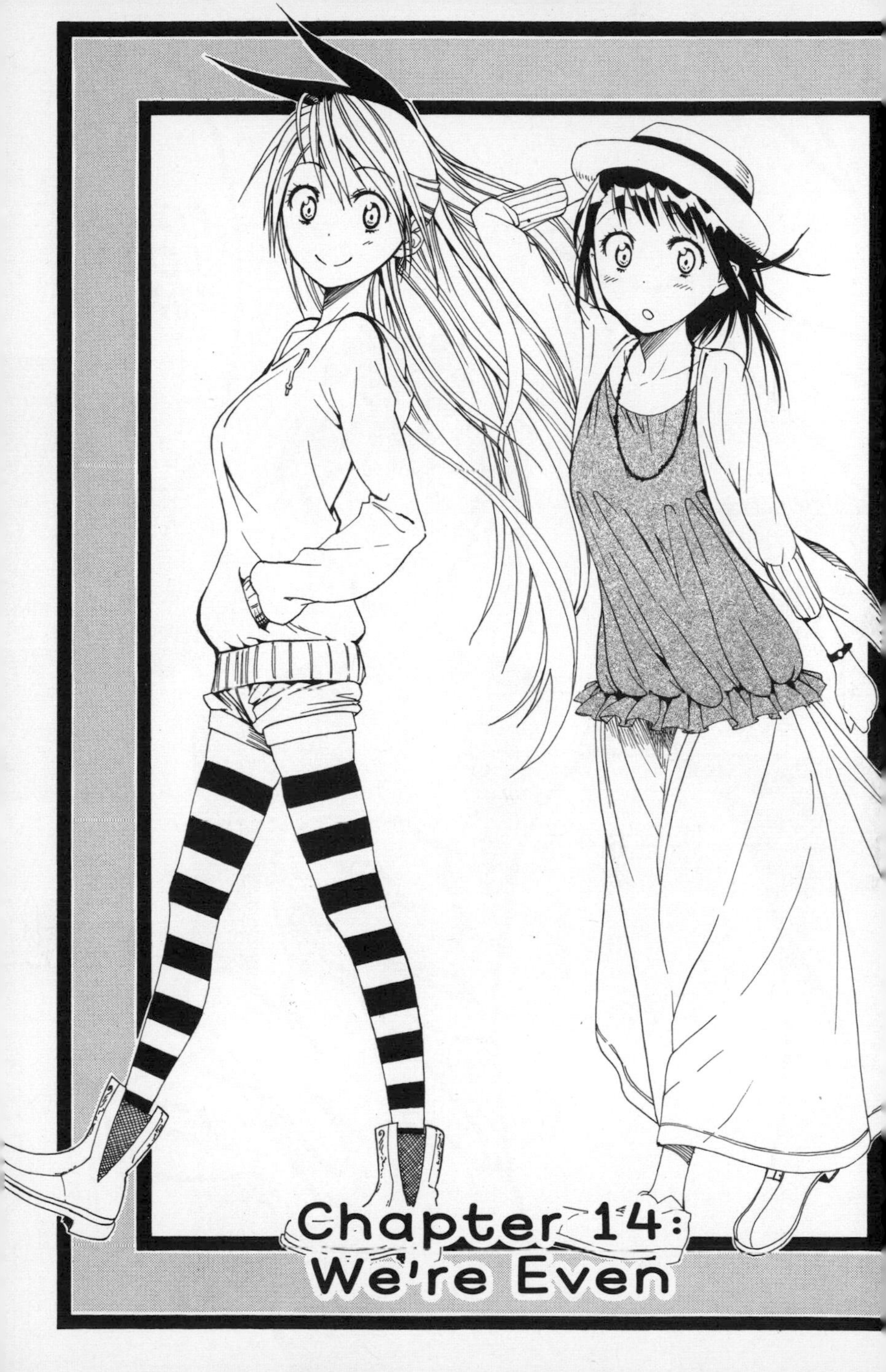

Chapter 14: We're Even

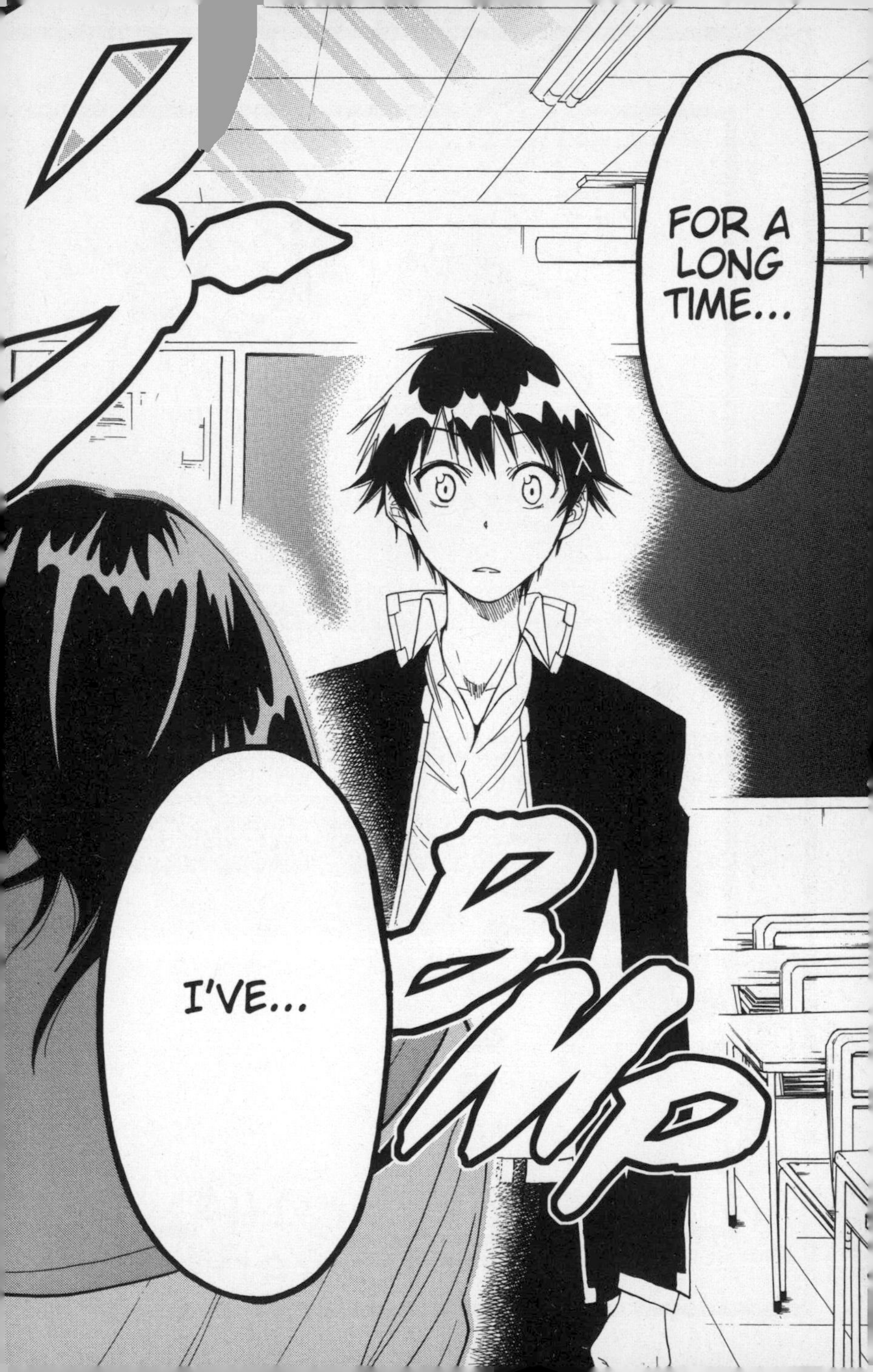
FOR A LONG TIME...
I'VE...

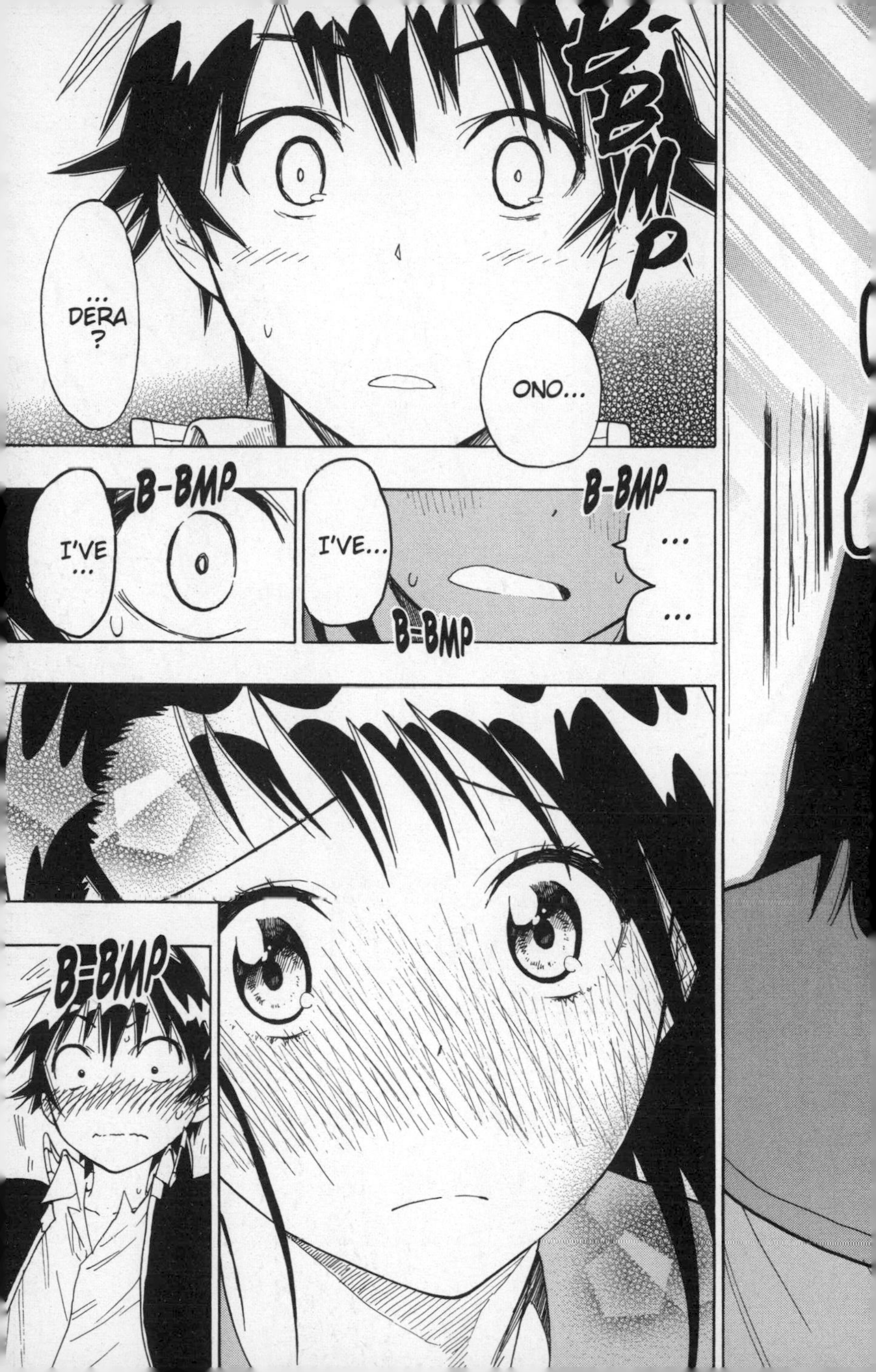
B-BMP
ONO...
... DERA?
B-BMP
...
...
B-BMP
I'VE...
B-BMP
I'VE ...
B-BMP

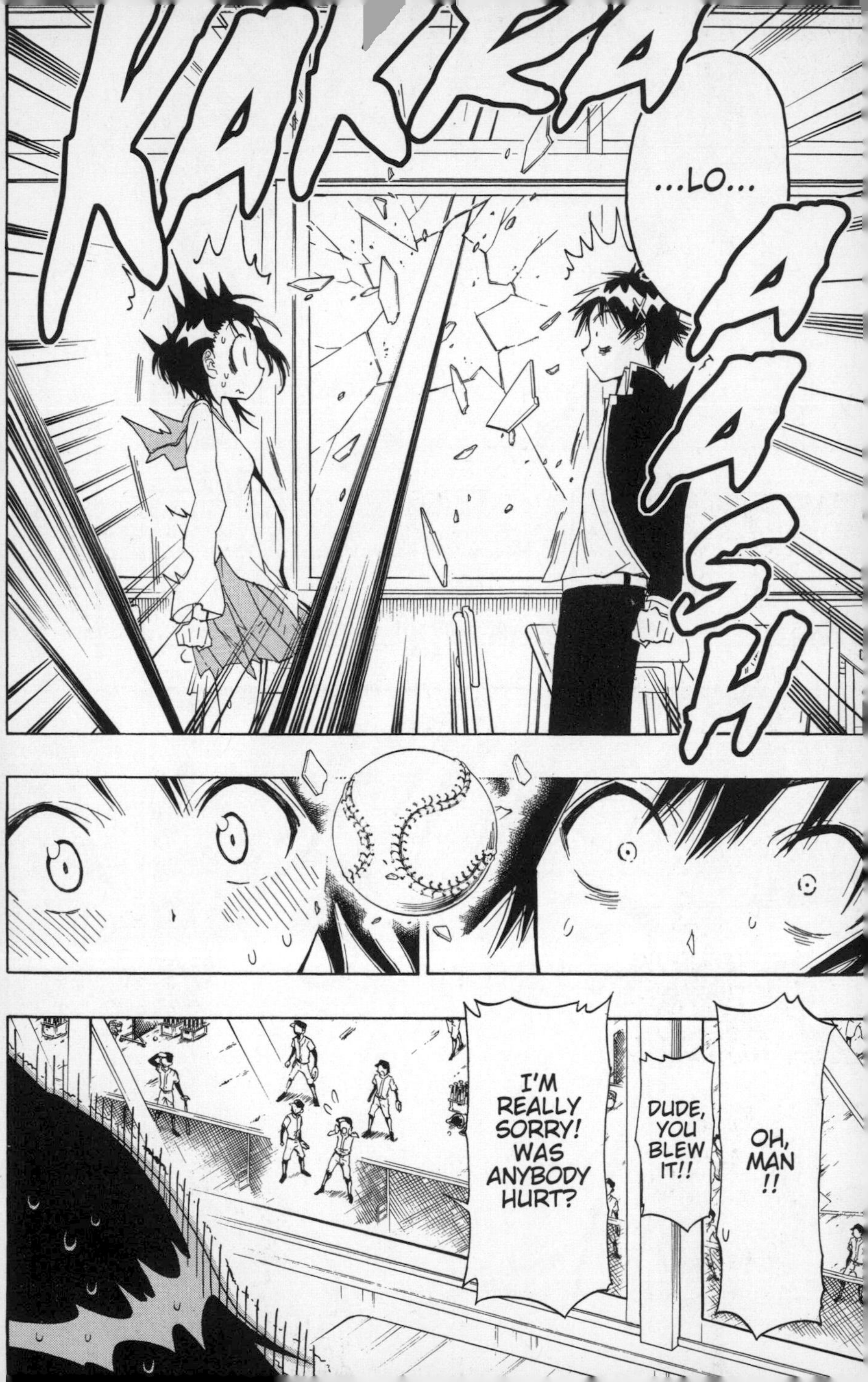
...LO...
OH, MAN!!
DUDE, YOU BLEW IT!!
I'M REALLY SORRY! WAS ANYBODY HURT?

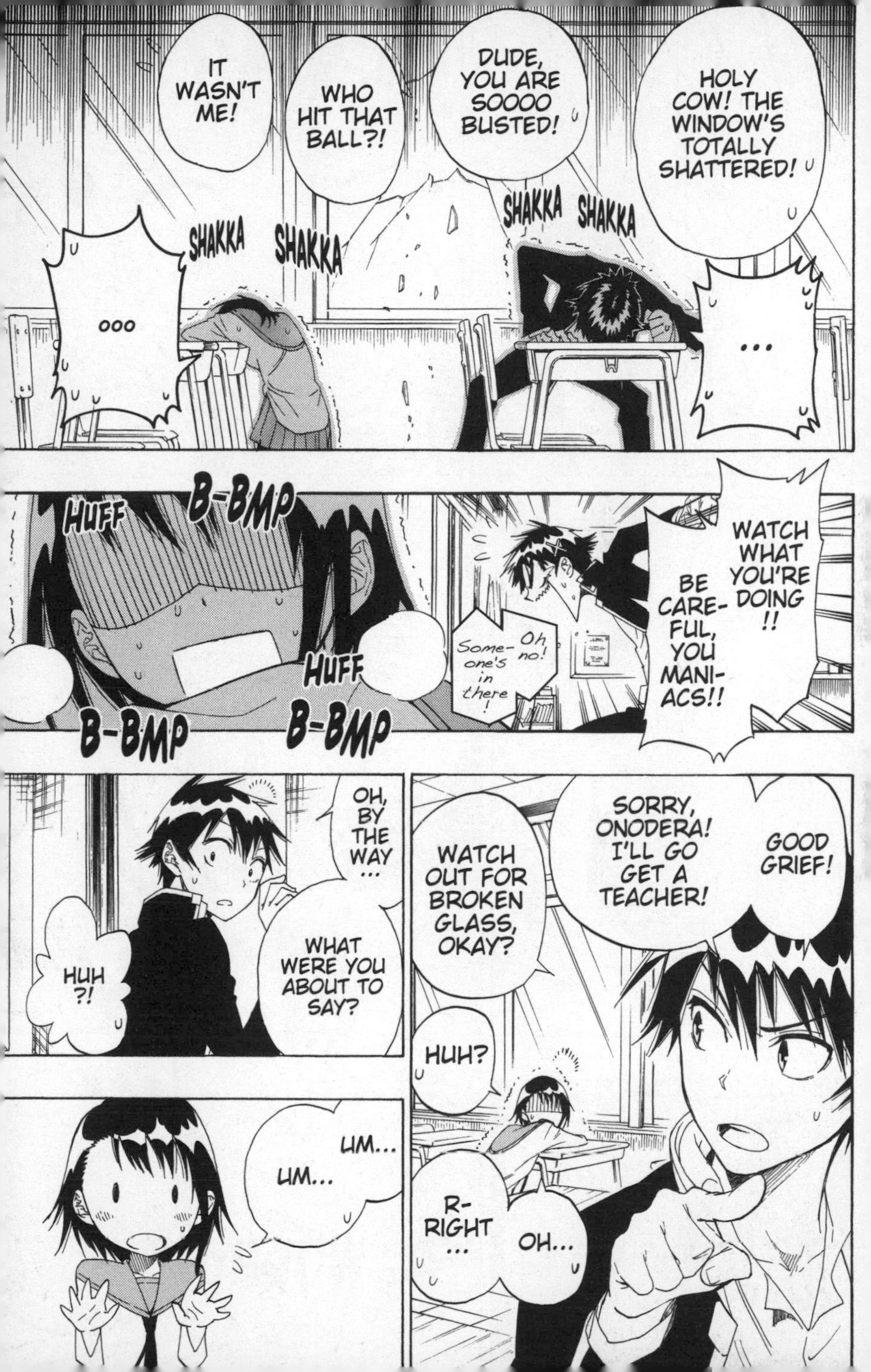
HOLY COW! THE WINDOW'S TOTALLY SHATTERED!
DUDE, YOU ARE SOOOO BUSTED!
WHO HIT THAT BALL?!
IT WASN'T ME!
SHAKKA SHAKKA
...
SHAKKA SHAKKA
OOO
WATCH WHAT YOU'RE DOING!!
BE CAREFUL, YOU MANIACS!!
Oh no! Someone's in there!
B-BMP
HUFF
HUFF
B-BMP
B-BMP
GOOD GRIEF!
SORRY, ONODERA! I'LL GO GET A TEACHER!
WATCH OUT FOR BROKEN GLASS, OKAY?
HUH?
OH...
R-RIGHT...
OH, BY THE WAY...
WHAT WERE YOU ABOUT TO SAY?
HUH?!
UM...
UM...

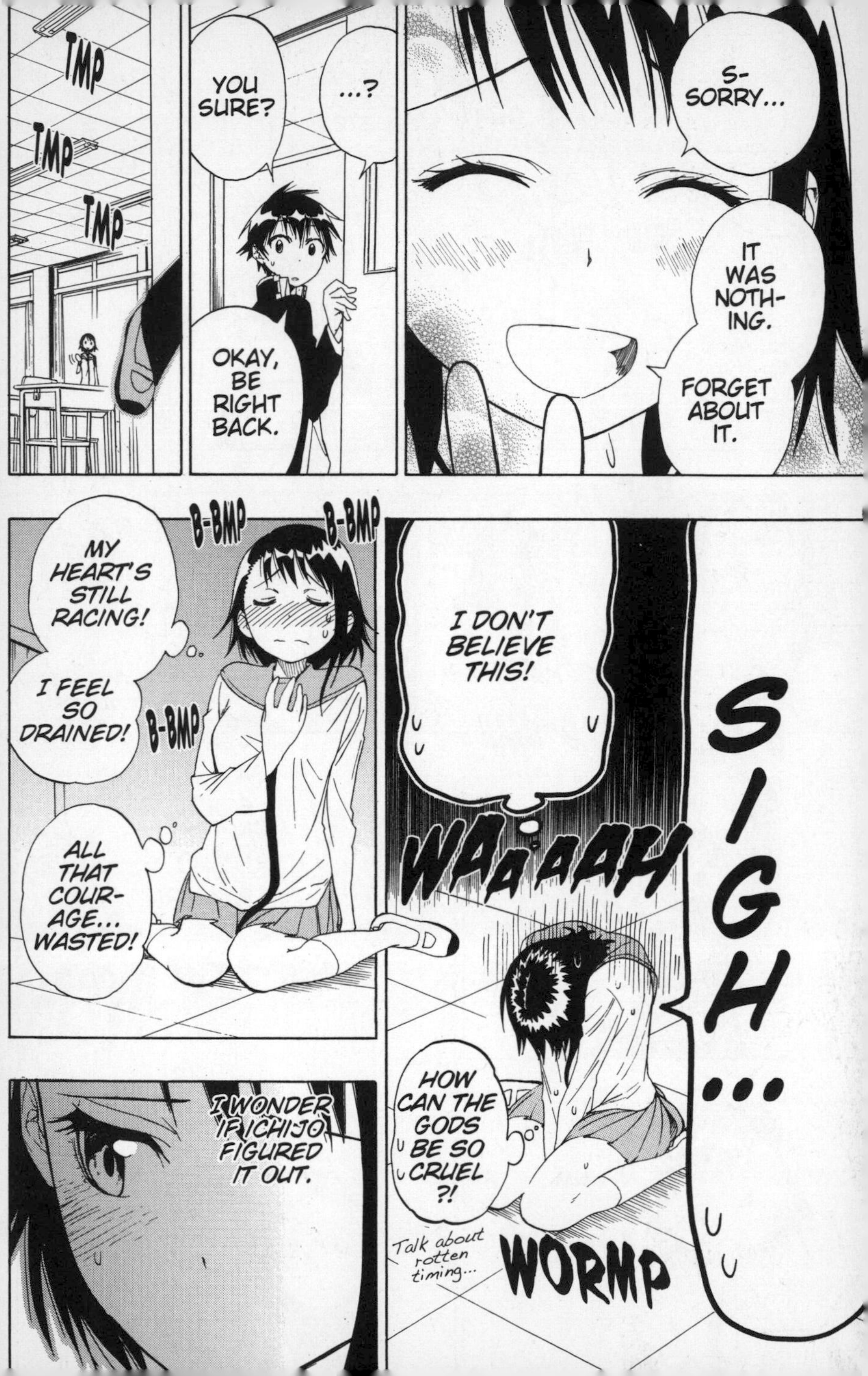
S-SORRY...
IT WAS NOTHING.
FORGET ABOUT IT.
...?
YOU SURE?
OKAY, BE RIGHT BACK.
TMP
TMP
TMP
I DON'T BELIEVE THIS!
SIGH...
WAAAAH
HOW CAN THE GODS BE SO CRUEL?!
WORMP
Talk about rotten timing...
B-BMP
B-BMP
MY HEART'S STILL RACING!
I FEEL SO DRAINED!
B-BMP
ALL THAT COURAGE... WASTED!
I WONDER IF ICHIJO FIGURED IT OUT.

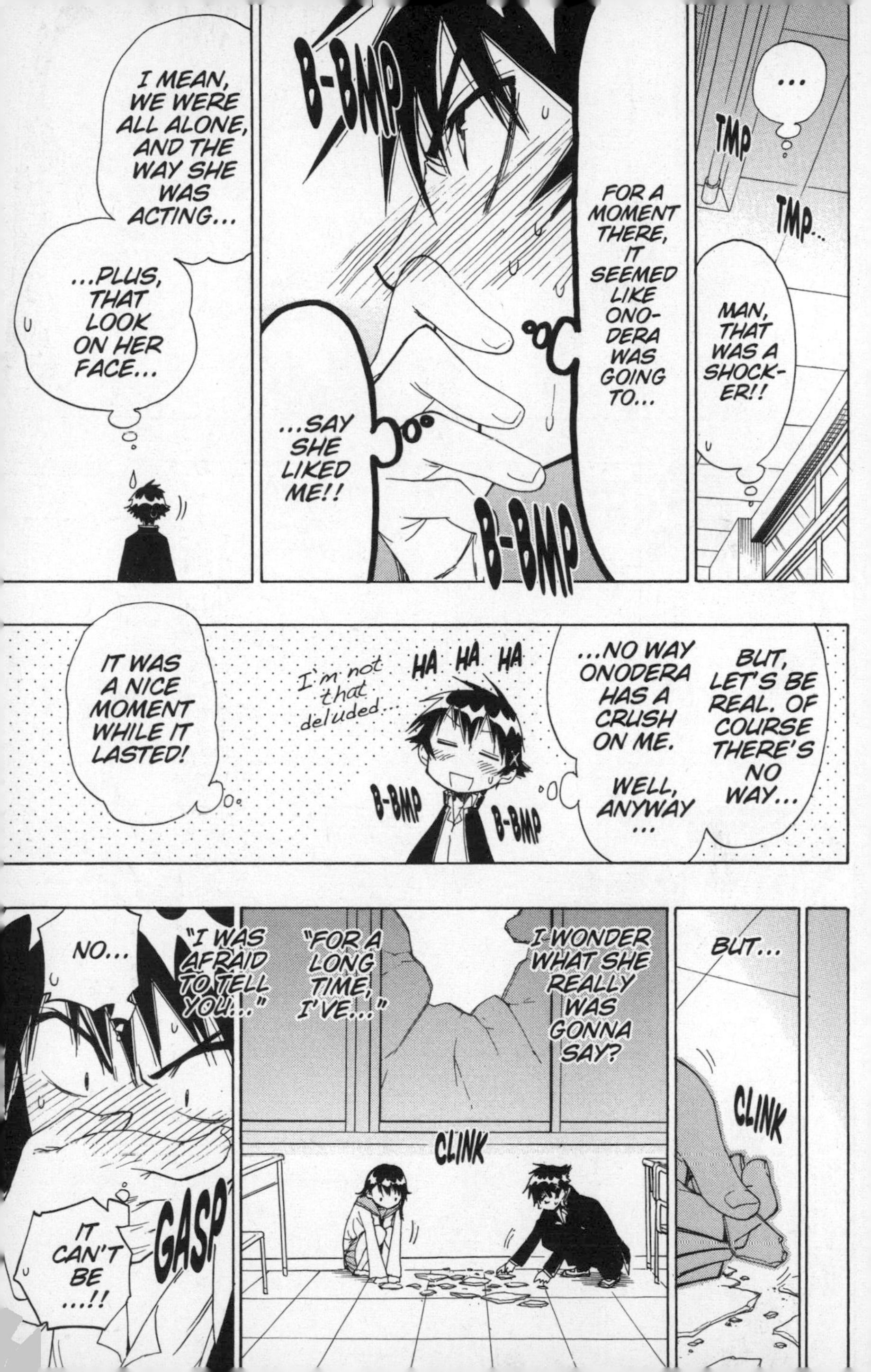
...
TMP
TMP...
MAN, THAT WAS A SHOCKER!!
FOR A MOMENT THERE, IT SEEMED LIKE ONODERA WAS GOING TO...
B-BMP
...SAY SHE LIKED ME!!
B-BMP
I MEAN, WE WERE ALL ALONE, AND THE WAY SHE WAS ACTING...
...PLUS, THAT LOOK ON HER FACE...
BUT, LET'S BE REAL. OF COURSE THERE'S NO WAY...
...NO WAY ONODERA HAS A CRUSH ON ME.
WELL, ANYWAY...
HA HA HA
I'm not that deluded...
B-BMP
B-BMP
IT WAS A NICE MOMENT WHILE IT LASTED!
BUT...
CLINK
I-WONDER WHAT SHE REALLY WAS GONNA SAY?
"FOR A LONG TIME, I'VE..."
"I WAS AFRAID TO TELL YOU..."
CLINK
NO...
GASP
IT CAN'T BE ...!!

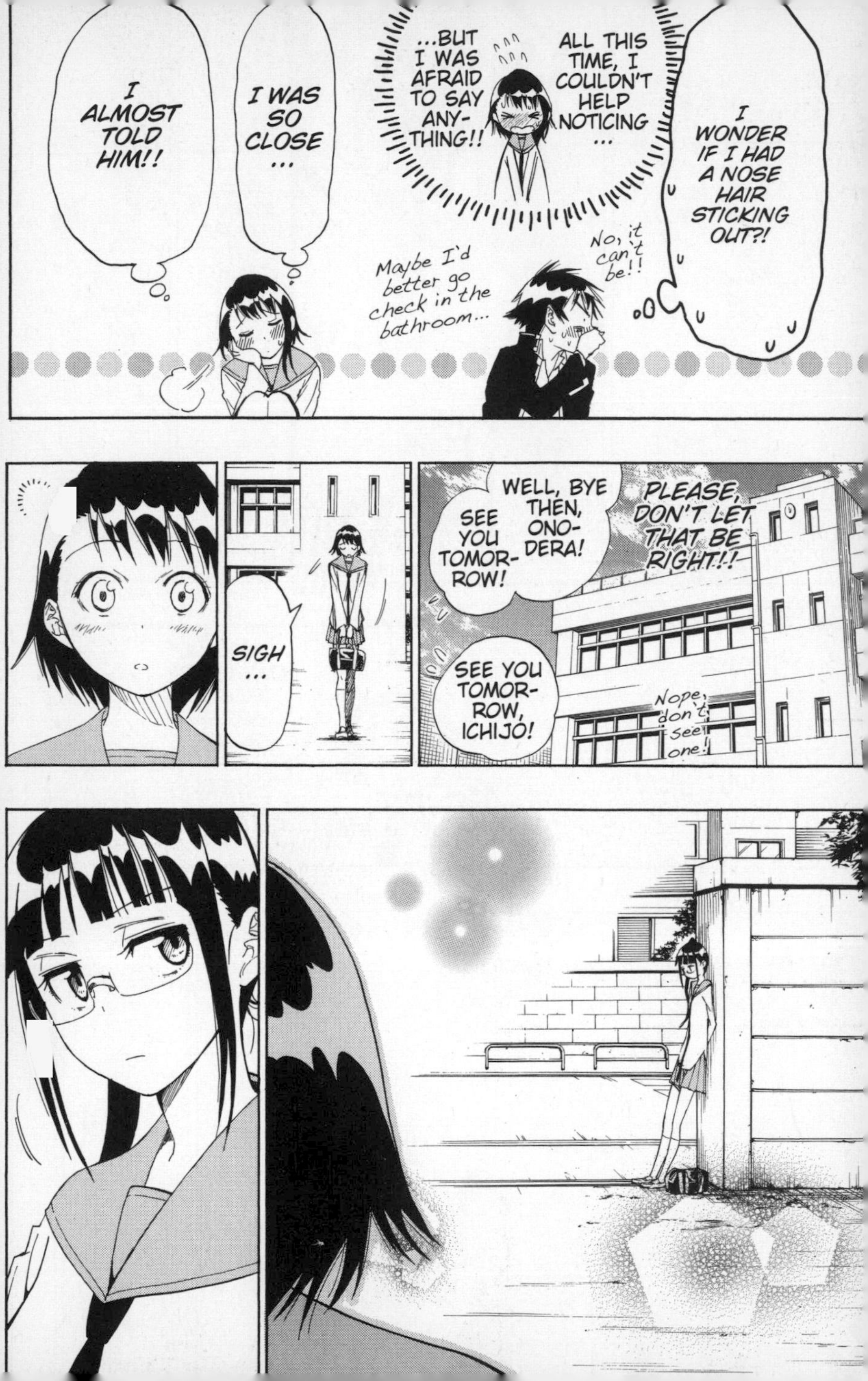
I WONDER IF I HAD A NOSE HAIR STICKING OUT?!
No, it can't be!!
ALL THIS TIME, I COULDN'T HELP NOTICING...
...BUT I WAS AFRAID TO SAY ANY-THING!!
Maybe I'd better go check in the bathroom...
I WAS SO CLOSE...
I ALMOST TOLD HIM!!
PLEASE, DON'T LET THAT BE RIGHT!!
WELL, BYE THEN, ONO-DERA!
SEE YOU TOMOR-ROW!
Nope, don't see one!
SEE YOU TOMOR-ROW, ICHIJO!
SIGH...

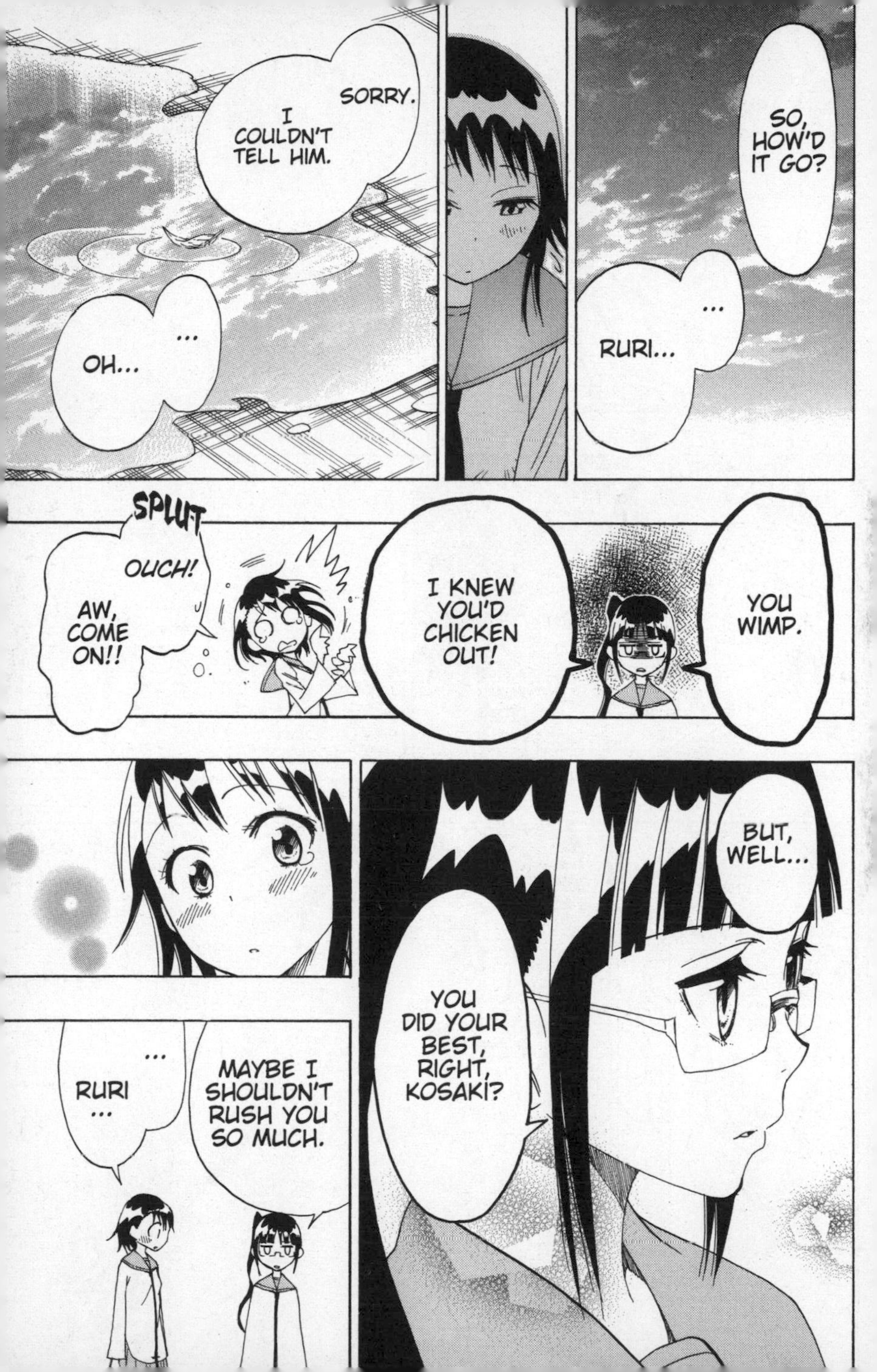
SO, HOW'D IT GO?
... RURI...
SORRY. I COULDN'T TELL HIM.
... OH...
YOU WIMP.
I KNEW YOU'D CHICKEN OUT!
SPLUT
OUCH! AW, COME ON!!
BUT, WELL...
YOU DID YOUR BEST, RIGHT, KOSAKI?
MAYBE I SHOULDN'T RUSH YOU SO MUCH.
... RURI ...

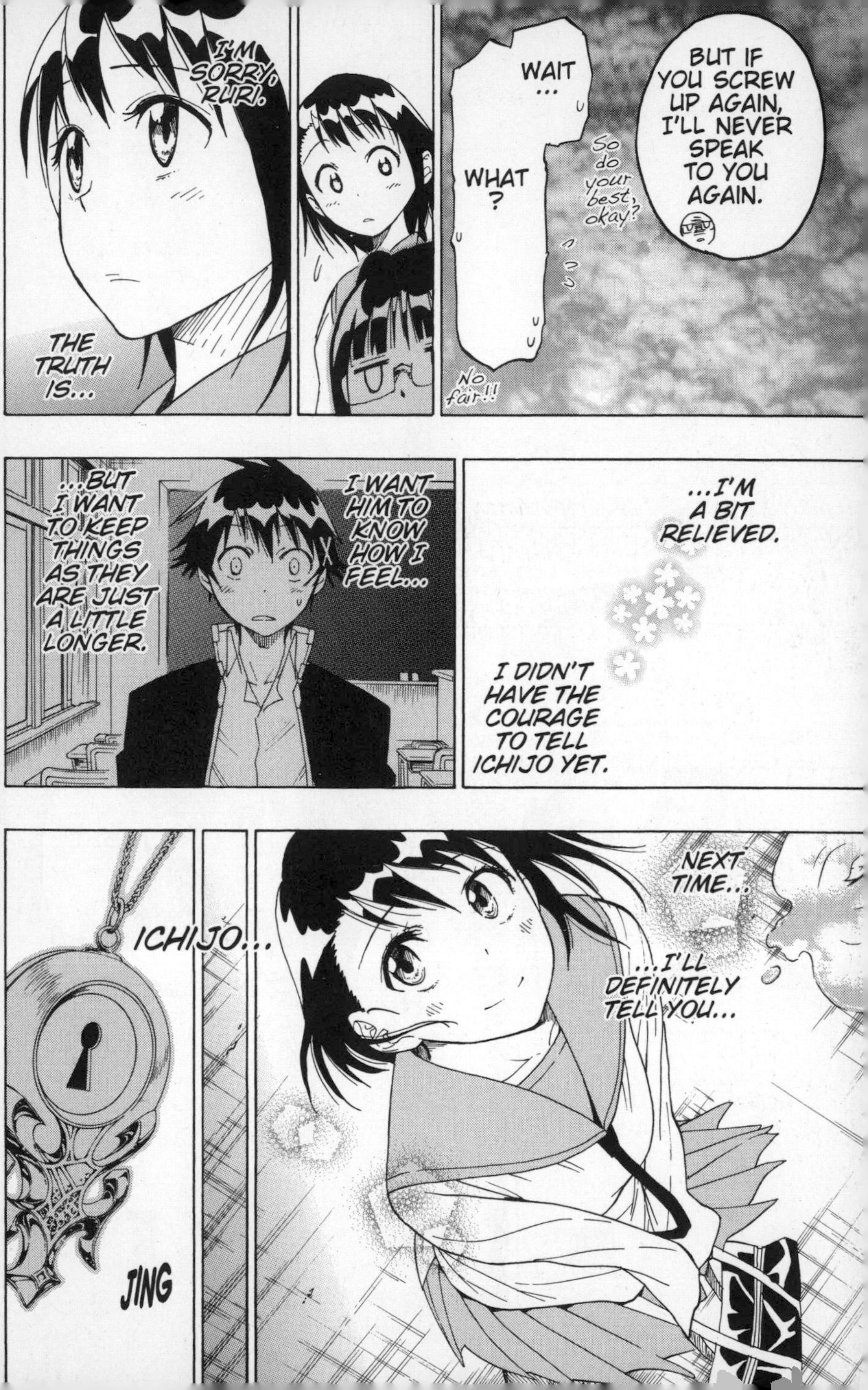
BUT IF YOU SCREW UP AGAIN, I'LL NEVER SPEAK TO YOU AGAIN.
So do your best, okay?
WAIT...
WHAT?
No fair!!
I'M SORRY, RURI.
THE TRUTH IS...
...I'M A BIT RELIEVED.
I DIDN'T HAVE THE COURAGE TO TELL ICHIJO YET.
I WANT HIM TO KNOW HOW I FEEL...
...BUT I WANT TO KEEP THINGS AS THEY ARE JUST A LITTLE LONGER.
NEXT TIME...
...I'LL DEFINITELY TELL YOU...
ICHIJO...
JING

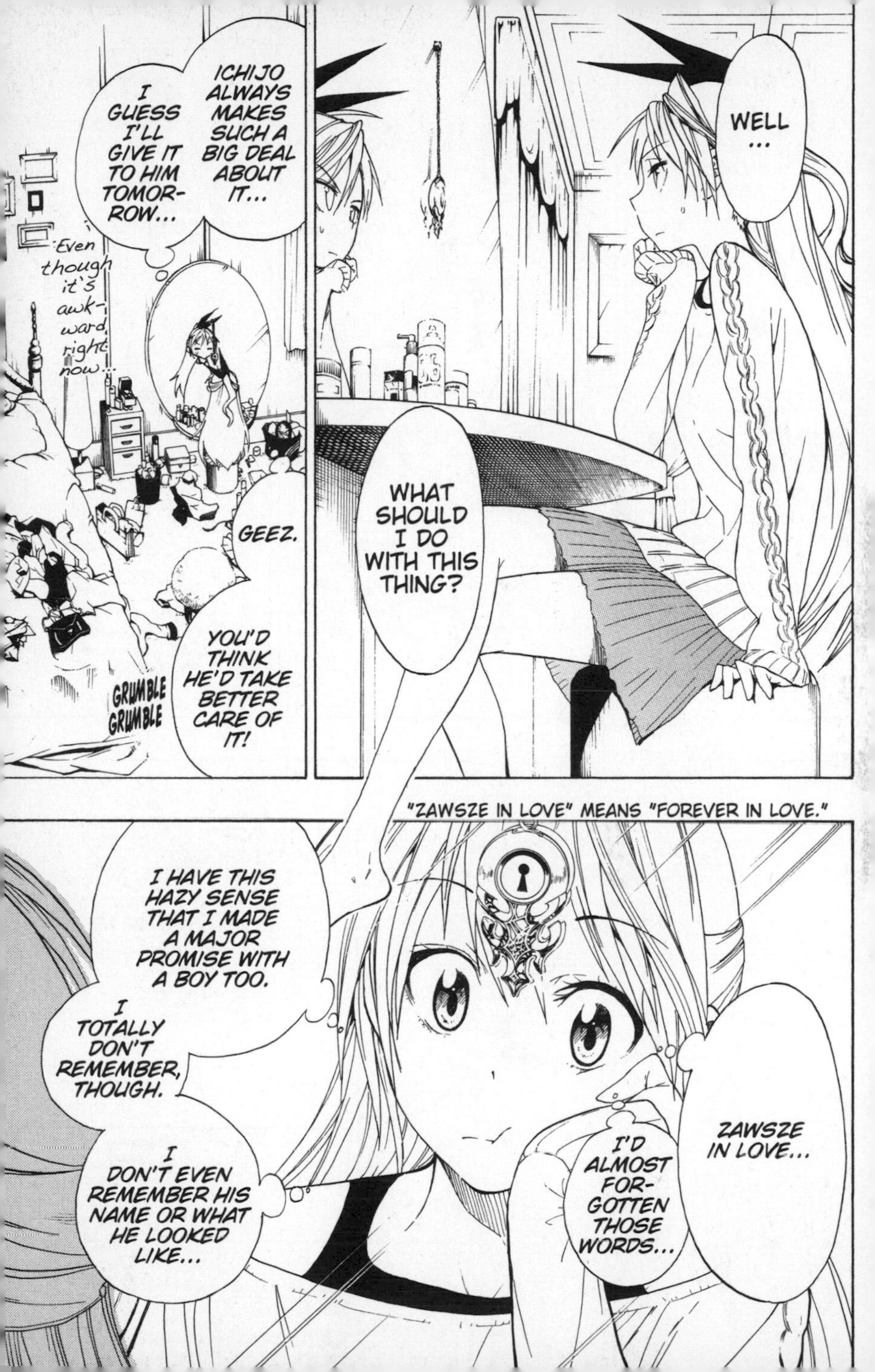
WELL ...
WHAT SHOULD I DO WITH THIS THING?
ICHIJO ALWAYS MAKES SUCH A BIG DEAL ABOUT IT...
I GUESS I'LL GIVE IT TO HIM TOMORROW...
Even though it's awkward right now...
GEEZ.
YOU'D THINK HE'D TAKE BETTER CARE OF IT!
GRUMBLE GRUMBLE
"ZAWSZE IN LOVE" MEANS "FOREVER IN LOVE."
ZAWSZE IN LOVE...
I'D ALMOST FORGOTTEN THOSE WORDS...
I HAVE THIS HAZY SENSE THAT I MADE A MAJOR PROMISE WITH A BOY TOO.
I TOTALLY DON'T REMEMBER, THOUGH.
I DON'T EVEN REMEMBER HIS NAME OR WHAT HE LOOKED LIKE...

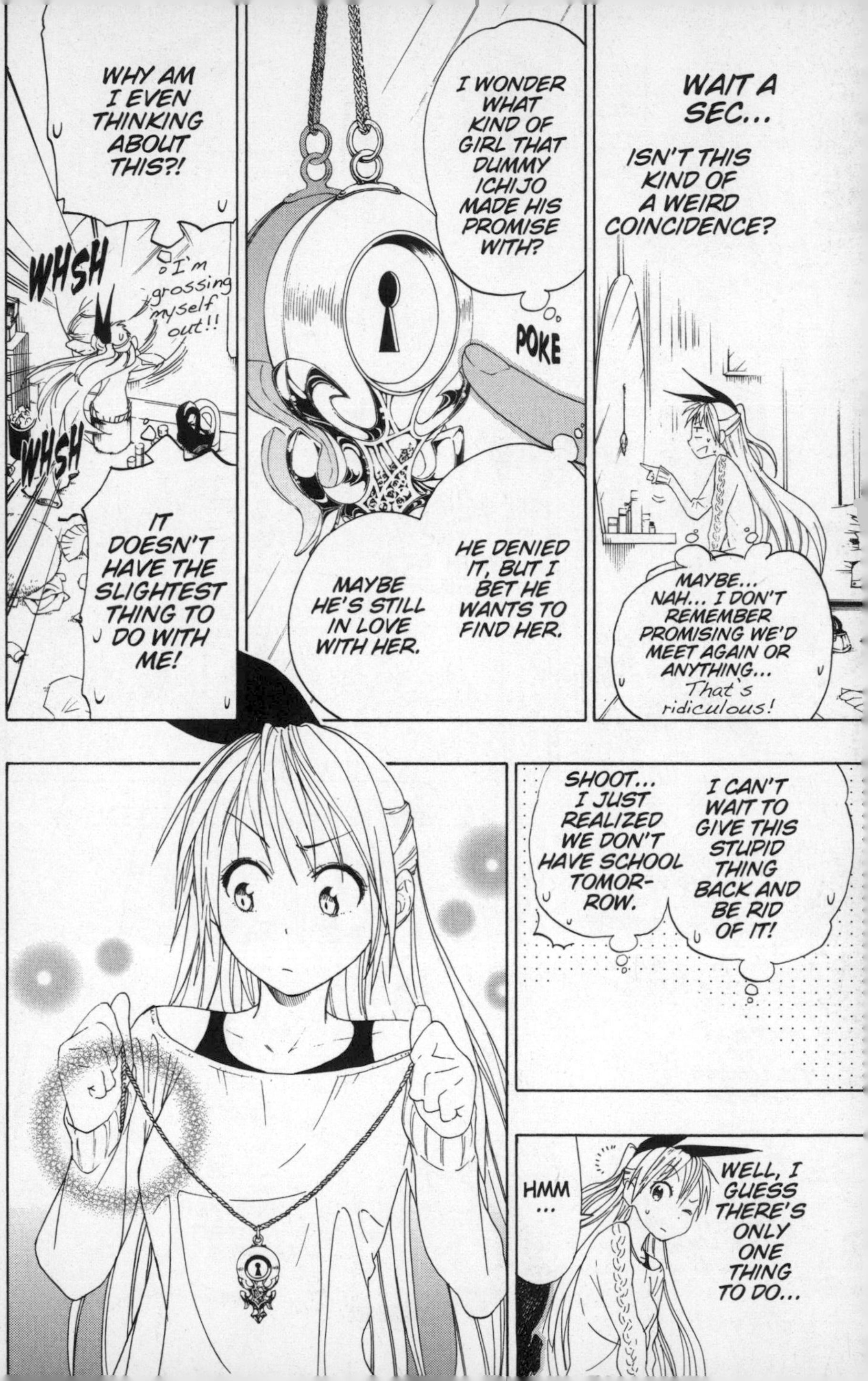
WAIT A SEC...
ISN'T THIS KIND OF A WEIRD COINCIDENCE?
MAYBE... NAH... I DON'T REMEMBER PROMISING WE'D MEET AGAIN OR ANYTHING... That's ridiculous!
I WONDER WHAT KIND OF GIRL THAT DUMMY ICHIJO MADE HIS PROMISE WITH?
POKE
HE DENIED IT, BUT I BET HE WANTS TO FIND HER.
MAYBE HE'S STILL IN LOVE WITH HER.
WHY AM I EVEN THINKING ABOUT THIS?!
WHSH
I'm grossing myself out!!
WHSH
IT DOESN'T HAVE THE SLIGHTEST THING TO DO WITH ME!
I CAN'T WAIT TO GIVE THIS STUPID THING BACK AND BE RID OF IT!
SHOOT... I JUST REALIZED WE DON'T HAVE SCHOOL TOMOR-ROW.
WELL, I GUESS THERE'S ONLY ONE THING TO DO...
HMM...

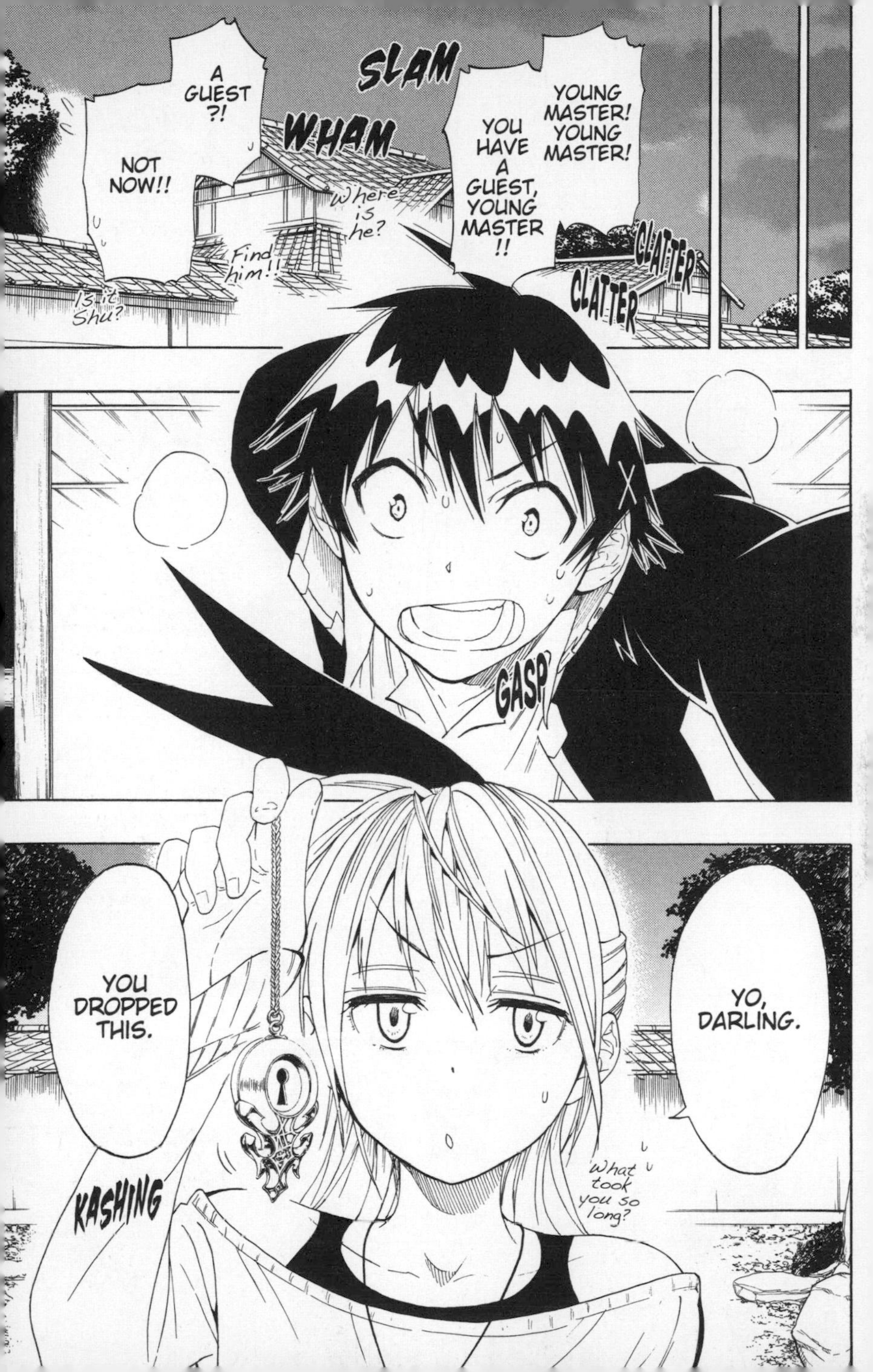
YOUNG MASTER! YOUNG MASTER!
YOU HAVE A GUEST, YOUNG MASTER!!
SLAM
WHAM
Where is he?
Find him!!
A GUEST?!
NOT NOW!!
Is it Shu?
CLATTER
CLATTER
GASP
YO, DARLING.
What took you so long?
YOU DROPPED THIS.
KASHING

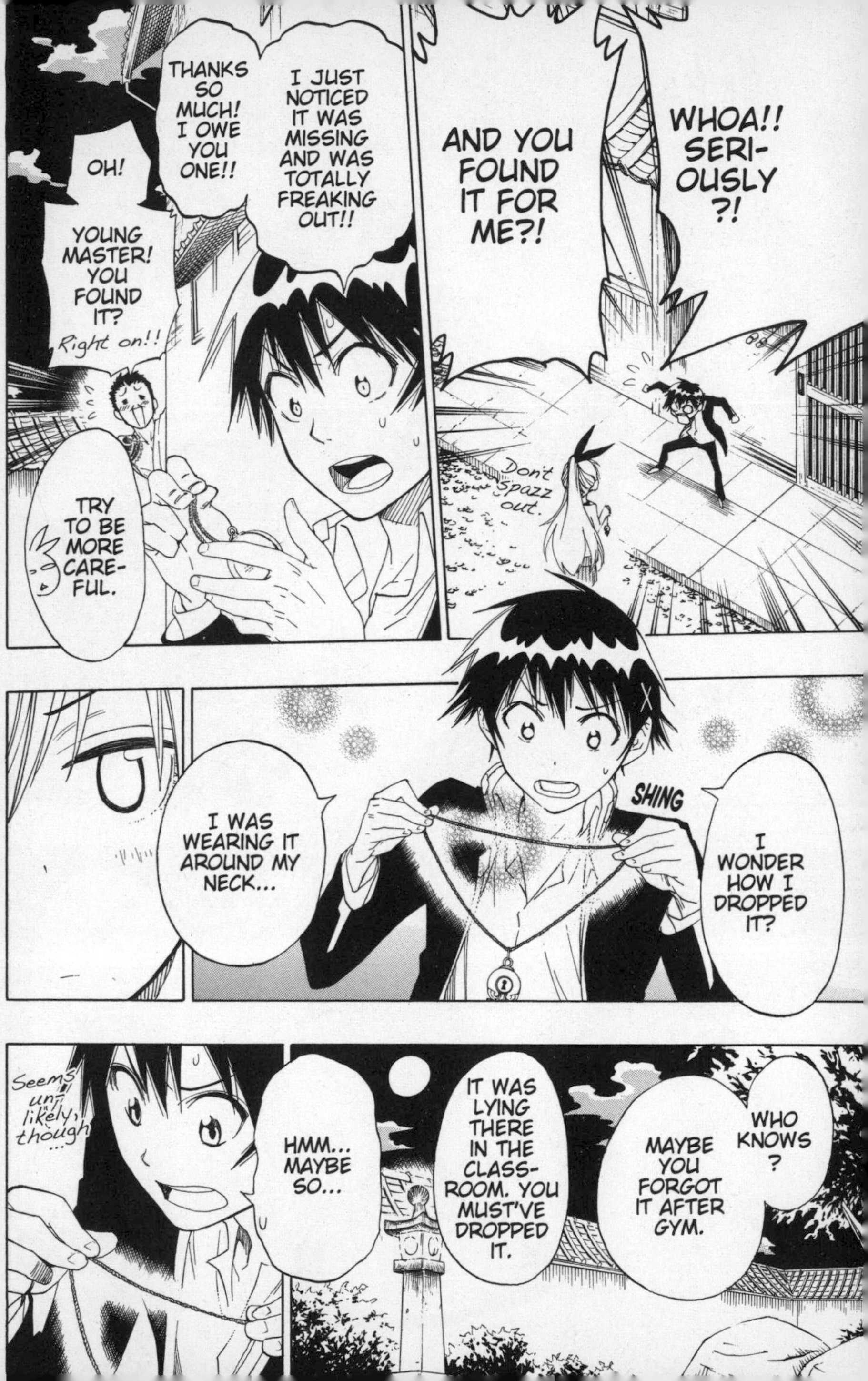
WHOA!! SERIOUSLY?!
AND YOU FOUND IT FOR ME?!
Don't spazz out.
I JUST NOTICED IT WAS MISSING AND WAS TOTALLY FREAKING OUT!!
THANKS SO MUCH! I OWE YOU ONE!!
OH!
YOUNG MASTER! YOU FOUND IT?
Right on!!
TRY TO BE MORE CAREFUL.
I WONDER HOW I DROPPED IT?
SHING
I WAS WEARING IT AROUND MY NECK...
WHO KNOWS?
MAYBE YOU FORGOT IT AFTER GYM.
IT WAS LYING THERE IN THE CLASSROOM. YOU MUST'VE DROPPED IT.
HMM... MAYBE SO...
Seems unlikely, though...

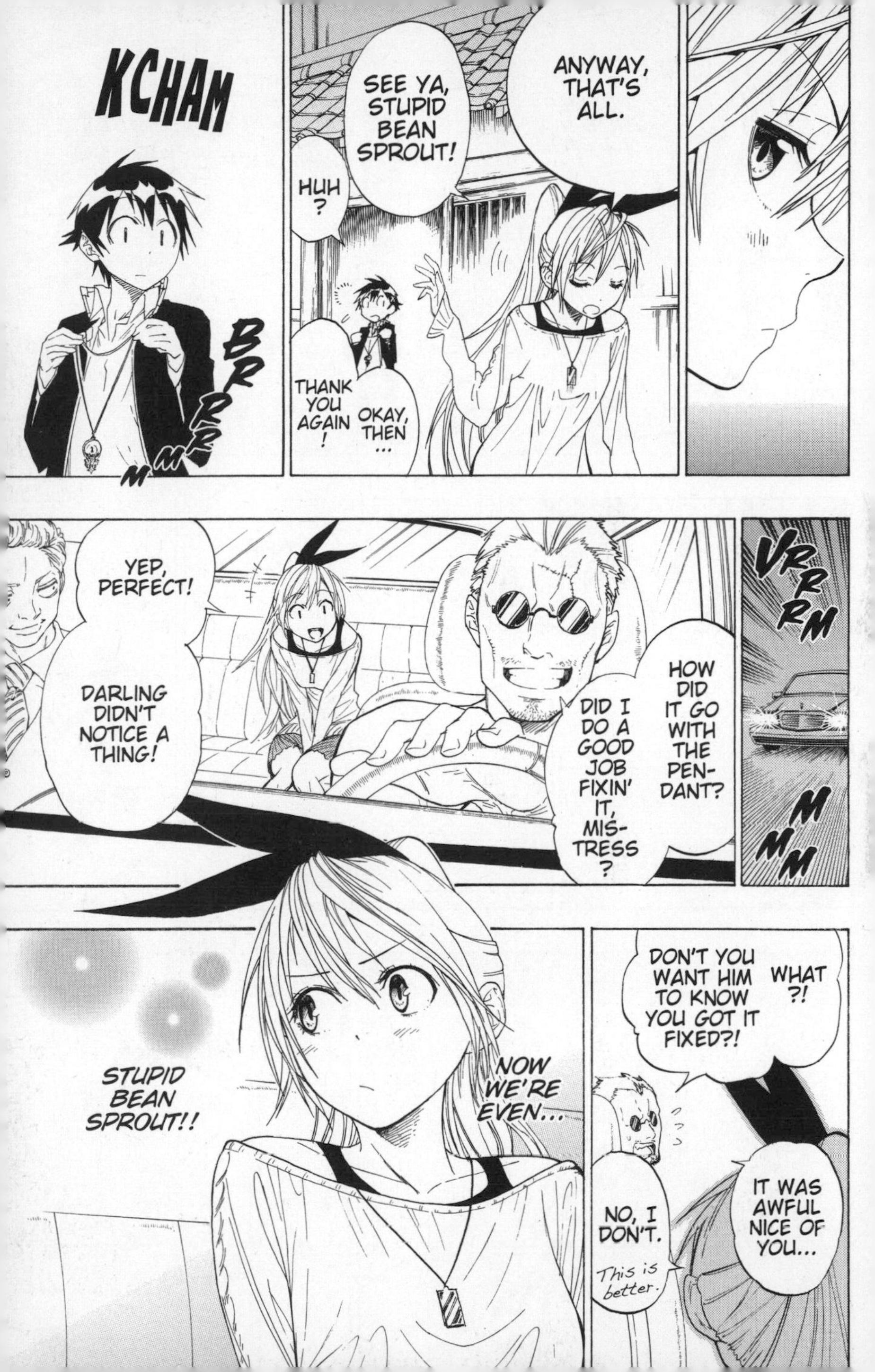
ANYWAY, THAT'S ALL.
SEE YA, STUPID BEAN SPROUT!
HUH?
OKAY, THEN...
THANK YOU AGAIN!
KCHAM
BRRRRMMM
VRRRRMMMM
HOW DID IT GO WITH THE PEN-DANT?
DID I DO A GOOD JOB FIXIN' IT, MIS-TRESS?
YEP, PERFECT!
DARLING DIDN'T NOTICE A THING!
WHAT?!
DON'T YOU WANT HIM TO KNOW YOU GOT IT FIXED?!
IT WAS AWFUL NICE OF YOU...
NO, I DON'T.
This is better.
NOW WE'RE EVEN...
STUPID BEAN SPROUT!!

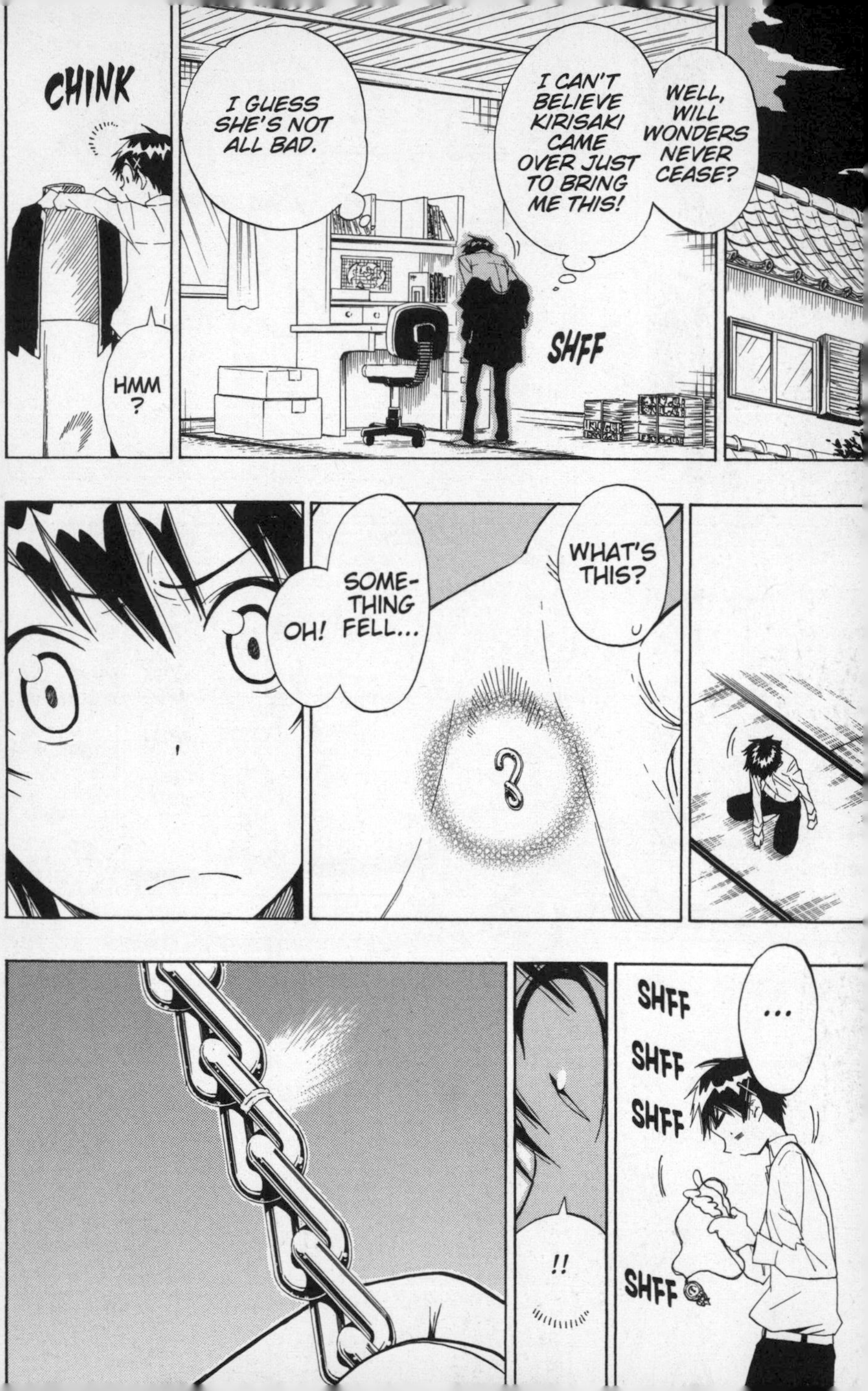
WELL, WILL WONDERS NEVER CEASE?
I CAN'T BELIEVE KIRISAKI CAME OVER JUST TO BRING ME THIS!
I GUESS SHE'S NOT ALL BAD.
SHFF
CHINK
HMM?
WHAT'S THIS?
SOME-THING FELL...
OH!
...
SHFF
SHFF
SHFF
SHFF
!!

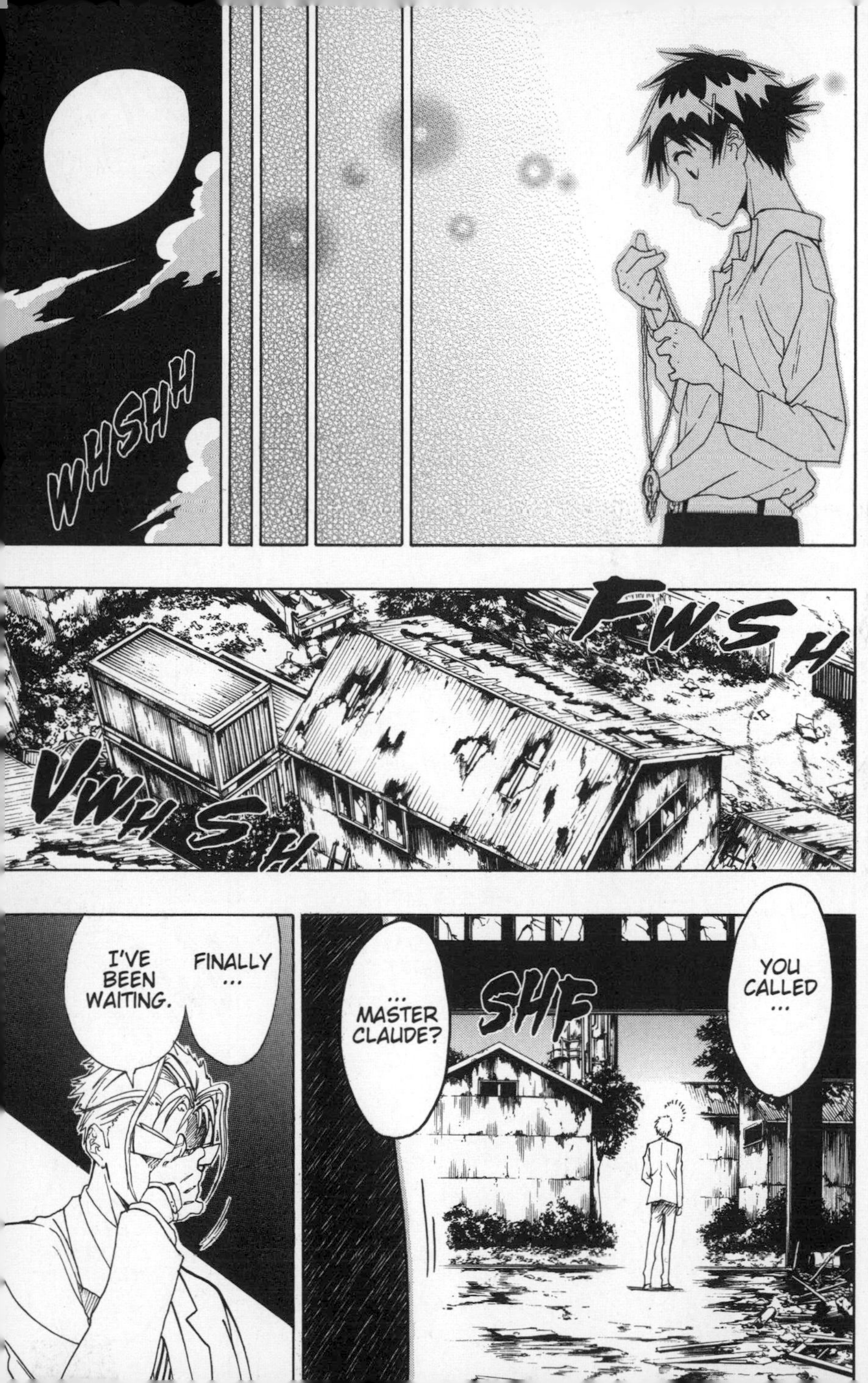
WHSHH
FWSH
VWHSH
YOU CALLED ...
... MASTER CLAUDE?
SHF
FINALLY ...
I'VE BEEN WAITING.

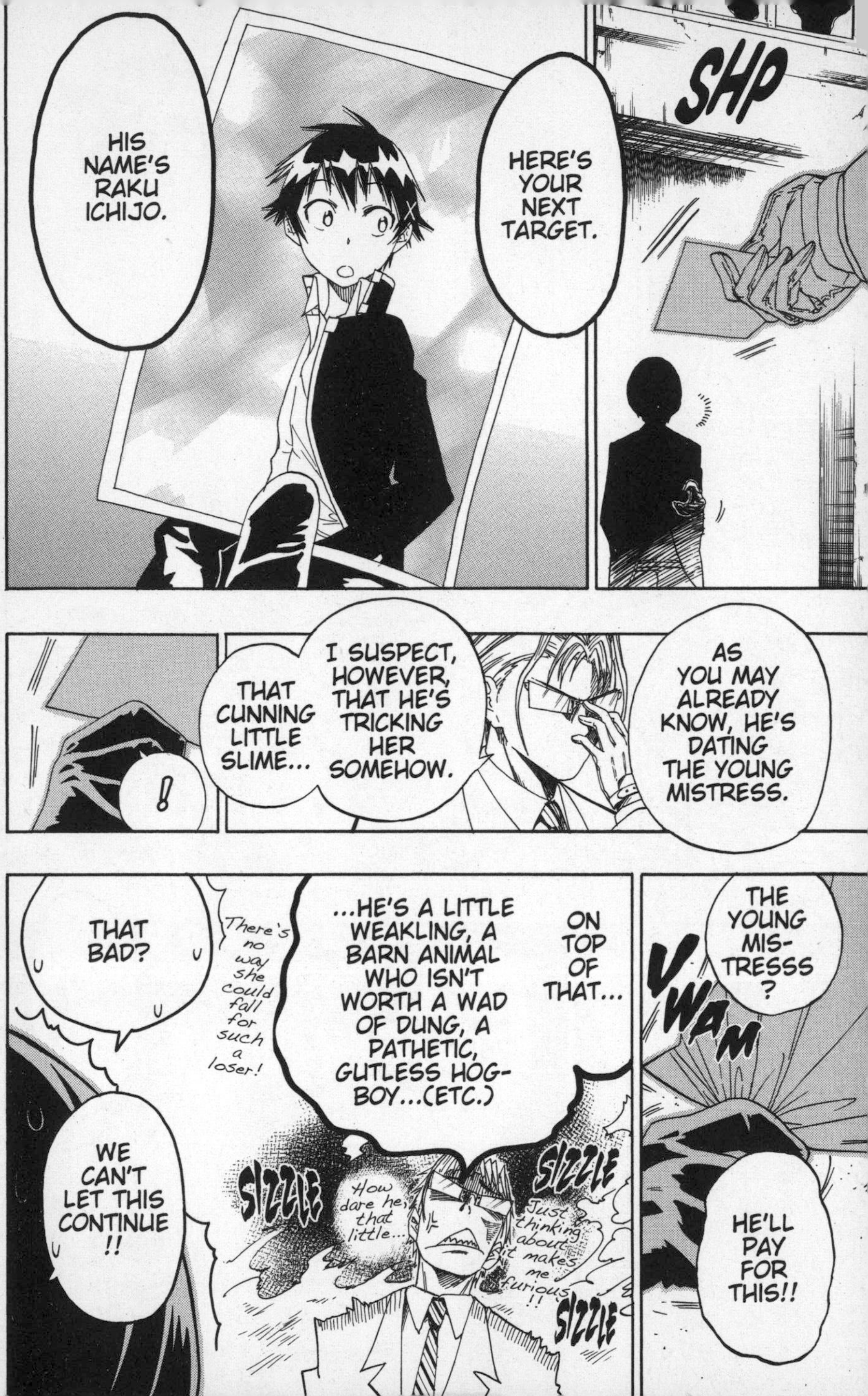
SHP
HERE'S YOUR NEXT TARGET.
HIS NAME'S RAKU ICHIJO.
AS YOU MAY ALREADY KNOW, HE'S DATING THE YOUNG MISTRESS.
I SUSPECT, HOWEVER, THAT HE'S TRICKING HER SOMEHOW.
THAT CUNNING LITTLE SLIME...
!
THE YOUNG MIS-TRESSS?
VWAM
HE'LL PAY FOR THIS!!
ON TOP OF THAT...
...HE'S A LITTLE WEAKLING, A BARN ANIMAL WHO ISN'T WORTH A WAD OF DUNG, A PATHETIC, GUTLESS HOG-BOY...(ETC.)
SIZZLE
How dare he, that little...
Just thinking about it makes me furious!!
SIZZLE
SIZZLE
THAT BAD?
There's no way she could fall for such a loser!
WE CAN'T LET THIS CONTINUE!!

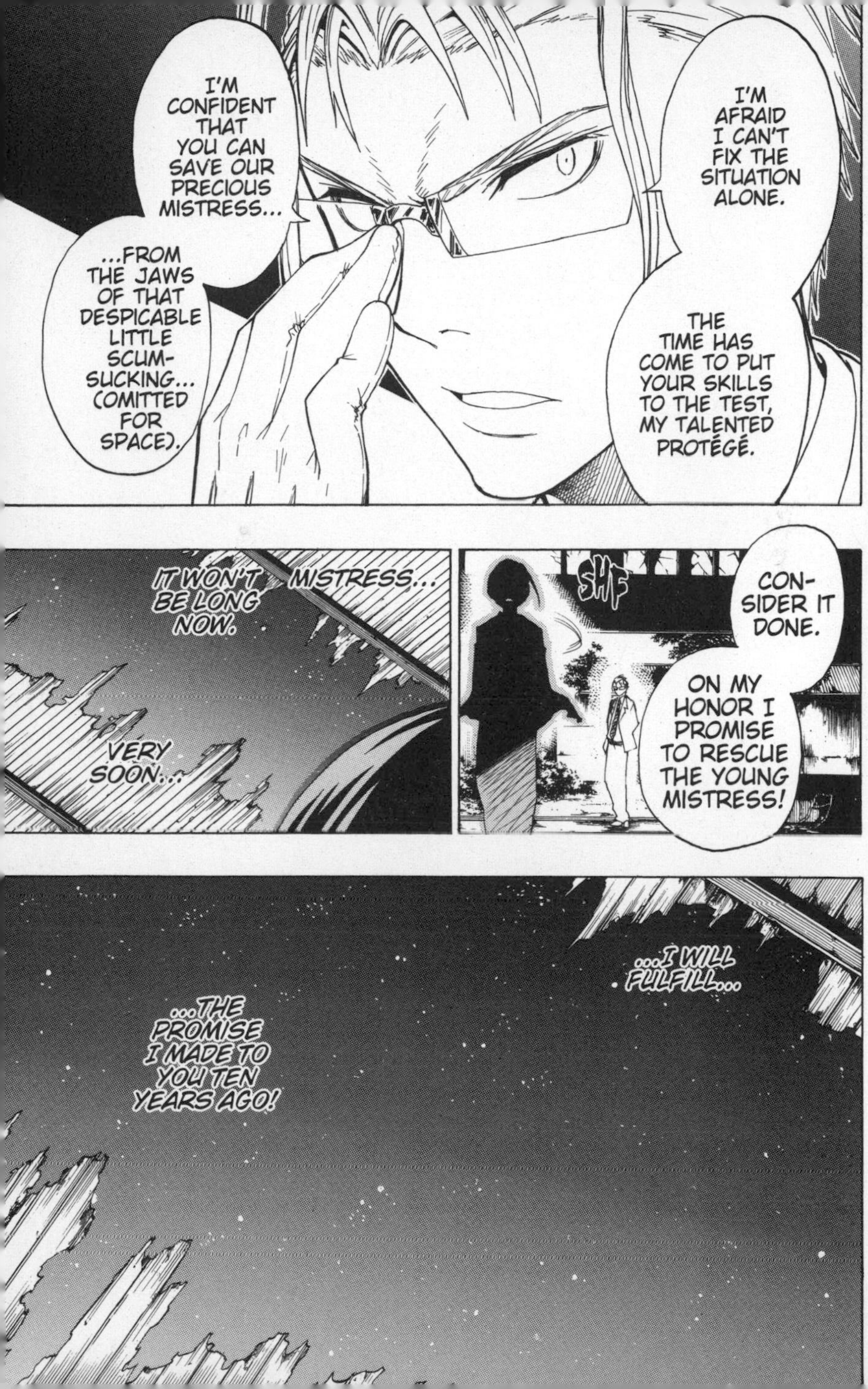
I'M AFRAID I CAN'T FIX THE SITUATION ALONE.
THE TIME HAS COME TO PUT YOUR SKILLS TO THE TEST, MY TALENTED PROTÉGÉ.
I'M CONFIDENT THAT YOU CAN SAVE OUR PRECIOUS MISTRESS...
...FROM THE JAWS OF THAT DESPICABLE LITTLE SCUM-SUCKING... (COMITTED FOR SPACE).
SHF
CONSIDER IT DONE.
ON MY HONOR I PROMISE TO RESCUE THE YOUNG MISTRESS!
MISTRESS...
IT WON'T BE LONG NOW.
VERY SOON...
...I WILL FULFILL...
...THE PROMISE I MADE TO YOU TEN YEARS AGO!

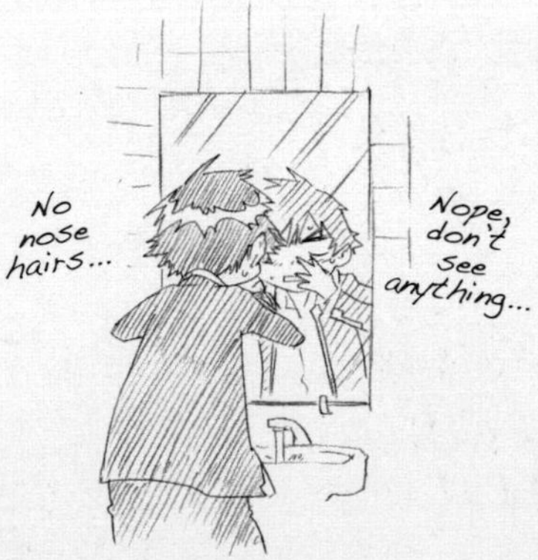
Nope, don't see anything...
No nose hairs...

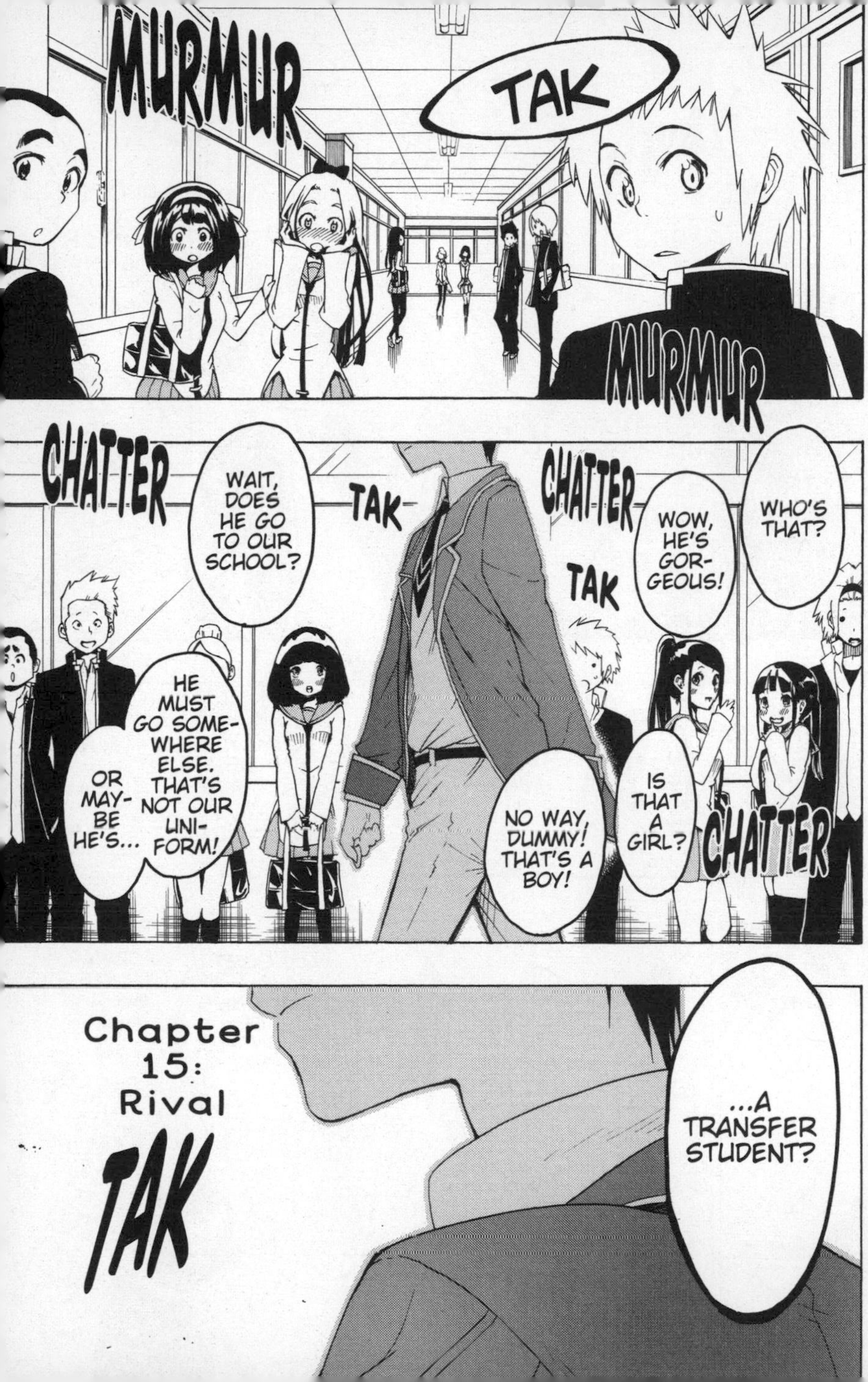
TAK
MURMUR
MURMUR
WHO'S THAT?
WOW, HE'S GOR-GEOUS!
CHATTER
TAK
IS THAT A GIRL?
NO WAY, DUMMY! THAT'S A BOY!
CHATTER
TAK
WAIT, DOES HE GO TO OUR SCHOOL?
CHATTER
HE MUST GO SOME-WHERE ELSE. THAT'S NOT OUR UNI-FORM!
OR MAY-BE HE'S...
...A TRANSFER STUDENT?
Chapter 15: Rival
TAK

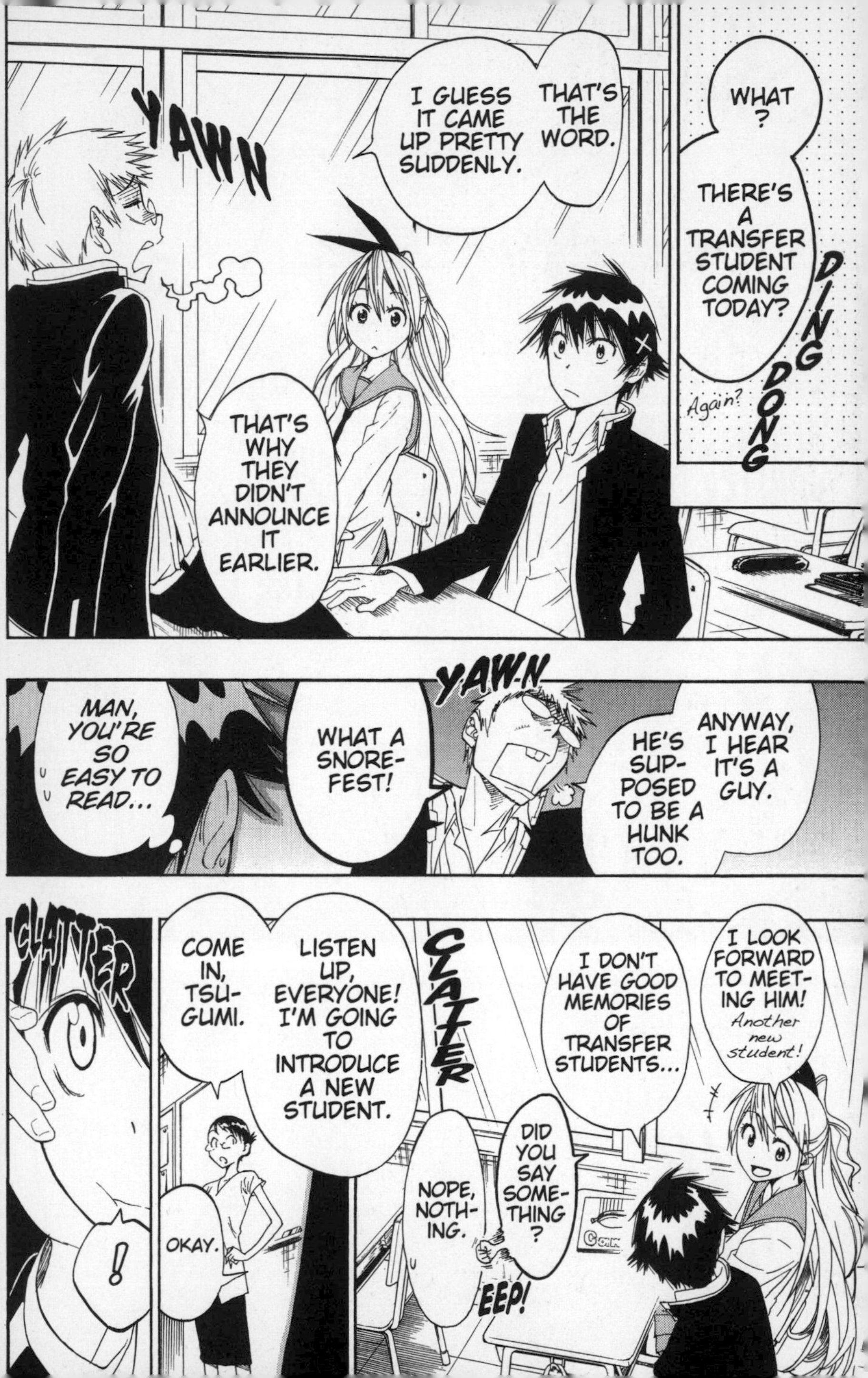
WHAT?
THERE'S A TRANSFER STUDENT COMING TODAY?
DING DONG
Again?
THAT'S THE WORD.
I GUESS IT CAME UP PRETTY SUDDENLY.
YAWN
THAT'S WHY THEY DIDN'T ANNOUNCE IT EARLIER.
ANYWAY, I HEAR IT'S A GUY.
HE'S SUP-POSED TO BE A HUNK TOO.
YAWN
WHAT A SNORE-FEST!
MAN, YOU'RE SO EASY TO READ...
I LOOK FORWARD TO MEET-ING HIM!
Another new student!
I DON'T HAVE GOOD MEMORIES OF TRANSFER STUDENTS...
DID YOU SAY SOME-THING?
NOPE, NOTH-ING.
EEP!
CLATTER
LISTEN UP, EVERYONE! I'M GOING TO INTRODUCE A NEW STUDENT.
COME IN, TSU-GUMI.
OKAY.
CLATTER
!

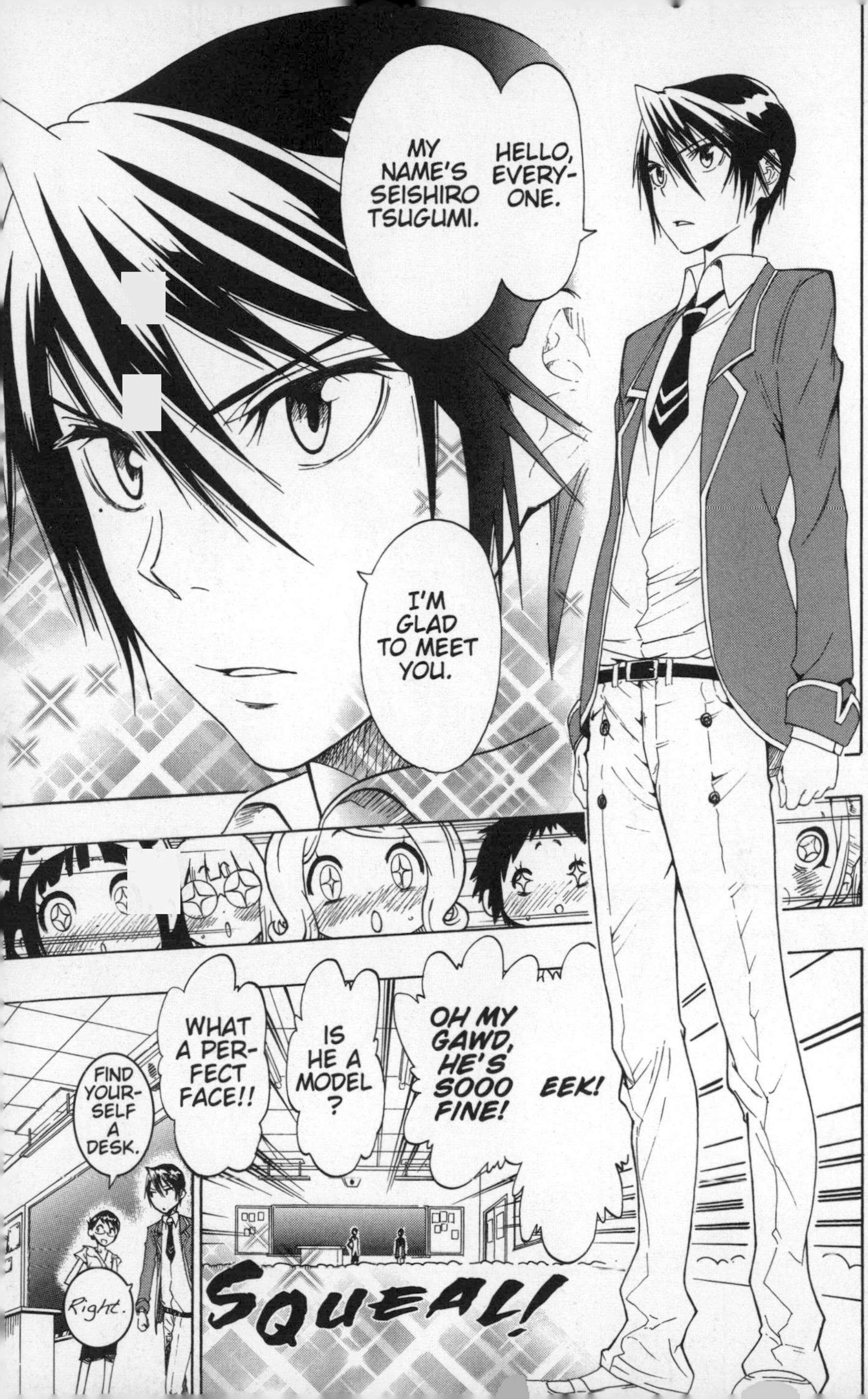
HELLO, EVERY-ONE.
MY NAME'S SEISHIRO TSUGUMI.
I'M GLAD TO MEET YOU.
EEK!
OH MY GAWD, HE'S SOOO FINE!
IS HE A MODEL?
WHAT A PER-FECT FACE!!
SQUEAL!
FIND YOUR-SELF A DESK.
Right.

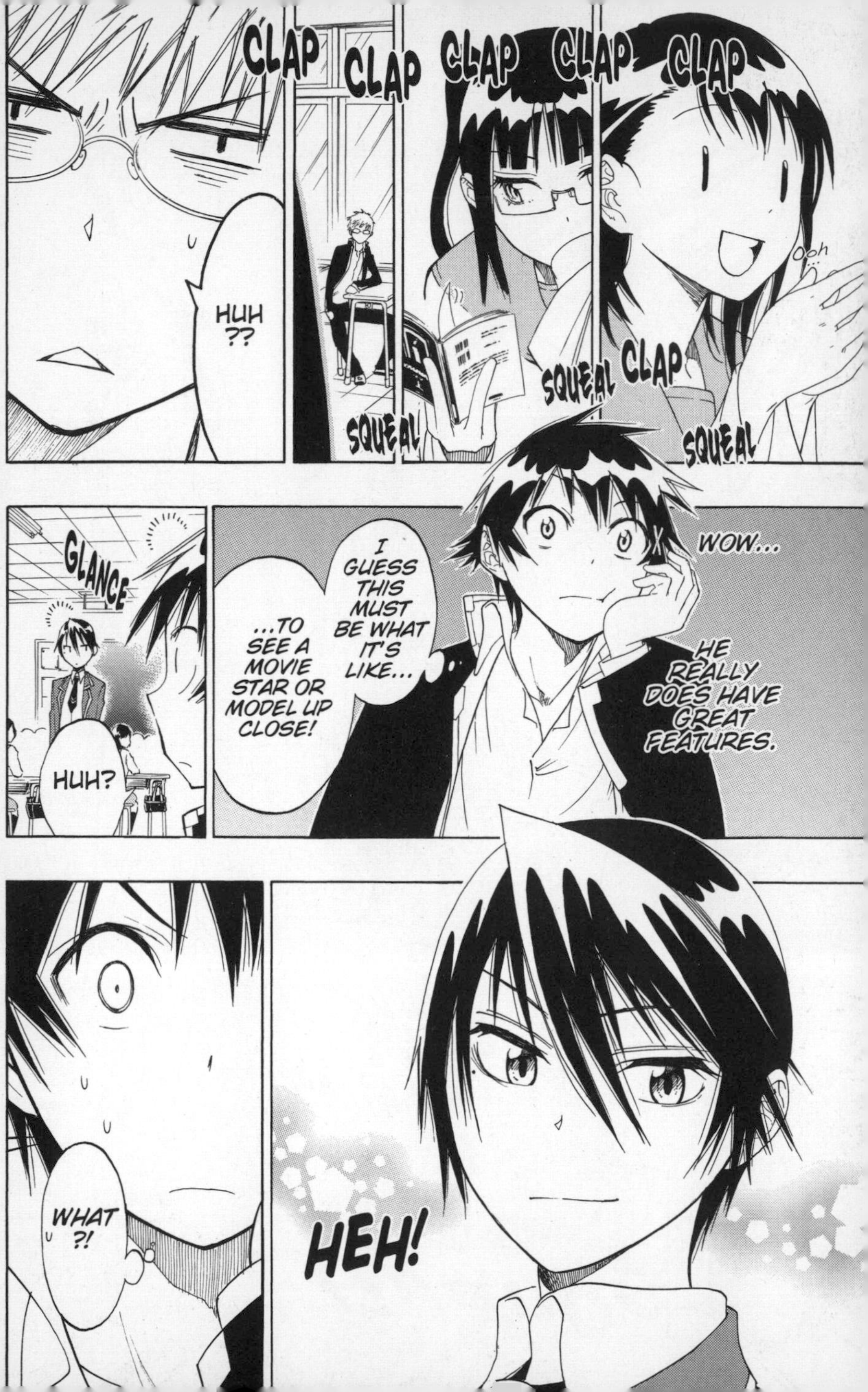
CLAP
Ooh...
SQUEAL
CLAP
SQUEAL
CLAP
CLAP
SQUEAL
CLAP
CLAP
HUH ??
WOW...
HE REALLY DOES HAVE GREAT FEATURES.
I GUESS THIS MUST BE WHAT IT'S LIKE...
...TO SEE A MOVIE STAR OR MODEL UP CLOSE!
GLANCE
HUH?
HEH!
WHAT ?!

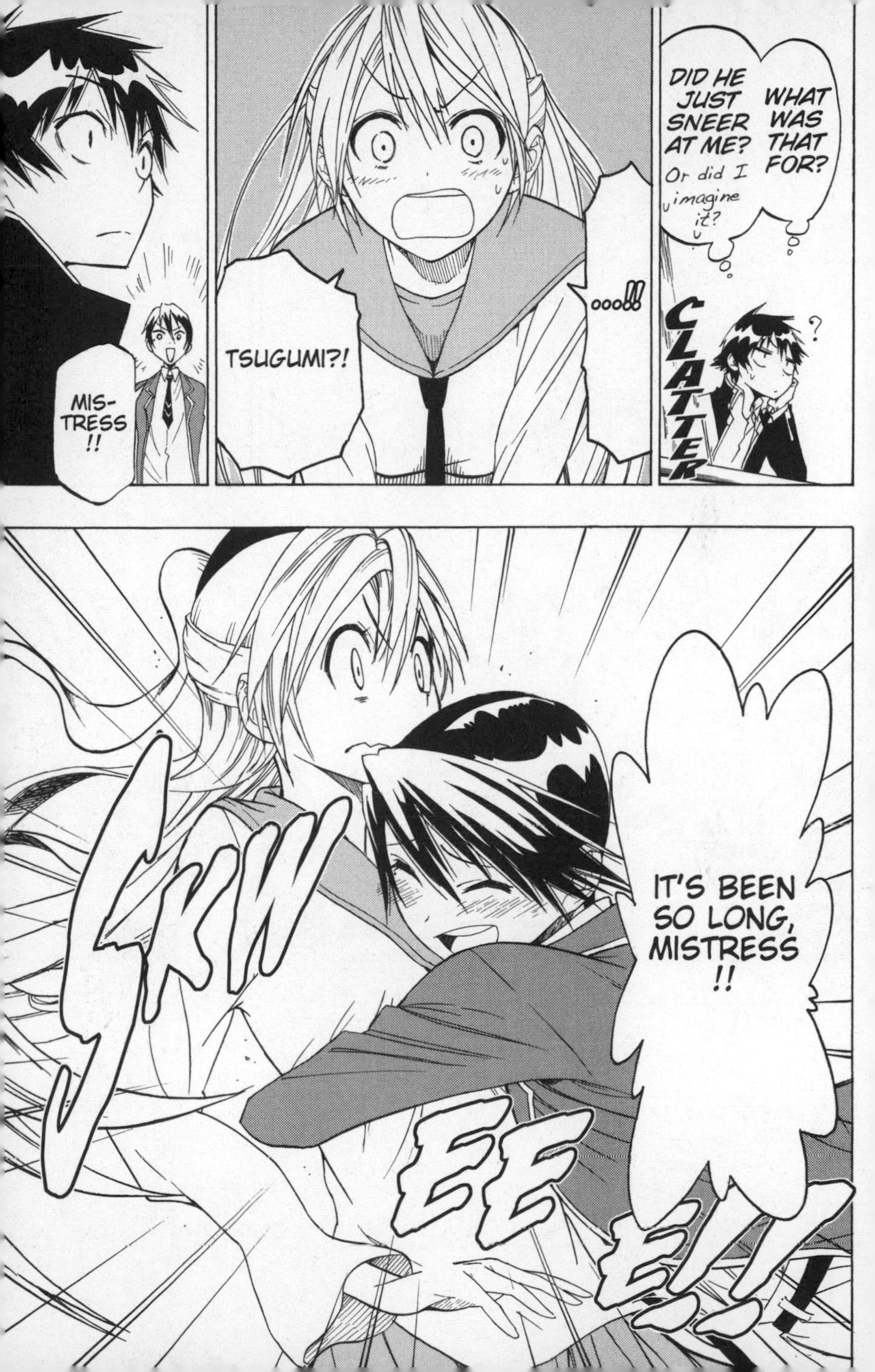

WHAT WAS THAT FOR?
DID HE JUST SNEER AT ME?
Or did I imagine it?
CLATTER
ooo!!
TSUGUMI?!
MIS-TRESS !!
IT'S BEEN SO LONG, MISTRESS !!
SKW
EE
EE!

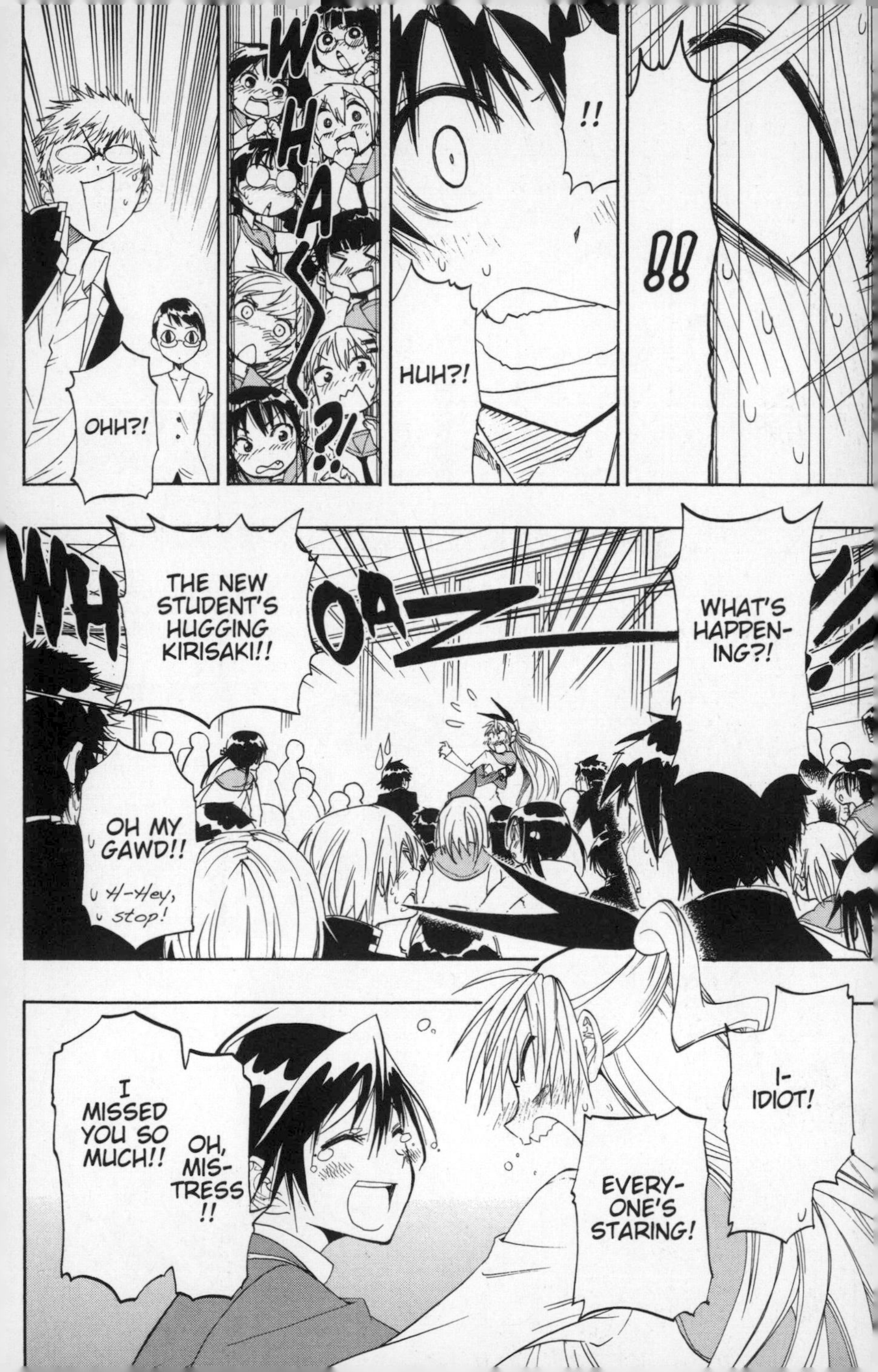
!!
!!
HUH?!
WHA
?!
OHH?!
!!
WHAT'S HAPPEN-ING?!
THE NEW STUDENT'S HUGGING KIRISAKI!!
OH MY GAWD!!
H-Hey, stop!
I- IDIOT!
EVERY-ONE'S STARING!
OH, MIS-TRESS!!
I MISSED YOU SO MUCH!!

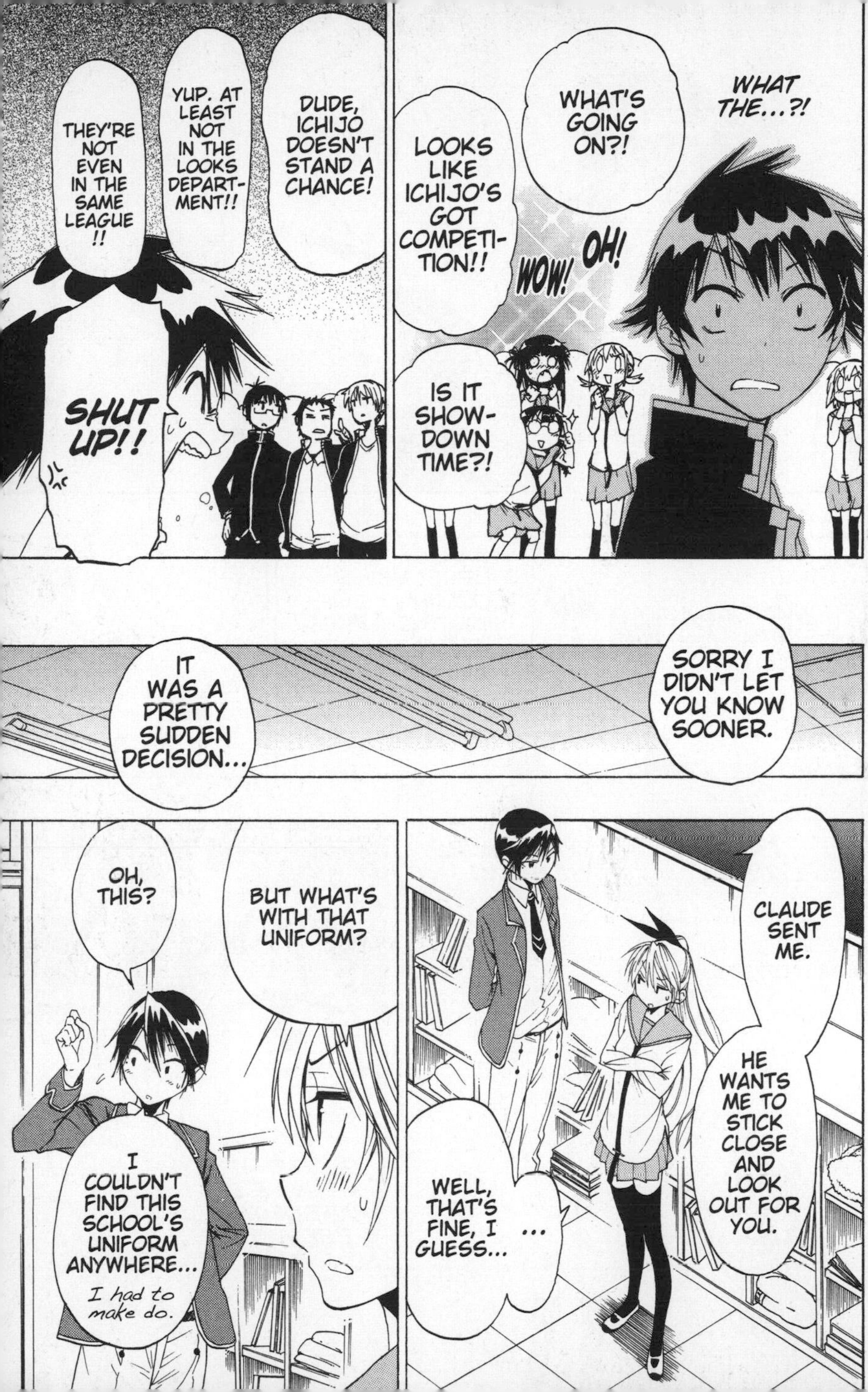
WHAT THE...?!
WHAT'S GOING ON?!
LOOKS LIKE ICHIJO'S GOT COMPETITION!!
OH!
WOW!
IS IT SHOWDOWN TIME?!
DUDE, ICHIJO DOESN'T STAND A CHANCE!
YUP. AT LEAST NOT IN THE LOOKS DEPARTMENT!!
THEY'RE NOT EVEN IN THE SAME LEAGUE!!
SHUT UP!!
SORRY I DIDN'T LET YOU KNOW SOONER.
IT WAS A PRETTY SUDDEN DECISION...
CLAUDE SENT ME.
HE WANTS ME TO STICK CLOSE AND LOOK OUT FOR YOU.
...
WELL, THAT'S FINE, I GUESS...
BUT WHAT'S WITH THAT UNIFORM?
OH, THIS?
I COULDN'T FIND THIS SCHOOL'S UNIFORM ANYWHERE...
I had to make do.

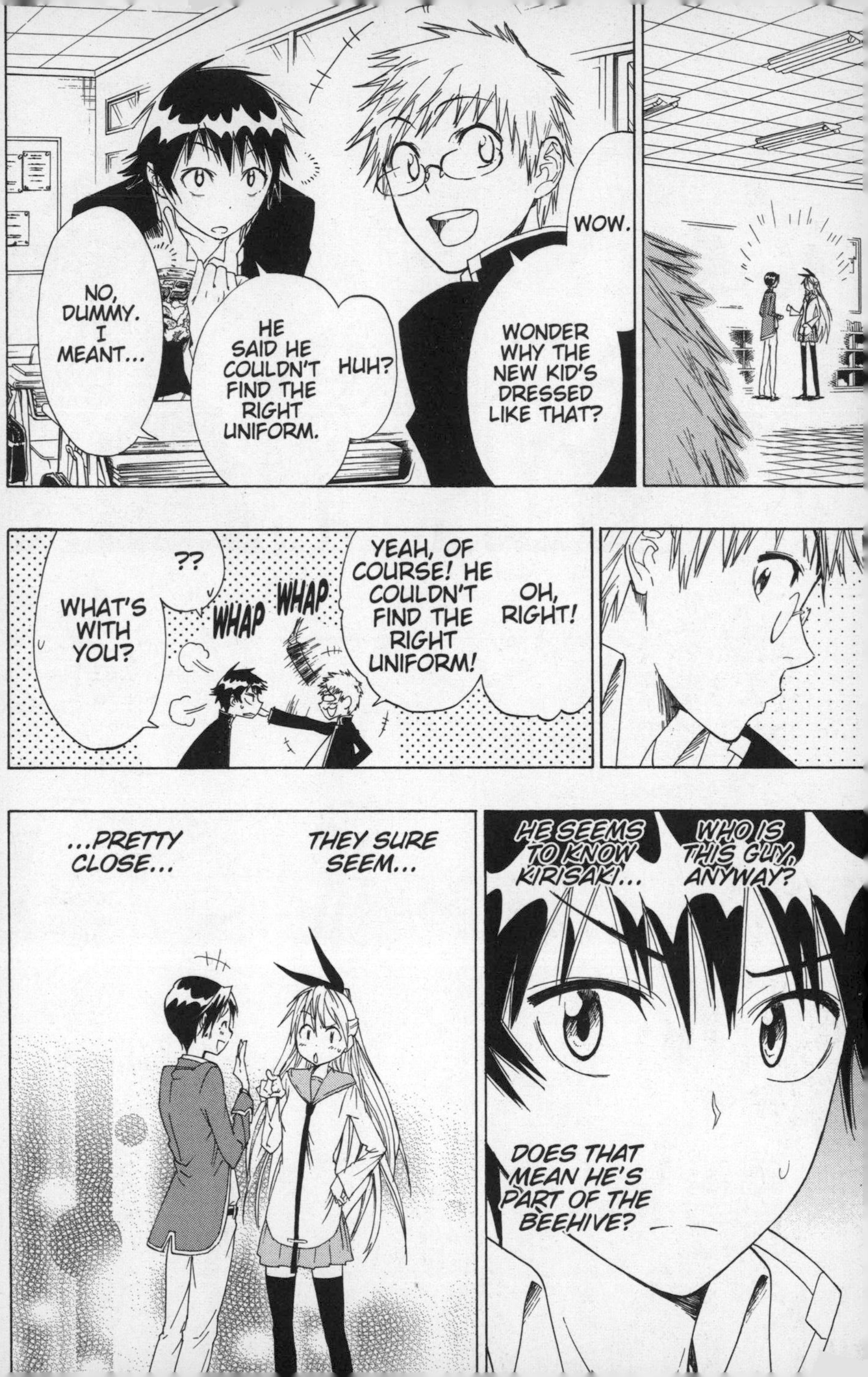
WOW.
WONDER WHY THE NEW KID'S DRESSED LIKE THAT?
HUH?
HE SAID HE COULDN'T FIND THE RIGHT UNIFORM.
NO, DUMMY. I MEANT...
OH, RIGHT!
YEAH, OF COURSE! HE COULDN'T FIND THE RIGHT UNIFORM!
WHAP
WHAP
??
WHAT'S WITH YOU?
WHO IS THIS GUY, ANYWAY?
HE SEEMS TO KNOW KIRISAKI...
DOES THAT MEAN HE'S PART OF THE BEEHIVE?
THEY SURE SEEM...
...PRETTY CLOSE...

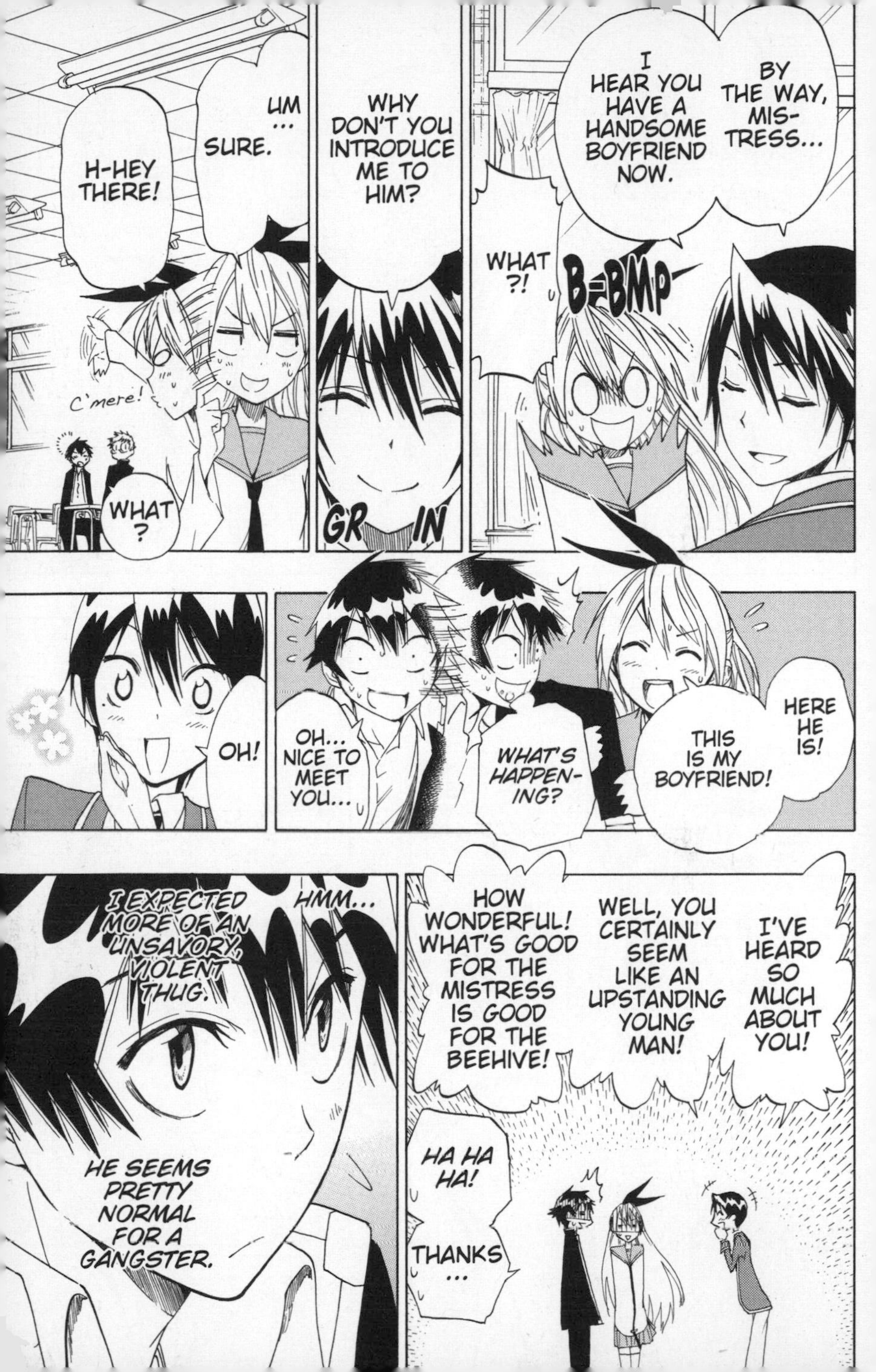
BY THE WAY, MIS-TRESS...
I HEAR YOU HAVE A HANDSOME BOYFRIEND NOW.
WHAT ?!
B-BMP
WHY DON'T YOU INTRODUCE ME TO HIM?
GR IN
UM ... SURE.
H-HEY THERE!
C'mere!
WHAT ?
HERE HE IS!
THIS IS MY BOYFRIEND!
WHAT'S HAPPEN-ING?
OH... NICE TO MEET YOU...
OH!
I'VE HEARD SO MUCH ABOUT YOU!
WELL, YOU CERTAINLY SEEM LIKE AN UPSTANDING YOUNG MAN!
HOW WONDERFUL! WHAT'S GOOD FOR THE MISTRESS IS GOOD FOR THE BEEHIVE!
HA HA HA!
THANKS ...
HMM...
I EXPECTED MORE OF AN UNSAVORY, VIOLENT THUG.
HE SEEMS PRETTY NORMAL FOR A GANGSTER.

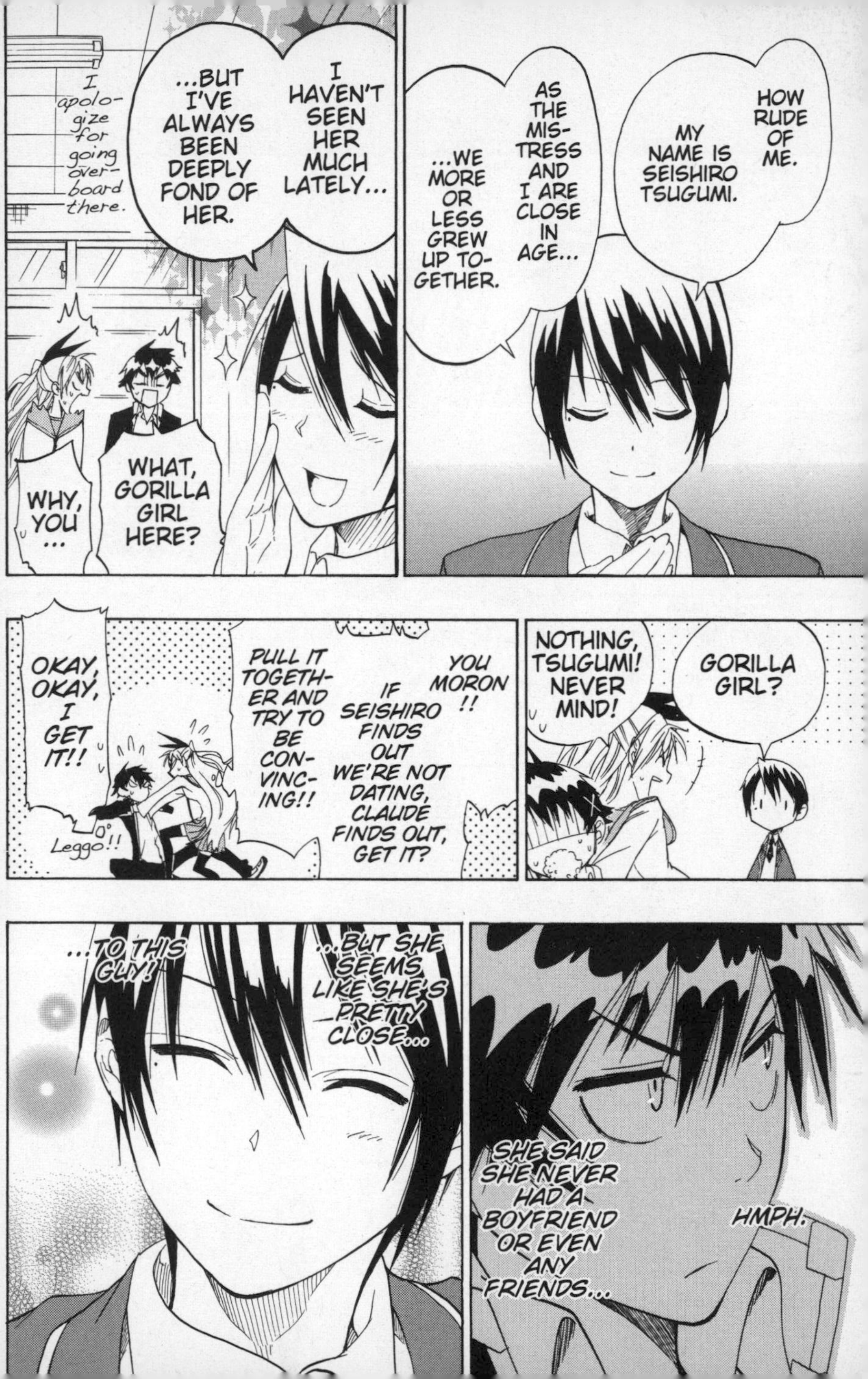
HOW RUDE OF ME.
MY NAME IS SEISHIRO TSUGUMI.
AS THE MISTRESS AND I ARE CLOSE IN AGE...
...WE MORE OR LESS GREW UP TOGETHER.
I HAVEN'T SEEN HER MUCH LATELY...
...BUT I'VE ALWAYS BEEN DEEPLY FOND OF HER.
I apologize for going overboard there.
WHAT, GORILLA GIRL HERE?
WHY, YOU...
GORILLA GIRL?
NOTHING, TSUGUMI! NEVER MIND!
YOU MORON!!
IF SEISHIRO FINDS OUT WE'RE NOT DATING, CLAUDE FINDS OUT, GET IT?
PULL IT TOGETHER AND TRY TO BE CONVINCING!!
OKAY, OKAY, I GET IT!!
Leggo!!
HMPH.
SHE SAID SHE NEVER HAD A BOYFRIEND OR EVEN ANY FRIENDS...
...BUT SHE SEEMS LIKE SHE'S PRETTY CLOSE...
...TO THIS GUY!

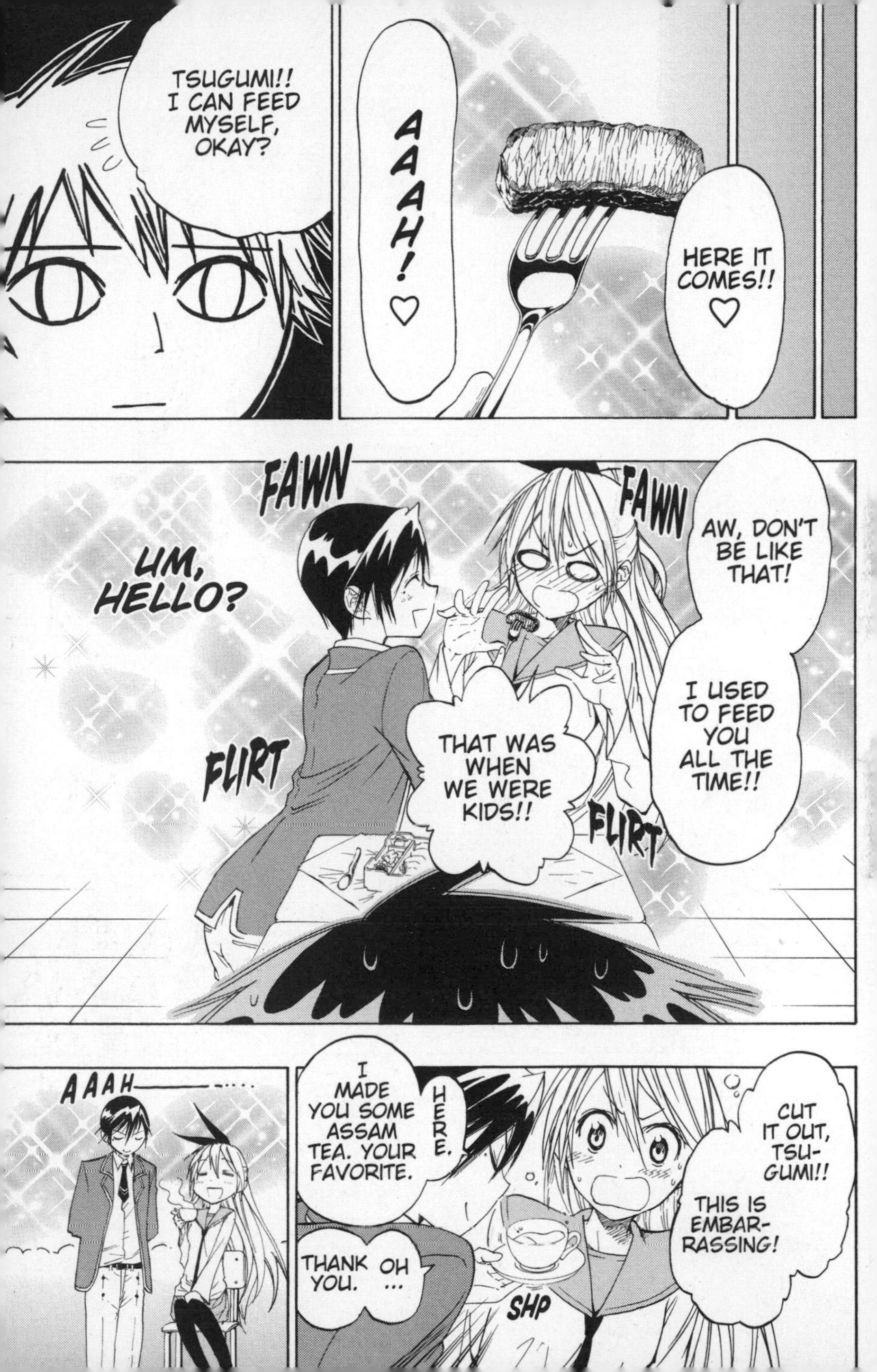
HERE IT COMES!! ♡
AAAAH! ♡
TSUGUMI!! I CAN FEED MYSELF, OKAY?
FAWN
AW, DON'T BE LIKE THAT!
I USED TO FEED YOU ALL THE TIME!!
FAWN
UM, HELLO?
THAT WAS WHEN WE WERE KIDS!!
FLIRT
FLIRT
CUT IT OUT, TSU-GUMI!!
THIS IS EMBAR-RASSING!
HERE.
I MADE YOU SOME ASSAM TEA. YOUR FAVORITE.
OH ...
THANK YOU.
SHP
AAAH——.....

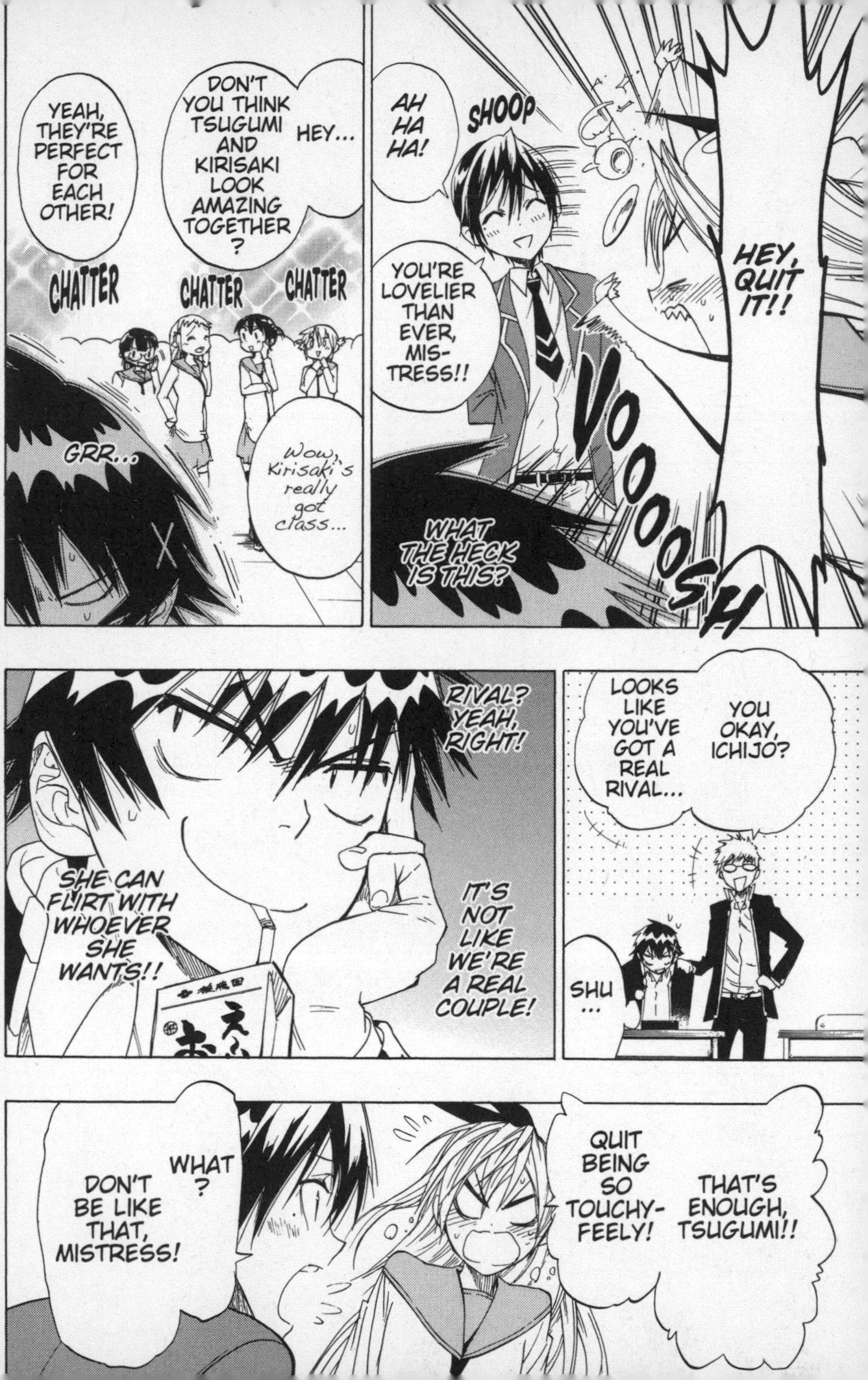
HEY, QUIT IT!!
SHOOP
AH HA HA!
YOU'RE LOVELIER THAN EVER, MIS-TRESS!!
VOOOOOSH
WHAT THE HECK IS THIS?
HEY...
DON'T YOU THINK TSUGUMI AND KIRISAKI LOOK AMAZING TOGETHER?
YEAH, THEY'RE PERFECT FOR EACH OTHER!
CHATTER
CHATTER
CHATTER
Wow, Kirisaki's really got class...
GRR...
YOU OKAY, ICHIJO?
LOOKS LIKE YOU'VE GOT A REAL RIVAL...
SHU...
RIVAL? YEAH, RIGHT!
IT'S NOT LIKE WE'RE A REAL COUPLE!
SHE CAN FLIRT WITH WHOEVER SHE WANTS!!
THAT'S ENOUGH, TSUGUMI!!
QUIT BEING SO TOUCHY-FEELY!
WHAT?
DON'T BE LIKE THAT, MISTRESS!

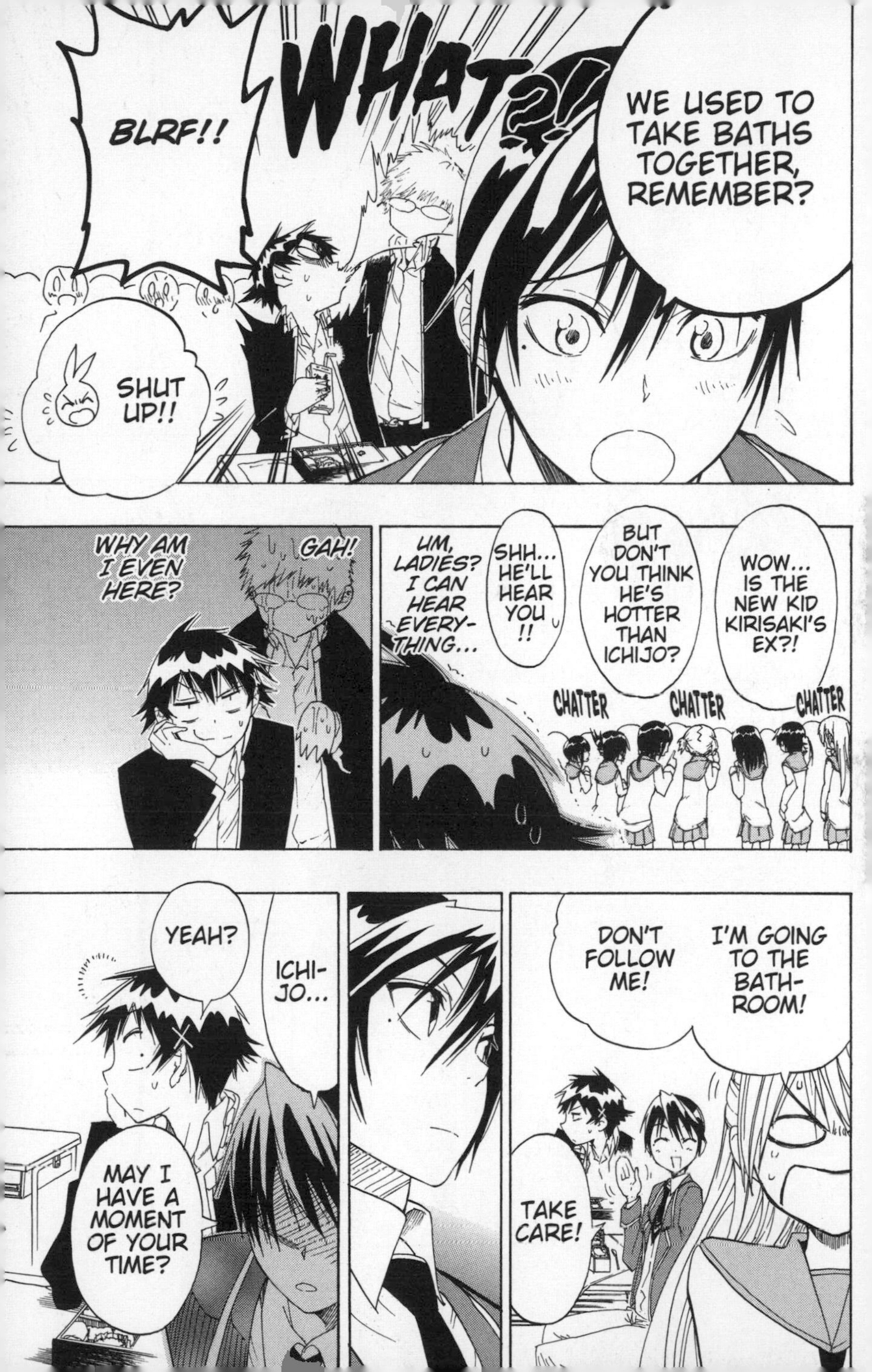
WE USED TO TAKE BATHS TOGETHER, REMEMBER?
WHAT?!
BLRF!!
SHUT UP!!
WOW... IS THE NEW KID KIRISAKI'S EX?!
CHATTER
CHATTER
CHATTER
BUT DON'T YOU THINK HE'S HOTTER THAN ICHIJO?
SHH... HE'LL HEAR YOU!!
UM, LADIES? I CAN HEAR EVERY-THING...
GAH!
WHY AM I EVEN HERE?
I'M GOING TO THE BATH-ROOM!
DON'T FOLLOW ME!
TAKE CARE!
ICHI-JO...
YEAH?
MAY I HAVE A MOMENT OF YOUR TIME?

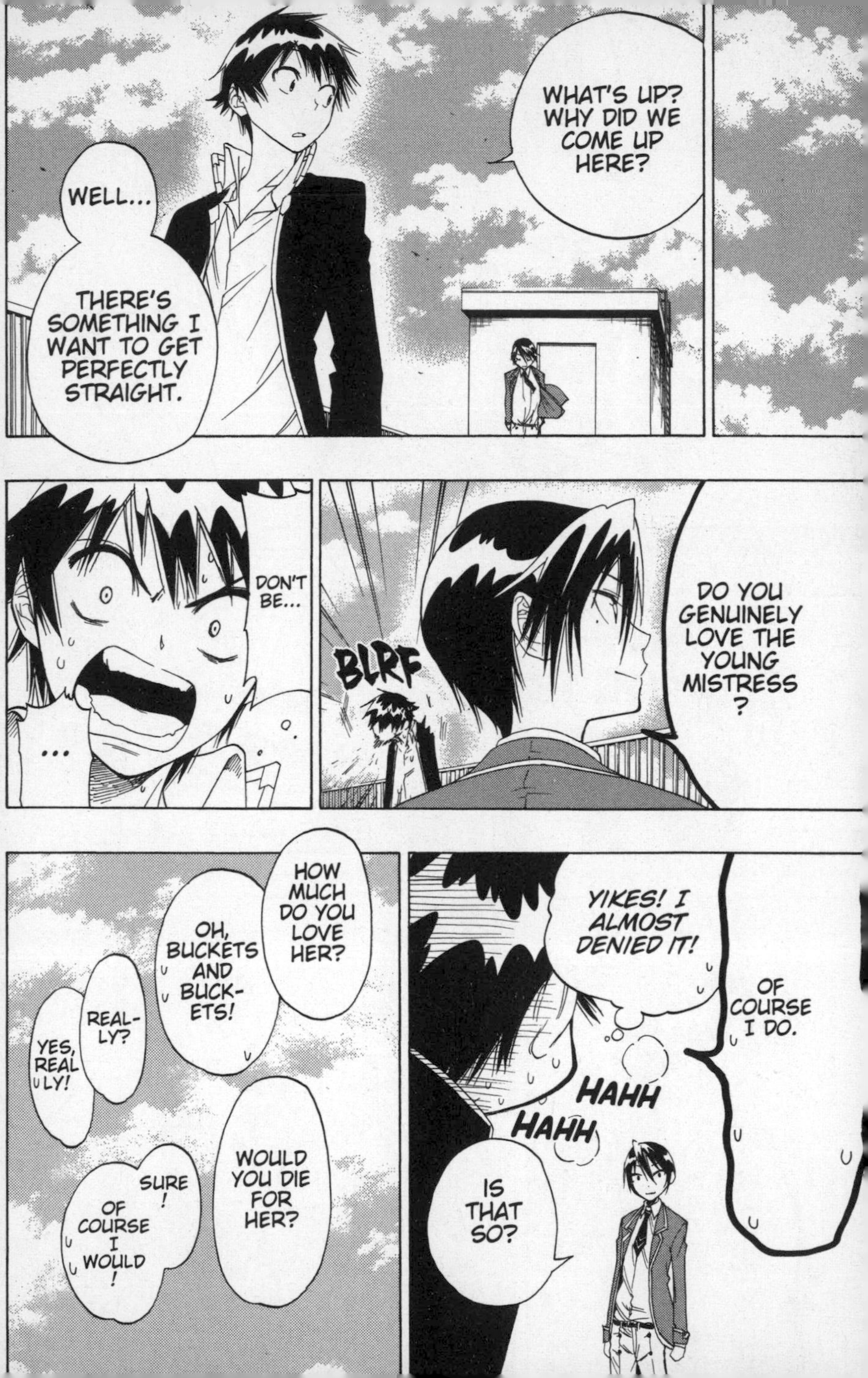
WHAT'S UP? WHY DID WE COME UP HERE?
WELL...
THERE'S SOMETHING I WANT TO GET PERFECTLY STRAIGHT.
DO YOU GENUINELY LOVE THE YOUNG MISTRESS?
BLRF
DON'T BE...
...
OF COURSE I DO.
YIKES! I ALMOST DENIED IT!
HAHH HAHH
IS THAT SO?
HOW MUCH DO YOU LOVE HER?
OH, BUCKETS AND BUCK-ETS!
REAL-LY?
YES, REAL LY!
WOULD YOU DIE FOR HER?
SURE!
OF COURSE I WOULD!

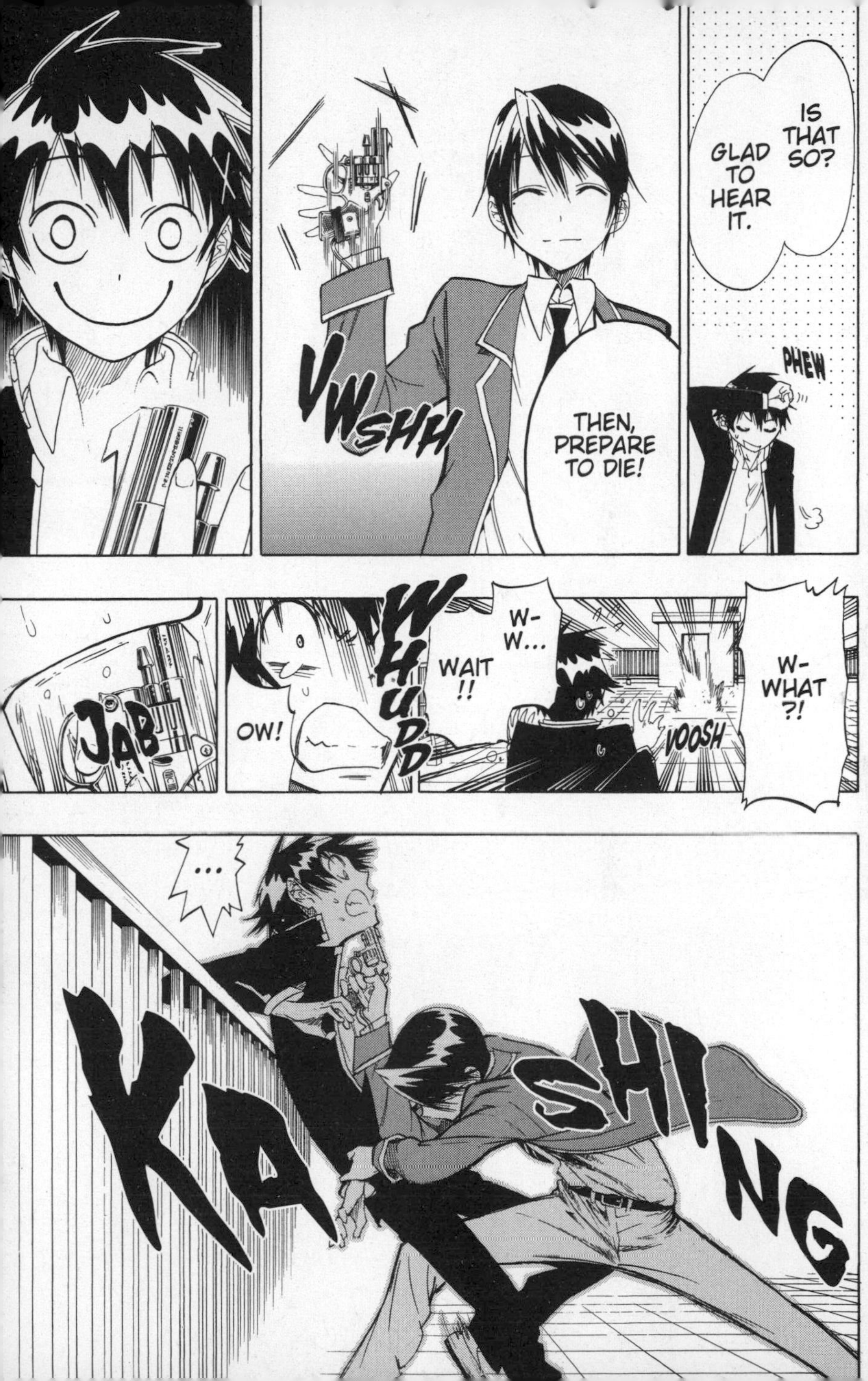
IS THAT SO?
GLAD TO HEAR IT.
PHEW
VWSHH
THEN, PREPARE TO DIE!
W-WHAT?!
VOOSH
W-W...
WAIT!!
WHUDD
OW!
JAB
...
KA
SHING

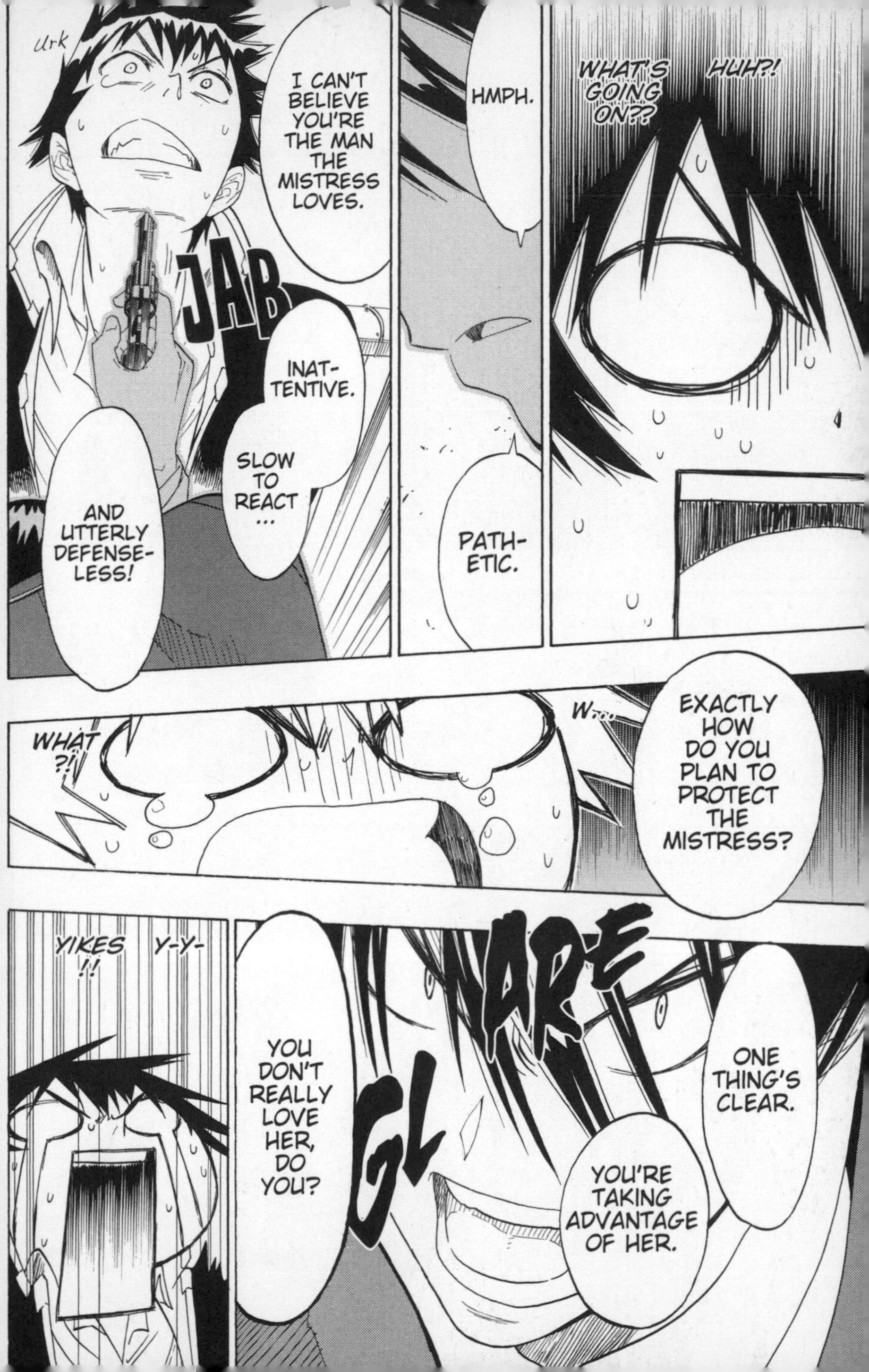
HUH?!
WHAT'S GOING ON??
HMPH.
PATHETIC.
I CAN'T BELIEVE YOU'RE THE MAN THE MISTRESS LOVES.
Urk
JAB
INATTENTIVE.
SLOW TO REACT...
AND UTTERLY DEFENSELESS!
EXACTLY HOW DO YOU PLAN TO PROTECT THE MISTRESS?
W...
WHAT?!
ONE THING'S CLEAR.
YOU'RE TAKING ADVANTAGE OF HER.
GLARE
YOU DON'T REALLY LOVE HER, DO YOU?
Y-Y-
YIKES!!

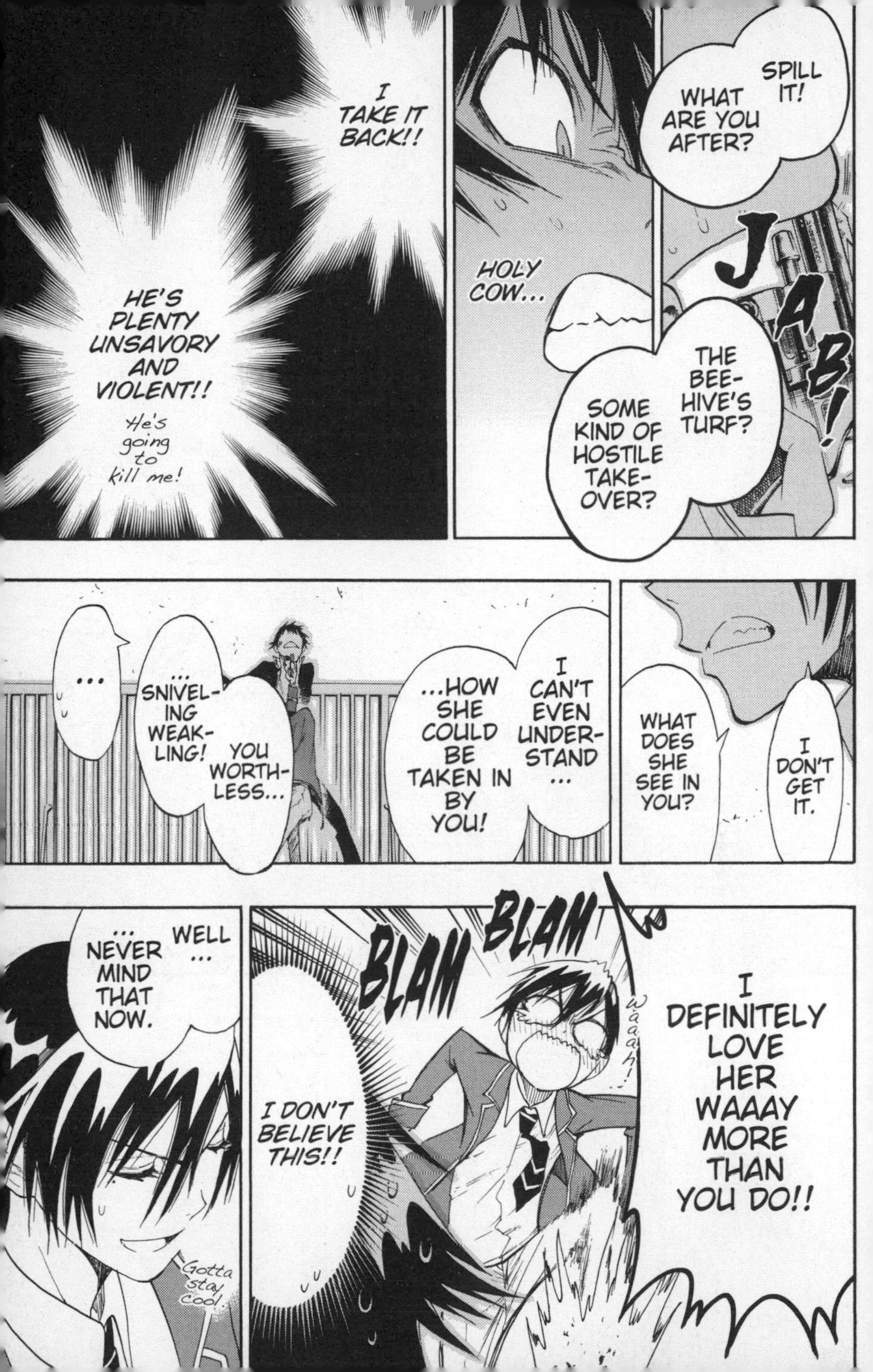
SPILL IT!
WHAT ARE YOU AFTER?
JAB!
THE BEE-HIVE'S TURF?
SOME KIND OF HOSTILE TAKE-OVER?
HOLY COW...
I TAKE IT BACK!!
HE'S PLENTY UNSAVORY AND VIOLENT!!
He's going to kill me!
I DON'T GET IT.
WHAT DOES SHE SEE IN YOU?
I CAN'T EVEN UNDERSTAND...
...HOW SHE COULD BE TAKEN IN BY YOU!
YOU WORTHLESS...
...SNIVELING WEAKLING!
...
I DEFINITELY LOVE HER WAAAY MORE THAN YOU DO!!
BLAM
BLAM
BLAM
Waaah!
I DON'T BELIEVE THIS!!
WELL...
...NEVER MIND THAT NOW.
Gotta stay cool.

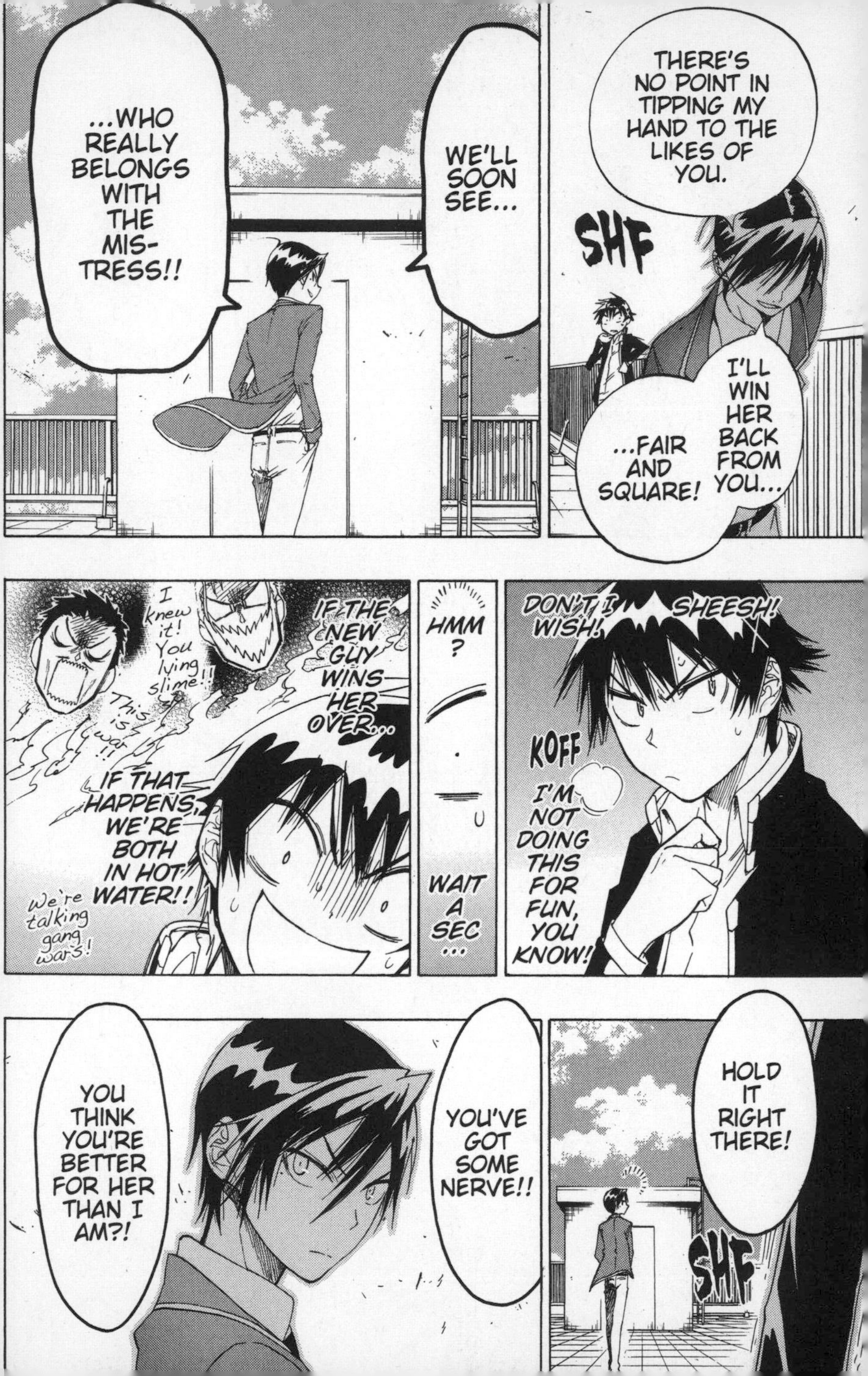
THERE'S NO POINT IN TIPPING MY HAND TO THE LIKES OF YOU.
SHF
I'LL WIN HER BACK FROM YOU...
...FAIR AND SQUARE!
WE'LL SOON SEE...
...WHO REALLY BELONGS WITH THE MIS-TRESS!!
DON'T I WISH!
SHEESH!
KOFF
I'M NOT DOING THIS FOR FUN, YOU KNOW!
HMM?
WAIT A SEC...
IF THE NEW GUY WINS HER OVER...
I knew it! You lying slime!!
This is war!!
IF THAT HAPPENS, WE'RE BOTH IN HOT WATER!!
We're talking gang wars!
HOLD IT RIGHT THERE!
SHF
YOU'VE GOT SOME NERVE!!
YOU THINK YOU'RE BETTER FOR HER THAN I AM?!

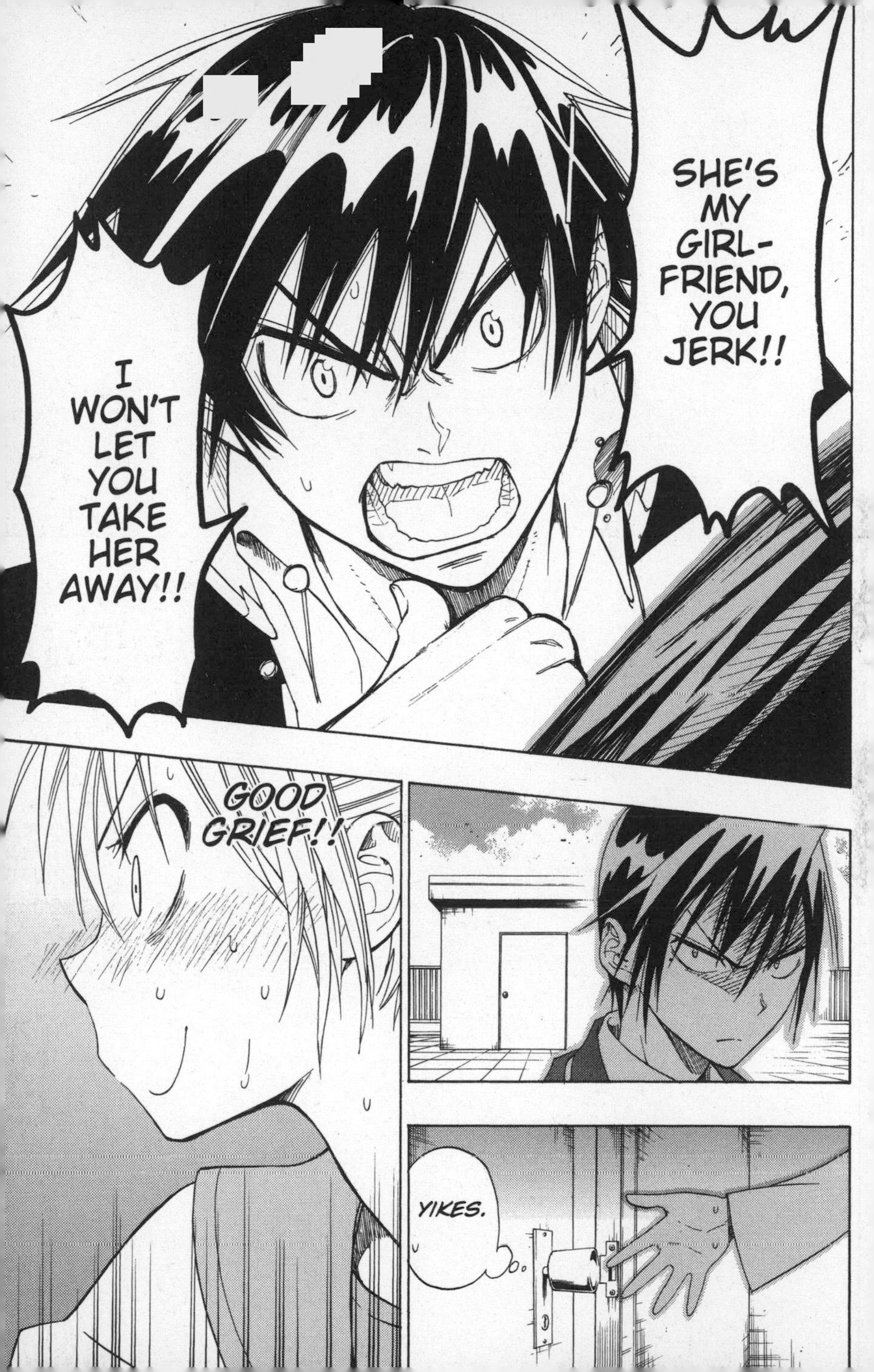
SHE'S MY GIRL-FRIEND, YOU JERK!!
I WON'T LET YOU TAKE HER AWAY!!
YIKES.
GOOD GRIEF!!

Five minutes earlier...
Hey...
Where did Tsugumi and my darling go?
I think they went up to the roof.
How come you're all wet, Maiko?

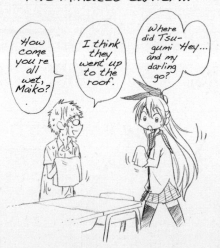

Chapter 16: Showdown

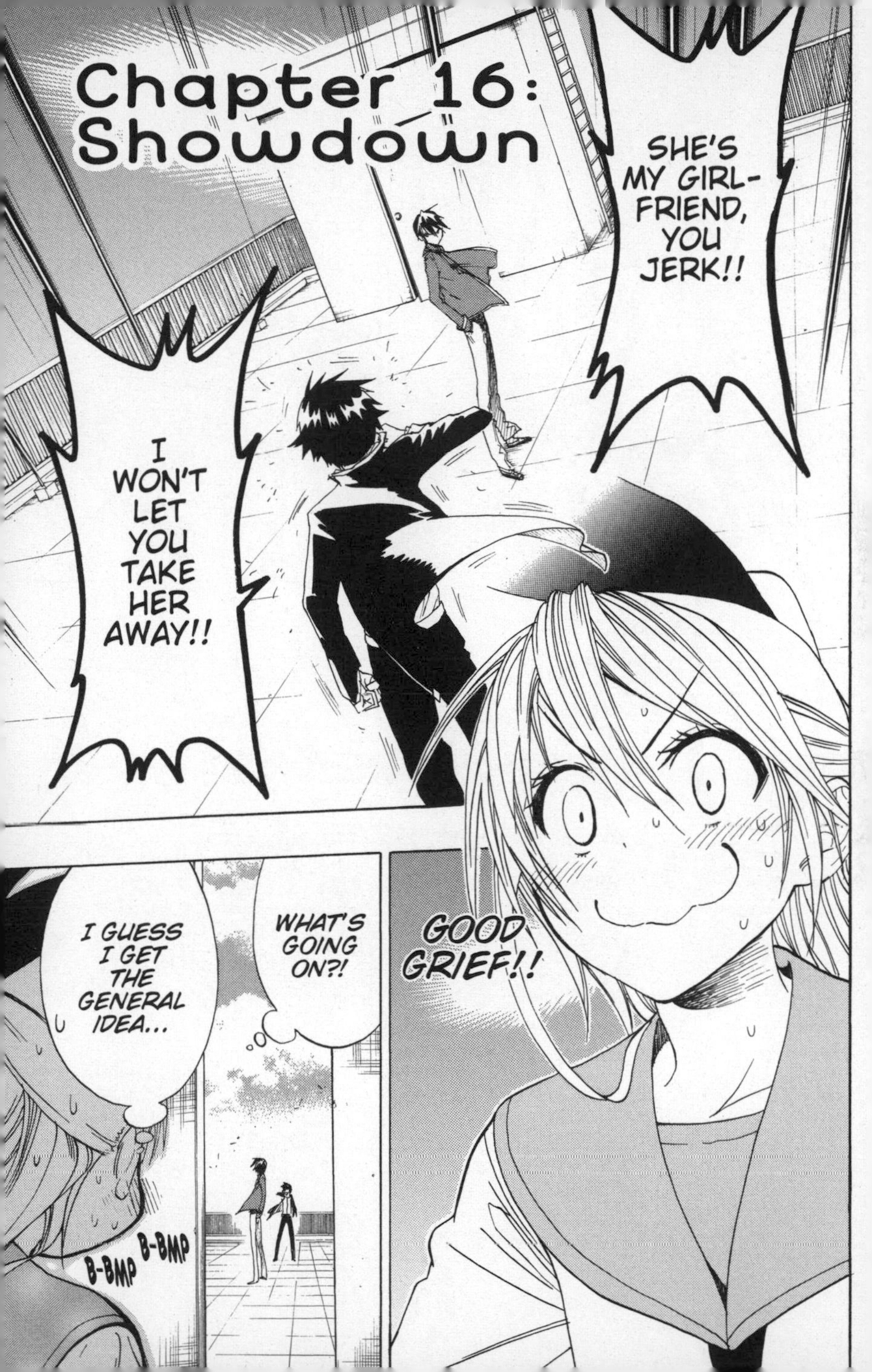

SHE'S MY GIRL-FRIEND, YOU JERK!!
I WON'T LET YOU TAKE HER AWAY!!
GOOD GRIEF!!
WHAT'S GOING ON?!
I GUESS I GET THE GENERAL IDEA...
B-BMP
B-BMP

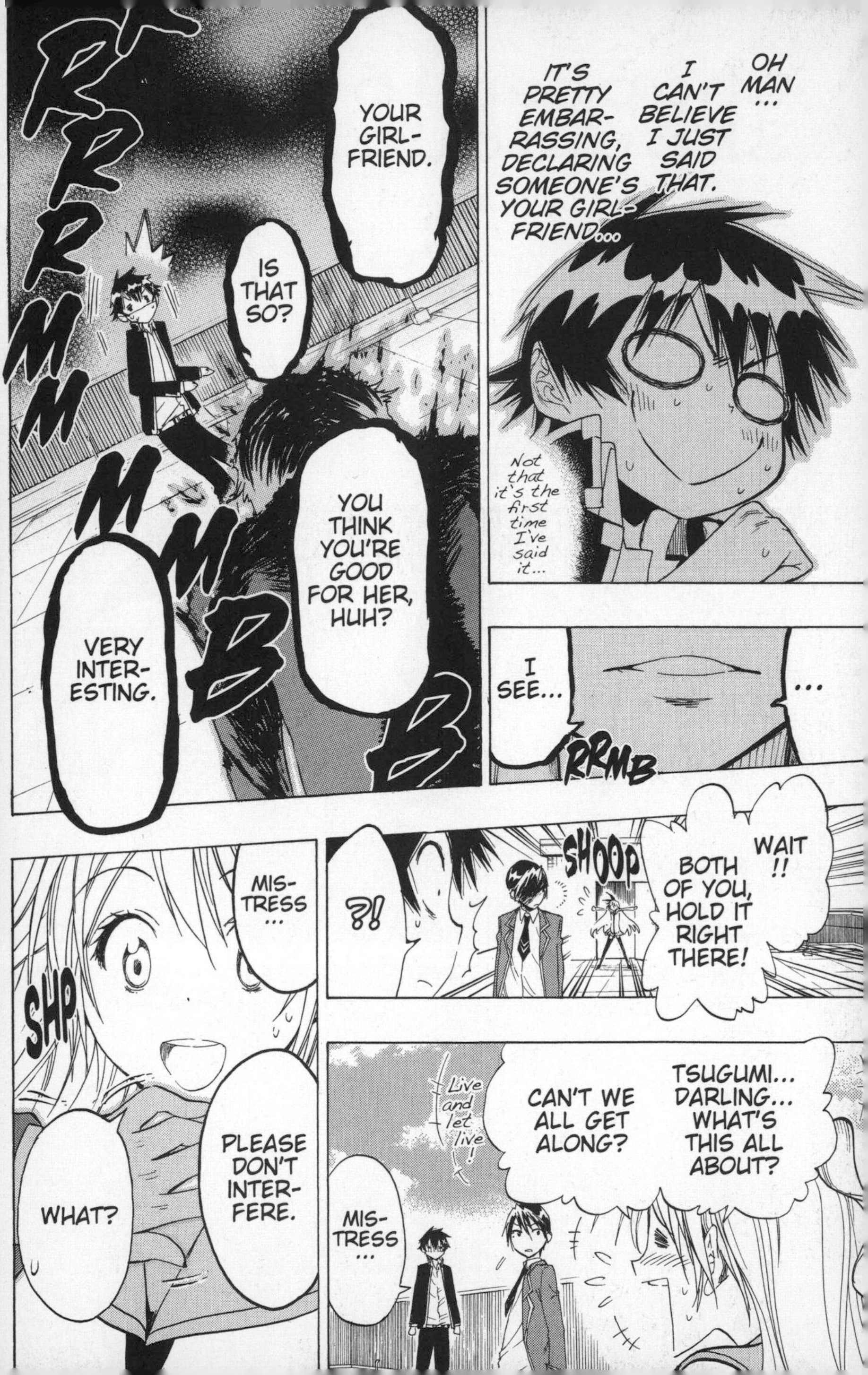
OH MAN...
I CAN'T BELIEVE I JUST SAID THAT.
IT'S PRETTY EMBARRASSING, DECLARING SOMEONE'S YOUR GIRLFRIEND...
Not that it's the first time I've said it...
...
I SEE...
RRMB
YOUR GIRLFRIEND.
IS THAT SO?
YOU THINK YOU'RE GOOD FOR HER, HUH?
VERY INTERESTING.
WAIT!!
BOTH OF YOU, HOLD IT RIGHT THERE!
SHOOP
?!
TSUGUMI... DARLING... WHAT'S THIS ALL ABOUT?
CAN'T WE ALL GET ALONG?
Live and let live!
MISTRESS...
MISTRESS...
SHP
PLEASE DON'T INTERFERE.
WHAT?

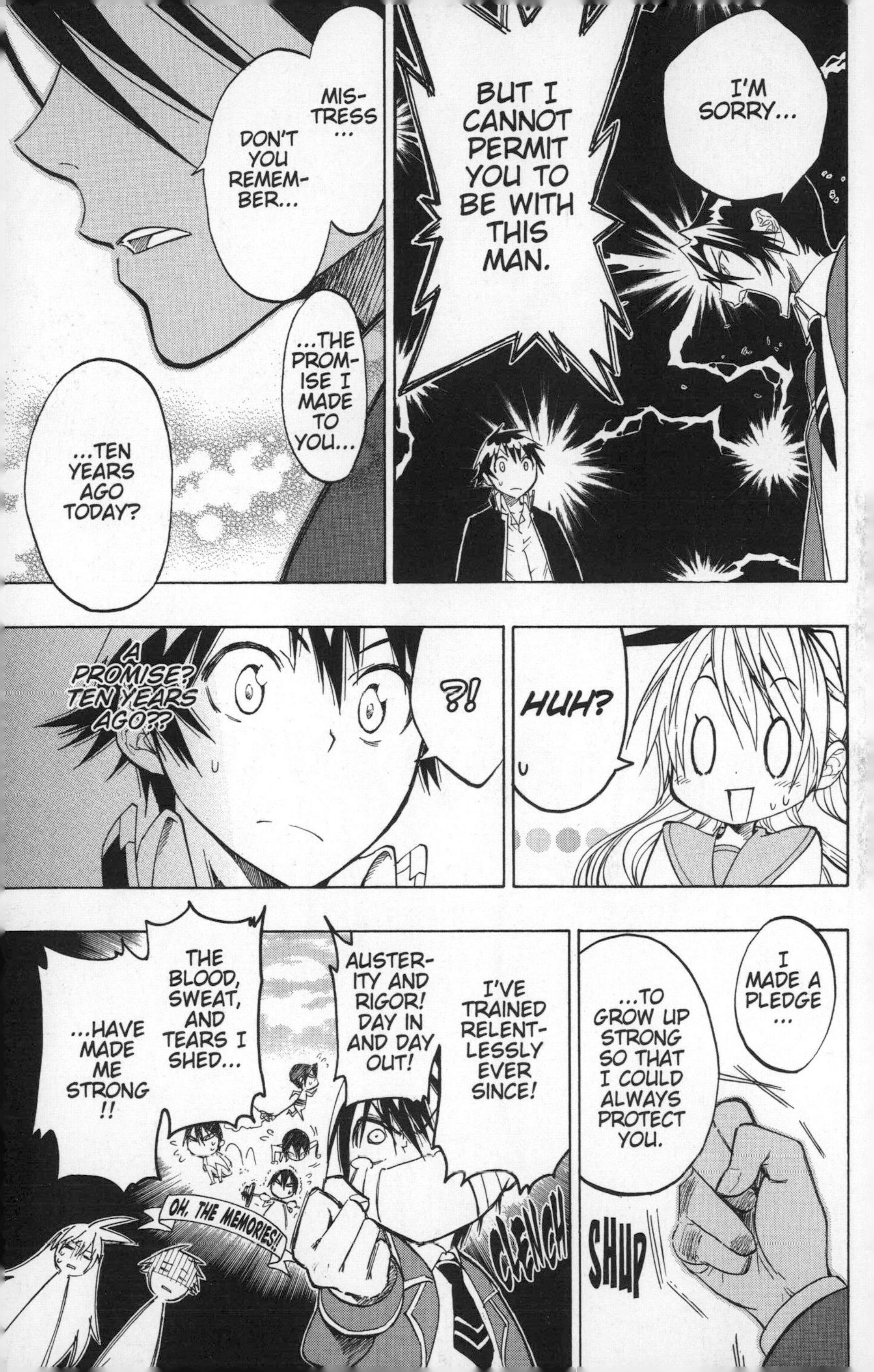
I'M SORRY...
BUT I CANNOT PERMIT YOU TO BE WITH THIS MAN.
MIS-TRESS...
DON'T YOU REMEM-BER...
...THE PROM-ISE I MADE TO YOU...
...TEN YEARS AGO TODAY?
HUH?
?!
A PROMISE? TEN YEARS AGO??
I MADE A PLEDGE...
...TO GROW UP STRONG SO THAT I COULD ALWAYS PROTECT YOU.
SHUP
I'VE TRAINED RELENT-LESSLY EVER SINCE!
AUSTER-ITY AND RIGOR! DAY IN AND DAY OUT!
CLENCH
THE BLOOD, SWEAT, AND TEARS I SHED...
...HAVE MADE ME STRONG!!
OH, THE MEMORIES!!

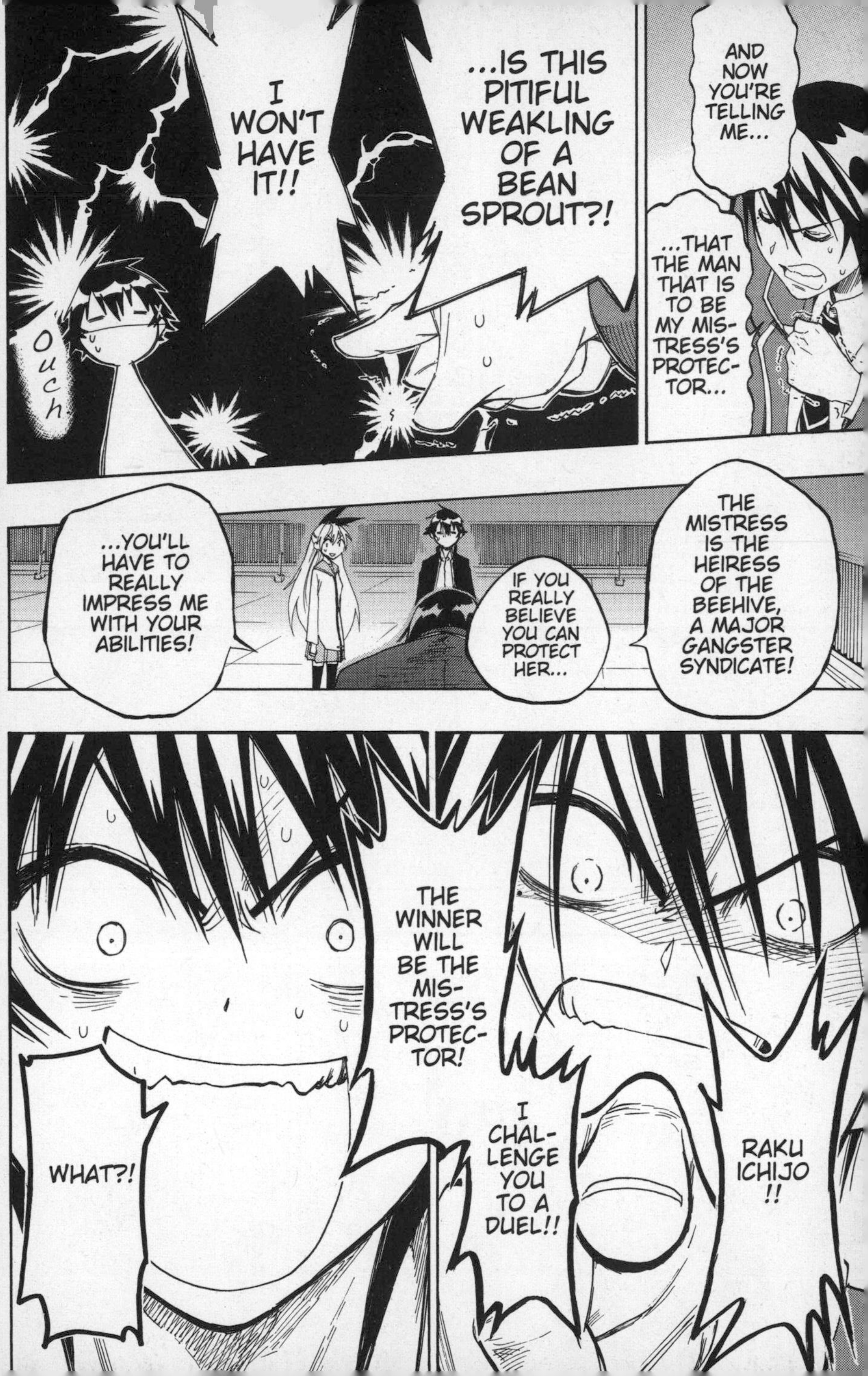
AND NOW YOU'RE TELLING ME...
...THAT THE MAN THAT IS TO BE MY MISTRESS'S PROTECTOR...
...IS THIS PITIFUL WEAKLING OF A BEAN SPROUT?!
I WON'T HAVE IT!!
Ouch
THE MISTRESS IS THE HEIRESS OF THE BEEHIVE, A MAJOR GANGSTER SYNDICATE!
IF YOU REALLY BELIEVE YOU CAN PROTECT HER...
...YOU'LL HAVE TO REALLY IMPRESS ME WITH YOUR ABILITIES!
RAKU ICHIJO!!
I CHALLENGE YOU TO A DUEL!!
THE WINNER WILL BE THE MISTRESS'S PROTECTOR!
WHAT?!

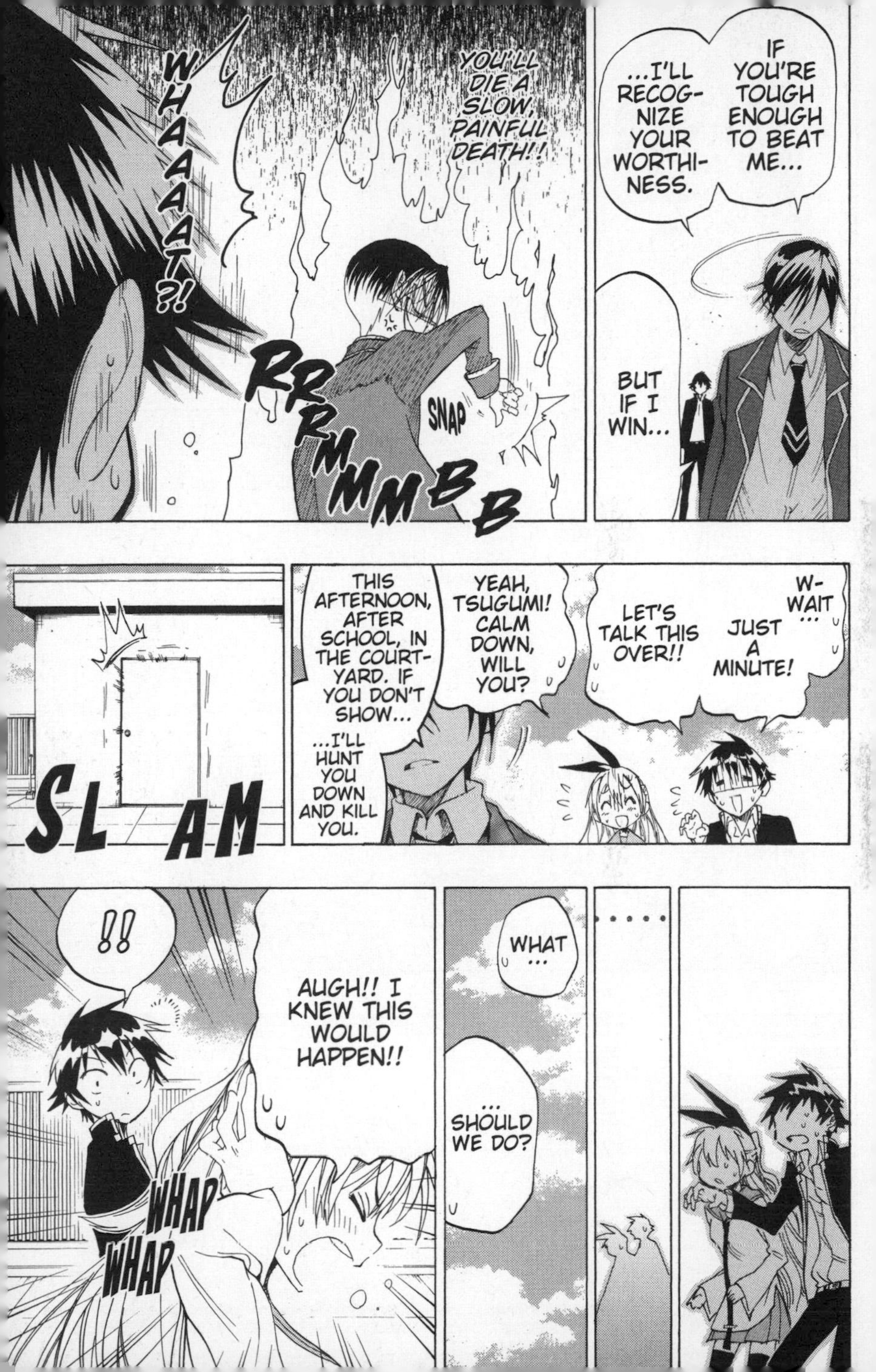
IF YOU'RE TOUGH ENOUGH TO BEAT ME...
...I'LL RECOG-NIZE YOUR WORTHI-NESS.
BUT IF I WIN...
YOU'LL DIE A SLOW, PAINFUL DEATH!!
SNAP
RRRMMMMBB
WHAAAAAT?!
W-WAIT... JUST A MINUTE!
LET'S TALK THIS OVER!!
YEAH, TSUGUMI! CALM DOWN, WILL YOU?
THIS AFTERNOON, AFTER SCHOOL, IN THE COURT-YARD. IF YOU DON'T SHOW...
...I'LL HUNT YOU DOWN AND KILL YOU.
SLAM
.....
WHAT...
...SHOULD WE DO?
!!
AUGH!! I KNEW THIS WOULD HAPPEN!!
WHAP WHAP

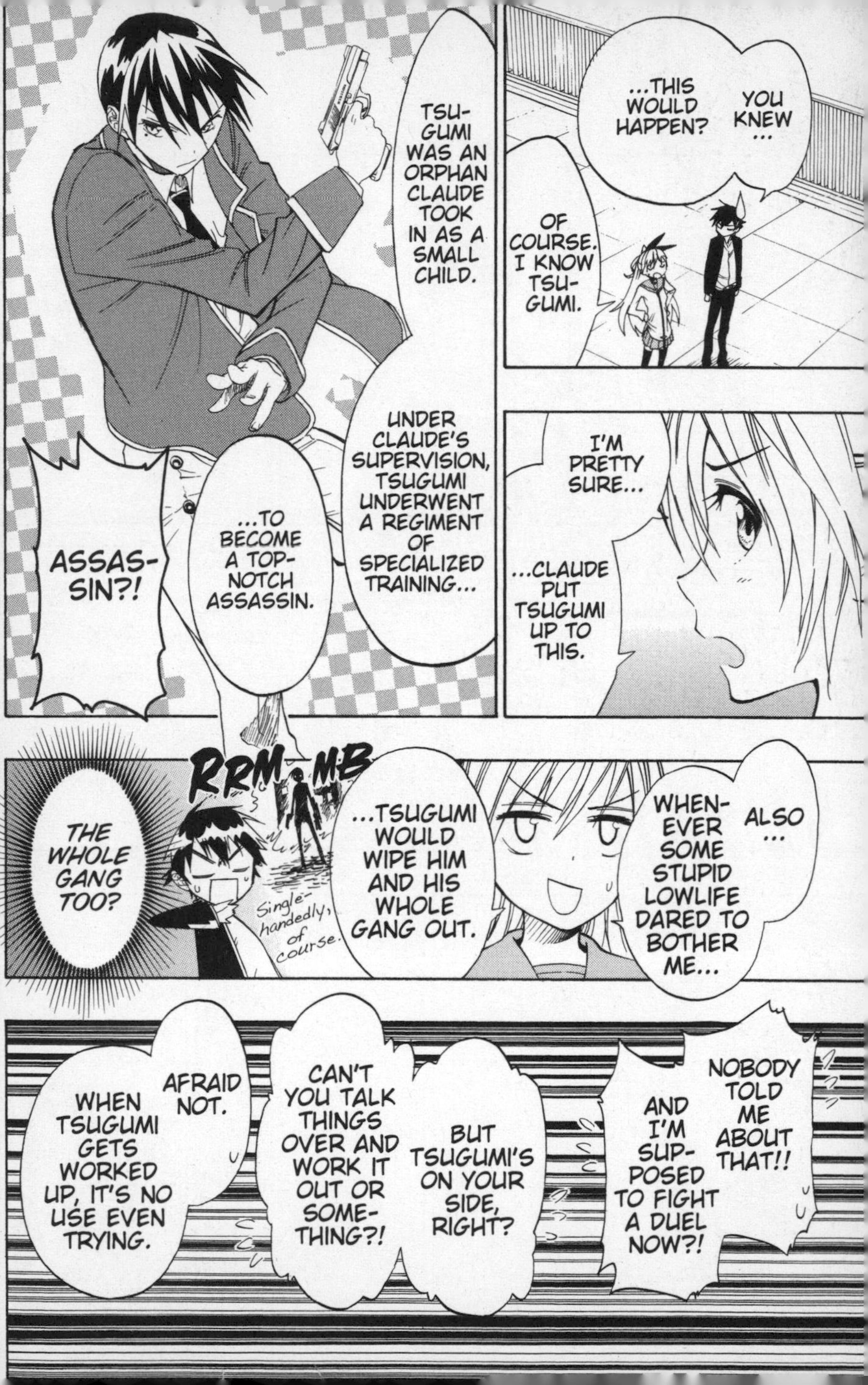
YOU KNEW...
...THIS WOULD HAPPEN?
OF COURSE. I KNOW TSUGUMI.
I'M PRETTY SURE...
...CLAUDE PUT TSUGUMI UP TO THIS.
TSUGUMI WAS AN ORPHAN CLAUDE TOOK IN AS A SMALL CHILD.
UNDER CLAUDE'S SUPERVISION, TSUGUMI UNDERWENT A REGIMENT OF SPECIALIZED TRAINING...
...TO BECOME A TOP-NOTCH ASSASSIN.
ASSASSIN?!
ALSO...
WHENEVER SOME STUPID LOWLIFE DARED TO BOTHER ME...
...TSUGUMI WOULD WIPE HIM AND HIS WHOLE GANG OUT.
RRMMB
Single-handedly, of course.
THE WHOLE GANG TOO?
NOBODY TOLD ME ABOUT THAT!!
AND I'M SUPPOSED TO FIGHT A DUEL NOW?!
BUT TSUGUMI'S ON YOUR SIDE, RIGHT?
CAN'T YOU TALK THINGS OVER AND WORK IT OUT OR SOMETHING?!
AFRAID NOT.
WHEN TSUGUMI GETS WORKED UP, IT'S NO USE EVEN TRYING.

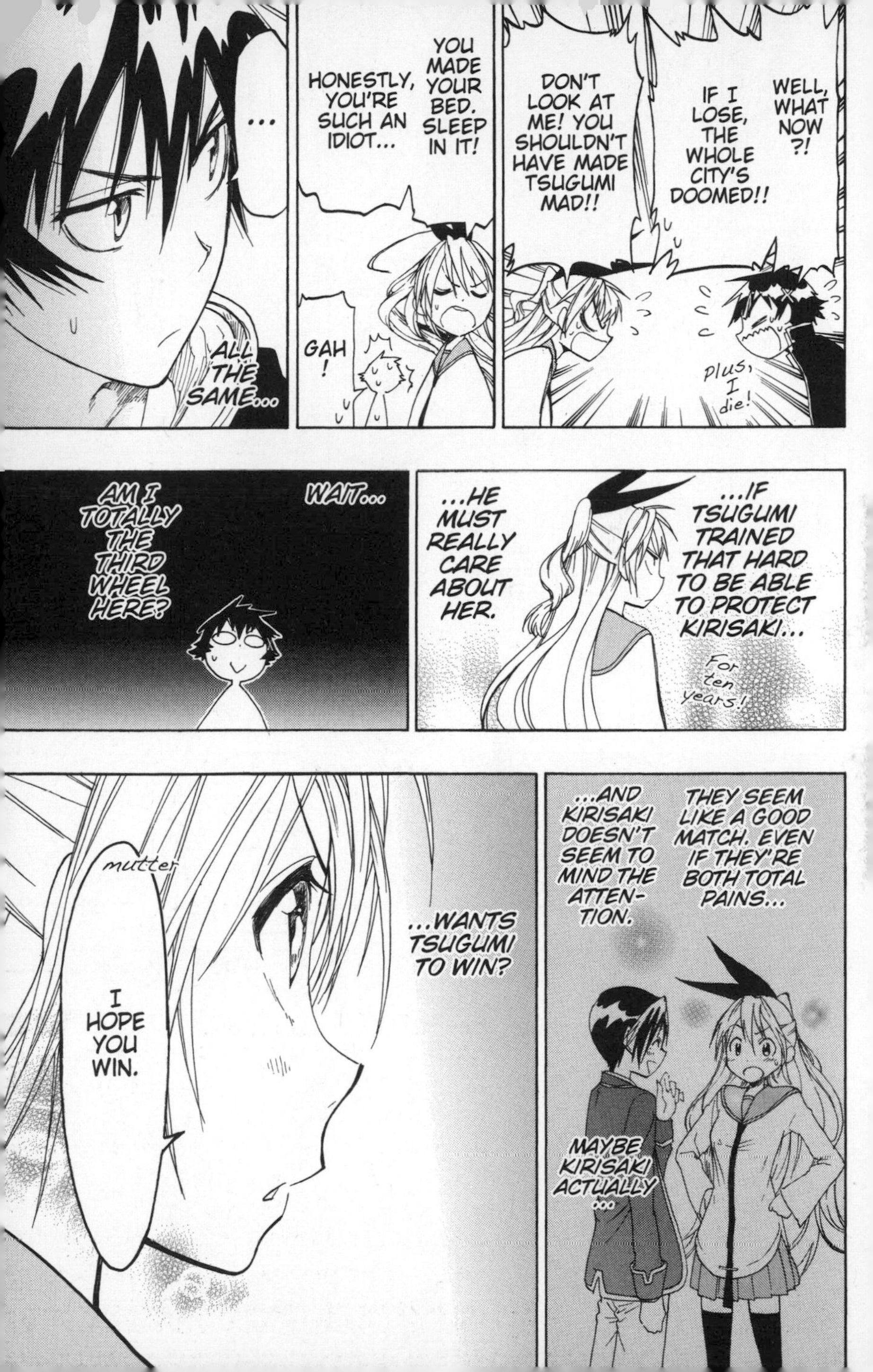
WELL, WHAT NOW?!
IF I LOSE, THE WHOLE CITY'S DOOMED!!
DON'T LOOK AT ME! YOU SHOULDN'T HAVE MADE TSUGUMI MAD!!
Plus, I die!
YOU MADE YOUR BED. SLEEP IN IT!
HONESTLY, YOU'RE SUCH AN IDIOT...
GAH!
...
ALL THE SAME...
...IF TSUGUMI TRAINED THAT HARD TO BE ABLE TO PROTECT KIRISAKI...
For ten years!
...HE MUST REALLY CARE ABOUT HER.
WAIT...
AM I TOTALLY THE THIRD WHEEL HERE?
THEY SEEM LIKE A GOOD MATCH. EVEN IF THEY'RE BOTH TOTAL PAINS...
...AND KIRISAKI DOESN'T SEEM TO MIND THE ATTEN-TION.
MAYBE KIRISAKI ACTUALLY...
...WANTS TSUGUMI TO WIN?
mutter
I HOPE YOU WIN.

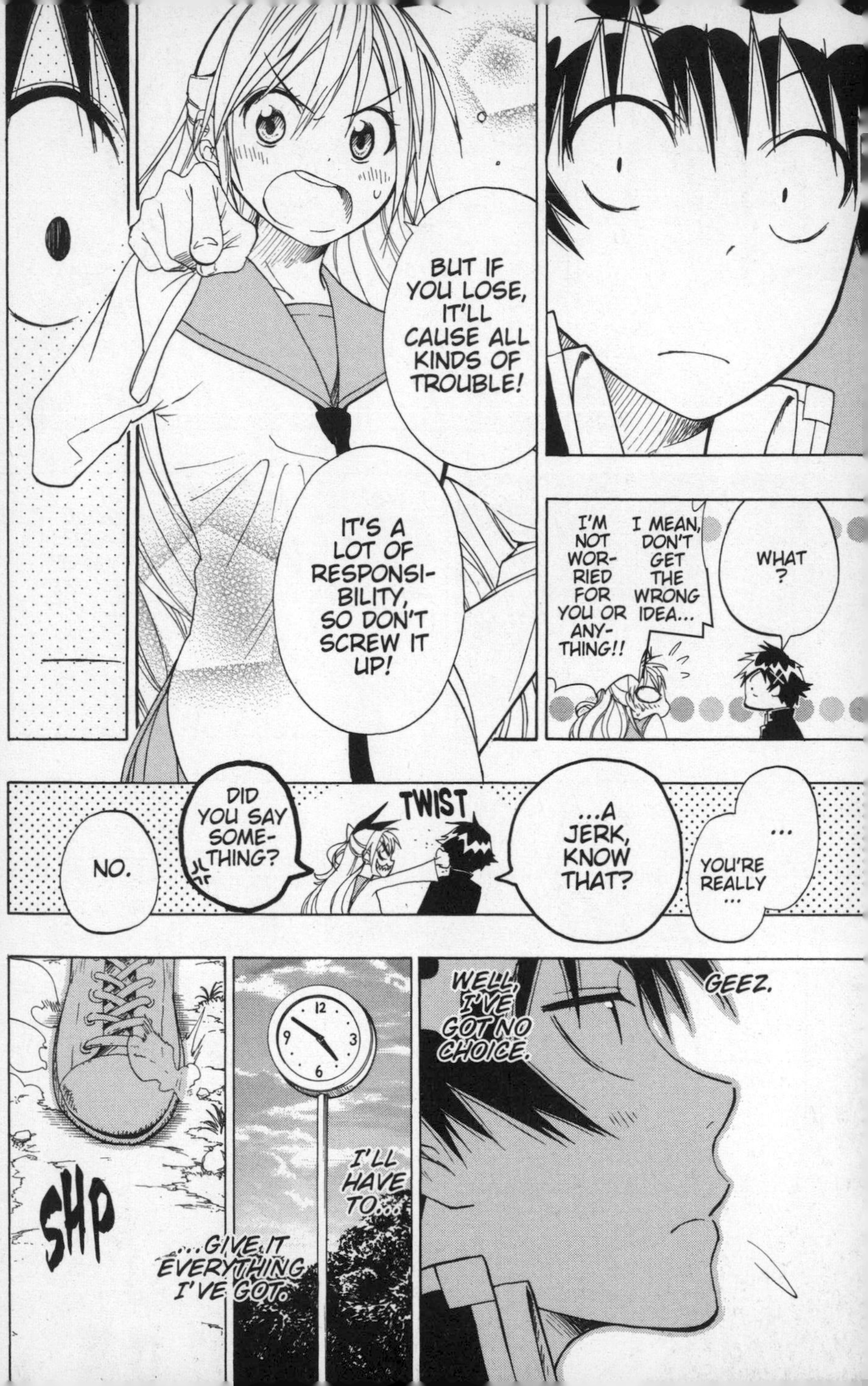
WHAT?
I MEAN, DON'T GET THE WRONG IDEA...
I'M NOT WORRIED FOR YOU OR ANYTHING!!
BUT IF YOU LOSE, IT'LL CAUSE ALL KINDS OF TROUBLE!
IT'S A LOT OF RESPONSIBILITY, SO DON'T SCREW IT UP!
... YOU'RE REALLY ...
...A JERK, KNOW THAT?
TWIST
DID YOU SAY SOMETHING?
NO.
GEEZ.
WELL, I'VE GOT NO CHOICE.
I'LL HAVE TO...
...GIVE IT EVERYTHING I'VE GOT.
SHP

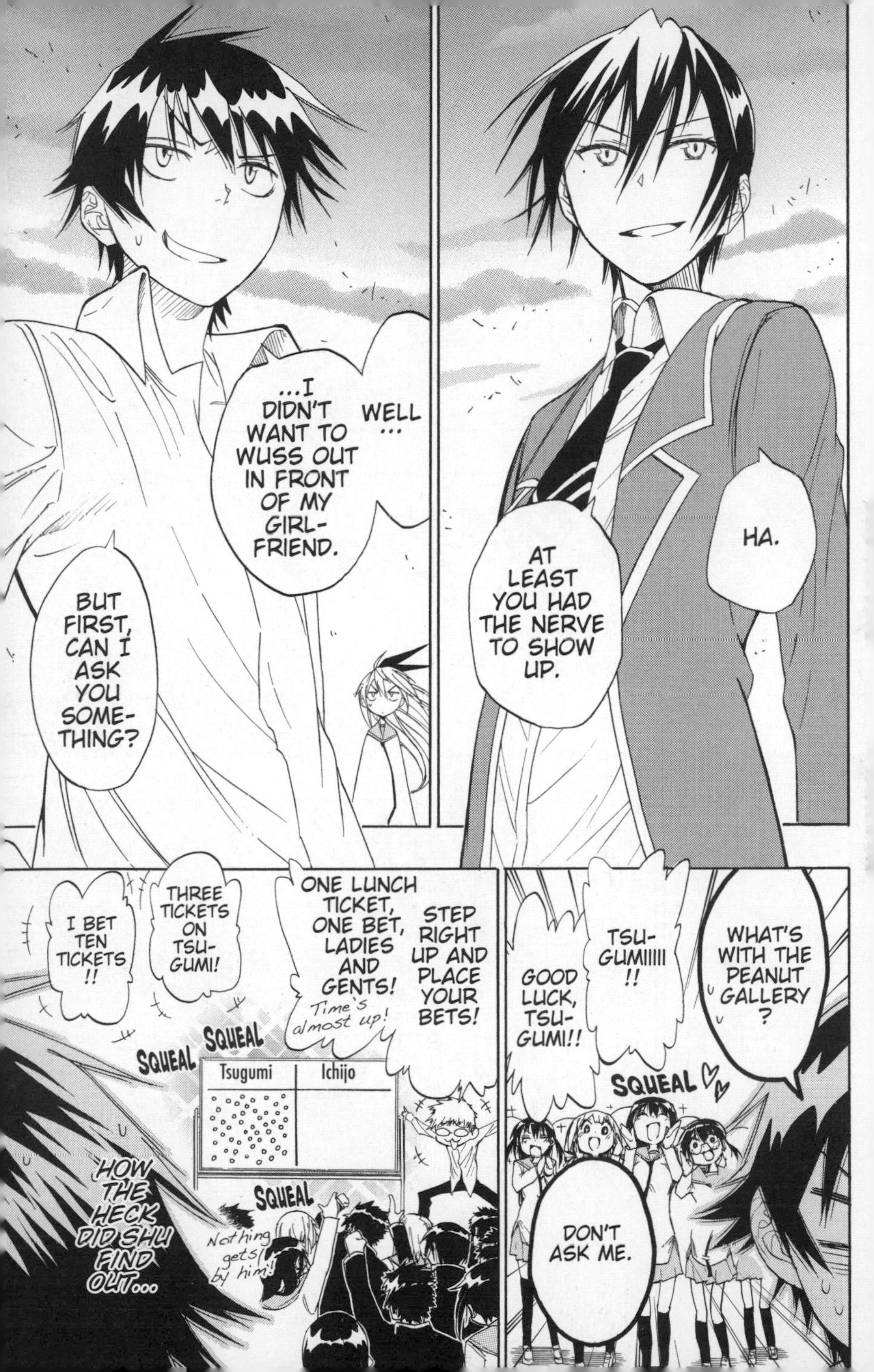
HA.
AT LEAST YOU HAD THE NERVE TO SHOW UP.
WELL...
...I DIDN'T WANT TO WUSS OUT IN FRONT OF MY GIRL-FRIEND.
BUT FIRST, CAN I ASK YOU SOME-THING?
WHAT'S WITH THE PEANUT GALLERY?
TSU-GUMIIIII!!
GOOD LUCK, TSU-GUMI!!
SQUEAL
DON'T ASK ME.
STEP RIGHT UP AND PLACE YOUR BETS!
ONE LUNCH TICKET, ONE BET, LADIES AND GENTS!
Time's almost up!
THREE TICKETS ON TSU-GUMI!
I BET TEN TICKETS!!
SQUEAL
SQUEAL
Tsugumi
Ichijo
SQUEAL
Nothing gets by him!
HOW THE HECK DID SHU FIND OUT...

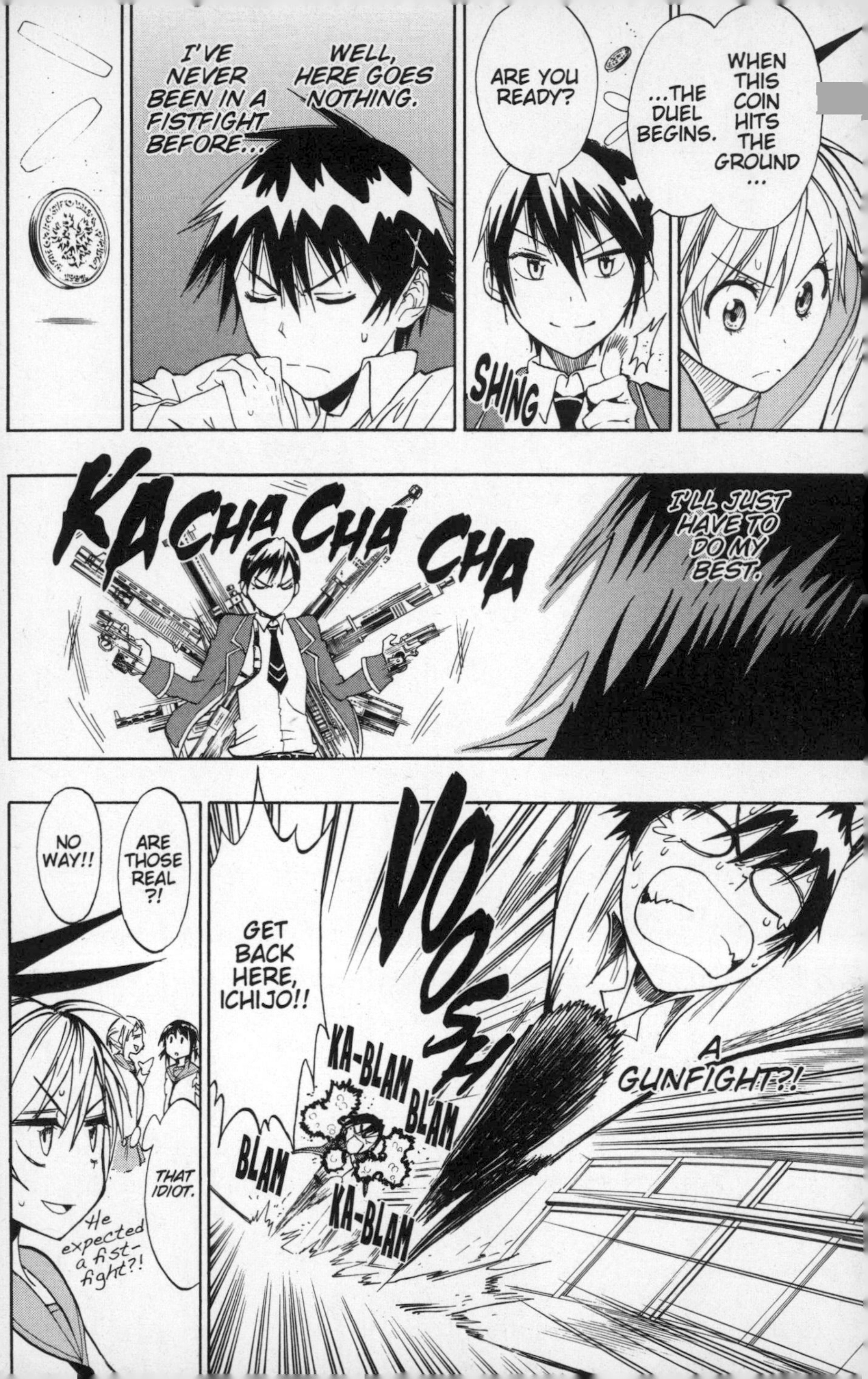
WHEN THIS COIN HITS THE GROUND...
...THE DUEL BEGINS.
ARE YOU READY?
SHING
WELL, HERE GOES NOTHING.
I'VE NEVER BEEN IN A FISTFIGHT BEFORE...
I'LL JUST HAVE TO DO MY BEST.
KACHACHACHA CHA
A GUNFIGHT?!
VOOSH
GET BACK HERE, ICHIJO!!
KA-BLAM BLAM
BLAM
KA-BLAM
ARE THOSE REAL?!
NO WAY!!
THAT IDIOT.
He expected a fist-fight?!

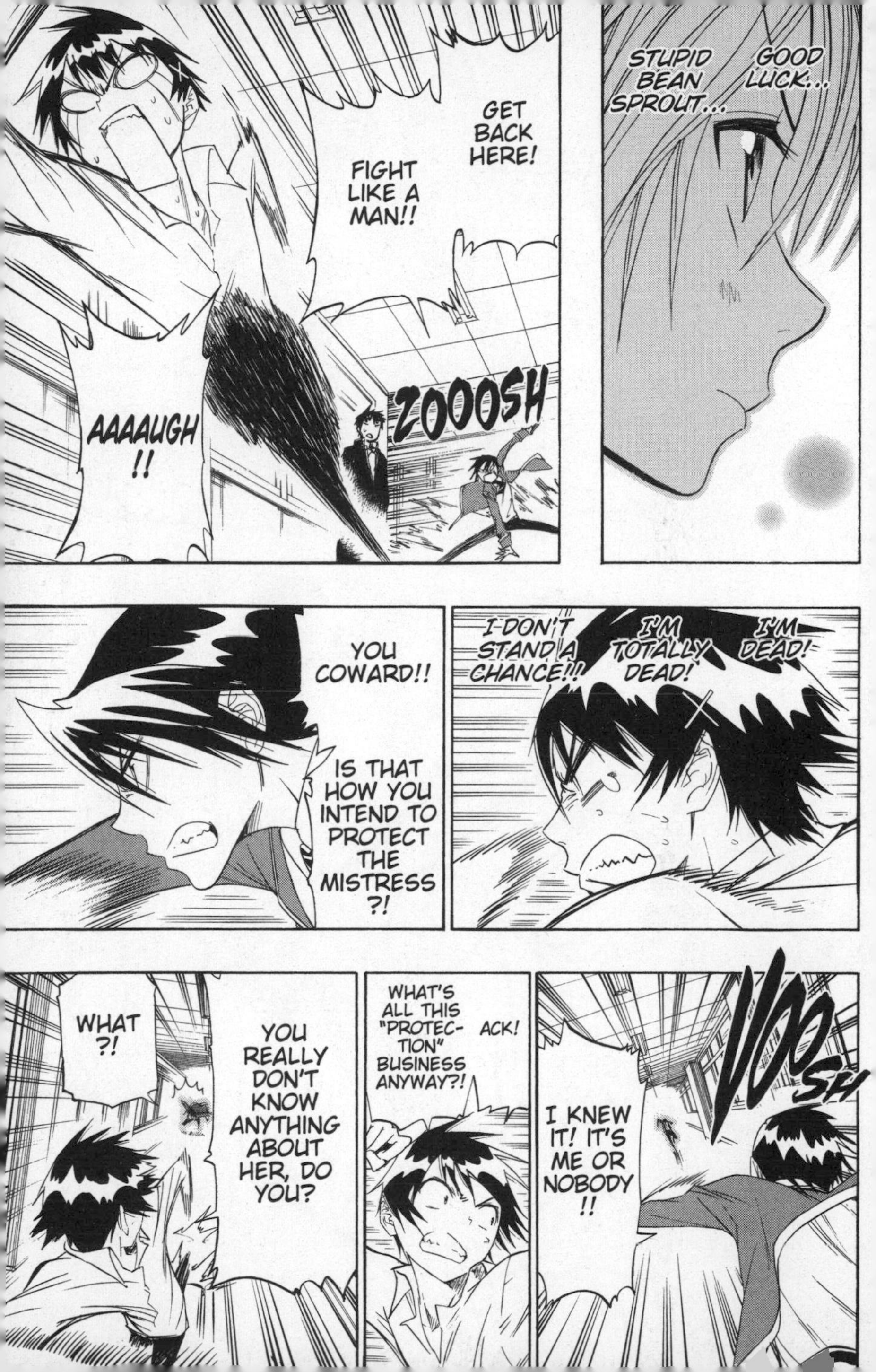
GOOD LUCK...
STUPID BEAN SPROUT...
GET BACK HERE!
FIGHT LIKE A MAN!!
ZOOOSH
AAAAUGH!!
I'M DEAD!
I'M TOTALLY DEAD!
I DON'T STAND A CHANCE!!
YOU COWARD!!
IS THAT HOW YOU INTEND TO PROTECT THE MISTRESS?!
VOOSH
I KNEW IT! IT'S ME OR NOBODY!!
ACK!
WHAT'S ALL THIS "PROTECTION" BUSINESS ANYWAY?!
YOU REALLY DON'T KNOW ANYTHING ABOUT HER, DO YOU?
WHAT?!

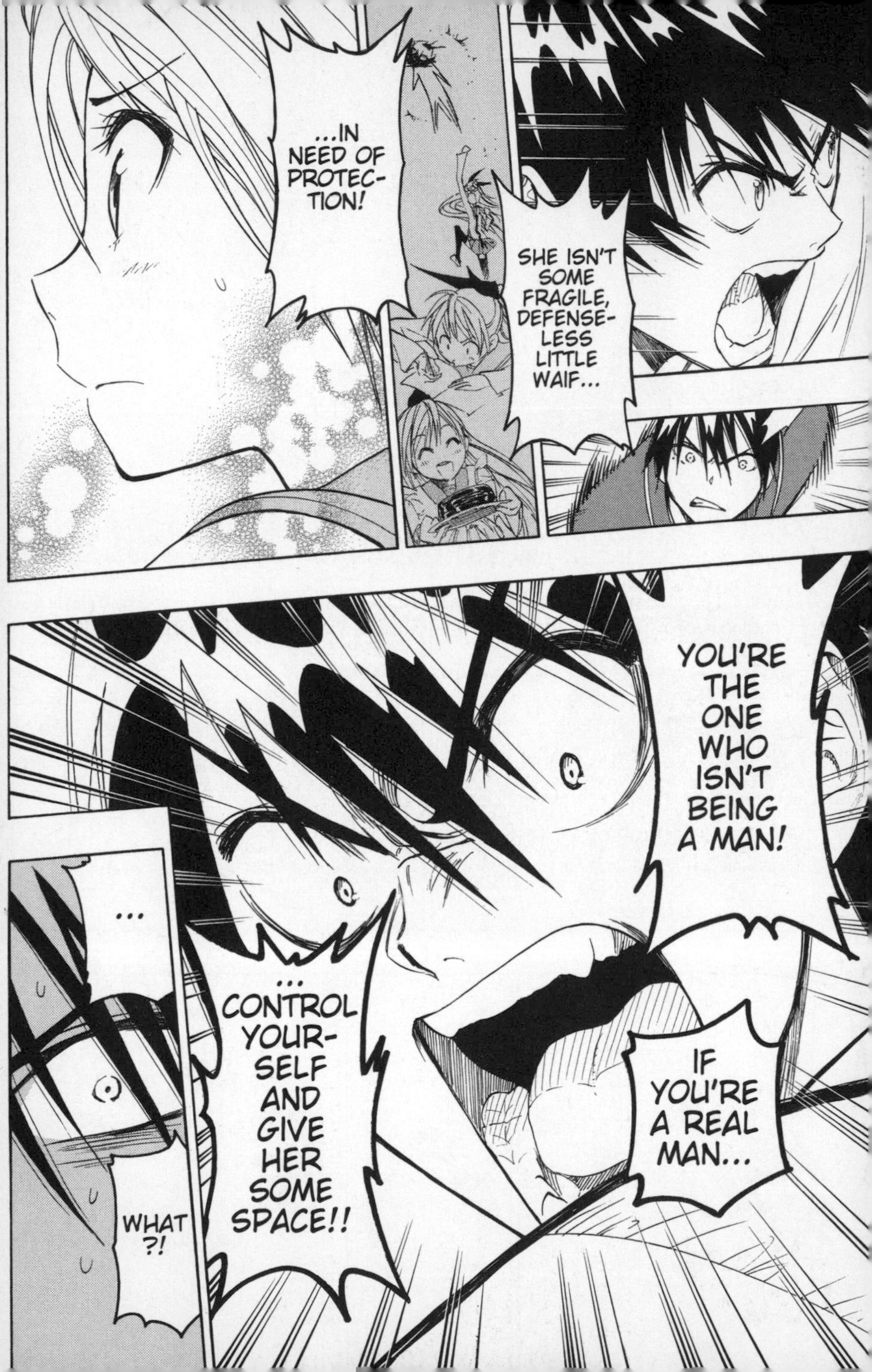
SHE ISN'T SOME FRAGILE, DEFENSELESS LITTLE WAIF...
...IN NEED OF PROTECTION!
YOU'RE THE ONE WHO ISN'T BEING A MAN!
IF YOU'RE A REAL MAN...
...CONTROL YOURSELF AND GIVE HER SOME SPACE!!
...
WHAT?!

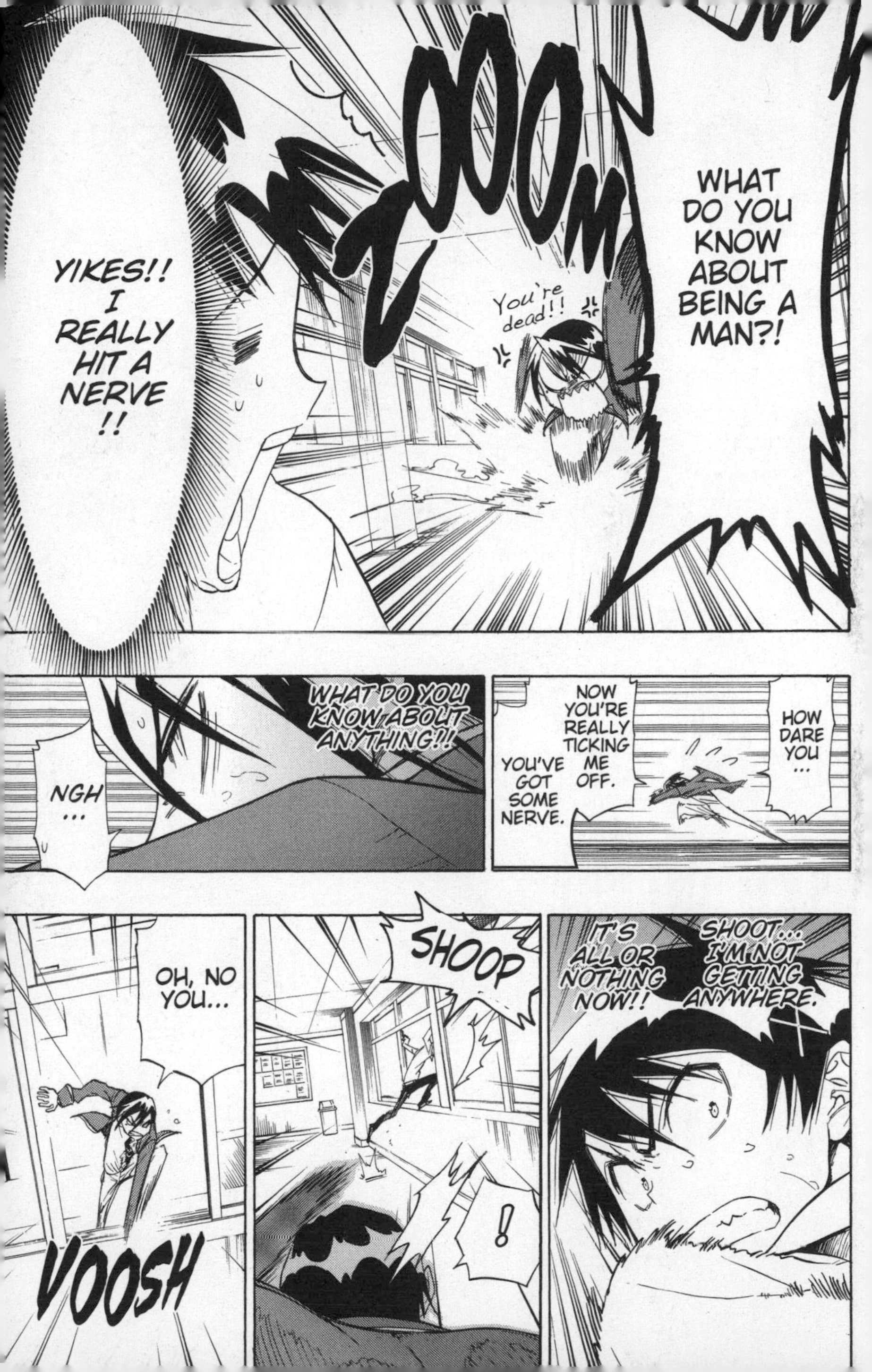
WHAT DO YOU KNOW ABOUT BEING A MAN?!
ZOOOOM
You're dead!!
YIKES!! I REALLY HIT A NERVE!!
HOW DARE YOU...
NOW YOU'RE REALLY TICKING ME OFF.
YOU'VE GOT SOME NERVE.
WHAT DO YOU KNOW ABOUT ANYTHING!!
NGH...
SHOOT... I'M NOT GETTING ANYWHERE.
IT'S ALL OR NOTHING NOW!!
SHOOP
!
OH, NO YOU...
VOOSH

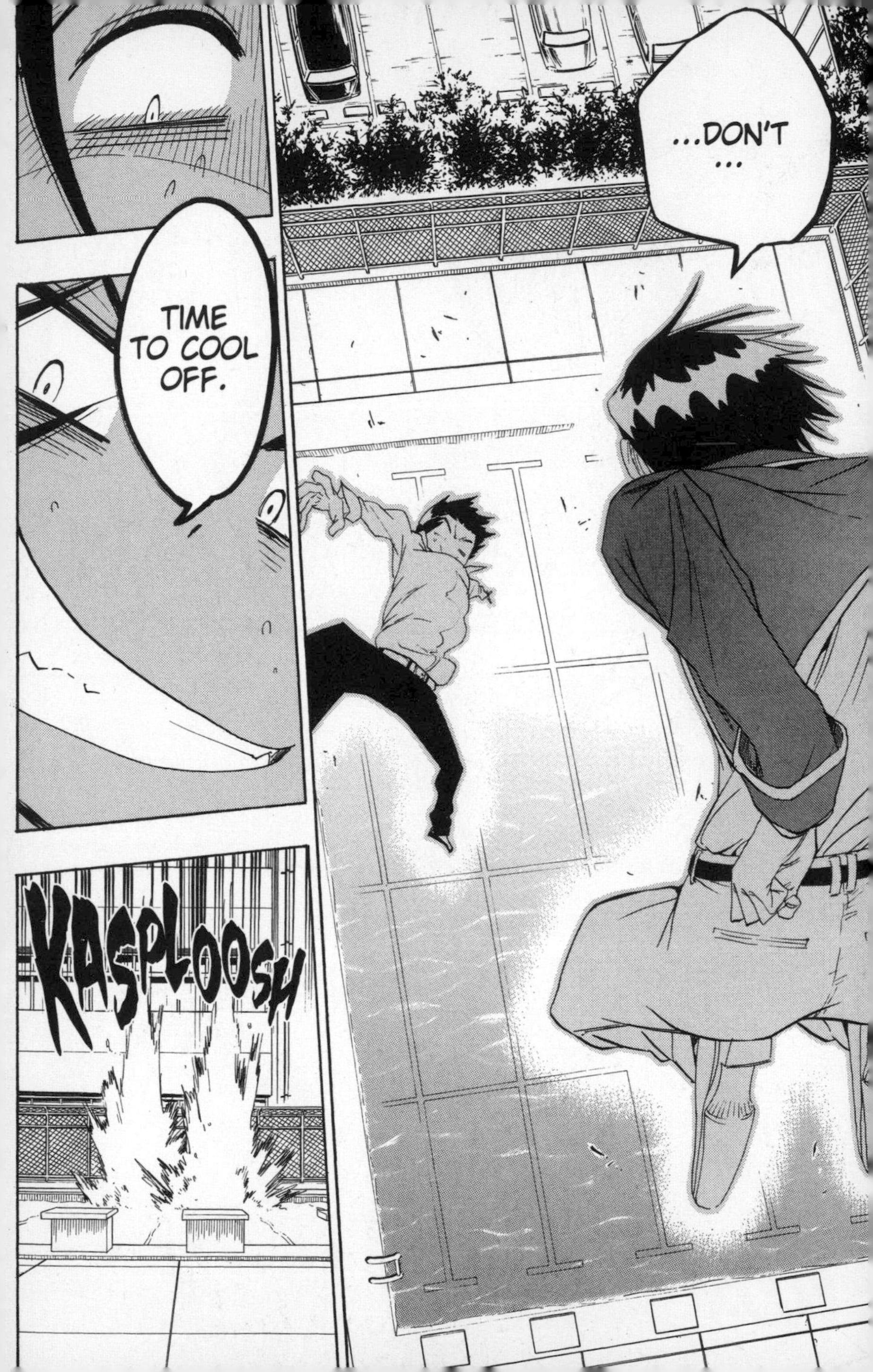
...DON'T ...
TIME TO COOL OFF.
KASPLOOSH

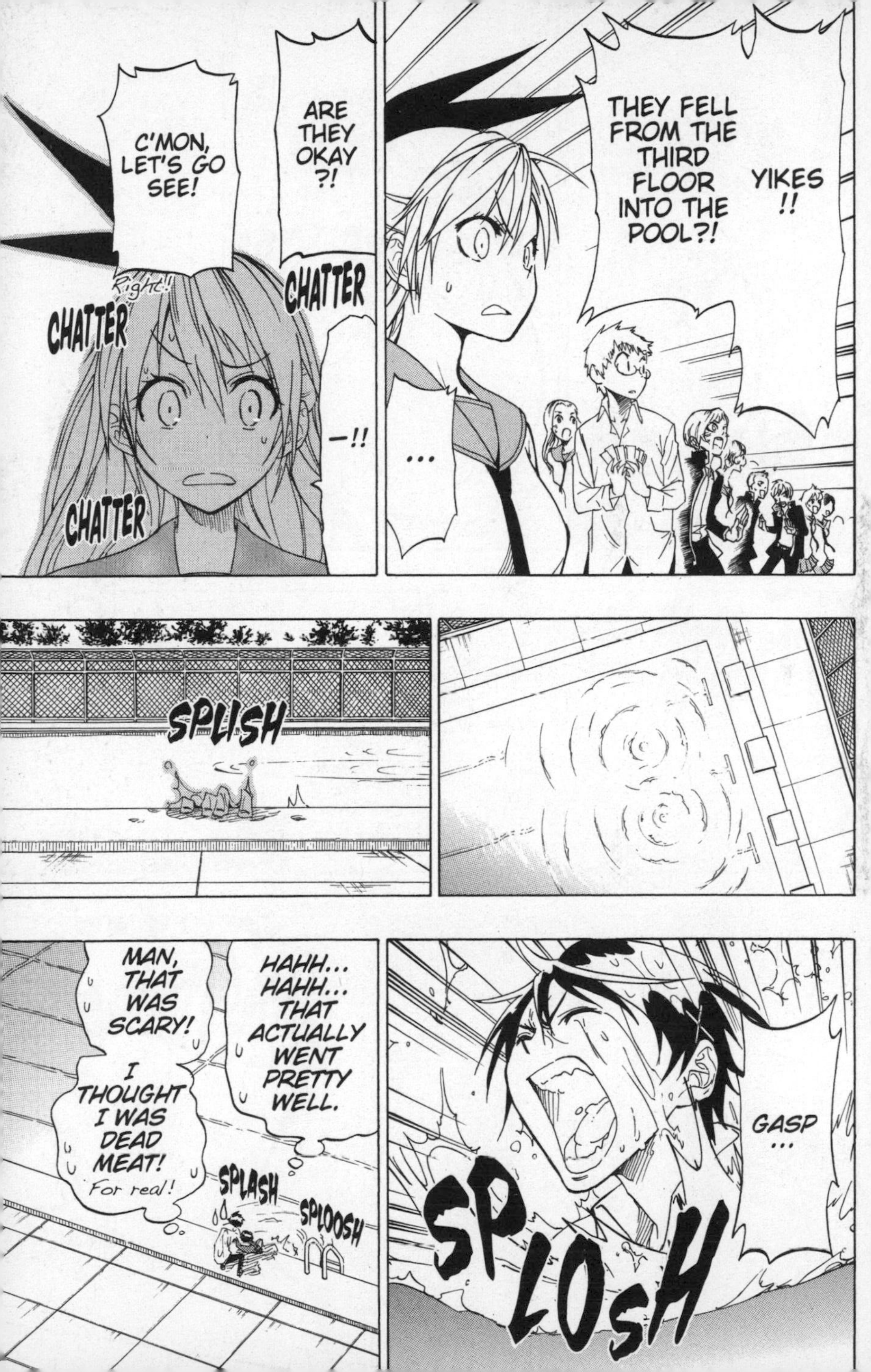
YIKES !!
THEY FELL FROM THE THIRD FLOOR INTO THE POOL?!
...
ARE THEY OKAY ?!
CHATTER
C'MON, LET'S GO SEE!
Right!
CHATTER
—!!
CHATTER
SPLISH
GASP ...
SPLOSH
HAHH... HAHH... THAT ACTUALLY WENT PRETTY WELL.
MAN, THAT WAS SCARY!
I THOUGHT I WAS DEAD MEAT!
For real!
SPLASH
SPLOOSH

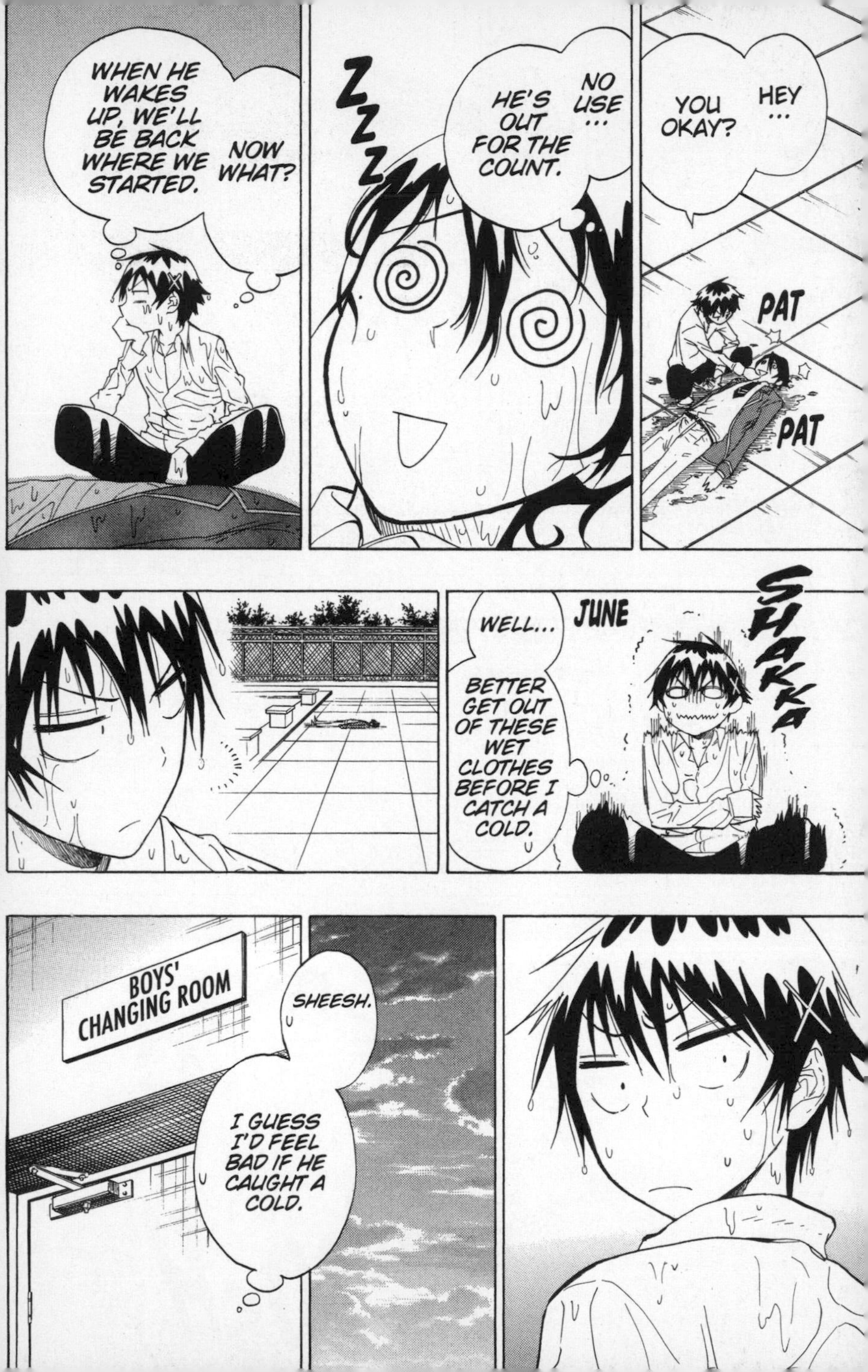
HEY...
YOU OKAY?
PAT
PAT
NO USE...
HE'S OUT FOR THE COUNT.
ZZZ
NOW WHAT?
WHEN HE WAKES UP, WE'LL BE BACK WHERE WE STARTED.
SHAKKA
JUNE
WELL...
BETTER GET OUT OF THESE WET CLOTHES BEFORE I CATCH A COLD.
BOYS' CHANGING ROOM
SHEESH.
I GUESS I'D FEEL BAD IF HE CAUGHT A COLD.

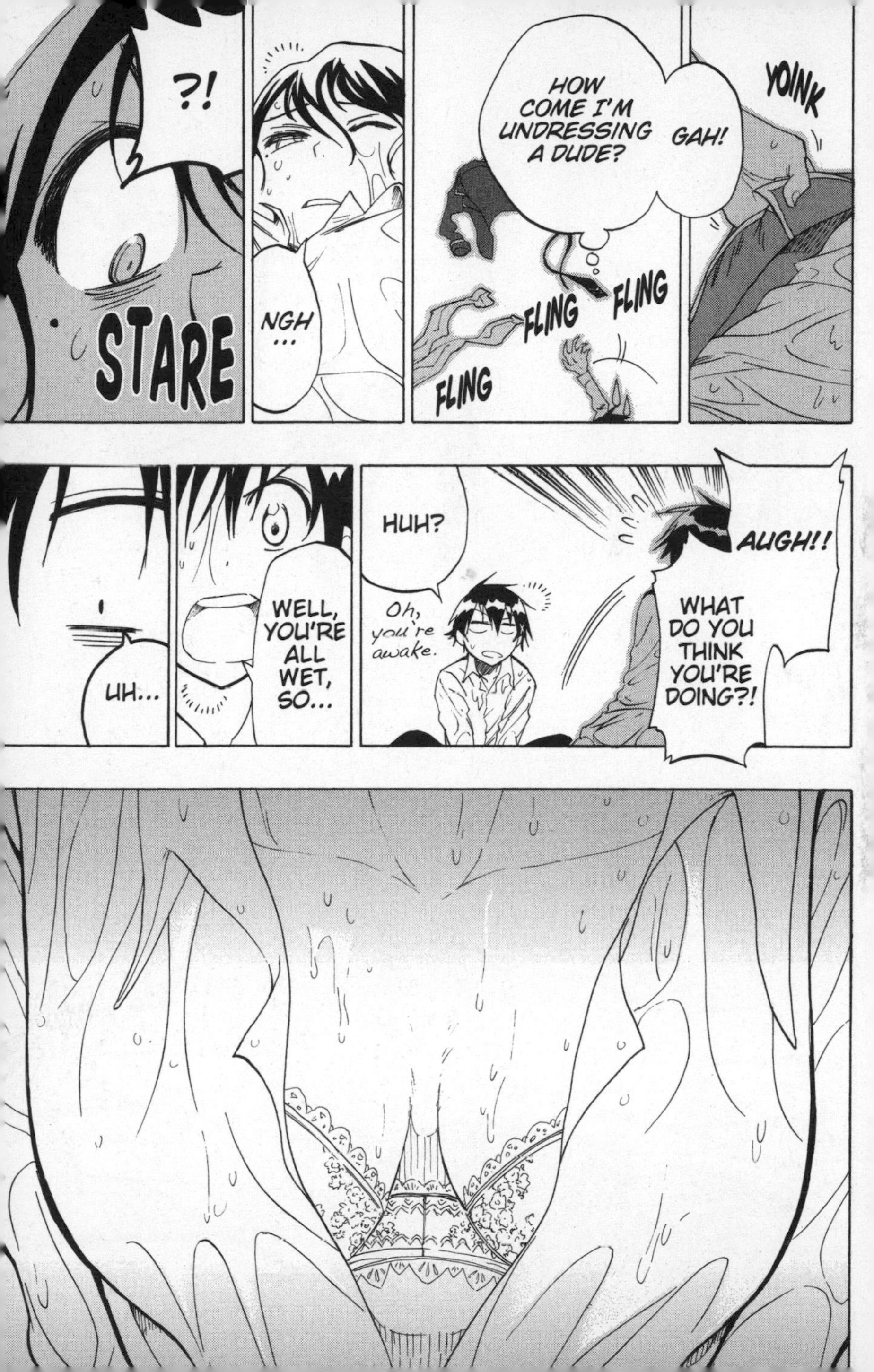
YOINK
GAH!
HOW COME I'M UNDRESSING A DUDE?
FLING
FLING
FLING
NGH ...
?!
STARE
AUGH!!
WHAT DO YOU THINK YOU'RE DOING?!
HUH?
Oh, you're awake.
WELL, YOU'RE ALL WET, SO...
UH...

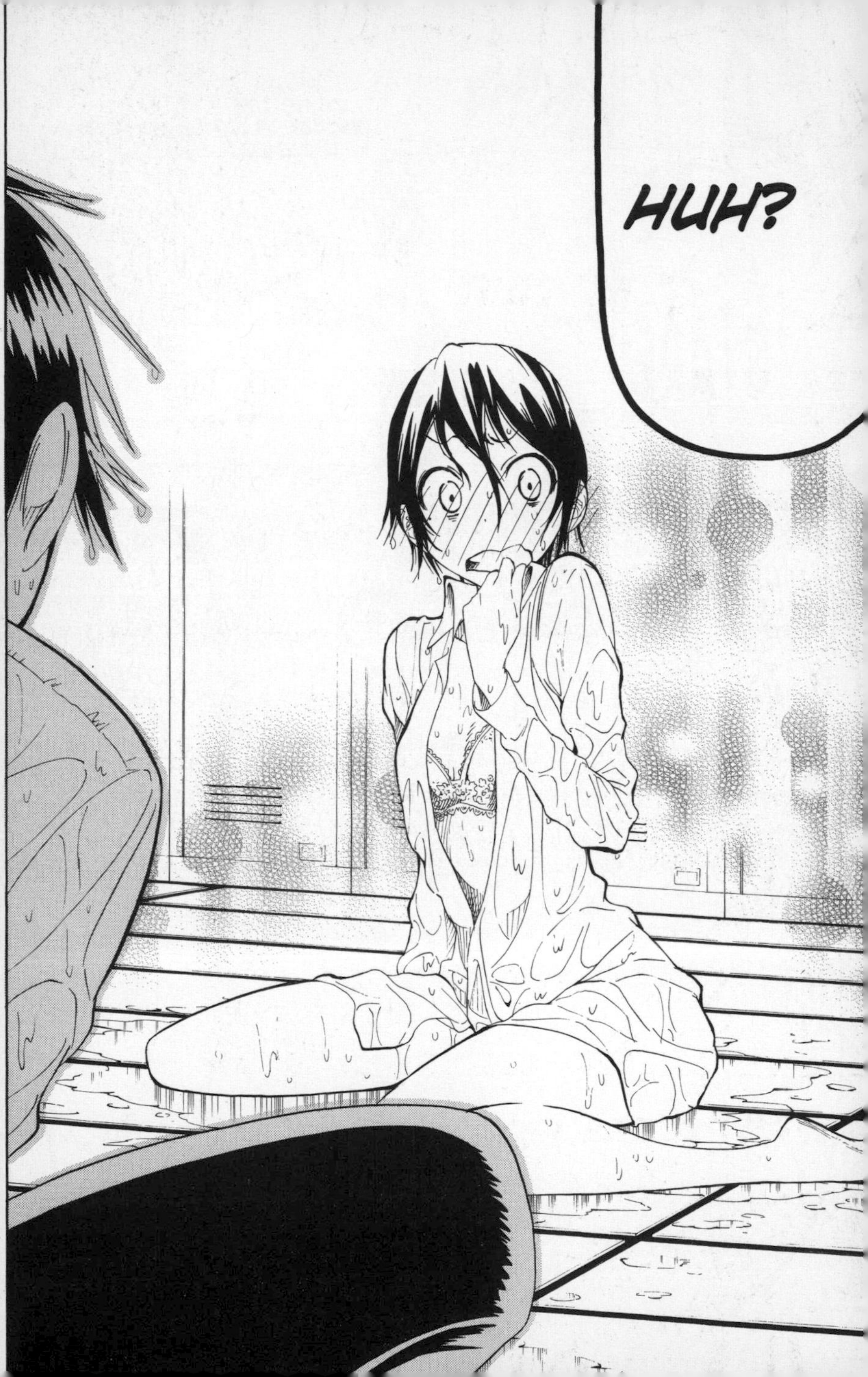
HUH?

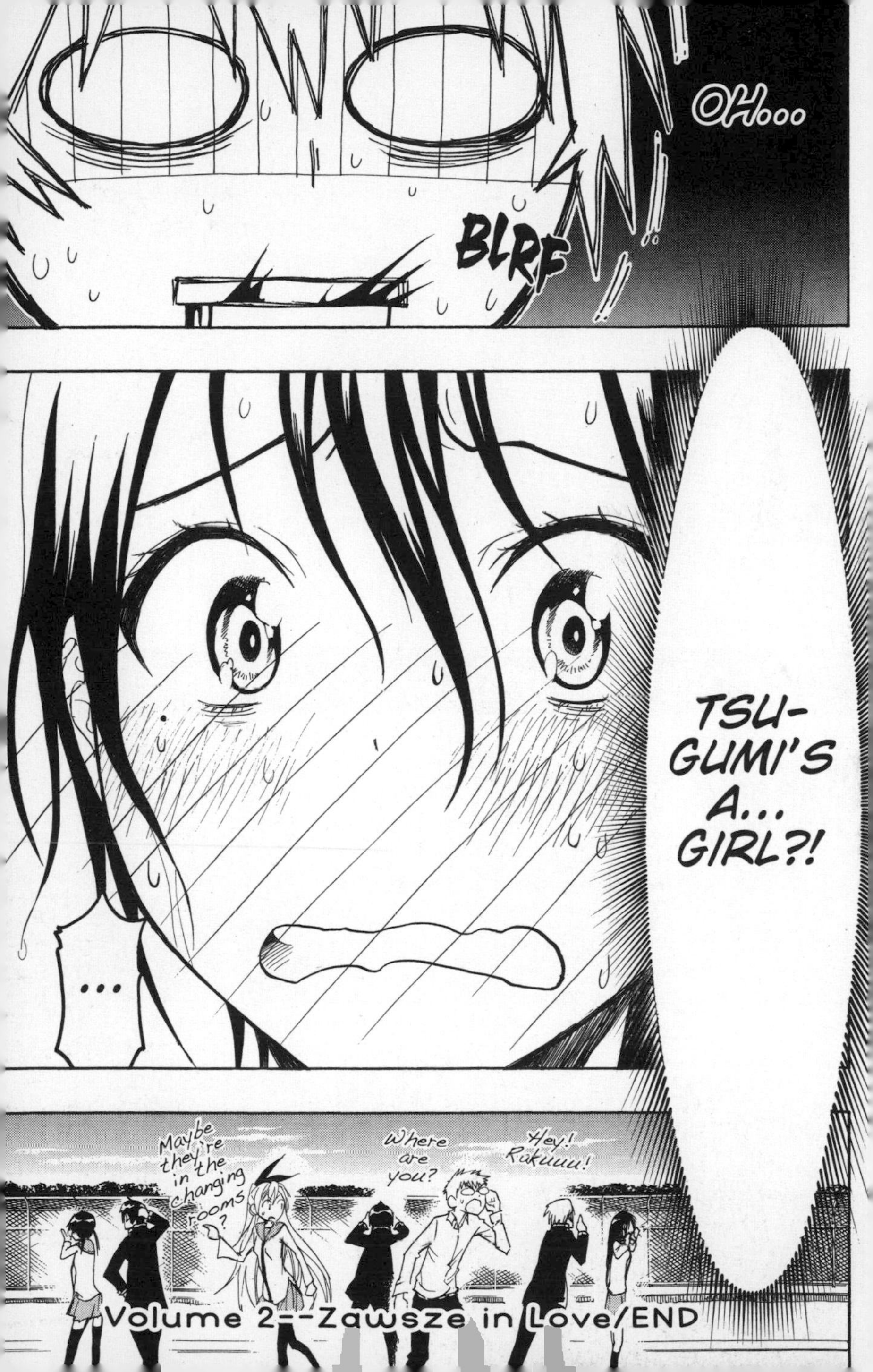
OH...
BLRF
TSU-GUMI'S A... GIRL?!
...
Hey! Rakuuu!
Where are you?
Maybe they're in the changing rooms?
Volume 2--Zawsze in Love/END

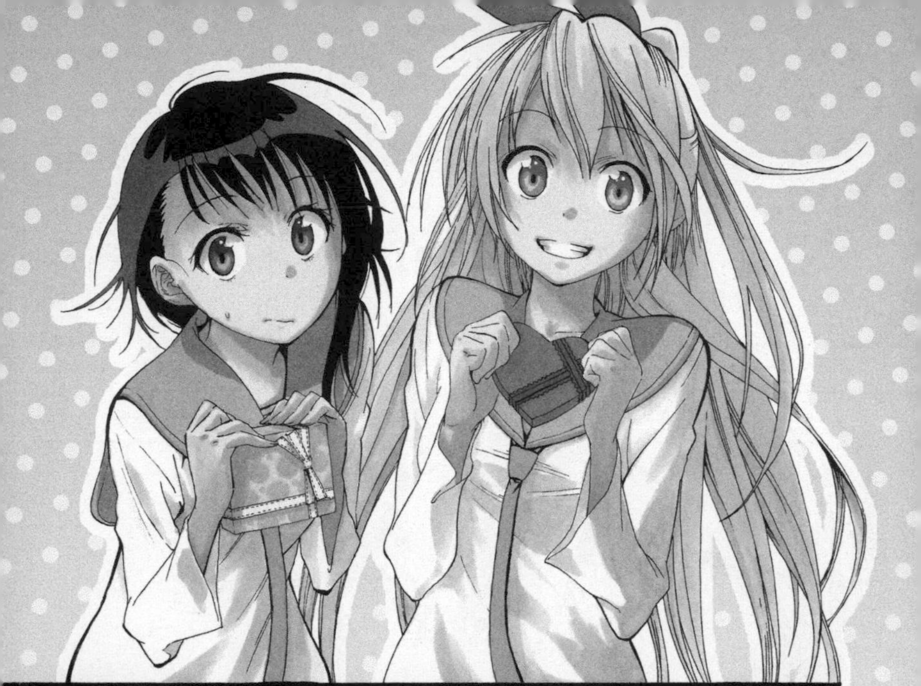

Chitoge in Junior High

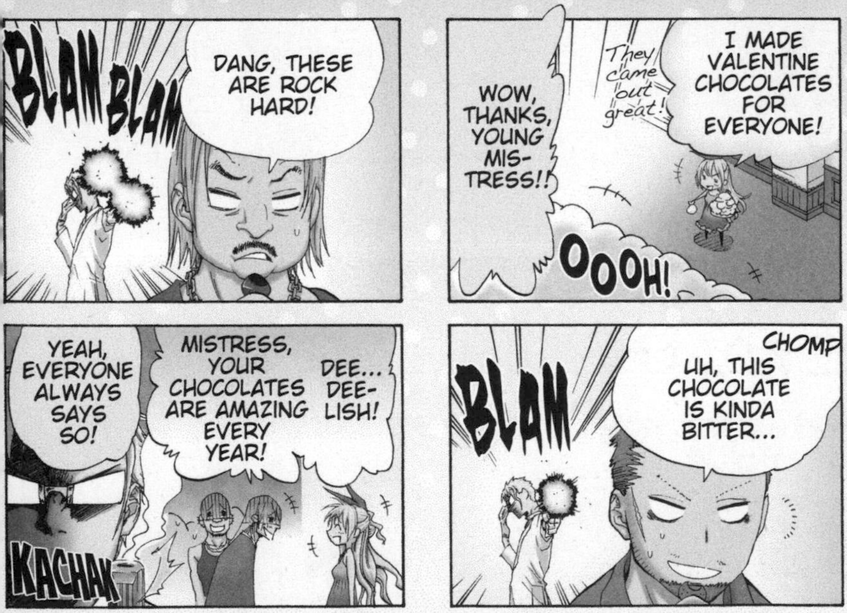
I MADE VALENTINE CHOCOLATES FOR EVERYONE!
They came out great!
WOW, THANKS, YOUNG MIS-TRESS!!
OOOH!
BLAM BLAM
DANG, THESE ARE ROCK HARD!
CHOMP
UH, THIS CHOCOLATE IS KINDA BITTER...
BLAM
DEE... DEE-LISH!
MISTRESS, YOUR CHOCOLATES ARE AMAZING EVERY YEAR!
YEAH, EVERYONE ALWAYS SAYS SO!
KACHAK

Raku in Junior High

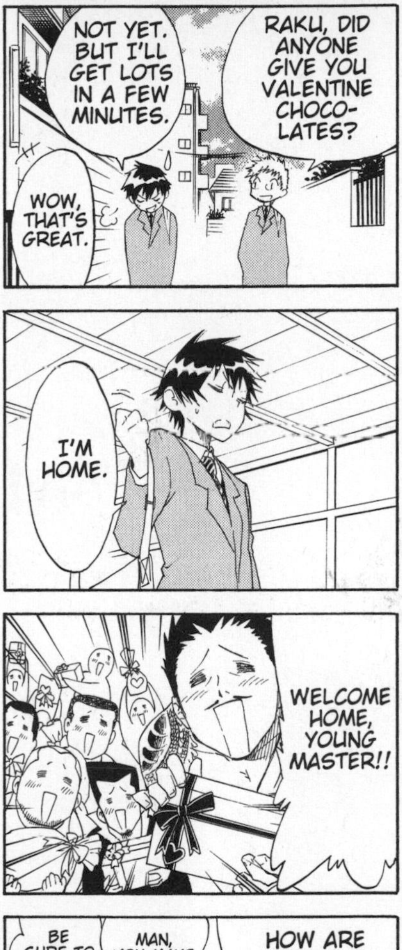
RAKU, DID ANYONE GIVE YOU VALENTINE CHOCOLATES?
NOT YET. BUT I'LL GET LOTS IN A FEW MINUTES.
WOW, THAT'S GREAT.
I'M HOME.
WELCOME HOME, YOUNG MASTER!!
HOW ARE THEY THIS YEAR? WE THINK THEY TURNED OUT AWESOME!!
MAN, YOU MAKE GOOD CHOCOLATE, BIG BRO!
BE SURE TO TASTE MINE TOO!

Onodera in Junior High

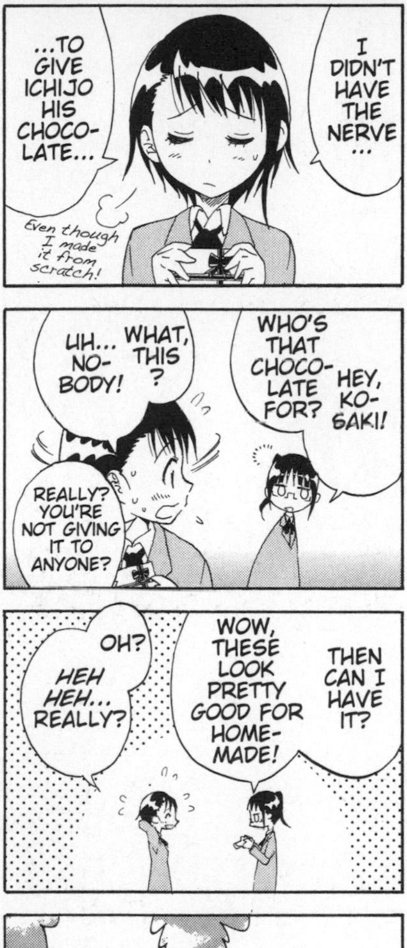
I DIDN'T HAVE THE NERVE...
...TO GIVE ICHIJO HIS CHOCOLATE...
Even though I made it from scratch!
HEY, KOSAKI!
WHO'S THAT CHOCOLATE FOR?
WHAT, THIS?
UH... NOBODY!
REALLY? YOU'RE NOT GIVING IT TO ANYONE?
THEN CAN I HAVE IT?
WOW, THESE LOOK PRETTY GOOD FOR HOMEMADE!
OH? HEH HEH... REALLY?
SENSEI!!
MIYAMOTO PASSED OUT!!
OH MY GOD!
SHE'S FOAMING AT THE MOUTH!!
What happened?!

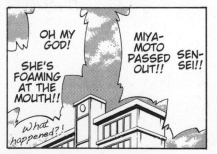

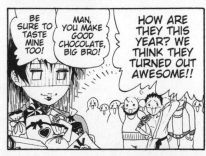

Bonus Comic: Shu Maiko and Ruri Miyamoto

☆Story #9: Intermission☆

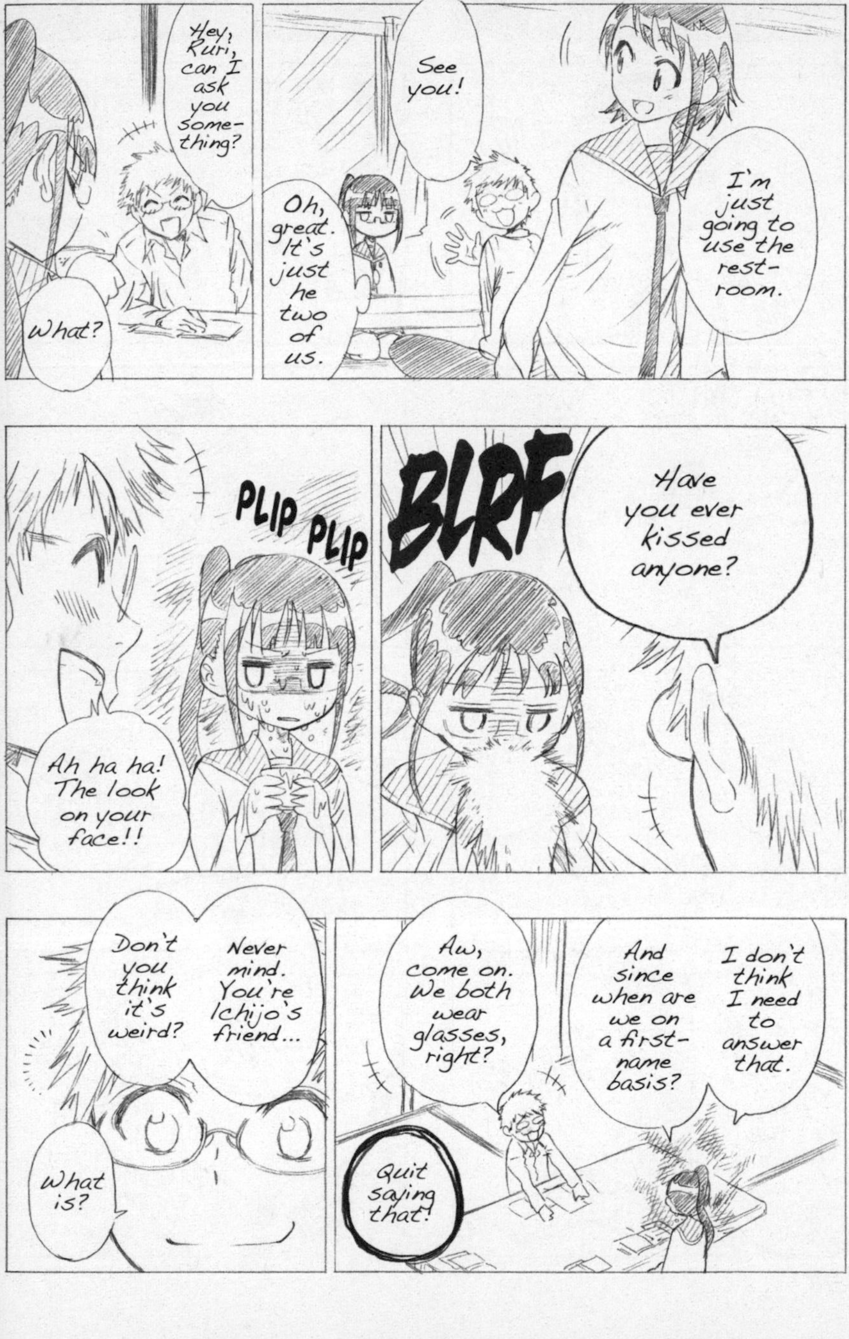
I'm just going to use the restroom.
See you!
Oh, great. It's just he two of us.
Hey, Ruri, can I ask you something?
What?
Have you ever kissed anyone?
BLRF
PLIP PLIP
Ah ha ha! The look on your face!!
I don't think I need to answer that.
And since when are we on a first-name basis?
Aw, come on. We both wear glasses, right?
Quit saying that!
Never mind. You're Ichijo's friend...
Don't you think it's weird?
What is?

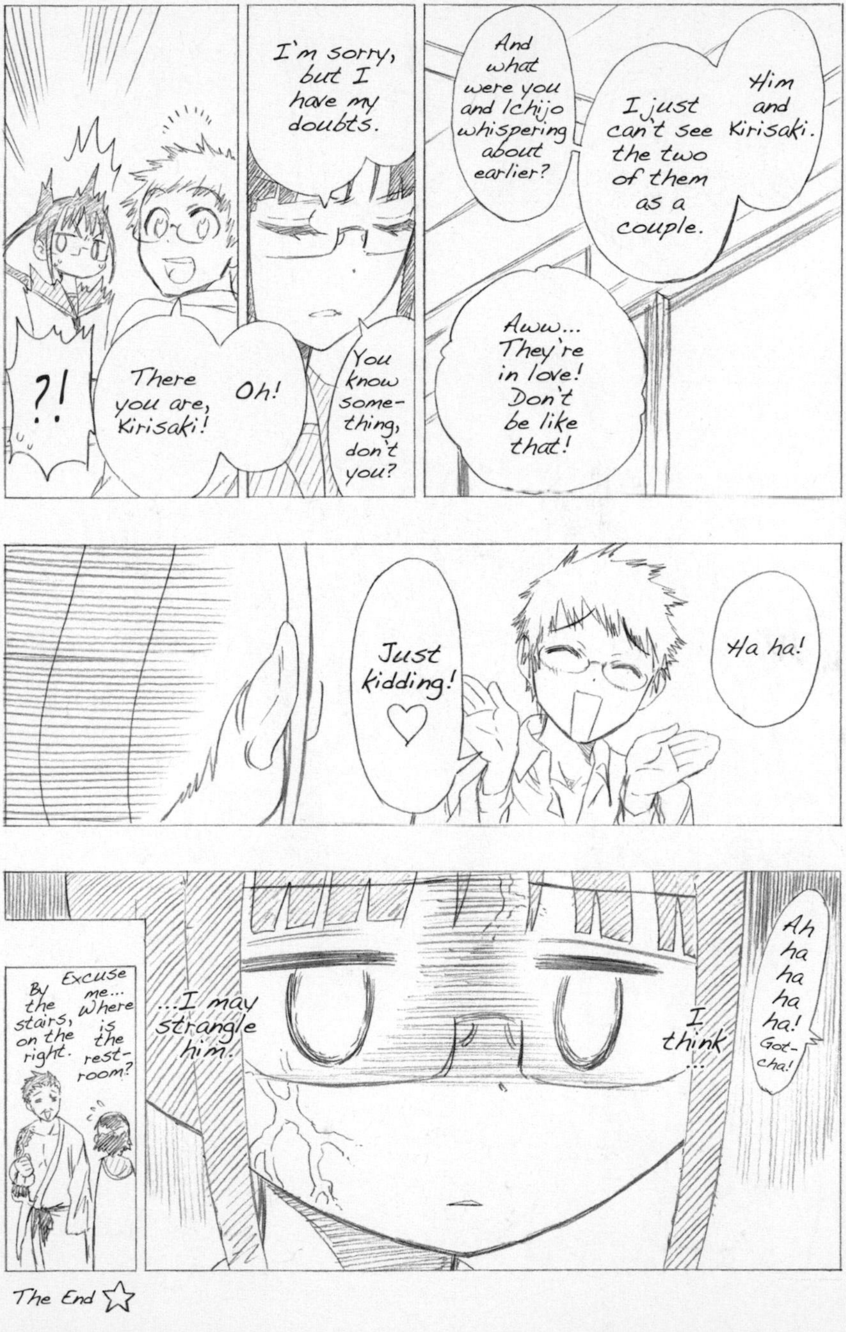
Him and Kirisaki.
I just can't see the two of them as a couple.
And what were you and Ichijo whispering about earlier?
Aww... They're in love! Don't be like that!
I'm sorry, but I have my doubts.
You know some-thing, don't you?
Oh!
There you are, Kirisaki!
?!
Ha ha!
Just kidding! ♥
Ah ha ha ha ha! Got-cha!
I think...
...I may strangle him.
Excuse me... Where is the rest-room?
By the stairs, on the right.

The End ☆

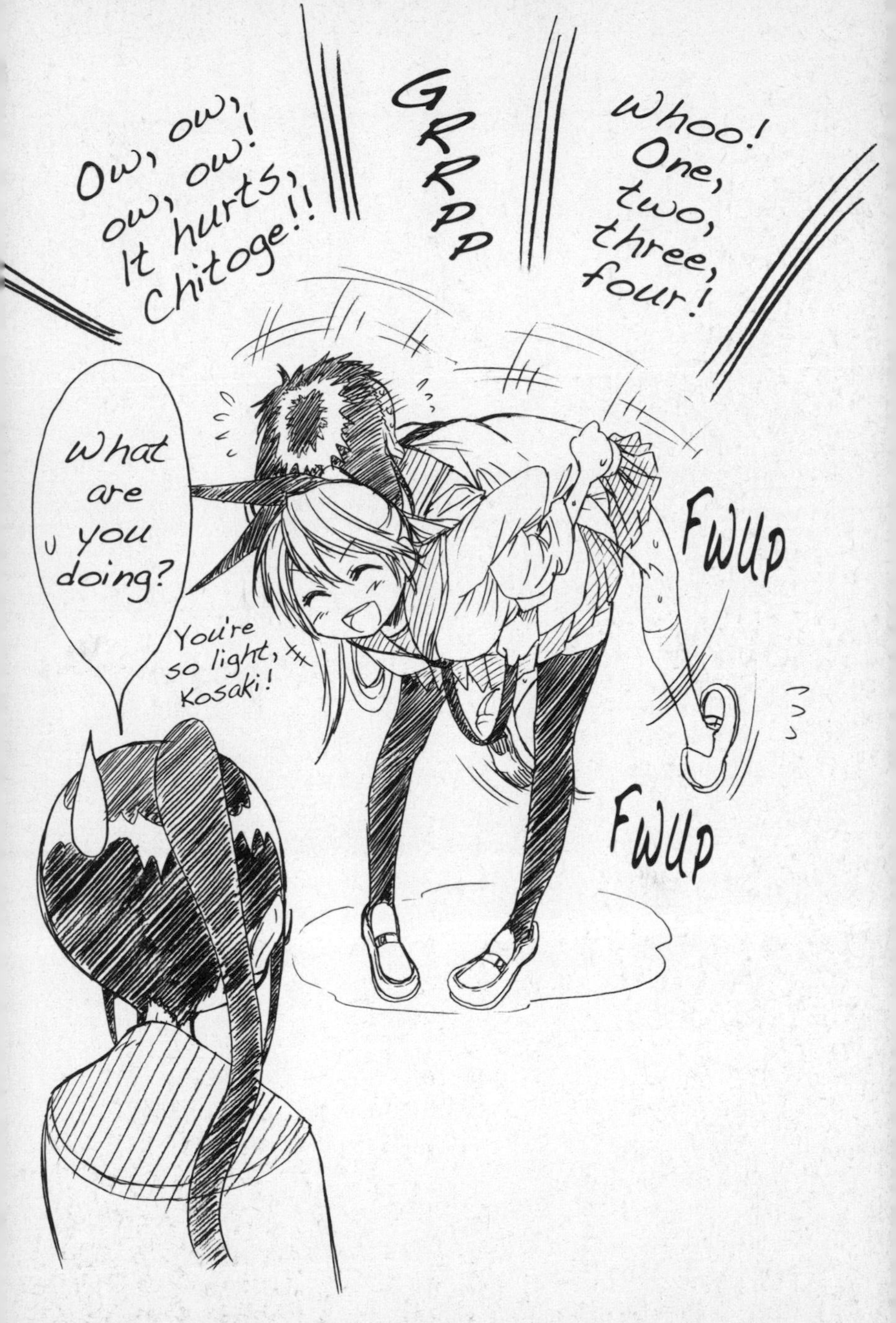
Whoo! One, two, three, four!
GRRPP
Ow, ow, ow, ow! It hurts, Chitoge!!
FWUP
You're so light, Kosaki!
FWUP
What are you doing?

You're Reading the WRONG WAY!

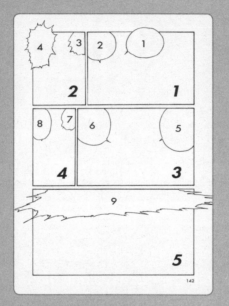

NISEKOI reads from right to left, starting in the upper-right corner. Japanese is read from right to left, meaning that action, sound effects, and word-balloon order are completely reversed from English order.